Java™ Oracle® Database Development

David J. Gallardo

PRENTICE HALL
Professional Technical Reference
Upper Saddle River, New Jersey 07458
www.phptr.com

A CIP catalog record for this book can be obtained from the Library of Congress.

Editorial/production supervision: *MetroVoice Publishing Services*
Cover design director: *Jerry Votta*
Cover design: *Nina Scuderi*
Art director: *Gail Cocker-Bogusz*
Interior design: *Meg Van Arsdale*
Manufacturing manager: *Alexis Heydt-Long*
Manufacturing buyer: *Maura Zaldivar*
Publisher: *Jeff Pepper*
Editorial assistant: *Linda Ramagnano*
Marketing manager: *Kate Hargett*
Full-service production manager: *Anne R. Garcia*

Publishing as Prentice Hall Professional Technical Reference
Upper Saddle River, New Jersey 07458

Prentice Hall books are widely used by corporations and government agencies for training, marketing, and resale.

For information regarding corporate and government bulk discounts please contact:
Corporate and Government Sales (800) 382-3419 or corpsales@pearsontechgroup.com

Printed in the United States of America

10 9 8 7 6 5 4 3 2 1

ISBN 0-13-046218-7

Pearson Education LTD.
Pearson Education Australia PTY, Limited
Pearson Education Singapore, Pte. Ltd.
Pearson Education North Asia Ltd.
Pearson Education Canada, Ltd.
Pearson Educación de Mexico, S.A. de C.V.
Pearson Education—Japan
Pearson Education Malaysia, Pte. Ltd.

*This book is dedicated to my wife Eni, my son Alejandro,
and my parents, whose love and support
made this adventure possible.*

About Prentice Hall Professional Technical Reference

With origins reaching back to the industry's first computer science publishing program in the 1960s, Prentice Hall Professional Technical Reference (PH PTR) has developed into the leading provider of technical books in the world today. Formally launched as its own imprint in 1986, our editors now publish over 200 books annually, authored by leaders in the fields of computing, engineering, and business.

Our roots are firmly planted in the soil that gave rise to the technological revolution. Our bookshelf contains many of the industry's computing and engineering classics: Kernighan and Ritchie's *C Programming Language,* Nemeth's *UNIX System Administration Handbook,* Horstmann's *Core Java,* and Johnson's *High-Speed Digital Design.*

PH PTR acknowledges its auspicious beginnings while it looks to the future for inspiration. We continue to evolve and break new ground in publishing by providing today's professionals with tomorrow's solutions.

Contents

Preface

Databases are unavoidable. That's probably the most important lesson I've learned in all my years as a programmer. I never explicitly sought out database-related development work at first; it always seemed to find me. I tried to pursue other technologies and avoid databases, but because of personal and general technological circumstances, was never entirely successful. Finally, I've learned it's best to accept database programming and enjoy it. I'm much happier now.

I was fortunate in that my introduction to databases was gradual as they were introduced slowly into companies and organizations. At the same time, the database programs for personal computers grew in sophistication. Now, standard relational database systems are ubiquitous, and a gradual introduction to their use is no longer a commonly available luxury. If you are a programmer, your programs will likely need to interact with a database sooner or later, but don't worry—while databases may be unavoidable, they can also be fun.

It's easy to become overwhelmed when first confronting database programming. First comes the culture shock of entering a well-established, densely populated realm with a distinct culture. The native language, SQL—a non-procedural language—is entirely alien.

Next comes the shock of realizing, that for any given task, there are at least three distinctly different approaches to accomplishing the task. Advice is easy to come by, but for every confident, well-supported, and well-argued opinion championing each approach, there is an equally confident, well-supported, and well-argued opinion denouncing it.

The answer to culture shock is acclimation: become acquainted with the lay of the land, the local ways, and the language. That is the purpose of the first half of this book: to provide a gentle but serviceable introduction to database design and SQL.

As for the shocks of choice and contradiction that arise from so many available solutions, there is no ready remedy. It is entirely possible for contradictory points of view to be valid, because underlying each conclusion is a unique set of premises, assumptions, priorities, and criteria. The second half of this book presents every major approach to using Java in database programming, outlines the strengths and weaknesses of each approach, and provides a primer for each.

For every point presented, an example is shown. In some cases, such as matters of syntax, this may be nothing but a code snippet. In other cases, demonstrating the use of a particular technology or technique, this may be a complete program. This fulfills two goals: First, providing a working example as a starting point makes learning easier and gives you something to incorporate into your own code. Second, the examples allow you to compare first hand the different approaches.

Throughout, I stress the standards-based, open-source, cross-platform approach that Java encourages. You may therefore justifiably question why this book concentrates solely on Oracle. The answer is that, unfortunately, the standards for relational databases, in particular the SQL standards, are weak. No major database is fully compliant with SQL and all require you to use proprietary extensions in one way or another. Trying to write a book about Java database programming that considered all popular databases would either need to be limited to isolated topics such as JDBC or would require numerous digressions covering the idiosyncrasies of each database.

Choosing to limit myself to Oracle is a practical matter but making it clear throughout what is a proprietary and what is a standard feature is, I believe, a fair compromise. To use quasi-object-oriented terms, you might think of database programming as an abstraction and Oracle database programming as an instantiation of that abstraction.

There are a number of reasons for choosing Oracle over other databases—a choice I justify a bit more in Chapter 1—but free, easy availability is a very immediate and practical one for developers seeking to learn database programming. All Oracle software and their documentation are freely available for download on the Internet (or on CD for minimal cost) for evaluation and non-commercial development purposes.

Resources and Reference

All of the software required to try the examples in this book, except for the JDO examples, is available from Sun and Oracle:

Java tutorials and API reference: *http://java.sun.com*

Oracle software and documentation: *http://otn.oracle.com*

In the case of Oracle documentation, and in particular, the Oracle9i SQL reference, you may wish to download the PDF versions for more convenient access.

The JDO examples require a JDO driver; I used a trial version of LiDO Professional Edition, available from LIBeLIS:

http://www.libelis.com

The source code for all significant examples is available for download from Prentice Hall:

http://www.phptr.com/gallardo

Typographical Conventions

The typographical conventions used throughout are fairly simple. In text, keywords and identifiers from case-insensitive languages such as SQL and HTML, are written in uppercase throughout. We might say, for example, that a query in SQL is performed using a SELECT statement. Keywords and identifiers from case-sensitive languages such as Java and XML are written using a code font. We might say, for example, that in JDBC, a query is performed using a `PreparedStatement` object. Code examples and examples to be typed at an interactive prompt (`command` prompt or `sqlplus` prompt) are set apart from the text and are also written in code font.

Sidebars

Throughout, I've found reason to digress from the main point, provide tips, or add a note. These asides are presented in sidebars.

ACKNOWLEDGMENTS

I would like to acknowledge and thank my friends and colleagues who provided valuable suggestions and advice: Ram Dash, Sylvia Nevarez, Jason Souza, Bing Zheng, and Drew Zimber. I would also like to thank the fine and patient folks at Prentice Hall who helped pull this book together: Victoria Jones, Jeff Pepper, Anne Garcia, and Scott Suckling.

CHAPTER 1

Java, Databases, and Oracle

Sun Microsystems' Java programming language seems to have strayed far from its origin in 1991 as a language for networking consumer gadgets, such as a set-top for interactive television. It's tempting to frame the story as a rags-to-riches tale of a tiny language that far surpassed the lowly aspirations that its creators, James Gosling and his colleagues, had for it. Instead of being embedded inside toasters, TVs, and ovens; it's now running on some of the most powerful servers on the Internet, serving information to millions of people around the world. But this really only proves how successful their design was for a programming language designed for networking all kinds of devices.

The tale turned especially interesting on May 23, 1995, when Sun officially announced that Java was being released and that support for it would be built into Netscape's dominant Navigator browser.

It's hard to imagine now the excitement that this created then. Web pages that had been static were suddenly electric—going online was transformed from a static, black and white landscape to a dynamic, colorful Oz. The *San Jose Mercury News* reported:

> Many leading-edge designers today are buzzing about Sun Microsystems, Inc.'s new software that the Mountain View-based company hopes will turn the Web into a rocking new medium. The software enables producers to make the Web as lively as a CD-ROM, but with the added advantages of continuous updates and real-time interaction between people.

Java's platform independence made it possible to write and compile a client-side application that would run in any user's browser, regardless of whether their machine was a Unix box, a Macintosh, a Windows PC, or anything else supported by Netscape. These mostly tiny applications—applets—

introduced scrolling text, sound, motion, and games that made browsing the Web a dynamic experience while strong security features preventing malicious actions by programs made it a more secure experience.

Java on the client side was one of the important forces that contributed to the Web's explosive growth over the next five years. It was this growth that set the stage for a new role for Java, on the server side.

The World Wide Web has grown from a virtual conference center for the academic community to a cosmopolitan bazaar of commerce, entertainment, and information exchange available to users of nearly every age, education level, and nationality. To develop and serve this new market, a diverse variety of applications have been and continue to be developed. And as it turns out, Java has matured into an excellent programming language for building these new applications and services, due to features such as network support, platform independence, and robustness, features that have been inherent in its core design from the beginning.

As the importance of Java as a server-side programming language has increased, Sun has dramatically expanded the number and types of features that support networking and distributed computing. According to Sun, the number of classes and interfaces in the Java standard edition has increased by an order of magnitude in a little over five years: from 212 in version 1.0 to 2,738 in version 1.4. Many of these new features are in packages supporting such things as security, networking, XML (Extensible Markup Language), RMI (Remote Method Invocation), naming services, and database connectivity.

The Right Tool at the Right Time

The Java programming language got to where it is today not simply by being in the right place at the right time, but by being the right tool in the right place at the right time.

There's been a lot of research into object-oriented design since the 1960s, and there are now quite a few object-oriented languages, but before Java, no purely object-oriented language had come into widespread use for general-purpose programming. Undeniably, C++ has achieved great popularity, but because it is a hybrid language, it is all too easy to lapse into non-object-oriented ways and to abuse the features it has inherited from C. Java, for many people, has turned out to be a better C++. Java is C++ stripped of the unsafe features that can lead to programming errors. After all, consumer gadgets, such as VCRs and toasters, should not crash and require rebooting.

Java enforces object-oriented programming because it was designed from the beginning as an object-oriented language. Though this is not a book about object-oriented design or programming, the fact that Java is so thoroughly object-oriented means that our approach must, by necessity, be object-oriented, as well. It will especially affect the way we approach using a database. In the end, to use Java effectively, we need to be true to its object-oriented nature.

Networking is Fundamental

The key to the growth of the Internet and the Web is networking. In the famous formula immortalized as Metcalf's Law, Robert Metcalf, inventor of Ethernet and founder of 3Com, observed that a network increases in proportion to the square of the number of participants. (Actually, the formula is $n^2 - n$, which approaches n^2 for large numbers.) This is because, as the number of participants increases, the number of possible links and interactions between them increases geometrically. Synergy is obtained as more people work together and interact with each other.

Tapping this new market/community/cyberspace and harnessing that synergistic energy is an exciting challenge. Java and databases are fundamental building blocks for building network-based applications that meet this challenge.

Networks and Applications

Despite the hype, not all network applications are Web applications. There are two principal types of applications designed to run on a network: *client-server* and *multitier* (or n-tier) applications.

Client-server applications are the most traditional type. Typically, client-server applications involve a database on the server and an application running on the users' computers, where most of the processing takes place (Figure 1–1). The main drawback of this architecture is maintainability. When a new version of the application is introduced, it must be distributed to many users at the same time, lest incompatibilities between versions cause problems. Another drawback is that the client machine must typically be fairly powerful, because most of the processing takes place on the client machine.

Multitier applications introduce an intermediate layer, called *middleware*, which, like the database, runs on a server—possibly, but not necessarily, the same server as the database. In a multitier application, much of the processing that ran on each user's machine is moved into this middleware

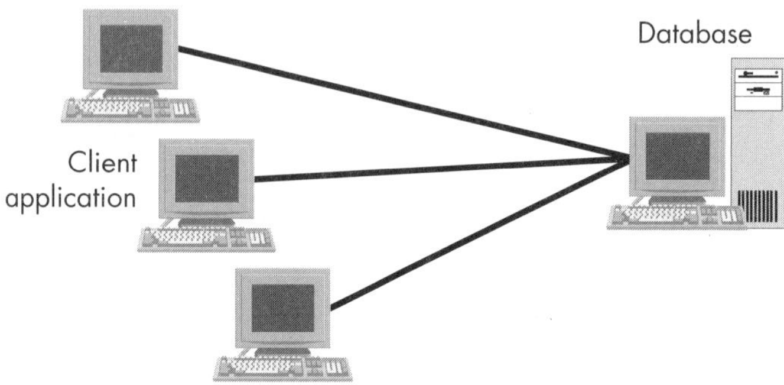

FIGURE 1–1 Client-server architecture.

layer and is shared by all users. The user's machine is typically responsible only for presenting the information to the user and allowing the user to interact with the display and provide input (Figure 1–2).

Organizations of all sizes use distributed applications, and these applications can be built using either the client-server or the multitier model. Some examples of these applications include:

- Library reference database
- Enterprise resource planning (ERP) systems
- Customer Relationship Management (CRM) systems
- Procurement systems
- Document storage

A *Web application* is a specific variety of multitier application. Where a more traditional architecture would use a stand-alone application on the client machine, a Web application generates HTML documents and interacts with a Web browser on the client, using the HTTP protocol.

Some examples of the types of Web sites using this architecture include:

- Information, news sites
- Catalog sales
- Entertainment, gaming
- Brokerages, auctions

All of these distributed applications have one important thing in common: Except for possibly games, they all exist primarily to move and process information. This information must be reliably stored and retrieved—it must be *persistent*.

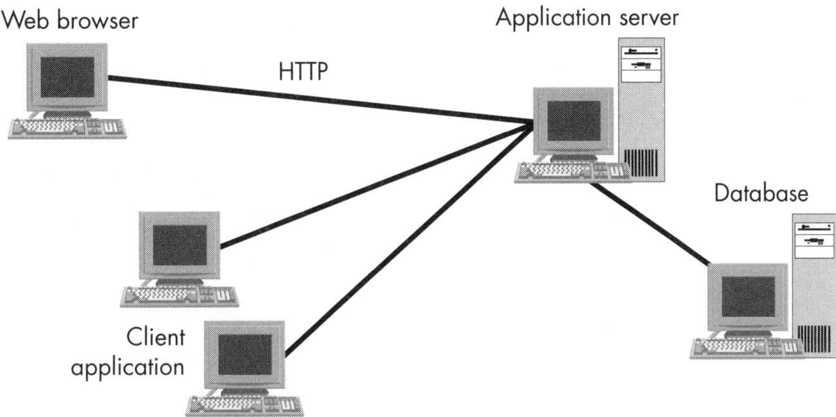

FIGURE 1–2 Multitier architecture.

The Value of Persistence

Virtually all applications, not just network applications, need some degree of persistence. The importance of persistence is easy to overlook at first. Imagine a student writing a research paper, using a PC to format and print it. Imagine that the PC was unable, for some reason, to save the file to disk. The student would probably be wise to (at least) print out the paper once in while, in case the electricity is shut off. Paper isn't usually the best way to store information that is in a digital format but it's better than not storing the information at all.

Similarly, when a user places an order from an online catalog or a writer submits a story to a Web magazine, this information needs to be stored somehow. The easiest way may be to keep these records in memory, but as was the case with the poor student, this isn't very safe, because a system crash or a power outage would permanently erase them. It would be better to write them out to a file or a set of files in the operating system.

Consider a Web magazine. It may be sufficient simply to create a file for each article. Perhaps there is a single editor or a webmaster responsible for putting the article in the right place in the Web server's file system and updating the appropriate Web pages to link in the new story.

Other types of Web sites have more complex needs. They need to keep track of such things as user names, passwords, preferences, and orders. Writing these bits of information out to files and managing them quickly becomes a major development task. The issues involved are far from trivial.

Database management system vendors have already solved the issues that arise from managing lots of information for lots of users: such things as allowing concurrent access, combining information from different sets of data on a record-by-record basis, providing different levels of access according to user, and treating a set of changes as a single transaction to ensure integrity of the data.

If a distributed application requires more than trivial persistence, a database system is almost always the best solution.

TYPES OF DATABASES

One of Java's chief strengths is that it enforces object-oriented programming. To get a database to work effectively with Java, we have to start with a database that supports objects or, if it doesn't, we must somehow find a way to bridge that gap, translating between Java's objects and whatever the database considers its basic unit of storage. This problem of bridging the gap between object-oriented Java and non-object-oriented databases is often called the *mismatched impedance problem.*

Object Databases

Considering that such a thing exists, it might seem that the easiest thing to do is to use a database that supports objects directly. That is probably true. In fact, for a while, there was quite a bit of excitement and optimism in the market and in the development community about object databases. A few years ago, the future couldn't have looked brighter for object databases. Unfortunately, for a number of reasons, they have since largely failed in the market except in certain niches, such as embedded databases and multimedia applications.

The main problem with object databases is that they do one thing really well—provide persistence for objects. It is relatively easy to build an object-oriented system using an object database. Unfortunately, the overall performance is not very good; in particular, they are slow in performing ad hoc queries. There is also some question about their ability to scale—that is, the ability to handle large amounts of data and transactions, which is a requirement for large distributed systems, such as popular Web sites.

Object-Relational Databases

Object-relational database are relational databases with object-oriented features added. Among the main characteristics are that the tables can store user-defined datatypes, such as objects; that tables or objects can be nested; and that methods can be associated with the objects in the tables.

Oracle has had object-relational features in its database since release 8. We will explore these features in depth in Chapter 6, "Oracle Object-Relational Features" and its use with Java in Chapter 9, "Advanced JDBC Features." In summary, although it does allow us to model our data as objects within the database, it is still difficult to integrate with a program written in Java. In particular, mapping between Oracle database objects and Java objects is complicated. Oracle database objects support methods, but this is of questionable value, because they are not easily mapped to the Java objects either; this may lead to having similar code in two places, which is certainly not desirable.

Despite these concerns, however, Oracle's object-relational features are useful for developing objects and methods that need to be shared by different applications, especially if those applications are written in different languages.

Relational Databases

Relational database management systems (RDBMSs) are the most popular type of database in the market today. E.F. Codd at IBM established much of the theory behind relational databases in the 1970s. There is an absolute set of criteria that defines a relational database, but because no database product at this writing totally meets it, the following informal description is probably more useful:

- Data consists of records stored in tables as rows.
- Each record includes a fixed set of fields, with each field corresponding to the columns of the table.
- One column must be a primary key—a required and unique value—so each record can be exclusively located.
- Views—alternate ways of looking at a table or a set of tables—must include support for inserting, updating, and deleting the appropriate data in the underlying table or tables.
- The database must support null—an unknown value not equivalent to zero or a blank.
- A high-level relational language—not necessarily, but usually Structured Query Language (SQL)—must be provided to support data definition, data manipulation, and database administration.
- Data constraints must be enforced by the database and cannot be bypassed.

RDBMSs are the standard today for a number of simple reasons: They are well studied and well understood. They scale well. Companies such as Oracle have invested extraordinary amounts of time and money in developing versatile, flexible, and powerful products. RDBMSs are so well established that we really need to change the question from, "What is the best way to provide persistence in an object-oriented system?" to "What is the best way to use a relational database to provide persistence for an object-oriented system?" That is, given that relational databases are the industry standard (and for good reasons), what is the best way to bridge the impedance mismatch?

One way to bridge the gap between an object-oriented system and a relational database is to use a mapping layer. (This is covered in Chapter 12, "Object Relational Mapping and Java Data Objects.) Because this layer creates a degree of independence between the database and the rest of the system, it can protect each from the effects of changes in the other. This can improve the maintainability and reusability of the system, both key goals of object-oriented design.

Oracle and Java

There are numerous good reasons to choose Oracle over its competitors in the RDBMS market. These include, in no particular order:

- Oracle has the best support for Java and has had that support for the longest time—though other vendors, particularly IBM and Sybase, are moving quickly to catch up.
- With regard to the market share, Oracle is the market leader. However, as of 2002, IBM is not far behind. Although Oracle is far and away the leader on Unix, IBM makes up the difference to a large extent in the mainframe market.
- Of the top three databases—IBM DB2 and Microsoft SQL Server being the other two—Oracle is the most platform-independent.

These are good reasons for choosing Oracle over its competitors. But to an extent, it doesn't really matter because this is also a book about Java database programming, and the mantra of Java programmers is: "Write once, run anywhere."

Portability is one of the biggest selling points for Java. In a perfect world, it wouldn't make any difference which database we used, as long as it has support for Java. But there are imperfections in the current database world.

- Java support is not complete in any database—not even Oracle.
- Even where two databases implement a particular Java feature or technology, they are not always fully compatible.
- Relational databases do not implement relational standards in compatible ways.
- Sometimes we need to rely on a relational database's proprietary features.

To the extent possible, this book will stick to platform- and database-independent code and techniques. It will clearly be identified where this is not possible. Recommendations will be provided where it is appropriate. It should not be difficult to carry over what you learn here to other databases.

Overview of Oracle's Java Features

There are many ways that we can use Java together with Oracle:

- Use Java and SQLJ (with embedded SQL statements) outside the database.
- Use Java and Java database connectivity (JDBC) outside the database.
- Use Java inside the database as stored procedures.
- Use a middleware layer to manage the connection between Java and the database.
- Use a mapping layer to provide more-or-less transparent persistence for Java—transparent meaning that Java does not need to manage persistence explicitly.

As we will see, these are not mutually exclusive options.

SQLJ

SQLJ is the easiest way to perform database access from Java. It is an ANSI standard way of embedding static SQL statements in Java code. A precompiler is used to translate the SQLJ + Java code into a pure Java source file. In the case of Oracle's SQLJ implementation, at least, the underlying connectivity is actually achieved with JDBC, and it is possible to mix SQLJ code with JDBC.

JDBC: Java Database Connectivity

The fundamental technology linking Java and databases is Java database connectivity (JDBC; Figure 1–3). The JDBC specification defines a way to access any form of tabular data from Java—from text files to spreadsheets to databases. Java provides a set of interfaces in the core language, the java.sql package. The database vendor typically provides an actual implementation in the

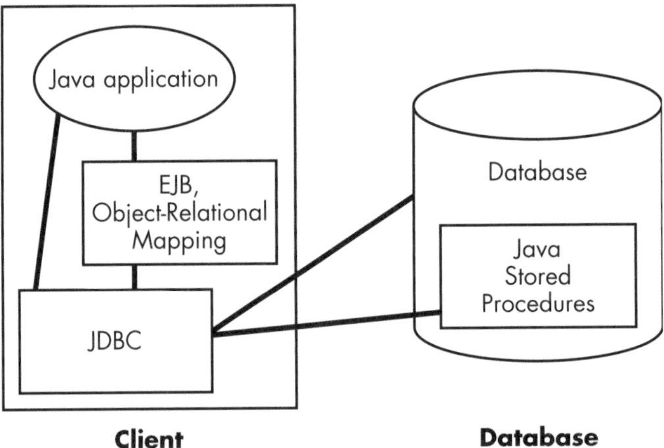

FIGURE 1–3 Java and the database.

form of a JDBC driver. After loading the driver in our code, we can connect to the database, send SQL statements to the database, and retrieve results.

Java Stored Procedures

Java methods can be loaded and run in the database in three different ways:

- Procedures can be called from interfaces such as SQLJ or JDBC, or interactively from SQL*Plus, using the CALL statement. Procedures can optionally have input and output parameters.
- Triggers are set up to run automatically when data is inserted, deleted, or updated. These are typically used to maintain a dependent column, write to a log, or enforce complicated constraints.
- Functions are similar to procedures but are required to return a single value. They can be used just like built-in SQL functions in SQL statements, such as SELECT, DELETE, INSERT, and UPDATE.

Procedures, triggers, and functions differ in the way they are loaded, published, and called, but they are more alike than different. They are all included in the term *stored procedure*.

There are numerous advantages to running a program on the database server, rather than on the client machines. If a program is data-intensive, running it on the server will significantly reduce the amount of data traffic over the network. This will benefit the client, but it may also benefit other users, too, even though additional processing takes place on the shared server. A procedure can be set up to provide limited access to data.

Stored procedures were traditionally written in Oracle's native procedural language, PL/SQL. (Actually, PL/SQL is still worth considering for use in stored procedures where performance is more important than portability.) We'll encounter a bit of this legacy later, when we find that we must publish the interface of our Java method as a mapping to PL/SQL.

J2EE, Application Servers, and JDO

In addition to using a database for persistence, networked Java applications often need additional or enhanced services, such as messaging, naming and directory services, Web services, connection pooling, and transaction services.

J2EE and Application Servers. In its J2EE specification (Java 2, Enterprise Edition), Sun defines a specific set of these features, including a technology, EJB (Enterprise JavaBeans), that can manage persistence automatically for applications. A product that implements J2EE services is called an application server. The most popular application servers are BEA WebLogic and IBM WebSphere but Oracle also has one that is largely compatible with the others and easy to use.

In order for a product to claim J2EE compliance, it must be able to provide the full set of J2EE functionality specified by Sun. But the single compelling use that many people find for an application server is as an EJB container. Because the container can manage persistence automatically, the developers of the application can largely or entirely avoid SQL and many of the details of database programming.

Java Data Objects. In addition to J2EE, Sun has published a specification for Java Data Objects (JDO)—an API for Java persistence. JDO provides a framework for mapping Java objects to a database of any kind and, therefore, isn't an object-relational API, per se. But naturally, implementations for relational databases, by definition, provide object-relational mapping. JDO provides nearly perfect transparent persistence. At the time of this writing—just six months since the release of the specification—there are at least nine commercial implementations already available and several open source projects underway.

CHAPTER 2

Database Design Essentials

A relational database is essentially just a set of tables of data that are related to each other. These tables are useful because we can use a high-level language, such as SQL, to add, change, or delete the tables or the data in the tables. We can query the database and obtain the results of selecting data based on simple or complex relations. We can perform set operations, such as joins, on the data. These capabilities let us store, manage, and make use of even very large amounts of data.

Tables can hold data of different types, allowing us to store, primarily, numbers, dates, and text. We can perform calculations, sort, or change these types of data. (There are also types used to store arbitrary data—which could be images or sounds, for example—but they are just "stuff" to the database and we cannot perform operations on these types apart from storing it and retrieving it. These cannot be manipulated using SQL and won't be considered until Chapter 9, "Advance JDBC Features.") The Oracle SQL datatypes correspond only roughly to Java types and mapping from one to the other requires some care.

Designing a database is largely a matter of determining the types of data in each table and determining the relationships between each of the tables in the database. Exploring a little of the theory behind relational database design will prevent problems such as redundant data or a database that is difficult to use.

Tables, Columns, and Rows

The table is the fundamental organizing unit in a database. There are several terminologies used, but generally we describe a table as having columns and rows. Let's take as an example a table designed to hold information about the CDs in our collection. There are a number of different pieces of information we would like to keep about each CD, such as artist, title, and release date. We call each of these a *column*, and we define them when we create the table.

As we start to enter data into our table, each item that we enter—in our example, the information for each CD—is called a *row* in the table.

Sometimes the columns in a table are called *fields*, and sometimes the rows are called *records*. In other words, for each CD, we will have a record in the table, and each record will have fields identifying the artist, the album title, etc. In general, we'll stick to the row and column terminology.

One of the requirements of a relational database is that it must have a high-level relational language. In practice, this language is SQL (Structured Query Language). The main purpose of SQL is to define and manipulate data through statements that apply to tables, rows, and sets of rows. Each SQL statement is independent of all others, and each one is executed, effectively, all at once. There is no provision in standard SQL (at least, as it is now most commonly implemented) for step-by-step, conditional processing. If we need to do that, we need to use a *host* procedural language, such as Java, that allows us to execute SQL statements sequentially, making decisions as we go, based on conditional expressions in constructs such as `if` statements and `while` loops.

Because SQL was intended to be hosted by another language, it has datatypes that are intended to be mapped to the datatypes of typical procedural languages. Perhaps because of this intention to be so generally useful, these mappings are not particularly ideal for any language. To complicate things further, different database vendors support the SQL standard types in different ways. Oracle, specifically, has a small set of native types that map to a larger set of standard SQL types. As a matter of principle, we should try to do things in as standard a way as possible, but in this case, we'll use the Oracle datatypes, rather than add an additional layer of complexity by struggling to maintain the illusion that we are using the standard SQL types.

Oracle Datatypes

To store data in a database, an appropriate set of tables must first be created, with columns of the appropriate types defined. These are the basic Oracle datatypes we have to choose from:

String types	
CHAR*(length)*	Fixed-length character data: max limit, 2,000
VARCHAR2*(length)*	Variable-length string: max limit: 4,000
Numeric	
NUMBER	Float, 38-digit decimal significance: max scale, 127
NUMBER*(precision)*	Integer (fixed precision)
NUMBER*(precision, scale)*	Fixed point
Time and date	
DATE	Date and time Jan 1, 4712 BCE– Dec 31, 9999 CE; 1-second precision
TIMESTAMP	Extension of date—fractional seconds with 0- to 9-digit precision, default 6

There are a few other types, particularly BLOB (Binary Large Objects) and CLOB (Character Large Objects), which are used to store arbitrary data. These types are opaque to the database—meaning that the database cannot access and perform operations on the contents. BLOBs and CLOBs require special processing that is difficult to perform using SQL alone. As mentioned earlier, we'll look at these types in Chapter 9.

String Types

There are two basic types for storing string data, CHAR and VARCHAR2. The difference between them is that CHAR has a fixed length up to a limit of 2,000 bytes, whereas VARCHAR2 has a variable length up to 4,000 bytes. A fixed amount of space is always used for a CHAR entry; if the entry is shorter than the reserved length, it is padded with blanks. This can lead to surprising results when doing string comparisons, for example. A VARCHAR2 entry, however, will take only as much space as necessary. Except perhaps for small, fixed-length fields, such as identifiers, it's generally preferable to use VARCHAR2.

Strings in SQL statements are delimited with single quotes. If we wish to include a single quote as part of a string, we need to escape it—that is, we need to precede it with a special character that indicates that it is to be treated as a literal single quote and not as a delimiter. To escape a single quote, we use another single quote. This is something like the backslash in Java: The backslash is the escape character, so in order to use it as a literal backslash, we have to precede it by another backslash. For example, if we want to use the string "Let's go" in an SQL statement, we write:

```
'Let''s go'
```

Numeric Types

The numeric types in Oracle are three variations on NUMBER. The default option, NUMBER, with no parameters, allows 38-digit precision, with a maximum scale of 127 (i.e., the decimal point can be moved right or left up to 127 places). The second option, NUMBER(*precision*), implies a scale of zero, so it is an integer with the specified precision. The third option, NUMBER(*precision, scale*), allows fixed-length (as specified by *precision*), floating point numbers, where the *scale* parameter specifies the minimum number of digits preceding the decimal point if positive, and the minimum number of digits following the decimal point if negative.

Because the default, NUMBER, is basically good enough to store any Java numeric type, the easiest thing to do is simply use NUMBER for everything. The drawback of not specifying realistic limits for precision and scale is that it can lead to inefficient storage of numbers and potentially poor performance in applications with large amounts of floating point data; in this case, it would be better to determine appropriate limits for precision and scale.

Although any Java numeric type can be stored in a NUMBER, the same is not true when we need to store a NUMBER in a Java type. We need to identify the type of data that the NUMBER is holding; this is usually obvious, and integer values are the most common. For NUMBERs known to be integer values, the safest choice in Java is the `long` type. For NUMBERs with a specified precision, we can choose `int`, if the precision is relatively small—9 or less; if the precision is larger, we need to use the `long` type.

For floating point values similar considerations apply. For NUMBERS known to be floating point values, the safest choice is the Java `double` type. For NUMBERs with a specified precision and scale, we can use the Java `float` type if the precision is 6 or less and the scale is not greater than 38—if either scale or precision are larger than these values, we need to use the `double` type.

Date Types

DATE is a bit misleading because it actually represents both date and time in Oracle SQL. There are two ways to consider a DATE, depending on whether we are using an interactive interface, such as SQL*Plus, or using it inside a host language, such as Java. In Java, the JDBC interface will perform the appropriate mapping to the Java `Date` class, so we can deal with it strictly in Java terms.

In SQL*Plus, we can generally use a string representation of the date, based on the default format (e.g., '12-July-02') or a format that we specify. We need to be aware that there is an underlying numerical representation because, depending on the format, when we perform a query we may see only part of the information that is actually stored. For example, a DATE field that stores the date and time July 12, 2001, 10:54:45 a.m. would display only the date portion by default: 12-JUL-02.

When we insert or change data in the database, we may inadvertently omit some of the information we intended. If we insert the value '12-JUL-2000', the time will be zero minutes, zero seconds after midnight on that date.

This behavior makes sense, but we need to be aware of it, because if we were to compare the values, they would not be equal, even though, by default, when we print them out they appear to be the same. If we wanted to know whether two values are the same date, without regard to the time, we need to truncate them before comparing them.

TIMESTAMP(precision), an extension of DATE, was introduced in Oracle 9i and is accurate to fractions of a second. DATE is accurate only to a second, which may not be sufficient for logging events or timing processes. The default precision of TIMESTAMP, 6 decimal places, means it is accurate to a microsecond. The maximum precision, 9, is accurate to a nanosecond. Note that this precision reflects only the ability of Oracle to store a value; using the operating system to obtain a time value, for example, is restricted to the accuracy to the resolution of the system clock, which is typically on the order of a millisecond.

Null

The value NULL is one of the most problematic features in relational databases, and we'll be revisiting it in different contexts as we expand our database experience. In short, it can be described as representing an unknown value. For example, when we enter information about our CDs into a database, we might not know the release date of a CD—in which case, we could enter NULL.

NULL can cause several problems for the unwary. For example, comparing NULL with anything, including NULL, is always false. (This may remind you of the Not a Number [NaN] value in Java.) When NULL is used in arithmetic operations, the value of NULL propagates through the results.

We'll explore this topic in more depth when we learn more about queries in the next chapter.

Designing a Database

Let's design a database for our CD collection. Assume that, until now, we've been keeping all the information about our CDs on index cards and that, for each CD, we've written down the artist's name, what country the artist is from, the title of the album, the release date, the label, and a list of the songs on the album. We want to convert this system of cards into an Oracle database.

Based on our index cards, we first design a table with the following columns, omitting for now the list of songs:

```
CD_COLLECTION
  TITLE
  ARTIST
  COUNTRY
  RELEASE_DATE
  LABEL
```

Our database table is shown in Figure 2–1.

Notice that, to identify each CD uniquely, we can use the combination of the two columns TITLE and ARTIST. This combination is called the *primary key* for the table.

A primary key isn't required by Oracle, and for our current purposes, we could probably get by without one, but a primary key is required by the defi-

CD_COLLECTION				
TITLE	ARTIST	COUNTRY	RELEASE_DATE	LABEL

Rows

Columns

FIGURE 2–1 CD database table.

nition of a relational database. A relational database requires that we must be able to address the intersection of any row and column uniquely.

We'll assume that a database is available for you to use in order to follow along with the examples. If you've installed Oracle and didn't choose to have a database created at installation time, you can use the Oracle Database Configuration Assistant to create one now.

In general, you shouldn't be logged in as administrator except when you need to do database administration work. If you don't have a regular user account already, you should create one and log in as that user. To create a user account, using SQL*Plus, connect to the database as administrator and type the following command at the sqlplus prompt:

```
CREATE USER username IDENTIFIED BY password
```

Next, grant the rights to connect and create and use objects:

```
GRANT CONNECT, RESOURCE TO username
```

Now you can connect to the database as the user you created:

```
CONNECT username/password
```

If you are using a database created by someone else, you should get the administrator of that database to create a user account for you, perhaps in your own tablespace. You should ensure that you have the sufficient rights to create and drop tables.

In this chapter, we will be using SQL*Plus to create tables and enter information into the database using SQL. At this stage, apart from noticing that CREATE TABLE is used to create a table, INSERT is used to put a row of data into it, and SELECT is used to list the contents, you shouldn't worry about the details of SQL.

To create the table, we'll type the following at the sqlplus prompt:

```
CREATE TABLE CD_COLLECTION (
  ALBUM_TITLE    VARCHAR2(100),
  ARTIST         VARCHAR2(100),
  COUNTRY        VARCHAR2(25),
  RELEASE_DATE   DATE,
  LABEL          VARCHAR2(25),
  PRIMARY KEY (ALBUM_TITLE, ARTIST)
);
```

The reason that we've omitted the songs from this table is that relational databases don't have a list or array type, so there is no natural way to store them in this table. A table in a relational database should store only items that have a one-to-one relationship with the other items in the tables.

If it were just a matter of storing the titles of the songs, it would be easy to fake it by having a series of columns SONG_1, SONG_2, SONG_3, etc. But this quickly gets unmanageable if we later decide to store more information about each song, such as length and composer. Also, there is no absolute way to determine the maximum number of songs we should allow per CD. Instead, we'll need to create a separate table for the songs on the CDs.

Let's enter a couple of CDs into this table with the following SQL statements:

```
INSERT INTO CD_COLLECTION VALUES('Black Sheets of Rain', 'Bob Mould',
'USA','1-JAN-1992', 'Virgin');

INSERT INTO CD_COLLECTION VALUES('Candy Apple Grey', 'Husker Du',
'USA','1-JAN-1986', 'Warner Brothers');
```

Representing the relationship between a whole, such as a CD, to its parts, such as the songs on the CD, is a fundamental part of designing a database and is termed a *one-to-many relationship*. The process of properly organizing data into tables—what the tables are, what the keys are, and what columns are in each table—is called *normalization*. We took the first step toward normalizing our database when we decided not to include songs in the CD_COLLECTION table.

Normalization

Normalization is not a simple, all-or-nothing process—it's a step-by-step process. As we normalize, we apply a specific new rule at each step to our database. Each of these steps is called a *normal form*. We'll look at the first three: the first, second, and third normal forms. Each is stricter than the next, and its requirements are in addition to those of the previous forms. Thus, a database in third normal form, by definition, meets the requirements of second and first normal forms, as well.

First Normal Form

The first normal form formalizes the principle that we've already stated about the songs on our CDs; we shouldn't have aggregate or repeating types, such as lists or arrays, in a table. Where there is a one-to-many relationship, each type of data should be in its own table—the wholes in one and the parts in another.

In the case of our CD collection, this means that the songs should be in a separate table of their own. We'll have a table that lists each of the songs (many) on each of the tracks (many) on each (one) of our CDs. This one-to-many relationship is illustrated in Figure 2–2.

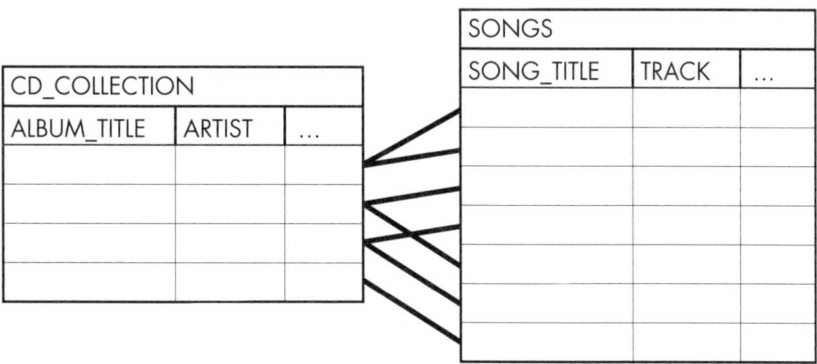

FIGURE 2–2 One-to-many relationship.

We'll also include the length of the song and the composer, using the following columns:

SONGS

```
SONG_TITLE
COMPOSER
LENGTH
TRACK
ARTIST
TITLE
```

In this table, the primary key consists of three columns, TRACK, ARTIST, and TITLE, all of which are sufficient together to identify each song on each CD uniquely. To tie a set of songs in this table with a CD in the CD_COLLECTION table, we need to include the primary key (which identifies a unique CD) from the CD_COLLECTION table; here, in the SONGS table, this key is called a *foreign key.* In addition to including columns for ARTIST and ALBUM_TITLE, we explicitly identify the foreign key, in addition to the primary key, when we create the table:

```
CREATE TABLE SONGS (
  SONG_TITLE      VARCHAR2(100),
  COMPOSER        VARCHAR2(100),
  LENGTH          NUMBER,
  TRACK           NUMBER,
  ARTIST          VARCHAR2(100),
  ALBUM_TITLE     VARCHAR2(100),
FOREIGN KEY (ARTIST, ALBUM_TITLE) REFERENCES
CD_COLLECTION(ARTIST, ALBUM_TITLE),
  PRIMARY KEY (SONG_TITLE, ARTIST, ALBUM_TITLE)
);
```

Associating the ARTIST and TITLE columns in this table with the ARTIST and TITLE columns of the CD_COLLECTION table by specifying with a foreign key forms a *referential constraint*. The database will enforce this constraint to ensure that any songs we enter into this table are associated with a CD that we've entered in the CD_COLLECTION table. This means that we must first enter CD information before we enter song information.

Let's insert a couple of songs for each of our CDs:

```
INSERT INTO SONGS VALUES('Black Sheets of Rain','Mould', NULL,1, 'Bob
Mould', 'Black Sheets of Rain);
INSERT INTO SONGS VALUES('Crystal','Mould', 3.28, 1, 'Husker Du',
'Candy Apple Grey');
INSERT INTO SONGS VALUES('Don''t want to know if you are lonely
','Hart', 3.28, 2, 'Husker Du', 'Candy Apple Grey');
INSERT INTO SONGS VALUES('I don''t know for sure','Mould', 3.28, 3,
'Husker Du', 'Candy Apple Grey');
```

As we'll see later, SQL will allow us to query the two tables in ways that will put the information back together like it was on our index card. But because we have not thrown information away about the individual songs by lumping them together with the CD-as-a-whole information, we can also do new things that would've been hard to do with index cards, such as determining how many CDs contain a given song or finding all songs by a given composer.

Second Normal Form

The second normal form says that a column in a table should not depend on just part of the key. This is actually a problem in our first table with the column COUNTRY. Assume that our CD collection has CDs from around the world. Our primary key for this table is ARTIST and TITLE, but COUNTRY depends only on ARTIST. To straighten this out, we'll need to remove the COUNTRY column from our CD_COLLECTION table and add a new table, an ARTISTS table that lists information, including at least COUNTRY, about each of the artists represented in our CD collection:

```
ARTISTS
  ARTIST
  COUNTRY
```

We can probably add more information to this later, such as date of birth, Web site URL, etc. This is already starting to show one of the typical effects of normalization—lots of smaller tables.

Third Normal Form

The third normal form states that a column in the table must not depend on any other column of the table. To put it another way, all columns in the table must depend directly on the whole key and nothing but the key. There is no example of this in our database now, but it's not hard to see how a situation could arise if we extend our example a bit. Suppose that we wanted to use our database for a music store and that one of the pieces of information we needed to store was the list price. Our first thought might be to add a column LIST_PRICE to the CD_COLLECTION tables:

```
CD_COLLECTION
  ALBUM_TITLE
  ARTIST
  COUNTRY
  RELEASE_DATE
  LABEL
  LIST_PRICE
```

Now suppose that each label sets the list price, the same price, for all of its CDs. Because LIST_PRICE does not vary for each individual CD but instead depends on the non-key column LABEL, the third normal form suggests that we need to remove the LIST_PRICE column and add instead a new table, LIST_PRICES, which lists the price by label:

```
LIST_PRICES
  LABEL
  LIST_PRICE
```

This has clear advantages. When a recording label changes its list price, there's only one value to change. Further, consistency is also ensured because it eliminates the possibility of entering wrong values on individual CDs.

This is as far as we'll take normalization here. These first three forms cover most of the issues that we need to deal with common database designs. Finding a way to resolve them is usually as straightforward as we've seen. It's usually much harder to fix problems with databases involving fourth and fifth normal forms, where the solutions are more varied, depending largely on the specifics of each situation.

If your application attempts to solve a large and complex data-modeling problem, you may wish to consult with someone who has more experience or refer to a book dealing more specifically with data modeling.

Denormalization

As we saw above, there is at least one drawback to normalizing a database: You get more tables, some of which can be quite small. This will make your queries more complex and may require more programming, because the new tables may, for example, require new user interfaces for data input.

In our example, if the only information that we are keeping specific to each artist is COUNTRY, we may decide that the programming necessary to maintain a separate table is not worth the effort. The major drawback is that, unless we restrict what we allow as a valid entry in some other way, we may end up with different, inconsistent values for different CDs by the same artist. Maybe that's acceptable.

The best way to determine whether you've normalized your data enough (or perhaps gone too far) is to test your data model before investing significant development time in developing an application that uses it. Using SQL*Plus manually or, preferably, using scripts, create the database, add some data, and try out typical queries.

In later chapters, we will occasionally revisit this CD collection example, and as we do so, we'll find that we'll need to make changes as we take more considerations into account. This evolution of a database is a common part of the development process and needs to be taken into account when planning a project.

CHAPTER 3

SQL Essentials

SQL is a special-purpose language, sometimes described as a relational language, which can be used with a database for a number of different purposes. SQL can be considered a standard language, with some qualification. There are two significant standards, SQL-92 and SQL-99. Most database vendors, including Oracle, are largely compliant with SQL-92. SQL-99 greatly extends the scope of SQL, introducing new features such as persistent modules and multidimensional analytical capabilities. Most database vendors are largely compliant with the core features of SQL-99, but not the new features. This core compliance allows them to claim that they are compliant with SQL-99, even though this is virtually the same as being compliant with SQL-92. To confuse things further, most vendors, including Oracle, also have extensions to standard SQL, which are sometimes unavoidable. SQL commands can generally be grouped into a number of general categories, according to their purpose:

- Data Definition Language (DDL), used for defining tables and the relationships between the tables and the data in them.
- Data Manipulation Language (DML), used for adding, retrieving, modifying, and deleting data.
- Transaction control commands, used to group sets of DML statements into a single unit of work; used to ensure data integrity.
- Database administration commands.
- SQL/PSM, used for writing procedural programs using persistent stored modules.

The first two categories of commands, DDL and DML, are the core SQL commands used for defining data models and for storing and querying data. These are the commands we will be concentrating on in this chapter. These commands are generally implemented in a standard way by vendors. We will generally adhere to the features defined in the SQL-92 standard for DML and DDL commands.

Transaction control commands are used to isolate groups of commands so that they can be treated as a unit. SQL-92 defines very basic support for transactions; there is no command to mark the start of a transaction, for example. We will largely use this basic model, but we will also consider SQL-99 features as implemented in Oracle.

Database administration commands are largely vendor-dependent. In Oracle, they are used to maintain the physical structure of the database, create users, grant rights to users, create database policies of various sorts, etc. Database administration is a large topic in its own right and well beyond the scope of this book. We'll cover only a few essential commands incidentally, when we set up a sample database.

The last category is an optional part of the SQL standard to allow procedural programming. It defines persistent stored modules that provide control flow statements and bind variables, similar to Oracle's PL/SQL. This standard was accepted in 1996, but since then, vendors have begun to converge on Java stored procedures. So instead of SQL/PSM, we will cover Java stored procedures and PL/SQL in Chapter 5.

DATA DEFINITION LANGUAGE

SQL has three main commands for data definition: CREATE, for creating tables and databases; ALTER, for changing tables and databases; and DROP, for deleting tables and databases. Because creating, altering, and deleting databases are database administration tasks, we will consider only tables in this section.

Creating Tables

We used the CREATE TABLE command in the previous chapter when we started building our sample database. The most basic form of this command is:

```
CREATE TABLE table_name (
  column_1_name   column_1_type,
  column_2_name   column_2_type,
  column_n_name   column_n_type
);
```

which can have as few as one or as many as 1,000 columns. Although it is perfectly legal to omit a primary key in Oracle, it's a good practice to include one, as follows:

```
CREATE TABLE table_name (
  column_1_name   column_1_type,
  column_2_name   column_2_type,
  column_n_name   column_n_type,
  PRIMARY KEY (column_list)
);
```

This example shows only a single column as the key. This is commonly the case, especially when we use an identification number of some kind to identify each record uniquely. In some cases, the items in the tables have a unique number already associated with them that make a good key—for individuals in the United States, a Social Security number is sometimes used in this way. Sometimes, it is necessary or just convenient to create a number for this purpose. Oracle, in particular, provides a feature—sequences—that can be used to generate numbers for keys.

In some cases, a combination of an item's properties serve to identify it uniquely. In the example we started discussing in the previous chapter, we mentioned that we could use the combination of an album title and an artist as the key.

We created our CD_COLLECTION table in the previous chapter with the following SQL command:

```
CREATE TABLE CD_COLLECTION (
  ALBUM_TITLE       VARCHAR2(100),
  ARTIST            VARCHAR2(100),
  COUNTRY           VARCHAR2(25),
  RELEASE_DATE      DATE,
  LABEL             VARCHAR2(25),
  PRIMARY KEY (ALBUM_TITLE, ARTIST)
);
```

The primary key is treated as a separate object in the database and has a name associated with it. If we don't explicitly name it, Oracle will give it a name automatically—something fairly cryptic, such as SYS_C001427.

It's a good idea to name our objects explicitly whenever possible. It makes things easier to understand and simplifies maintaining our database. In this case, the way to do it is to name the PRIMARY KEY constraint when we create it. This is a better way to create a table:

```
CREATE TABLE table_name (
  column_1_name   column_1_type,
  column_2_name   column_2_type,
  column_n_name   column_n_type,
  CONSTRAINT name PRIMARY KEY (column_list)
);
```

If we were to do it all over again, we could use a command such as this to create our CD table:

```
CREATE TABLE CD_COLLECTION (
  ALBUM_TITLE      VARCHAR2(100),
  ARTIST           VARCHAR2(100),
  COUNTRY          VARCHAR2(25),
  RELEASE_DATE     DATE,
  LABEL            VARCHAR2(25),
  CONSTRAINT CD_COLLECTION_PK PRIMARY KEY (ALBUM_TITLE, ARTIST)
);
```

Another option that we should consider applies to the columns in a table, NOT NULL. We can add this to our column definition after the datatype if we wish to require that a value be provided for a particular column. (This is automatically a requirement for key columns.) We may, for example, want to make the COUNTRY a mandatory field in the CD_COLLECTION table. We can do that by changing the CREATE statement like this:

```
CREATE TABLE CD_COLLECTION (
  ALBUM_TITLE        VARCHAR2(100),
  ARTIST             VARCHAR2(100),
  COUNTRY            VARCHAR2(25) NOT NULL,
  RELEASE_DATE       DATE,
  LABEL              VARCHAR2(25),
  CONSTRAINT CD_COLLECTION_PK PRIMARY KEY (ALBUM_TITLE, ARTIST)
);
```

Throughout this chapter we will be creating, altering, and deleting the CD_COLLECTION and SONGS tables. Rather than typing these commands at the sqlplus prompt, you may wish to type the command into a text file then run it as a script because we will later need to re-create the tables in order to add and change data in them.

Although COUNTRY is the only column we explicitly declare NOT NULL, it is not the only column for which we must provide a value. Because the ALBUM_TITLE and ARTIST columns together are the primary key, they are implicitly NOT NULL also.

Finally, let's consider another type of constraint, a FOREIGN KEY. Before we knew we should name our constraints, we created our SONGS table with this statement:

```
CREATE TABLE SONGS (
  SONG_TITLE    VARCHAR2(100),
  COMPOSER      VARCHAR2(100),
  LENGTH        NUMBER,
  TRACK         NUMBER,
  ARTIST        VARCHAR2(100),
ALBUM_TITLE     VARCHAR2(100),
  PRIMARY KEY (SONG_TITLE),
FOREIGN KEY (ARTIST, ALBUM_TITLE)
               REFERENCES CD_COLLECTION(ARTIST, ALBUM_TITLE)
);
```

The FOREIGN KEY clause indicates that each record in this table is a child of a record in the CD_COLLECTION table. This means that we cannot enter a song in the SONGS table without first entering an album in the CD_COLLECTION table. This also means that we cannot delete any albums from the CD_COLLECTION table without first deleting the corresponding child records in the SONGS table. Were we to attempt to delete a record from CD_COLLECTION that had child records in SONGS, we would get an error like this:

```
SQL> delete from cd_collection;
delete from cd_collection
*
ERROR at line 1:
ORA-02292: integrity constraint (MYDB.SYS_C002745) violated - child
record found
```

We can add an option to the foreign key constraint that will automatically delete child records when the parent record is deleted, ON DELETE CASCADE.

This is the form our statement for creating the SONGS table takes after we name our constraints and add the ON DELETE CASCADE OPTION to it:

```
CREATE TABLE SONGS (
  SONG_TITLE    VARCHAR2(100),
  COMPOSER      VARCHAR2(100),
  LENGTH        NUMBER,
  TRACK         NUMBER,
  ARTIST        VARCHAR2(100),
  ALBUM_TITLE   VARCHAR2(100),
```

```
  CONSTRAINT SONGS_PK PRIMARY KEY (SONG_TITLE),
  CONSTRAINT SONGS_FK_CD_COLLECTION
FOREIGN KEY (ARTIST, ALBUM_TITLE)
        REFERENCES CD_COLLECTION(ARTIST, ALBUM_TITLE)
        ON DELETE CASCADE
);
```

Keys and Sequences

In the preceding examples we used an existing column or group of columns that uniquely identify a row as the primary key in a table. This is called a *natural key*. Sometimes, however, a natural key does not exist or it is not practical to use a natural key. If we have a list of names, for example, we may have many John Smiths. As mentioned earlier, one solution that is common in the United States is to use a person's Social Security number to identify unique individuals, but this is a practice that is often—and justifiably—criticized.

Using long and complex keys, such as combinations of columns, makes it more difficult to use a table. This is a problem with using the combination of ALBUM and TITLE as the primary key for the CD_COLLECTION table.

The way to avoid these problems with natural keys is to use an artificial key. This is an arbitrary unique number that is assigned to each row in the table. This is such a common requirement for relational databases that it is surprising there is no standard way to generate artificial keys for a table. Every RDBMS has its own special way of doing this.

In Oracle, the way to generate artificial keys is by using a SEQUENCE. This is a database object that generates numbers guaranteed to be unique, even for multiple clients in a distributed environment.

Let's redefine our CD_COLLECTION table to use an artificial primary key, CD_ID. But first, we need to drop the SONGS table because it contains a foreign key that refers to this table, then we can drop the CD_COLLECTION table.

```
DROP TABLE SONGS;
DROP TABLE CD_COLLECTION;
CREATE TABLE CD_COLLECTION (
     CD_ID                NUMBER,
     ALBUM_TITLE          VARCHAR2(100),
     ARTIST               VARCHAR2(100),
     COUNTRY              VARCHAR2(25) NOT NULL,
     RELEASE_DATE         DATE,
     LABEL                VARCHAR2(25),
     CONSTRAINT CD_COLLECTION_PK PRIMARY KEY
(CD_ID)
);
```

Next, we'll create a SEQUENCE to generate CD_IDs:

```
CREATE SEQUENCE CD_ID_SEQUENCE;
```

Now, when we want to add an album, in addition to the other information, we'll need to include a CD_ID, which we can obtain from CD_ID_SEQUENCE, using the NEXTVAL function:

```
INSERT INTO CD_COLLECTION (CD_ID, ...)
  VALUES(CD_ID_SEQUENCE.NEXTVAL, ...);
```

(We'll learn more about the INSERT statement later in this chapter; the important thing to note is that calling the CD_ID_SEQUENCE.NEXTVAL function returns a unique integer.)

In the same way, we can recreate the SONGS table to use a sequence for the primary key. Notice that we need to change the foreign key (and the corresponding columns) to reflect the new primary key in the CD_COLLECTION table, from ARTIST and ALBUM_TITLE to CD_ID:

```
CREATE TABLE SONGS (
    SONG_ID         NUMBER,
    CD_ID           NUMBER,
    SONG_TITLE      VARCHAR2(100),
    COMPOSER        VARCHAR2(100),
    LENGTH          NUMBER,
    TRACK           NUMBER,
    CONSTRAINT SONGS_PK PRIMARY KEY (SONG_ID),
    CONSTRAINT SONGS_FK_CD_COLLECTION
FOREIGN KEY (CD_ID)
      REFERENCES CD_COLLECTION(CD_ID)
      ON DELETE CASCADE
);
CREATE SEQUENCE SONG_ID_SEQUENCE;
```

We don't need any of the details of the numbers that a sequence generates, other than their uniqueness. In fact, because they are entirely arbitrary, our applications should use them only internally, should not depend on their having any particular properties, and should not expose them to users.

By default, sequences generate consecutive numbers starting at 1, but as an optimization in a distributed environment—to minimize the number of round trips between the client application and the server—the client session may reserve a set of numbers for later use. If it doesn't use all of these numbers, they are silently discarded. This means that there will be gaps in the numbers that get used as primary keys in the database. This shouldn't matter, but if the number appears in the user interface, as a sales order number, for example, nonconsecutive numbers will be perceived as a bug, not a performance feature!

Indexes and Functional Indexes

When we insert data into a database, the data typically is entered in an unordered fashion. One of the benefits of identifying a primary key for a table is that we are indicating to the database that we will be using this key to locate records in the database. Rather than keeping the data sorted by this key, the database creates an index behind the scenes by keeping a separate table of our primary keys in sorted order, together with a pointer to the record in our table.

Creating Indexes

If we know we will be searching the table often, using a specific set of criteria, we sometimes want to create additional indexes of our own. This is especially the case where we are using an artificial key. Using a CD_ID in our COLLECTION_TABLE will make programming easier, as we will see later, but we still will find ourselves frequently searching for ARTIST and ALBUM_TITLE. We may want to create additional indexes for ARTIST and TITLE or the combination of the two, to speed up queries.

There is a cost for indexes, however; each time we add a record to a table in the database, each index for that table must be updated. Adding indexes to support every likely query can make inserting records, especially into large tables, noticeably slow. This might be acceptable if the table is primarily used for queries (particularly ad hoc queries), but more typically, a balance must be struck, and we must be selective about what columns to index.

Suppose we anticipate that we will most frequently query our CD_COLLECTION by ARTIST and only occasionally by ARTIST and ALBUM_TITLE. We might decide to create a single column index for ARTIST. We do this as follows:

```
CREATE INDEX CD_COLL_ARTIST_IDX ON CD_COLLECTION(ARTIST);
```

But now let's suppose that, as we develop our application, we realize that although querying on ARTIST is, in fact, a common query, this returns a list of the ARTIST's albums, from which the user will typically then select a specific album. In other words for every search based on ARTIST, there will be another search based on ARTIST plus TITLE. We may want to create instead an index based on the combination of ARTIST and ALBUM_TITLE:

```
CREATE INDEX CD_COLL_ART_ALB_IDX
ON CD_COLLECTION(ARTIST, ALBUM_TITLE);
```

Because ARTIST is the first column in this index, the database can use this composite index as an index for the ARTIST column too, so we don't need the single-column index we created above.

If, on the other hand, we found that we were often searching on the combination of ARTIST and ALBUM_TITLE, and never on ARTIST, we may want to reverse the order of the columns in this index. It is more efficient if the column with the most unique values appears first in an index. In this case, we can expect that each artist will have multiple albums and album titles for the most part will be unique.

Creating Function-Based Indexes

In Oracle 9i, it is also possible to create indexes based on functions. To support case-insensitive searches, for example, we may want to create a *functional index*. A functional index is like a regular index, except that instead of specifying a column name, we specify the function (including, of course, any applicable columns). The following will create an index on the uppercase version of ARTIST:

```
CREATE INDEX CD_COLL_UC_ARTIST_IDX
  CD_COLLECTION(UPPER(ARTIST));
```

As each record is inserted into the database, the UPPER() value of the ARTIST column will be indexed. This can greatly ameliorate the performance problems that using functions as part of a search criterion can cause.

Indexes and Performance

It's important to understand the purpose of indexes and their interaction on the code we write—this understanding often leads us to make better choices in how we design our queries. But as a practical matter, in a development environment, with small test databases, indexes make little or no difference.

Setting up indexes properly in a production environment is a complex task. Typically, indexes are assigned to their own tablespaces, which are usually on a separate disk drive than the data table. (The commands in the examples above default to using the same tablespace as the data tables.) Oracle provides a number of performance tools for verifying that queries are using indexes and other optimizations properly. If you will be deploying to such a system, you likely need to work together with the DBA (or refer to additional resources, such as Oracle's documentation) to build the appropriate indexes and make sure your application's queries are properly tuned to use these indexes.

Altering Existing Tables

Once a table is created, it's not too late to modify it. We can add, alter, or drop columns, and disable or enable the constraints, among other things. Here are some of the most commonly used formats that the ALTER command can take:

```
ALTER TABLE tablename ADD(column_name column_type);
ALTER TABLE tablename ADD(CONSTRAINT constraint_name
  PRIMARY KEY (column_list));
ALTER TABLE tablename MODIFY(column_name, column_type)
ALTER TABLE tablename ENABLE CONSTRAINT constraint_name;
ALTER TABLE tablename DISABLE CONSTRAINT constraint_name;
ALTER TABLE tablename DROP COLUMN column_name;
ALTER TABLE tablename DROP CONSTRAINT constraint_name [CASCADE];
ALTER TABLE tablename DROP CONSTRAINT PRIMARY KEY [CASCADE];
ALTER TABLE tablename RENAME table_name TO new_table_name;
```

We'll first take a look at how to change the name of the primary key. Because there are no commands to rename columns or constraints, in order to rename our primary key, we first need to drop it, then add a new one with the correct name.

To drop a constraint, we need to know its name. If we've used a reasonable naming convention, we can guess what that name is. Otherwise we can find out from the database's data dictionary—a set of views (views are a type of virtual table) that we can query to obtain information about the database. The view USER_CONSTRAINTS contains information about constraints such as primary keys. The following query displays the constraints associated with our SONGS table.

```
SQL> SELECT CONSTRAINT_NAME
  2  FROM USER_CONSTRAINTS
  3  WHERE TABLE_NAME='SONGS';

CONSTRAINT_NAME
------------------------------
SONGS_PK
SONGS_FK_CD_COLLECTION
```

Knowing the constraint's name, we can drop it:

```
ALTER TABLE SONGS DROP CONSTRAINT SONGS_PK;
```

Now we can add a new primary key:

```
ALTER TABLE SONGS ADD CONSTRAINT SONGS_NEW_PK
  PRIMARY KEY(SONG_ID);
```

Querying again for the constraints for this table, we find:

```
SQL> SELECT CONSTRAINT_NAME
  2  FROM USER_CONSTRAINTS
  3  WHERE TABLE_NAME='SONGS';

CONSTRAINT_NAME
------------------------------
SONGS_NEW_PK
SONGS_FK_CD_COLLECTION
```

Probably the most common changes we will make to tables are to add columns or to change the type or size of an existing column. Let's take a look at the SONGS table, using the SQL*Plus DESCRIBE table command.

```
SQL> DESC SONGS
Name                              Null?    Type
--------------------------------- -------- -----------
SONG_ID                           NOT NULL NUMBER
CD_ID                                      NUMBER
SONG_TITLE                                 VARCHAR2(100)
COMPOSER                                   VARCHAR2(100)
LENGTH                                     NUMBER
TRACK                                      NUMBER
```

(Notice that we can abbreviate DESCRIBE as DESC and that we don't need to add a semicolon at the end because it is an SQL*Plus command, not an SQL command.)

First we'll add a column:

```
ALTER TABLE SONGS ADD(PUBLISHER VARCHAR2(50));
```

We can use DESCRIBE again to see that it has been added:

```
SQL> DESC SONGS
Name                                      Null?    Type
----------------------------------------- -------- -------------
SONG_ID                                   NOT NULL NUMBER
CD_ID                                              NUMBER
SONG_TITLE                                         VARCHAR2(100)
COMPOSER                                           VARCHAR2(100)
LENGTH                                             NUMBER
TRACK                                              NUMBER
PUBLISHER                                          VARCHAR2(50)
```

Next, we'll change an existing column. But before we do that, we need to consider that existing data may interfere with our ability to do that. If we try to shorten the length of the SONG_TITLE field, but we have data that would not fit in the shortened column, the following error would occur:

```
SQL>    ALTER TABLE SONGS MODIFY(SONG_TITLE VARCHAR2(20));
        ALTER TABLE SONGS MODIFY(SONG_TITLE VARCHAR2(20))
                                      *
ERROR at line 1:
ORA-01441: cannot decrease column length because some value is too big
```

As we'll see later, we can use an SQL UPDATE statement to find and change the value that is too long, then run this command again.

Another alternative is to drop the table and start fresh. In fact, this isn't as drastic an alternative as it may seem. It's not generally a good idea to create and alter tables ad hoc at an SQL*Plus prompt. To properly plan, document, and manage a database schema, it's better to write scripts to perform DDL commands. If our database is being used for development, we would modify our scripts for creating tables, rather than adding additional scripts to alter tables. In a development environment, we often create and recreate our tables, as we'll see, so scripts for creating tables often begin with a command to drop the table first. If we were in a production environment, we would need to consider preserving user data; we don't need to worry about that, because we also have scripts for creating test data—although if we were to decide to change the column length of the SONG_TITLE column, we'd have to remember to change the data to fit within the length restriction.

Dropping Tables

The command for dropping a table is easy. The format is:

```
DROP TABLE table_name;
```

But if we try this with our CD_COLLECTION table, we find that it fails, with a complaint from Oracle about the primary key in this table being referenced as a foreign key by another table:

```
SQL> drop table cd_collection;
drop table cd_collection
           *
ERROR at line 1:
ORA-02449: unique/primary keys in table referenced by foreign keys
```

There are two ways to solve this problem, depending on our intention. If we are going to delete all the tables in our database—in order to rebuild it, perhaps—we can do this by deleting the tables in an order that doesn't violate these dependencies. In this case, it means dropping the SONGS table first, which removes the reference to the CD_COLLECTION table's primary key, allowing us to drop CD_COLLECTION next.

If we have a large database, however, determining the right order to drop tables can be nontrivial. (It may even be impossible, given that it is possible to create circular dependencies.) We can find out which constraints reference other constraints by looking at the USER_CONSTRAINTS table using the following query:

```
SQL> SELECT CONSTRAINT_NAME, R_CONSTRAINT_NAME, TABLE_NAME
FROM USER_CONSTRAINTS;

CONSTRAINT_NAME          R_CONSTRAINT_NAME        TABLE_NAME
----------------------   ----------------------   ----------
CD_COLLECTION_PK                                  CD_COLLECTION
SONGS_NEW_PK                                      SONGS
SONGS_FK_CD_COLLECTION   CD_COLLECTION_PK         SONGS

3 rows selected.
```

Notice that the constraint SONGS_FK_CD_COLLECTION belonging to the SONGS table references the constraint CD_COLLECTION_PK, as listed under R_CONSTRAINT_NAME. If it weren't already clear from the name, we could also see that the CD_COLLECTION_PK constraint belongs to the CD_COLLECTION table. If there were more tables with additional dependencies, we could continue going through this listing to determine how to proceed. As it is, we can drop the tables with two commands:

```
DROP TABLE SONGS;
DROP TABLE CD_COLLECTION;
```

Another way of deleting the CD_COLLECTION table is to remove the dependency between the two tables. We can do that by dropping the constraint in the SONGS table. If there were other tables that referenced CD_COLLECTION, we would need to drop the constraints in those, as well. We can do that in one step, however, by dropping the referenced constraint in CD_COLLECTION with option CASCADE, like this:

```
ALTER TABLE CD_COLLECTION
  DROP CONSTRAINT CD_COLLECTION_PK CASCADE;
```

In one step, this drops the CD_COLLECTION primary key constraint, CD_COLLECTION_PK, as well as any other constraints that reference it. Now we can drop the CD_COLLECTION table without a complaint from Oracle:

```
DROP TABLE CD_COLLECTION;
```

Data Manipulation Language

Once we've created tables using DDL, we use DML to add, modify, delete, and query the data. In the process of creating and exploring our database, we've had a chance to become briefly acquainted with a few of these commands already.

This is the set of SQL DML statements that we will learn to use in this section:

Adding, changing, and deleting data

```
INSERT
UPDATE
DELETE
```

Querying data

```
SELECT
```

Transaction control statements

```
COMMIT
ROLLBACK
SAVEPOINT
SET TRANSACTION
```

If you've followed the examples in the last section, you no longer have the CD_COLLECTION and SONGS tables that were created earlier in this last chapter. If you followed the recommendation to create these tables using scripts, you can re-run the most recent scripts to re-create them now. Otherwise, you will need to type the appropriate CREATE TABLE commands again. The latest version of the CD_COLLECTION table is found in the "Keys and Sequences" section and the latest version of the SONGS table is found in the "Creating Tables" section.

Adding Records

The command for adding new records to a database table is INSERT. There are two general formats for the INSERT command:

```
INSERT INTO tablename VALUES (value1, value2, …);
INSERT INTO tablename (column_name1, column_name2, …)
  VALUES (value1, value2, …);
```

In the first format we do not list the columns that we will be supplying values for. The values must exactly match the type and default order of all the columns in the table. We can find this out with the DESC command.

This is the result for the CD_COLLECTION table:

```
SQL> DESC CD_COLLECTION
Name                                  Null?     Type
------------------------------------ --------- -----------
CD_ID                                 NOT NULL  NUMBER
ALBUM_TITLE                                     VARCHAR2(100)
ARTIST                                          VARCHAR2(100)
COUNTRY                                         VARCHAR2(25)
RELEASE_DATE                                    DATE
LABEL                                           VARCHAR2(25)
```

To add a row, we need to provide values for all six columns, in order:

```
INSERT INTO CD_COLLECTION VALUES
   (CD_ID_SEQUENCE.NEXTVAL, 'Horses', 'Patti Smith', 'USA',
   '1-JAN-1975', 'Arista');
```

If we wish to omit a value (and it is valid to do so), we can use the keyword NULL, as in this example:

```
INSERT INTO CD_COLLECTION VALUES
   (CD_ID_SEQUENCE.NEXTVAL, 'Doolittle', 'Pixies', 'USA',
   '1-JAN-1989', NULL);
```

You may be wondering whether it is true that all the albums we've entered so far really have a release date of 1 January. Actually, in most cases, the only available information is the year. Oracle, however, is very particular about the format of dates, so we need to provide a day and a month, as well. (In addition, hours and minutes are implied, so this really means zero hours, zero minutes, zero seconds after midnight on 1 Jan 1989.) We are essentially setting a convention that we will use only the year part of a date. Another way of representing just years would be to use a character field.

One problem with using an INSERT statement that doesn't specify a column list is that the table might change, and the statement will no longer be valid. If a column were added to the CD_COLLECTION table, for example, the previous INSERT statements would fail with the complaint from Oracle of not enough values. It is usually better to write INSERT statements with an explicit column list:

```
INSERT INTO CD_COLLECTION (CD_ID, ARTIST, ALBUM_TITLE)
   VALUES(CD_ID_SEQUENCE.NEXTVAL, 'The Breeders', 'Last Splash');
```

Notice that this INSERT statement has only the CD_ID, ARTIST, and ALBUM_TITLE columns and the order in which the values appear corresponds to the statement's column list, not the table as listed by the DESCRIBE command.

Updating Records

After a record has been entered, we may wish to change it or add more information to it. The SQL UPDATE statement is used to add information to existing records. The basic format is:

```
UPDATE tablename SET column_name1=value1, column_name2=value2, …
[WHERE condition]
```

The WHERE clause is optional and can be used to select which record or records are to be updated. If we omit it, all records will be updated. WHERE clauses can be very complicated and powerful, as we will see when we examine queries, but for now, we can get by with knowing just the basics. WHERE is followed by a logical expression; every record for which this expression is true is updated. We'll see a complete list of logical operators later, but for now, we need to know only that the comparison operator for equality is the equal sign (=). (It is distinguished from the assignment operator, which is also an equal sign, by context.) We also need to know that we can combine logical expressions with the Boolean operators AND and OR.

In the last two examples of the INSERT statement, we deliberately omitted some information. We'll correct that now. To identify a record in a table uniquely, we need to specify either its primary key or a set of columns that we know will identify the record uniquely. In the CD_COLLECTION table, we can use the ALBUM_TITLE and the ARTIST columns. (You may remember that these two columns previously served as a natural primary key.) The WHERE clause to identify the Pixies album, "Doolittle," is:

```
WHERE ARTIST='The Pixies' AND ALBUM_TITLE='Doolittle'
```

We can use this clause in an UPDATE statement to supply the LABEL, which we previously specified as NULL:

```
UPDATE CD_COLLECTION SET LABEL='Elektra'
WHERE ARTIST='The Pixies' AND ALBUM_TITLE='Doolittle';
```

There is more information to add to the Breeders album, but the format is similar:

```
UPDATE CD_COLLECTION SET RELEASE_DATE='1-JAN-1993',
   COUNTRY='USA', LABEL='4AD/Elektra'
   WHERE ARTIST='The Breeders'
   AND ALBUM_TITLE='Last Splash';
```

Used without a WHERE clause, an UPDATE statement will change the specified field or fields for all records. The following statement will change the COUNTRY column to USA for every record in the CD_COLLECTION table:

```
UPDATE CD_COLLECTION SET COUNTRY='USA';
```

As it happens, the COUNTRY column for all the albums so far was USA anyway, so no harm has been done by this command.

Deleting Records

The DELETE statement for deleting records from the database is similar to the UPDATE statement in that it takes an optional WHERE clause for specifying which records to delete:

```
DELETE FROM tablename
[WHERE condition]
```

Like the UPDATE command, omitting the WHERE clause means the command will be performed on all records: All records will be deleted. It is frightening—but worth remembering—how easy it is to delete all records.

Let's suppose that these are the songs in the SONGS table:

```
SQL> SELECT SONG_TITLE FROM SONGS;

SONG_TITLE
------------------------------------------------
Black Sheets of Rain
Crystal
Don't want to know if you are lonely
I don't know for sure
```

If we wanted to delete `I don't know for sure` we would enter the following DELETE statement (remembering to use two single quotes for the literal single quote in the title):

```
SQL> DELETE FROM SONGS
  2  WHERE SONG_TITLE='I don''t know for sure';

1 row deleted.
Listing the songs again:
SQL> SELECT SONG_TITLE FROM SONGS;

SONG_TITLE
-------------------------------------------------
Black Sheets of Rain
Crystal
Don't want to know if you are lonely
```

Now let's see what albums are in the CD_COLLECTION table and delete one of them:

```
SQL> SELECT ALBUM_TITLE FROM CD_COLLECTION;

ALBUM_TITLE
-------------------------------------------------------
Black Sheets of Rain
Candy Apple Grey
Horses
Doolittle
Last Splash

SQL> DELETE FROM CD_COLLECTION
  2  WHERE ALBUM_TITLE='Candy Apple Grey';

1 row deleted.
```

When we created the SONGS table, you may have noticed that we added the ON DELETE CASCADE option to the foreign key constraint, as we suggested in the section on DDL. This means that when a parent record is deleted from the CD_COLLECTION table, the children records in the SONGS table are deleted, as well. If we now list the SONGS table, we'll see that the songs from this album have silently been removed, as well:

```
SQL> SELECT SONG_TITLE FROM SONGS;

SONG_TITLE
-----------------------------------------------------
Black Sheets of Rain
```

Querying Data

The most important statement in SQL is the one we use to query tables, the SELECT statement. At its simplest, it can be used to select data from a single table, as we've already seen in previous examples. However, because of the many ways it can be used to combine tables and conditions, it has a versatility that we can only begin to explore here.

We'll be using the following table for this section:

```
FRUIT        COLOR        QUANTITY  PRICE  PICKED
----------   ----------   --------  -----  ---------
Apple        Green              12     .5  12-SEP-02
Apple        Red                12     .5  15-SEP-02
Mango        Yellow             10    1.5  22-SEP-02
Mangosteen   Purple              5      2  25-SEP-02
Durian                           2     15
Orange       Orange             10      1  28-AUG-02
```

These are the commands needed to create this table:

```
CREATE TABLE FRUITS (
  FRUIT VARCHAR2(12),
  COLOR VARCHAR2(12),
  QUANTITY NUMBER,
  PRICE NUMBER,
  PICKED DATE
);

INSERT INTO FRUITS VALUES('Apple', 'Green', 12, 0.50, '12-Sep-2002');
INSERT INTO FRUITS VALUES('Apple', 'Red', 12, 0.50, '15-Sep-2002');
INSERT INTO FRUITS VALUES('Orange', 'Orange', 10, 1.50, '28-Aug-2002');
INSERT INTO FRUITS VALUES('Durian', 'NULL', 2, 15.00, NULL);
INSERT INTO FRUITS VALUES(NULL, NULL, NULL, NULL, NULL);
```

This is the basic format of the SELECT statement:

```
SELECT select_list
FROM table_name
[WHERE condition]
```

When executed, the SELECT statement returns one or more rows, called the *result set*. If we don't specify a WHERE clause, it simply returns one row for every row in the table.

The select list specifies the columns that are returned in the result set. The simplest form of the column list is an asterisk, which represents all the columns. This statement, therefore, returns all the columns and rows of the table:

```
SQL> SELECT * FROM FRUITS;

FRUIT      COLOR        QUANTITY      PRICE PICKED
---------- ---------- ---------- ---------- ---------
Apple      Green              12         .5 12-SEP-02
Apple      Red                12         .5 15-SEP-02
Mango      Yellow             10        1.5 22-SEP-02
Mangosteen Purple              5          2 25-SEP-02
Durian                         2         15
Orange     Orange             10          1 28-AUG-02

6 rows selected.
```

Tables sometimes contain columns that we are not interested in. We can select the columns we want displayed by specifying them in the select list:

```
SQL> SELECT FRUIT, PRICE FROM FRUITS;

FRUIT           PRICE
---------- ----------
Apple              .5
Apple              .5
Mango             1.5
Mangosteen          2
Durian             15
Orange              1

6 rows selected.
```

Select list items can include not just column names, but also expressions, including combinations of columns, SQL functions, and literal values. For example, we can calculate the total value of each type of fruit we have by multiplying the quantity by the price:

```
SQL> SELECT FRUIT, QUANTITY*PRICE FROM FRUITS;

FRUIT      QUANTITY*PRICE
---------- --------------
Apple                   6
Apple                   6
Mango                  15
Mangosteen             10
Durian                 30
Orange                 10

6 rows selected.
```

We can also change the name of a column by giving it a column alias. Oracle lets us do this by simply following the column name or expression with the alias:

```
SELECT FRUIT, QUANTITY*PRICE VALUE FROM FRUITS;
```

Standard SQL, however, uses the keyword AS to indicate the alias. Because Oracle supports this as well, we'll use that instead, in an effort to remain as standard as possible:

```
SQL> SELECT FRUIT, QUANTITY*PRICE AS VALUE FROM FRUITS;

FRUIT           VALUE
---------- ----------
Apple               6
Apple               6
Mango              15
Mangosteen         10
Durian             30
Orange             10

6 rows selected.
```

Column aliases are important, not because they provide us with nicer headings in SQL*Plus but because later, they will provide us with a way of accessing the value of SQL expressions and functions in Java, particularly when we use SQLJ.

The WHERE Clause

In the examples we have just seen, the SELECT statement returns one row of results for every row it finds in the table. One of the more powerful and commonly used abilities of SQL is to specify criteria for selecting subsets of the data in a table. The WHERE clause is used to set a condition that each row must meet in order to be included in the result set.

A condition can be a simple condition with a single comparison, such as:

```
FRUIT='Apple'
```

A condition can also be a compound condition, including multiple single conditions joined logically using AND or OR:

```
FRUIT='Apple' AND COLOR='Red'
```

Comparison Operators

The following comparison operators (Table 3–1) are available in Oracle SQL:

TABLE 3–1 Comparison Operators in Oracle SQL

=	Equivalent
>	Greater than
>=	Greater than or equal to
<	Less than
<=	Less than or equal to
<>, !=	Not equivalent
BETWEEN...AND	In range (closed interval)
IN	In set
IS NULL	Is NULL
IS NOT NULL	Is not NULL
LIKE	String comparison

The first set of operators should be familiar from Java. But unlike Java, where they can be used only with primitive types, in SQL, the comparison operators can also be used with any of the basic datatypes or expressions, including strings and dates.

There are two other differences between the SQL operators and Java. The first is that the equality comparison and assignment operators, both represented by a single equal sign (=), are the same in SQL. Which is meant is determined by context. The second is that the standard SQL inequality operator is represented by angle brackets (<>), though Oracle also supports the Java-style (!=).

The last set of operators may be unfamiliar. BETWEEN...AND and IN are a kind of wordy shorthand for comparisons that you can also perform using the other operators. BETWEEN...AND is used to compare a value with a range. IN is used to find whether a value is a member of a set of values.

The next two, IS NULL and IS NOT NULL, are necessary to test specifically for the presence or absence of a NULL value. They are necessary because when NULL is compared with other values, the result is neither TRUE nor FALSE, but NULL. Because NULL represents an unknown value, the result of a comparison remains unknown, as well. This is true even (or maybe especially) if both values being compared are NULL. It may seem counterintuitive, but the condition NULL=NULL is neither TRUE nor FALSE, it is NULL.

The final comparison operator, LIKE, is a special comparison operator for strings. Unlike the equivalence (=) operator, LIKE also supports wildcards.

Comparisons with Numbers

Comparisons are most frequently done with numbers, so we'll begin by very briefly looking at some examples comparing numbers—familiar territory for a Java programmer.

To find a specific value in the database, we use the equivalence operator—the equal sign. The following query finds any fruit with a price of 1:

```
SQL> SELECT FRUIT, PRICE
  2  FROM FRUITS WHERE PRICE = 1;

FRUIT           PRICE
---------- ----------
Orange              1
```

We don't need to limit our comparisons to simple values; we can also use expressions. For example, we can search for any fruits with a combined value, QUANTITY*PRICE, greater than 10:

```
SQL> SELECT FRUIT, QUANTITY*PRICE
  2  FROM FRUITS
  3  WHERE QUANTITY*PRICE > 10;

FRUIT      QUANTITY*PRICE
---------- --------------
1 Mango                15
2 Durian               30
```

We can also select records that are within a given range. BETWEEN...AND is used to select a closed interval—one that includes the end points. For example, the range BETWEEN 1 AND 15 includes both 1 and 15, as the following query demonstrates:

```
SQL> SELECT FRUIT, PRICE
  2  FROM FRUITS
  3  WHERE PRICE BETWEEN 1 AND 15;

FRUIT           PRICE
---------- ----------
Mango             1.5
Mangosteen          2
Durian             15
Orange              1
```

Using BETWEEN...AND is exactly the same as using the inequality operators (>=) and (<=):

```
SQL> SELECT FRUIT, PRICE
  2  FROM FRUITS
  3  WHERE PRICE >= 1 AND PRICE <= 15;

FRUIT           PRICE
---------- ----------
Mango             1.5
Mangosteen          2
Durian             15
Orange              1
```

Using inequality operators is more flexible than using the BETWEEN...AND syntax, because we can choose whether to include either, both, or neither of the end points.

To select an open interval, one that excludes the end points, we can use (>) and (<). The following searches for fruit with prices between $1 and $15, not including $1 and $15—finding none, of course:

```
SQL> SELECT FRUIT, PRICE
  2  FROM FRUITS
  3  WHERE PRICE > 1 AND PRICE < 15;

FRUIT           PRICE
---------- ----------
Mango             1.5
Mangosteen          2
```

Half-open intervals are important for sorting things into categories; otherwise, you end up with values that don't belong in any category. For example, we bought these fruits from a grower who gives us a discount, depending on the quantity of each type of fruit purchased. Someone purchasing less than 5 gets no discount, someone purchasing at least 5 but less that 10 gets a 10% discount, someone purchasing at least 10 but less than 50 gets a 20% discount, and someone purchasing 50 or more gets a 20% discount.

These ranges are:

```
No discount:QUANTITY < 5
10%: QUANTITY >= 5 AND QUANTITY < 10
20%  QUANTITY >= 10 AND QUANTITY < 50
30%  QUANTITY >= 50
```

There are two ways to calculate the discount for each type of fruit: either with a somewhat complex SQL statement or procedurally, as separate SQL statements, using Java, for example. SQL can be extraordinarily powerful, and a single statement can replace many lines of code. Sometimes, however, that statement can be quite complex and difficult to compose and debug. If it can't be solved with a simple query, programmers tend to use a procedural approach to combine multiple simple queries instead. This is usually inefficient for three reasons: first, using multiple queries to arrive at a single result means multiple round trips between the client application and the database; second, the database can perform data-related operations, such as searching and sorting, much more efficiently than a procedural program (not to mention that database servers tend to be much more powerful than client machines); and finally, if the operation is performed in the database, it is often possible to improve the performance even further, using indexes and other optimization techniques.

Programmers often find it surprising how much can be accomplished with an SQL statement. We don't mean to suggest that programmers need to become SQL experts, only that we need to be aware of the possibilities as much as possible. That way, we can make an informed decision about whether we should find a database expert to help us with the query, do the research necessary to write the query ourselves, or resort to a procedural approach—perhaps because, in fact, that is the only way to do it.

As we'll see in the next chapter, the SQL solution in this case, using a union, is actually quite straightforward.

Simple String Comparisons

String comparisons are performed using the numeric value of the characters. These values are determined by the database character set—something that we selected when we created our database. We can generally assume that the character set is compatible with ASCII, as long as we limit ourselves to the Latin characters, without diacritical marks. The decimal values of the numbers and letters, for example, are found in Table 3–2.

TABLE 3–2 Decimal Values of ASCII Numbers and Letters

Character range	*Decimal value range*
0–9	48–39
A–Z	65–90
a–z	97–122

This limits the usefulness of making simple string comparisons for two related reasons: First, it defies intuition that 'Zoo' < 'animal'. Second, and more generally, it fails to take into account cultural conventions, such as rules regarding diacritics and non-Western European characters. We could almost go as far as to say that comparing two strings with the inequality operators (>), (>=), (<), and (<=) is usually meaningless. A better way to compare strings in a linguistically meaningful way is to use the NLSSORT function, which we will cover in the next chapter.

The most useful simple comparisons for strings are done with the equality and inequality operators "=" and "<>". They can be used to select or omit specific records. For example, to find the price of apples, we can query the database:

```
SQL> SELECT FRUIT, COLOR, PRICE
  2  FROM FRUITS
  3  WHERE FRUIT='Apple';

FRUIT      COLOR           PRICE
---------- ---------- ----------
Apple      Green              .5
Apple      Red                .5
```

Supposing we have an aversion to green fruits, we could also query to find out which fruits are not green:

```
SQL> SELECT FRUIT, COLOR, PRICE
  2  FROM FRUITS
  3  WHERE COLOR<>'Green';

FRUIT      COLOR           PRICE
---------- ---------- ----------
Apple      Red                .5
Orange     Orange              1
```

The comparison operators, when used with strings, have the drawback that we must match case correctly. In order for queries to work reliably, we need to make sure that our text strings are stored in a consistent manner. There are SQL functions that we can use to convert strings in the database to all upper- or lowercase, so we can enter our criterion in all upper- or lowercase to find a case-insensitive match:

```
SQL> SELECT FRUIT, COLOR, PRICE
  2  FROM FRUITS
  3  WHERE UPPER(COLOR)<>'GREEN'
  4  ;

FRUIT      COLOR           PRICE
---------- ---------- ----------
Apple      Red                .5
Orange     Orange              1
```

We'll see more about functions later. But keep in mind that, for large tables, we need to be careful when using functions in complex WHERE clauses.

String Comparisons with Wildcards

We've seen that we can compare character strings for equality, using the same comparison operators that we use for dates and numbers. However, this works only if we want to compare entire strings for exact matches. SQL provides a special comparison operator, LIKE, which allows us to match portions of strings by using wildcard characters as placeholders in pattern strings to perform the comparison. There are two wildcard characters in SQL, underscore and percent, as shown in Table 3–3:

TABLE 3–3 Wildcard Characters in SQL

_	Matches any one single character
%	Matches any number of occurrences (including zero) of any character

These are similar to the wildcards (?) and (*), respectively, used in the DOS and Unix environments.

The underscore (_), is easiest to understand. To match a pattern string, one character—any character—must appear wherever the (_) appears. Any literals in the rest of the string (anything except the percent symbol, in other words) must appear exactly as it appears in the pattern strings. Table 3–4 shows some examples:

TABLE 3–4 Examples of the Underscore Wildcard

Pattern	*Matches*
'_'	Any single letter string
'__'	Any string two letters long
'_BC'	Any string three letters long, ending in BC
'A_C'	Any string three letters long, beginning with A and ending with C
'_A_'	Any string three letters long, with middle letter A

The percent sign (%) is probably harder to explain than it is to understand. It can represent any number of any character or characters, including none. However, if there are any literals in the string or (_) in the string, these must be matched, as well. For example (Table 3–5):

TABLE 3–5 Examples of the Percent Sign Wildcard

Pattern	*Matches*
'%'	Any string, but not NULL
'%A'	Any string that ends with A
'A%'	Any string that begins with A
'%A%'	Any string that contains the letter A
'_%A%'	Any string that contains the letter A, except as the first letter

We'll try a few sample queries. For the first one, we'll select all fruits that begin with *Mango*:

```
SQL> SELECT FRUIT FROM FRUITS WHERE FRUIT LIKE 'Mango%'

FRUIT
----------
Mango
Mangosteen
```

Next, we'll look for those that contain the letters *an*

```
SQL> SELECT FRUIT FROM FRUITS WHERE FRUIT LIKE '%an%';

FRUIT
----------
Mango
Mangosteen
Durian
Orange
```

Next, those that contain the letters *an*, except at the end:

```
SQL> SELECT FRUIT FROM FRUITS WHERE FRUIT LIKE '%an%_';

FRUIT
----------
Mango
Mangosteen
Orange
```

Finally, those that end with the letters *an*:

```
SQL> SELECT FRUIT FROM FRUITS WHERE FRUIT LIKE '%an';

FRUIT
----------
Durian
```

Date and Time Comparisons

Date and time comparisons are similar to comparisons with numbers because underlying every date and time is a number. The only thing that makes this a little more difficult is that, in Oracle, there is a single datatype, DATE, that represents both date and time with a single number.

If we want to compare a date column with another date, the easiest thing to do is use a string literal in the default date format and let Oracle perform the conversion for us behind the scenes, like this:

```
SQL> SELECT FRUIT, PICKED FROM FRUITS WHERE PICKED>'20-SEP-2002';

FRUIT      PICKED
---------- ---------
Mango      22-SEP-02
Mangosteen 25-SEP-02
```

We can get the current date and time in Oracle by using the pseudo-column, SYSDATE. A pseudo-column is an Oracle function that we use as though it were a column that automatically exists in any table—we can use it anywhere we'd use any of the table's real column names. Now let's suppose that today is 25 September 2002. This query will list all of the fruits in our table, the day they were picked, and the current system date:

```
SQL> SELECT FRUIT, PICKED, SYSDATE FROM FRUITS;

FRUIT      PICKED    SYSDATE
---------- --------- ---------
Apple      12-SEP-02 25-SEP-02
Apple      15-SEP-02 25-SEP-02
Mango      22-SEP-02 25-SEP-02
Mangosteen 25-SEP-02 25-SEP-02
Durian               25-SEP-02
Orange     28-AUG-02 25-SEP-02

7 rows selected.
```

It looks as though one of the fruits, mangosteen, was picked today: SYSDATE and PICKED are the same. But if we query for fruits picked today using SYSDATE, we won't find any. When we entered the PICKED dates, we entered the date using the default date format that doesn't have a time part. The time defaulted to 12:00:00 a.m. SYSDATE, the current date and time, does have a time part, even though only the date part displays by default:

```
SQL> SELECT FRUIT, PICKED FROM FRUITS
  2  WHERE PICKED=SYSDATE;

no rows selected
```

To remove the time part of an Oracle DATE, we can use the TRUNC function. This way, we can compare the dates in the table with today's date, disregarding any hours, minutes, or seconds:

```
SQL> SELECT FRUIT, PICKED FROM FRUITS
2  WHERE PICKED=TRUNC(SYSDATE);

FRUIT      PICKED
---------- ---------
Mangosteen 25-SEP-02
```

Logic in SQL: AND, OR, NOT, and NULL

Now that we've seen how to create simple conditions, we'll look at how conditions can be negated using NOT or combined with AND or OR to form a compound condition. We'll also look at how the unknown value, NULL, complicates things.

In SQL, there are three logical values, TRUE, FALSE, and NULL. Every condition, simple or compound, evaluates to one of these three values. In a

WHERE clause, if this condition evaluates to TRUE, the row is returned if it's part of a SELECT statement, for example. If it's FALSE or NULL, it is not.

NOT

FALSE and NULL are not the same, though. When we negate FALSE, we get TRUE. But when we negate NULL, we still get NULL. Table 3–6 is the truth table for NOT:

TABLE 3–6 Truth Table for NOT

	NOT
TRUE	FALSE
FALSE	TRUE
NULL	NULL

If we query the FRUIT table with the condition COLOR='Green', we can see that only one row meets this criterion:

```
SQL> SELECT FRUIT, COLOR FROM FRUITS
  2  WHERE COLOR='Green';

FRUIT      COLOR
---------- ----------
Apple      Green
```

Now let's try the negation of this, NOT(COLOR='Green'):

```
SQL> SELECT FRUIT, COLOR FROM FRUITS
  2  WHERE NOT(COLOR='Green');

FRUIT      COLOR
---------- ----------
Apple      Red
Mango      Yellow
Mangosteen Purple
Orange     Orange
```

If you're used to regular Boolean logic, this result may seem strange, because between the fruits that are green and the fruits that are not, there appears to be some fruit missing. The entry for durian doesn't appear in either of these tables, because its color is unknown, NULL.

AND

AND is used to combine two conditions. In order to satisfy the combined condition, both must be true. If both are TRUE, the combination is TRUE. If either (or both) are FALSE, the combination is FALSE. If either (or both) are NULL, the combination is NULL.

Table 3–7 is the AND truth table:

TABLE 3–7 Truth Table for AND

AND	*TRUE*	*FALSE*	*NULL*
TRUE	TRUE	FALSE	NULL
FALSE	FALSE	FALSE	NULL
NULL	NULL	NULL	NULL

Here is a query combining conditions with AND:

```
SQL> SELECT FRUIT, COLOR FROM FRUITS
  2  WHERE FRUIT ='Apple' AND COLOR='Green';

FRUIT      COLOR
---------- ----------
Apple      Green
```

Only one entry, obviously, is both green and an apple. We already know that the other fruits are either not apples or not green. This doesn't demonstrate anything about the NULL entries in the truth table, however.

Because we previously demonstrated that NOT(NULL) evaluates to NULL, we can demonstrate that TRUE AND NULL evaluates to NULL in the following query:

```
SQL> SELECT FRUIT, COLOR FROM FRUITS
  2  WHERE FRUIT='Durian' AND NOT(COLOR='Green');

no rows selected
```

Because we know there is a row that satisfies the condition FRUIT='Durian', the condition NOT(COLOR='Green') is either FALSE or NULL for that row. If it's FALSE and we negate it again, it will be TRUE, and the following query should return this row:

```
SQL> SELECT FRUIT, COLOR FROM FRUITS
  2  WHERE FRUIT='Durian' AND NOT(NOT(COLOR='Green'));

no rows selected
```

Because it still doesn't return anything, we know that the original condition, NOT(COLOR='Green') was NULL. We still don't know, though, whether the row wasn't returned because the combined condition is NULL or because it is FALSE. We can find that out by negating the combined condition and seeing whether we get the durian in the results:

```
SQL> SELECT FRUIT, COLOR FROM FRUITS
  2  WHERE NOT(FRUIT='Durian' AND NOT(COLOR='Green'));

FRUIT      COLOR
---------- ----------
Apple      Green
Apple      Red
Mango      Yellow
Mangosteen Purple
Orange     Orange
```

If the combined condition had originally evaluated to FALSE, negating it would have made it TRUE. Because we still don't get the durian row in the results, we know that TRUE AND NULL evaluate to NULL.

OR

OR is also used to combine two conditions. In order to satisfy the combined condition, one (or both) must be TRUE. If both are FALSE, the result is FALSE. If one is UNKNOWN, and the other is FALSE or UNKNOWN, the result is UNKNOWN.

Table 3–8 is the OR truth table:

TABLE 3–8 Truth Table for OR

OR	*TRUE*	*FALSE*	*UNKNOWN*
TRUE	TRUE	TRUE	TRUE
FALSE	TRUE	FALSE	UNKNOWN
UNKNOWN	TRUE	UNKNOWN	UNKNOWN

Here is a sample query with OR:

```
SQL> SELECT FRUIT, COLOR FROM FRUITS
  2  WHERE FRUIT ='Durian'  OR COLOR='Green';

FRUIT      COLOR
---------- ----------
Apple      Green
Durian
```

We can see here, from the presence of the durian row, that if one of the conditions is NULL and the other is TRUE, the combined result is still TRUE.

SQL Functions

Oracle SQL has three main types of functions: single-row functions, user-defined functions, and aggregate functions. Single-row functions are usually referred to simply as functions and are the type we will be describing here. User-defined functions are functions that we write ourselves, using either Java or PL/SQL, and can be used like regular SQL functions; we will examine those in Chapter 5, "PL/SQL." Aggregate functions are a special kind of function that combines multiple values returned by a query that returns multiple rows of data—to calculate a total or an average, for example. Aggregate functions will be examined in the next chapter, "More SQL: Queries, Subqueries, and Views."

Single-row functions are similar to Java methods: They take zero or more parameters and return a single value. (Unlike Java, however, they must return a value; there is no equivalent to the void return type.) SQL functions can be used anywhere that a literal constant or a select list item can be used, and its parameters can be either constants or select list items.

We can use functions in a SELECT statement to modify a select list item. The following example, using the UPPER() function, will convert the names of fruits to uppercase:

```
SQL> SELECT UPPER(FRUIT) FROM FRUITS;

UPPER(FRUI
----------
APPLE
APPLE
MANGO
MANGOSTEEN
DURIAN
ORANGE
```

We can also use functions in a SELECT statement's WHERE clause. The following example selects fruits that have names that are six letters long:

```
SQL> SELECT FRUIT FROM FRUITS
  2  WHERE LENGTH(FRUIT)=6;

FRUIT
----------
Durian
Orange
```

Note that when we call the function for a value in the select list, the function is called once per each returned row. (If the table is large, we normally restrict the size of the result set to a manageable size by using a WHERE clause.) But if we use a function in the WHERE clause, it will be called for every row in the table; unless we have created a function-based index, this can cause performance problems for large tables.

There are four main categories of functions:

- Numeric
- Character
- Date
- Miscellaneous

Functions can be categorized either on the basis of the first and principal parameter or on the basis of the return value. The function LENGTH(), for example, would be a character function based on the parameter it takes, but a numeric function based on its return value. Here, they are categorized according to their first parameter. A few functions do not take any parameters and are categorized as miscellaneous.

Because Oracle has a very large number of functions, only a few common ones will be briefly covered. Refer to the Oracle SQL Reference for a complete list.

Numeric Functions

All numeric functions take one or more numeric values and return a numeric value. These typically perform mathematical operations, such as rounding, calculating the square root, raising to a power, etc. Here are a few commonly used functions:

- ABS(*n*)—Returns the absolute value of *n*.

  Example: ABS(-123)
  Returns: 123

- MOD(*m*, *n*)—Returns *m* modulo *n*, that is, the remainder that results from dividing *m* integrally by *n*.

  Example: MOD(15, 4)
  Returns: 3

- POWER(*m*, *n*)—Returns *m* raised to the power *n*. Both *m* and *n* can be floating point numbers, unless *m* is negative, in which case, *n* must be an integer.

  Example: POWER(2, 8)
  Returns: 256

- ROUND(*m* [, *n*])—Rounds *m* to the nearest integer, unless *n* is specified, in which case, *m* is rounded to the number of decimal places corresponding to *n*. If *n* is positive, it refers to places to the right of the decimal point; if *n* is negative it refers to places to the left of the decimal point.

  Example: ROUND(2.718281828459)
  Returns: 3

  Example: ROUND(2.718281828459, 5)
  Returns: 2.71828

  Example: ROUND(186282.397, -3)
  Returns: 186000

- SQRT(*n*)—Returns the square root of *n*.

  Example: SQRT(256)
  Returns: 16

Character Functions

Character functions take a string as the first parameter and sometimes additional character or numeric parameters. Most return a string, but a few, such as LENGTH(), return a numeric value. Here are some commonly used character functions:

- ASCII(*c*)—Returns decimal value of the character *c* in the database character set. Note that this function is misnamed, because the database character set is unlikely to actually be ASCII.

  Example: ASCII('Æ')
  Returns: 146
  (Assuming the database character set is WE8MSWIN1252)

- CHR(*n*)—Returns the character that the decimal value *n* represents in the current database character set.

Example: CHR(65)
Returns: A

- CONCAT(*string1*, *string2*)—Returns a string that is the concatenation of *string1* and *string2*. This is equivalent to the (||) concatenation operator.

  Example: CONCAT('top', 'hat')
  Returns: tophat

- LOWER(*string*)—Returns *string* with all letters in lowercase.

  Example: LOWER('Your VOICE!')
  Returns: your voice!

- LTRIM(*string* [, *chars*])—Returns *string* with all blanks preceding the first nonblank character removed. If a string *chars* is specified, any characters appearing in *chars* are removed up to the first character that does not appear in *chars*.

  Example: LTRIM('   ...uh, hello?')
  Returns: ...uh, hello?

  Example: LTRIM('   ...uh, hello?', ' .')
  Returns: uh, hello?

- SUBSTR(*string*, *start* [, *length*])—Returns the portion of *string* beginning with the character at position *start*. (The first character in the string is 1.) If *length* is specified, only the number of characters corresponding to *length* are returned; otherwise, the remainder of the string is returned.

  Example: SUBSTR('Supercalifragilisticexpialidocious', 21)
  Returns: expialidocious

  Example: SUBSTR('Supercalifragilisticexpialidocious', 15, 4)
  Returns: list

- UPPER(*string*)—Returns *string* with all letters in lowercase.

  Example: UPPER('crust')
  Returns: CRUST

Date Functions

- ADD_MONTHS(*date*, *n*)—Returns a date *n* months later than *date*. If the day of the month in *date* is greater than the last day of the resulting month, the last day of the resulting month is returned.

  Example: ADD_MONTHS('7-JUL-2000', 1)
  Returns: 07-AUG-00

  Example: ADD_MONTHS('31-DEC-2003', 2)
  Returns: 28-FEB-04

- CURRENT_DATE—Returns current date and time according to the current database session's time zone. Takes no arguments and, consequently, does not use parentheses. See TO_CHAR() below for formatting information.

  Example: CURRENT_DATE
  Returns: 14-SEP-02

- LAST_DAY(*date*)—Returns the date of the last day of the month that contains *date*.

  Example: LAST_DAY('19-DEC-2002')
  Returns: 31-DEC-02

- MONTHS_BETWEEN(*date1*, *date2*)—Returns the number of months between *date1* and *date2*. This includes a fractional part unless they are the same day of the month or both are the last day of the month. The value is positive if *date1* is later than *date2*, negative if *date1* is earlier than *date2*.

  Example: MONTHS_BETWEEN('21-MAR-2003', '15-JAN-2003')
  Returns: 2.19354839

  Example: MONTHS_BETWEEN('31-JAN-2003', '1-FEB-2003')
  Returns: -.03225806

- NEXT_DAY(*date*, *dayOfWeek*)—Returns the date of the next weekday corresponding to *dayOfWeek* (for example, Tuesday) following *date*. The weekday is in the current session language and can be abbreviated.

Example: NEXT_DAY('1-MAR-2003','FRI')
Returns: 07-MAR-03

- SYSDATE—Returns current date and time according to the database. Takes no arguments and, consequently, does not use parentheses.

  Example: SYSDATE
  Returns: 14-SEP-02

- TO_CHAR(*date* [,*format*])—Returns a string representing *date*. If *format* is not provided, the default date format is used. The optional format parameter is a string that provides a template for the date formatting. Table 3–9 lists the most common format elements that it can include:

TABLE 3–9 Most Common Format Elements

am	Meridian indicator (lowercase)
AM	Meridian indicator (uppercase)
Day	Name (initial uppercase)
DAY	Name of day of week (uppercase)
DD	Day of month (1–31)
DY	Abbreviated day of week
HH	Hour of day (12-hour clock)
HH12	Hour of day (12-hour clock)
HH24	Hour of day (24-hour clock)
MI	Minutes (0–59)
MM	Month (01–12)
MON	Abbreviated name of month (uppercase)
Mon	Abbreviated name of month (initial uppercase)
MONTH	Name of month (uppercase)
Month	Name of month (initial uppercase)
PM	Same as AM
pm	Same as am
SS	Seconds (0–59)
YYYY	Year (four digits)
YY	Year (two digits)

In addition to these elements, the format string can include punctuation and double-quoted text.

Example: TO_CHAR(TO_DATE('19-JAN-2003', 'Month DD,YYYY HH:MI:SS am')
Returns: January 19,2003 12:00:00 am

Example: TO_CHAR(CURRENT_DATE, '"Today is" Day')
Returns: Today is Saturday

TRANSACTIONS

A transaction is the logical unit of work when performing database operations. A transaction is created by grouping a sequence of one or more DML statements into a single, all-or-nothing proposition with the following characteristics.

- Atomicity—All statements must complete successfully or the entire set is aborted.
- Consistency—The statements' net effect is to leave the database in a consistent state.
- Isolation—Intermediate statements should not be visible to other transactions.
- Durability—When the transaction is complete, the changes are made permanent.

These four characteristics of a transaction are often abbreviated ACID. To ensure the consistency of the data, we need to identify the boundaries of a transaction and the SQL statements it comprises. Oracle then does the rest of the work necessary for ensuring that the transaction passes the ACID test.

The environment in which we are executing SQL, whether it's SQL*Plus, SQLJ, or JDBC, normally allows us to execute our statements in one of two modes, manual commit or auto-commit. In auto-commit mode, changes made to the database with DML statements are immediately made permanent in the database and are immediately visible to other transactions. In other words, transactions can include only a single SQL DML statement. In this case, Oracle ensures that the transaction meets the ACID requirements.

In manual commit mode, Oracle provides isolation and durability. Changes made to the database with DML are not visible to other transactions and are made permanent only once the transaction has been successfully completed. We take responsibility for atomicity and consistency. We determine what set of DML statements we want to group as an atomic set, and we perform any intermediate validation or error checking that might be necessary.

We group DML statements by marking the boundaries of the transaction—the beginning and the end. Oracle has no statement to mark the start of a transaction explicitly; a transaction begins either at the start of a session (or connection) or after the previous transaction has ended by being committed or cancelled. There are two statements used to mark the end of a transaction:

- COMMIT—Save the results of the transactions permanently in the database.
- ROLLBACK—Abort the transaction and return the database to its state at the beginning of the transaction.

In addition, DDL statements, such as CREATE TABLE, ALTER TABLE, and DROP TABLE, have an implied COMMIT.

A Transaction: All or Nothing

SQL*Plus, like other interfaces to Oracle, has an auto-commit feature. When this feature is enabled, every SQL statement is automatically committed as it is entered. By default, auto-commit is off in SQL*Plus, so we can manually control a transaction by entering a sequence of SQL statements, then decide at the end whether to call COMMIT or ROLLBACK.

In other interfaces, we need to be aware of the default and change it if necessary to support transaction processing. In SQLJ, auto-commit is off by default. In JDBC, it is on by default, meaning that each SQL statement we send to the database is committed automatically; this is less efficient and less flexible than auto-commit.

Suppose that we are adding a CD to our CD collection by typing SQL statements directly into SQL*Plus. We need to update two tables—the CD_COLLECTION table, which contains information about the CD as a whole, and the SONGS table, which contains information for all the songs. We don't want to have incomplete information available in the database, so we'll consider the SQL statement that inserts the CD information and the SQL statements that insert each of the songs into the database as a single transaction.

Assuming that the session just started or that we have just called either COMMIT or ROLLBACK for the previous transaction, we are ready to begin a new transaction:

```
INSERT INTO CD_COLLECTION
(CD_ID, ARTIST, ALBUM_TITLE, RELEASE_DATE, COUNTRY, LABEL)
VALUES
(100, 'PJ Harvey','Rid of Me','1-JAN-1993','UK','Island');

INSERT INTO SONGS
(SONG_ID, CD_ID, SONG_TITLE, COMPOSER, TRACK)
(1,100, 'Rid of Me','Harvey',1);

INSERT INTO SONGS
(SONG_ID, CD_ID, SONG_TITLE, COMPOSER, TRACK)
VALUES (2, 100, 'Missed','Harvey', 2);

INSERT INTO SONGS
(SONG_ID, CD_ID, SONG_TITLE, COMPOSER, TRACK)
VALUES (NULL, 100, 'Missed','Harvey', 3);
```

Suppose that, at this point, we realize it is far too tedious to enter each song manually and decide we'll write a script to do this, instead. We can undo all that we've done so far by typing ROLLBACK. All of the records that we entered up until that point in this session will be removed from the database.

If, on the other hand, we decide we'll just pick up from here later, either with a script or manually, we would commit the transaction so far by entering:

```
COMMIT;
```

Up until the time we enter the COMMIT statement, the records we enter into SQL*Plus are not visible in other users' sessions. We can stop partway through, for example, and query the database, and we will see any records we have entered into the CD_COLLECTION table or the SONGS table. But nobody else can see the new records. You can verify this by opening another SQL*Plus session and querying the databases in the second session. You will find that until you type COMMIT in the first, you will not see the updates in the second.

Partial Rollbacks

In addition to allowing us to commit or roll back a group of SQL statements as a whole, Oracle also allows us to mark intermediate points to allow a partial rollback. The commands to do this are:

- SAVEPOINT *savepoint_name*—Names a point to which we can selectively roll back a transaction.
- ROLLBACK TO *savepoint_name*—Rolls back a transaction to previously named SAVEPOINT.

This is not as generally useful as the basic COMMIT/ROLLBACK arrangement, but it allows creating a more sophisticated scheme for recovering from a partial failure while processing a transaction.

For example, suppose that we have an application with a user interface that allows a user to enter the information for a CD. Suppose we will allow the users to enter just the general CD information or the general information and all the songs. Now suppose that a user tries to enter information and songs, but an error occurs while inserting the songs. We can prompt the user with three choices:

1. Save just the general CD information.
2. Try to pick up where the error occurred.
3. Abandon the entire transaction.

We won't present the application code here to support this logic, but here is a sequence of SQL statements that could cause an error like this—notice NULL in the third INSERT into the SONGS table:

```
INSERT INTO CD_COLLECTION
(CD_ID, ARTIST, ALBUM_TITLE, RELEASE_DATE, COUNTRY, LABEL)
VALUES (100, 'PJ Harvey','Rid of Me','1-JAN-1993','UK','Island');
SAVEPOINT CD_INFO;

INSERT INTO SONGS
(SONG_ID, CD_ID, SONG_TITLE, COMPOSER, TRACK)
(1,100, 'Rid of Me','Harvey',1);
SAVEPOINT SONG_1;

INSERT INTO SONGS
(SONG_ID, CD_ID, SONG_TITLE, COMPOSER, TRACK)
VALUES (2, 100, 'Missed','Harvey', 2);
SAVEPOINT SONG_2;

INSERT INTO SONGS
(SONG_ID, CD_ID, SONG_TITLE, COMPOSER, TRACK)
VALUES (NULL, 100, 'Missed','Harvey', 3);
SAVEPOINT SONG_3;
```

Because the third insert is missing its primary key, this causes an error. At this point, if the user chose option 1, to save just the CD information, we would perform a partial rollback and commit:

```
/* Save just CD information */
ROLLBACK TO CD_INFO;
COMMIT;
```

If the user chose instead to pick up from where the error occurred, we could roll back to SONG_2, the last successful insert, and let the user start again from there:

```
/* Start again just before first error */
ROLLBACK TO SONG_2;
/* Continue inserting more songs … */
```

If the user chose to abandon the entire transaction, we would use an unqualified ROLLBACK, which returns the database to its state prior to starting the transaction:

```
/* Abandon transaction entirely */
ROLLBACK;
```

Partial rollbacks should be approached cautiously. It is easy to create complicated scenarios that can be hard to manage and which can leave the application in an invalid or undetermined state from which it is impossible to recover.

CHAPTER 4

More SQL: Queries, Subqueries, and Views

In the last chapter, we surveyed the different SQL statements that are available and learned the essentials that we need to create, maintain, and use a database. In this chapter, we will concentrate in detail on the most versatile SQL statement, the SELECT statement. We'll learn how to use SELECT statements to:

- Group data
- Put data in order
- Combine data from different tables
- Use as subqueries
- Create views

The first three topics are elaborations on the SELECT statement as we already know it. We'll learn a few new clauses for grouping and ordering data. We'll also learn a few new options for the FROM and WHERE clauses that allow us to combine data from multiple tables.

The next topic, subqueries, is an entirely new use for SELECT statements—as clauses of other SQL statements. Subqueries can be used with CREATE TABLE, INSERT, DELETE, and UPDATE. But they are especially useful within other SELECT statements. Queries with subqueries are another way of combining data from multiple tables.

The final topic in this chapter, views, provide us with a way of "freezing" a query and having the database make it appear as a virtual table.

AGGREGATE FUNCTIONS, GROUP BY AND HAVING

Aggregate functions are functions that take a set of values—a column or an expression including a column name—in a result set and return a single value. For example, we can query a table that contains students' test scores to find the average by using the AVG() function. In SQL, the basic aggregate functions are:

- AVG()—Calculates average
- COUNT()—Returns the number of rows
- MAX()—The highest value in the set of values
- MIN()—The smallest value in the set
- SUM()—The sum of the values

When we use an aggregate function in a select list, we can't use anything else but aggregate functions in the select list—unless we use a GROUP BY clause.

In the previous chapter, we considered a table of fruit.

```
Fruit       Color    Quantity  Price  Picked
----------  -------  --------  -----  ---------
Apple       Green          12     .5  12-SEP-02
Apple       Red            12     .5  15-SEP-02
Mango       Yellow         10    1.5  22-SEP-02
Mangosteen  Purple          5      2  25-SEP-02
Durian                      2     15
Orange      Orange         10      1  28-
```

This is what happens when we try to mix an aggregate function with regular select list items:

```
SQL> SELECT FRUIT, PRICE, AVG(PRICE) FROM FRUITS;
SELECT FRUIT, PRICE, AVG(PRICE) FROM FRUITS
       *
ERROR at line 1:
ORA-00937: not a single-group group function
```

The problem, of course, is that this SELECT statement would return six rows for FRUIT and PRICE but only one for AVG(PRICE).

```
SQL> SELECT AVG(PRICE) FROM FRUITS;

AVG(PRICE)
----------
3.41666667
```

We can't reconcile the difference between aggregate functions that return only a single row and select list items that can potentially return multiple rows. But we can break down rows into smaller subsets based on particular columns, using a GROUP BY clause. The basic format of a SELECT statement with a GROUP BY clause is:

```
SELECT select_list
FROM table_list
[WHERE condition]
GROUP BY group_by_list;
```

The group_by_list is essentially a select_list of columns that together are used to generate unique sets of values. In this table, if we were to group fruit together on the FRUIT column, all rows that have the same value in FRUIT would be combined into a single row. This, by itself, is no different than using the keyword DISTINCT with the select list. What is different is that when we use GROUP BY, aggregate functions, instead of applying to the whole result set, apply to each group of distinct rows.

When we use GROUP BY, items in the select list must either appear in the GROUP BY clause or they must include aggregate functions. Here we use the FRUIT column in the GROUP BY clause and in the select list; we additionally use the aggregate SUM() function in the select list.

```
SQL> SELECT FRUIT, SUM(QUANTITY) FROM FRUITS
  2      GROUP BY FRUIT;

FRUIT      SUM(QUANTITY)
---------- -------------
Apple                 24
Durian                 2
Mango                 10
Mangosteen             5
Orange                10
```

We have two types of apples, 12 of each type, and we can see that here they've been combined into a single row with the total quantity 24.

GROUP BY has an optional subclause, HAVING. HAVING is similar to a WHERE clause for groups. The principal difference is that you can use it only with aggregate functions or with the select list items specified in the GROUP BY clause. Suppose that we want to list only fruits with QUANTITY greater than or equal to 10:

```
SQL> SELECT FRUIT, SUM(QUANTITY) FROM FRUITS
  2  GROUP BY FRUIT
  3  HAVING SUM(QUANTITY)>=10;

FRUIT      SUM(QUANTITY)
---------- -------------
Apple                 24
Mango                 10
Orange                10
```

We cannot use columns that do not appear in the select list in the HAVING clause, but we can use aggregate expressions that don't appear elsewhere. For example, we can limit the results to fruits that have a value totaling 12 or more, even though this calculation doesn't appear in the select list:

```
SQL> SELECT FRUIT, SUM(QUANTITY) FROM FRUITS
  2  GROUP BY FRUIT
  3  HAVING SUM(QUANTITY*PRICE)>=12;

FRUIT      SUM(QUANTITY)
---------- -------------
Apple                 24
Durian                 2
Mango                 10
```

Here is an example with multiple columns in the GROUP BY list and a more complicated condition:

```
SQL> SELECT FRUIT, COLOR, SUM(QUANTITY) FROM FRUITS
  2  GROUP BY FRUIT, COLOR
  3  HAVING SUM(QUANTITY)>=10 AND AVG(PRICE)>1;

FRUIT      COLOR      SUM(QUANTITY)
---------- ---------- -------------
Mango      Yellow                10
```

The GROUP BY clause groups the rows where the combination of FRUIT and COLOR are unique (in this case, all rows are unique, so this returns six rows), finds anywhere the average price is greater than 1 (which rules out apples and oranges), and finally, finds those with a quantity greater than or equal to 10, which leaves only mangos.

Putting Data in Order

One of the most basic yet essential operations we can perform on data is to put it in order. Imagine how useless a phone book would be if the names appeared in random order. One of the most valuable features of a relational database is the flexibility it allows us in sorting our data.

To sort the data returned from a SELECT statement, we add an ORDER BY clause at the end of the other options we've seen so far. This is the basic format:

```
SELECT select_list
FROM table_list
[WHERE condition]
[GROUP BY clause]
ORDER BY order_list
```

The order_list is similar to the select list: It is a list of column names or expressions containing column names that are used in decreasing order of priority in determining the sort order.

For example, suppose that we have the following table of names:

FIRST_NAME	MIDDLE_INITIAL	LAST_NAME	PHONE
John	B	Smith	555-2121
John	A	Smith	555-1234
James	R	Smith	555-1212
Maria	T	Garcia	555-4321

A simple select will return the rows in arbitrary order (as a practical matter, this is most likely in the order in which they were entered). But there is no guarantee that repeating a query will return the results in the same order. (The order can change if data is exported then imported, for example; for this reason, it is better to consider the data unordered.) If we sort using only last name, all the Smiths will fall together, but the first names will be in an arbitrary order.

```
SQL> SELECT * FROM NAMES ORDER BY LAST_NAME;

FIRST_NAME   M LAST_NAME            PHONE_NUMBER
------------ - -------------------- -------------
Maria        T Garcia               555-4321
John         B Smith                555-2121
John         A Smith                555-1234
James        R Smith                555-1212
```

What we need, of course, is to use FIRST_NAME and MIDDLE_INITIAL in addition to LAST_NAME in our sort order to make sure that not only does James R. Smith come before the John Smiths, but also that the John Smiths are sorted correctly, according to their middle initials:

```
SQL> SELECT * FROM NAMES ORDER BY
  2  LAST_NAME, FIRST_NAME, MIDDLE_INITIAL;

FIRST_NAME   M LAST_NAME            PHONE_NUMBER
------------ - -------------------- -------------
Maria        T Garcia               555-4321
James        R Smith                555-1212
John         A Smith                555-1234
John         B Smith                555-2121
```

The default sort order, as you see, is ascending. We can change this for each order list item independently by adding DESC, for *descending*. (We can also explicitly specify ascending by adding ASC, but because it is the default, this isn't necessary.) In the following example, we sort the EMP sample table in descending order by salary but in ascending order by name:

```
SQL> SELECT ENAME,SAL FROM EMP
  2  ORDER BY SAL DESC, ENAME;

ENAME             SAL
---------- ----------
KING             5000
FORD             3000
SCOTT            3000
JONES            2975
BLAKE            2850
CLARK            2450
ALLEN            1600
TURNER           1500
MILLER           1300
MARTIN           1250
WARD             1250

ENAME             SAL
---------- ----------
ADAMS            1100
JAMES             950
SMITH             800

14 rows selected.
```

This ensures that within groups of people who have the same salary, such as FORD and SCOTT, names are listed in alphabetical order.

In addition to allowing ASC and DESC options, the order list also differs from a select list in another way. In the order list, instead of using column names or expressions, we can use numbers to refer to the columns in the select list by position. We can rewrite the SELECT statement in the previous expression, for example, using 1 in the order list to refer to ENAME in the select list, and 2 to refer to SAL:

```
SELECT ENAME, SAL FROM EMP ORDER BY 2 DESC, 1;
```

So far, we've avoided making an important distinction. There are two basic ways that we can sort strings. We can sort by numeric, or binary, value or we can sort according to linguistic rules. In the examples we've seen so far, we've sorted strings using the binary value of the characters in the string. In Oracle, this is the default for English. This generally works adequately—as long as we are consistent about the case of the strings in our table—mostly because we don't have to worry about messy things such as accent marks and expanding characters in English.

Linguistic Sorting

Human languages are complex, naturally arising systems that sometimes don't seem to develop in rational ways. Sorting, or collation, for most languages, is a complex problem. It can be especially vexing because it seems that sorting should be easy—exactly the type of simple-minded task for which a computer is designed. Fortunately, much of this complex functionality has been implemented in Oracle, and it is easy to enable.

The primary issue that arises for English, something to which we've already alluded, is the issue of case sensitivity. In most common applications, we don't expect a sort to be case-sensitive. We want all the A's, big and small, together, as well as all the B's together, etc. In a dictionary, we expect to find Erasmus between erase and erbium.

Suppose we have the following table of unsorted data:

INITIALS	LAST_NAME	BORN
ee	cummings	1894
WH	Auden	1907
TS	Eliot	1888

If we sort these names, we would want to find ee cummings after WH Auden but before TS Eliot. Sometimes, cumming's name is spelled with traditional capitalization to solve the problem. But if we respect his lowercase usage and our default sort is a binary sort, his name falls at the end. All names beginning with A–Z come before those beginning with a–z:

```
SQL> SELECT INITIALS, LAST_NAME, BORN
  2  FROM POETS
  3  ORDER BY LAST_NAME, INITIALS;

INITIALS LAST_NAME             BORN
-------- ------------ ----------
WH       Auden                 1907
TS       Eliot                 1888
ee       cummings              1894
```

One way to solve this in English is to convert all strings in the ORDER BY clause to uppercase (or lowercase):

```
SQL> SELECT INITIALS, LAST_NAME, BORN
  2  FROM POETS
  3  ORDER BY UPPER(LAST_NAME), UPPER(INITIALS);

INITIALS LAST_NAME             BORN
-------- ------------ ----------
WH       Auden                 1907
ee       cummings              1894
TS       Eliot                 1888
```

We need to be careful about using functions such as UPPER() in ORDER BY clauses because they can be very inefficient unless we create and enable function-based indexes.

A more general solution is to use Oracle's NLS (National Language Support) features. Oracle has built-in collation support for many languages that addresses not only case, but also other issues, such as characters with diacritical marks, expanding characters (single characters that are treated as two characters), and contracting characters (two characters that are treated as a single character). This collation support is controlled by a system parameter, NLS_SORT, which is set to value called a *linguistic definition* by Oracle. The basic linguistic definitions are generally named the same as the language name, for example, FRENCH or SWEDISH. Extended support for special cases is also available for many languages; these linguistic definitions begin with the prefix X, for example, XFRENCH or XSPANISH.

System parameters are used to configure the database and the client session, somewhat like environment variables in some operating systems. Many database features can be modified by changing a system parameter. When the database is first started, it reads system parameters from a parameter file, [ORACLE_HOME]/database/init[DB_NAME].ora, or from files included by this file using an IFILE parameter. System parameters not set in this file are derived from other system parameters or from the operating system environment, or else they default to some reasonable or arbitrary value. Finally, some system parameters can also be changed dynamically by a client using the ALTER SESSION command.

The NLS_SORT parameter, in particular, is derived from the NLS_LANGUAGE parameter, which, in turn, is derived from the operating system NLS_LANG variable; if the NLS_LANG variable is not set, NLS_LANGUAGE defaults to AMERICAN.

You can find out the current session's NLS parameters by querying the data dictionary as follows:

```
SELECT * FROM NLS_SESSION_PARAMETERS;
```

In addition to supporting correct linguistic sorting for a single language at a time as in Oracle 8i, Oracle 9i introduced support for sorting multiple languages. The general multilingual sort, based on the International Standards Organizations standard for multilingual sorting, ISO 14651, is GENERIC_M. There are other versions of this linguistic definition that provide additional specialized sorting for individual languages. For example, FRENCH_M is the ISO14651 multilingual sort but handles French diacritics in the proper order, from right to left. See the Oracle9i Globalization Support Guide or the Oracle 8i National Language Support Guide for a complete list of linguistic definitions.

Consider the following unordered table with multilingual names. Each name is included twice, once capitalized and once not, to demonstrate issues with case:

```
SQL> SELECT NAME FROM ML_NAMES;

NAME
----------
Zamboni
zamboni
Ångström
ångström
Amenhotep
amenhotep
Álvarez
álvarez
```

```
chytilova
Chytilova
capek
Capek
Havel
havel

14 rows selected.
```

Assuming that our database is set up for English, the default sort is BINARY. All uppercase letters will sort before all lowercase letters, because A–Z are encoded as decimal 65–90, and a–z are encoded as 97–122. (These are in the ASCII range, 0–127, which does not generally differ from one character set to another. Letters with diacritical marks, non-Roman letters, and other symbols are generally encoded above this range.) In ISO-8859-1 (Latin 1) and Windows 1252, which are commonly used character sets in Western Europe, uppercase letters with various diacritical marks are in the range 192–220, and lowercase letters with diacritical marks are in the range 224–252. Using a binary sort order, despite the ORDER BY clause, this list appears almost as unordered as before:

```
SQL> SELECT NAME FROM ML_NAMES ORDER BY NAME;

NAME
----------
Amenhotep
Capek
Chytilova
Havel
Zamboni
amenhotep
capek
chytilova
havel
zamboni
Álvarez
Ångström
álvarez
ångström

14 rows selected.
```

We can correct the problem with case by selecting a linguistic sort, such as WEST_EUROPEAN (or GENERIC_M in Oracle 9i) for our NLS_SORT parameter. We set the NLS_SORT parameter dynamically in the ALTER SESSION statement:

```
SQL> ALTER SESSION SET NLS_SORT='WEST_EUROPEAN';

Session altered.
```

This change to the NLS_SORT parameter will remain in effect until the end of the session or until we change it with another ALTER SESSION command. The ORDER BY clause will now sort uppercase and lowercase letters together, including those with diacritical marks:

```
SQL> SELECT NAME FROM ML_NAMES ORDER BY NAME;

NAME
----------
Álvarez
álvarez
Amenhotep
amenhotep
Ångström
ångström
Capek
capek
Chytilova
chytilova
Havel
havel
Zamboni
zamboni

14 rows selected.
```

This is clearly an improvement—and it's actually the best we can do with this multilingual list without favoring one language over another.

Several of the languages represented by the names in this multilingual list have rules that this generic sort ignores. For example, in Swedish, the letter A with a circle above it, Å, is considered a separate letter that sorts after Z. Setting the sort order to SWEDISH yields this list:

```
SQL> ALTER SESSION SET NLS_SORT='SWEDISH';

Session altered.

SQL> SELECT NAME FROM ML_NAMES ORDER BY NAME;

NAME
----------
Álvarez
```

```
álvarez
Amenhotep
amenhotep
Capek
capek
Chytilova
chytilova
Havel
havel
Zamboni
zamboni
Ångström
ångström

14 rows selected.
```

In some languages, certain combinations of letters are treated as a single character when sorting—this is called *contraction.* In Czech, for example, CH is sorted as a single letter that falls between H and I. If we set NLS_SORT to XCZECH to enable extended Czech collation, names beginning with CH, disregarding case, will fall after names beginning with H:

```
SQL> ALTER SESSION SET NLS_SORT='XCZECH';

Session altered.

SQL> SELECT NAME FROM ML_NAMES ORDER BY NAME;

NAME
----------
álvarez
Álvarez
amenhotep
Amenhotep
capek
Capek
havel
Havel
chytilova
Chytilova
Ångström
ångström
zamboni
Zamboni

14 rows selected.
```

In other languages, certain single characters are treated as though they were two characters—this is called *expansion*. In German, for example, vowels with an umlaut are sorted as though they were the combination of the base vowel (the vowel without the umlaut) plus the letter e. For example, *ä* is sorted as though it were *ae*.

There are many other issues involved in collation, especially in non-Western European languages, which are beyond the scope of this book. Eastern European languages, bidirectional languages, and Asian languages all present unique challenges. If your requirements include support for these languages, you will also need to consider related issues, such as character set support and language tagging.

Java's internationalization classes also include support for linguistic sorts (see the `Collator` class, in particular), but sorting is much more costly to perform in a client application than it is using the database. Even if you are using other internationalization features in Java such as date and currency formats, which you may find easier and more flexible to use than Oracle's, you should still rely on Oracle for linguistically correct sorting.

Combining Data from Different Tables

An important part of designing a relational database is deciding how to divide data into different tables. We imagined a CD collection that we originally organized on index cards, one card per CD, which we wanted to put in a database. To do this, we created one table to hold information that applied to the CD as a whole and another table for information about the songs. We called the process of finding relationships and creating tables to model the data with minimal redundancy *normalization*. We found that this process leads to multiple small tables. An important consequence of this is that, in order to use the data, create reports, or perform analyses—or, in our example, to recreate the information that was on each CD's index card—we need to combine the information from different tables.

Joins

Just as we can use a SELECT statement to retrieve subsets of data and to put the data in order, we can also use it to combine data from two tables. (We can combine any number of tables, but in practice, a join is usually between two tables.) A SELECT statement used in this way is called a *join*. Two clauses in the SELECT statement are used to create a join: the FROM clause identifies the tables that are to be combined, and the WHERE clause is used to specify the conditions that must be satisfied in order to match records in one table with those in the other.

SQL also provides an alternative to using the FROM and WHERE clauses to create a join—the JOIN clause. Both syntaxes provide the same functionality. There is no compelling reason to choose one syntax over the other. Many database programmers are most comfortable with the FROM...WHERE syntax because it's been around longer on more platforms, but that's largely a matter of personal preference. We'll take a look at examples of both.

Simple Joins

The simplest kind of join is called a *Cartesian join*. This is rarely useful and usually occurs when we accidentally omit the conditions in the WHERE clause. This causes the database to join every row in the first table unconditionally with every row in the second table. Let's use these two tables for example:

```
ANTIQUE_CARS
MODEL         MAKE
Terraplane    Hudson
Firedome      DeSoto
Bearcat       Stutz

CAR_CLUB
OWNER         MODEL
Bob           Terraplane
Sally         Corvette
Lou           Bearcat
Jane          Mustang
```

We can create a Cartesian join of these two tables with the following SELECT statement:

```
SQL> SELECT *
  2  FROM ANTIQUE_CARS, CAR_CLUB;

MODEL        MAKE         OWNER        MODEL
------------ ------------ ------------ ------------
Terraplane   Hudson       Bob          Terraplane
Firedome     DeSoto       Bob          Terraplane
Bearcat      Stutz        Bob          Terraplane
Terraplane   Hudson       Sally        Corvette
Firedome     DeSoto       Sally        Corvette
Bearcat      Stutz        Sally        Corvette
Terraplane   Hudson       Lou          Bearcat
Firedome     DeSoto       Lou          Bearcat
Bearcat      Stutz        Lou          Bearcat
```

```
Terraplane   Hudson       Jane         Mustang
Firedome     DeSoto       Jane         Mustang
Bearcat      Stutz        Jane         Mustang

12 rows selected.
```

Each of the four rows in the first table is matched with each of the three rows in the second table, resulting in twelve rows. If each table had 100 entries, the result would have 10,000 rows. While most of the rows are meaningless, there are a few rows that are interesting: where the entry in the MODEL column from one table matches the MODEL column in the other. In these rows, the OWNER column from one table is connected with the MAKE column in the other table by the MODEL column in each table. If we add a requirement for the MODEL columns to match as a condition of the join, we can, in effect, filter the Cartesian join to get a useful result:

```
SQL> SELECT *
  2  FROM ANTIQUE_CARS, CAR_CLUB
  3  WHERE ANTIQUE_CARS.MODEL=CAR_CLUB.MODEL;

MODEL        MAKE         OWNER        MODEL
------------ ------------ ------------ ------------
Bearcat      Stutz        Lou          Bearcat
Terraplane   Hudson       Bob          Terraplane
```

This tells which club members own antique cars, along with the make and model of their cars. We can eliminate the duplicate MODEL column by specifying a select list. But first notice that, because both tables have a MODEL column, we needed to distinguish between the two in our condition, so we had to specify the name of the table we meant for each one. A convenient feature in SQL is that we can create an alias for each of our tables in the FROM clause that we can use elsewhere in the SELECT statement. We do this by simply adding the table alias after the table name. Although the aliases can be any valid name, most commonly this is used to create an abbreviation.

```
SQL> SELECT C.OWNER, C.MODEL, A.MAKE
  2  FROM ANTIQUE_CARS A, CAR_CLUB C
  3  WHERE A.MODEL=C.MODEL;

OWNER        MODEL        MAKE
------------ ------------ ------------
Lou          Bearcat      Stutz
Bob          Terraplane   Hudson
```

Notice that we specified the table for each column in the select list. This is necessary for the MODEL column, because it appears in both tables; otherwise, Oracle will complain about a column being ambiguously defined. It's a good idea to be explicit about the table for all columns, anyway. This not only makes things clear, but also makes the SQL statement more robust. It won't break if we later add a MAKE column to the CAR_CLUB table, for example.

This type of join is called an *equijoin* because the join condition specifies that the join columns in the two tables must be equal. In this example, we link only on a single column, as illustrated in Figure 4–1, but it is also possible to include multiple columns in the join condition. If each of these tables included a column for the model year, we might want to make that part of the join condition, too.

In addition to the join condition, we can add other criteria to the WHERE clause to select a subset of the rows that meet the join criteria. For example, we can find out who in the car club owns a Stutz, as follows:

```
SQL> SELECT C.OWNER, C.MODEL, A.MAKE
  2  FROM ANTIQUE_CARS A, CAR_CLUB C
  3  WHERE A.MODEL=C.MODEL
  4  AND A.MAKE='Stutz';

OWNER        MODEL        MAKE
------------ ------------ ------------
Lou          Bearcat      Stutz
```

The syntax for this kind of join statement, using FROM and WHERE, has the following general format:

```
SELECT select_list
FROM table_name_1 [alias_1], table_name_2 [alias_2]
WHERE join_conditions
[AND select_conditions];
```

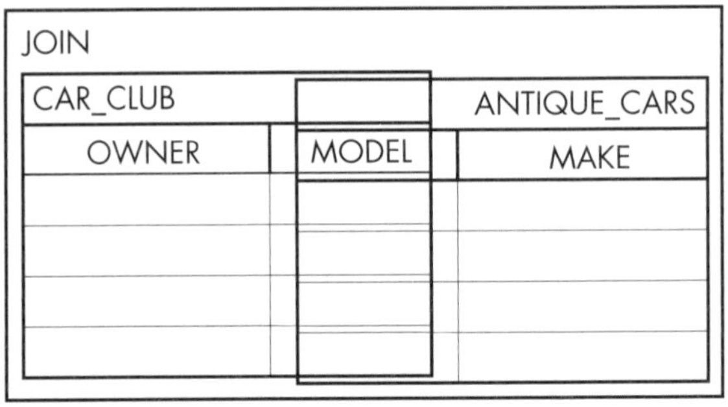

FIGURE 4–1 Join on a single column.

Note that there is no formal distinction between the join conditions and any other conditions, and no requirement that they be joined by AND, but it's a useful distinction, especially when we compare it with the JOIN syntax that makes this distinction between the join conditions and select conditions formal.

To perform a join using the JOIN command, we use this syntax:

```
  SELECT select_list
  FROM table_name_1 [alias_1] JOIN table_name_2 [alias_2]
  ON join_conditions
[WHERE select_conditions];
```

The previous example using the JOIN syntax is:

```
SQL> SELECT C.OWNER, C.MODEL, A.MAKE
     FROM ANTIQUE_CARS A JOIN CAR_CLUB C
     ON A.MODEL=C.MODEL
     WHERE A.MAKE='Stutz';

OWNER        MODEL        MAKE
------------ ------------ ------------
Lou          Bearcat      Stutz
```

The JOIN syntax has one variation that is particularly handy in a case like this where we are joining the tables based on columns that have the same name in both tables—the NATURAL JOIN. It automatically finds rows that have equal values in the common column.

The syntax is:

```
SELECT select_list
FROM table_name_1 [alias_1] NATURAL JOIN table_name_2 [alias_2]
[WHERE select_conditions];
```

Again, the previous example using the NATURAL JOIN syntax:

```
SQL> SELECT OWNER, MODEL, MAKE
     FROM ANTIQUE_CARS NATURAL JOIN CAR_CLUB
     WHERE MAKE='Stutz';

OWNER        MODEL        MAKE
------------ ------------ ------------
Lou          Bearcat      Stutz
```

Notice that we don't need to use table names with columns because there can be no ambiguity. Columns with the same name in each table—in this case, MODEL—necessarily have the same value because they are used for the join condition. In fact, if we try to qualify the join column with a table name, we'll get an error.

The NATURAL JOIN will also work on tables that have more than one column with the same name. Joins of all kinds are frequently done using key columns as the link. Consider the first version of the CD_COLLECTION table in our CD collection database—it had a natural primary key consisting of two columns, ARTIST and TITLE. We can link the songs in the first version of the SONGS table to this table based on these two columns, using a NATURAL JOIN, with the following statement.

```
SELECT ALBUM_TITLE, ARTIST, SONG_TITLE
FROM CD_COLLECTION NATURAL JOIN SONGS
```

This is functionally identical to the following join, using the FROM... WHERE syntax:

```
SELECT C.ALBUM_TITLE, C.ARTIST, S.SONG_TITLE
FROM CD_COLLECTION C, SONGS S
WHERE CD_COLLECTION.ALBUM_TITLE=SONGS.ALBUM_TITLE
  AND CD_COLLECTION.ARTIST=SONGS.ALBUM_ARTIST;
```

It's most common to perform a join on two tables, but we can have any number of tables. (We'll see the special case of joining a table with itself, the self-join, below.) To prevent a Cartesian product, for any number of tables *N*, we need to provide at least *N*-1 join conditions. Suppose that we've noticed a number of old cars around town and create a table listing where we usually see them:

CAR_SIGHTINGS

MAKE	**COMPANY**
Hudson	Acme Lumber
Studebaker	Central Supermarket
Edsel	Cup O' Java
Stutz	Ace Insurance

We might assume that if the car is usually parked in front of a place of business, the owner works there. This assumption may or may not be valid, but given this table, we can associate the owners of antique cars with places of business, as follows:

```
SQL> SELECT C.OWNER, S.COMPANY
  2  FROM CAR_CLUB C, ANTIQUE_CARS A, CAR_SIGHTINGS S
  3  WHERE C.MODEL=A.MODEL AND A.MAKE=S.MAKE;

OWNER        COMPANY
------------ --------------------
Lou          Ace Insurance
Bob          Acme Lumber
```

This is the most common use for multiple joins, navigating from data in one table that is linked via one or more intermediate tables to data in another table. In this case, to get from the COMPANY in the CAR_SIGHTINGS table to the OWNER in the CAR_CLUB table, we linked CAR_SIGHTING to the ANTIQUE_CARS table with the MAKE column, then we linked the ANTIQUE_CARS table to the CAR_CLUB table with the MODEL column.

Outer Joins

The simple joins that we've seen so far are called *inner joins.* They include the rows from both tables that meet the join condition and only those rows. Sometimes we want to include all the rows from one of the tables and use the other table to provide additional information, if it's available, for some rows. This is called an *outer join.*

There are three kinds of outer joins. When you are joining two tables in an SQL statement, the first one appears on the left and the second one on the right, if you list them on the same line in the join clause. Because of this obvious fact, we refer to the first table as the *left* table and the second table as the *right* table. If we specify that we want to include all rows for the first table, this is called a *left outer join.* If we specify that we want to include all rows for the second table, this is called a *right outer join.* We can also include all rows for both tables; this is called a *full outer join.*

For example, suppose we want to see what each member of the car club drives. The CAR_CLUB table lists the owner and the model of each car but not the make. We have the make information for antique cars in the ANTIQUE_CARS table, but not everyone drives an antique car. The following is a left outer join that will list all owners and models from the first table, unconditionally. If, for a given column, the make is available from the second table because the car is an antique, it will list that too; otherwise, it will leave the column for that row blank.

```
SQL> SELECT C.OWNER, C.MODEL, A.MAKE
     FROM CAR_CLUB C LEFT OUTER JOIN ANTIQUE_CARS A
     ON C.MODEL=A.MODEL;

OWNER        MODEL        MAKE
------------ ------------ ------------
Bob          Terraplane   Hudson
Lou          Bearcat      Stutz
Jane         Mustang
Sally        Corvette
```

This uses the newer ANSI JOIN syntax. The general format for a left outer join is:

```
SELECT select_list
FROM table_name_1 [alias_1] LEFT OUTER JOIN table_name_2 [alias_2]
ON join_conditions
[WHERE select_conditions];
```

The general format for a right outer join is:

```
SELECT select_list
FROM table_name_1 [alias_1] RIGHT OUTER JOIN table_name_2 [alias_2]
ON join_conditions
[WHERE select_conditions];
```

We can list all the cars in the ANTIQUE_CAR list plus any club members who own one, with a right outer join as follows:

```
SQL> SELECT C.OWNER, A.MODEL, A.MAKE
  2  FROM CAR_CLUB C RIGHT OUTER JOIN ANTIQUE_CARS A
  3  ON C.MODEL=A.MODEL;

OWNER        MODEL        MAKE
------------ ------------ ------------
Bob          Terraplane   Hudson
Lou          Bearcat      Stutz
             Firedome     DeSoto
```

Notice that we changed the select list as well. We include MODEL from the ANTIQUE_CARS table—not the CAR_CLUB, like we did before—because since no one in the car club owns a DeSoto, the MODEL column would otherwise be null.

A full outer join lists all rows of the joined tables, filling in the appropriate columns with null where a row in one table does not have a matching row in the other. Here is a full outer join of the CAR_CLUB and ANTIQUE_CARS table, listing all club members and all antique cars:

```
SQL> SELECT C.OWNER, C.MODEL, A.MODEL, A.MAKE
  2  FROM CAR_CLUB C FULL OUTER JOIN ANTIQUE_CARS A
  3  ON C.MODEL=A.MODEL;

OWNER        MODEL        MODEL        MAKE
------------ ------------ ------------ ------------
Bob          Terraplane   Terraplane   Hudson
Lou          Bearcat      Bearcat      Stutz
Jane         Mustang
Sally        Corvette
                          Firedome     DeSoto
```

We can perform outer joins using a variation of FROM...WHERE, syntax as well. To do this, we mark the join columns of the table that need to be *expanded* with (+). This means that if we are performing a *left* outer join, we must mark the join columns of the *right* table with (+). This last example is a left outer join, using the FROM...WHERE syntax:

```
SQL> SELECT C.OWNER, A.MODEL, A.MAKE
  2  FROM CAR_CLUB C, ANTIQUE_CARS A
  3  WHERE C.MODEL=A.MODEL(+);

OWNER        MODEL        MAKE
------------ ------------ ------------
Lou          Bearcat      Stutz
Sally
Jane
Bob          Terraplane   Hudson
```

This syntax for outer joins, using the (+) operator, is specific to Oracle, and it is subject to a number of restrictions that don't apply to the standard JOIN syntax. Two examples: If multiple join conditions are specified and you omit the (+) in any of them, a simple join will result, with no indication of the error. Join conditions cannot be combined with OR if you use the (+) operator. Oracle recommends that we use the ANSI standard RIGHT OUTER JOIN, LEFT OUTER JOIN, and FULL OUTER JOIN syntax, instead.

Self-Joins

Not only can we join a table with one or more other tables, we can also join a table with itself. This is useful when there are dependencies between the rows in a table.

Although it is generally best to avoid dependencies between rows in a table, sometimes this is the most convenient way to store the data. A common example is an employee table that lists employees and their managers; managers, in turn, are also employees. Another example is a product catalog that includes components as well as assemblies that may include components. The problem with these dependencies is that the self-joins are required to work with them, and self-joins are often complex and difficult to create and debug.

We'll use a table of the family relations between some early Egyptian gods for our examples:

EGYPTIAN_GODS

NAME	**FATHER**	**MOTHER**
Shu	Atum	
Tefnut	Atum	
Nut	Shu	Tefnut
Geb	Shu	Tefnut

```
Osiris     Geb        Nut
Isis       Geb        Nut
Horus      Osiris     Isis
Anubis     Osiris     Nephthys
```

It's easiest to think of a self-join as a join of two separate copies of the table. Consider one copy to be a list of children and another copy to be a list of parents. We can join the two by linking the FATHER column in the children table with the NAME column in the parents table. This links each child to information about the child's father; that information includes the father's mother and father, which is to say, the child's grandparents. This query will list each child's paternal grandfather and grandmother:

```
SQL> SELECT C.NAME, P.NAME AS FATHER,
     P.FATHER AS GRANDFATHER,
     P.MOTHER AS GRANDMOTHER
     FROM EGYPTIAN_GODS C, EGYPTIAN_GODS P
     WHERE C.FATHER=P.NAME;

NAME       FATHER     GRANDFATHE GRANDMOTHE
---------- ---------- ---------- ----------
Osiris     Geb        Shu        Tefnut
Isis       Geb        Shu        Tefnut
Horus      Osiris     Geb        Nut
Anubis     Osiris     Geb        Nut
Nut        Shu        Atum
Geb        Shu        Atum

6 rows selected.
```

If we join yet another copy of the same table to itself, we can list both maternal and paternal grandparents for each child. Notice that we have three tables in the join statement: one for the children, one for the fathers, and one for the mothers. The join conditions ensure that the FATHER column in the child table matches the NAME column in the fathers table, as before. We've added an additional join condition, to match the MOTHER column in the children table to the NAME column in the mothers table. This way, the FATHER and MOTHER columns in the fathers table are a child's paternal grandparents—as before—and the FATHER and MOTHER columns in the mothers table are a child's maternal grandparents:

```
SQL> SELECT C.NAME,
     C.MOTHER AS M, M.MOTHER AS M_GM, M.FATHER AS M_GF,
     C.FATHER AS F, F.MOTHER AS P_GM, F.FATHER AS P_GF
     FROM EGYPTIAN_GODS C, EGYPTIAN_GODS F, EGYPTIAN_GODS M
     WHERE F.NAME=C.FATHER AND M.NAME=C.MOTHER;
```

```
NAME     M       M_GM     M_GF     F        P_GM      P_GF
-------- ------- -------- -------- -------- --------- -----
Osiris   Nut     Tefnut   Shu      Geb      Tefnut    Shu
Isis     Nut     Tefnut   Shu      Geb      Tefnut    Shu
Horus    Isis    Nut      Geb      Osiris   Nut       Geb
Nut      Tefnut           Atum     Shu                Atum
Geb      Tefnut           Atum     Shu                Atum
```

(Where M = Mother, F = Father, M_GM = Maternal Grandmother, P_GF = Paternal Grandfather, etc.)

Combining Data with Set Operations: Unions, Intersect, and Minus

SQL provides a number of operators that allow us to perform common set operations on tables. The UNION operator lets us combine tables. The INTERSECT operator lets us find the data that two tables have in common. The MINUS operator lets us use one table to specify which rows to remove from another table.

The syntax of these operators is very straightforward. They are conjunctions that join two or more SELECT statements together.

Unions

Unions and joins are both ways of combining tables, but they are markedly different. A join is a single SELECT statement that combines tables by linking them together, using one or more join columns. This establishes a relationship. The rows that are selected from one table are related in some way to the rows selected from the other table or tables. A union, in contrast, is the combined result of multiple, independent SELECT statements, and there isn't any explicit relationship whatsoever between the SELECT statements. The only requirement for SELECT statements that are joined by UNION is that the select lists must all return the same number of columns of compatible types, so that their results can be pasted together into a single result.

The basic syntax for a union is:

```
select_statement
UNION [ALL]
select_statement
[UNION [ALL]
select statement
[…]]
[ORDER BY order_by_list]
```

In the car example that we used to explore joins we had a list of antique cars:

ANTIQUE_CARS

MODEL	**MAKE**
Terraplane	Hudson
Firedome	DeSoto
Bearcat	Stutz

Supposing we also had a lists of modern cars too:

MODERN_CARS

MODEL	**MAKE**
Mustang	Ford
Corvette	Chevrolet
Cherokee	Jeep

We can combine the two lists with a UNION statement as follows:

```
SQL> SELECT MODEL, MAKE FROM ANTIQUE_CARS
  2  UNION
  3  SELECT MODEL, MAKE FROM MODERN_CARS;

MODEL        MAKE
------------ ------------
Bearcat      Stutz
Cherokee     Jeep
Corvette     Chevrolet
Firedome     DeSoto
Mustang      Ford
Terraplane   Hudson

6 rows selected.
```

If we had other lists, such as a list of sports cars, we could combine those as well:

SPORTS_CARS

MODEL	**MAKE**
Bearcat	Stutz
Corvette	Chevrolet
Viper	Dodge

We might expect that, by adding this table with three more rows to the union, we'll get a result with a total of nine rows, but we don't:

```
SQL> SELECT MODEL, MAKE FROM ANTIQUE_CARS
  2  UNION
  3  SELECT MODEL, MAKE FROM MODERN_CARS
  4  UNION
  5  SELECT MODEL, MAKE FROM SPORTS_CARS;

MODEL        MAKE
------------ ------------
Bearcat      Stutz
Cherokee     Jeep
Corvette     Chevrolet
Firedome     DeSoto
Mustang      Ford
Terraplane   Hudson
Viper        Dodge

7 rows selected.
```

If we compare this result with the previous one, we'll see why. An important characteristic of the UNION statement is that it eliminates all duplicate rows. (Notice that one artifact of the process used to implement this is that the models are listed in alphabetical order.) This new table, SPORTS_CARS, contains two cars that were already listed in the previous two tables, so there is only one new car.

We can override this behavior so that all rows are included by adding the ALL option to the UNION command:

```
SQL> SELECT MODEL, MAKE FROM ANTIQUE_CARS
  2  UNION ALL
  3  SELECT MODEL, MAKE FROM MODERN_CARS
  4  UNION ALL
  5  SELECT MODEL, MAKE FROM SPORTS_CARS;

MODEL        MAKE
------------ ------------
Terraplane   Hudson
Firedome     DeSoto
Bearcat      Stutz
Mustang      Ford
Corvette     Chevrolet
Cherokee     Jeep
Bearcat      Stutz
Corvette     Chevrolet
Viper        Dodge

9 rows selected.
```

As stated before, there is only one requirement for the SELECT statements: They must have compatible select lists. This means that each SELECT statement must have the same number of items in its select lists and the datatypes of each must be the same. So far, our tables have had the same structure and the same column names. If we combine tables that are not alike, we need either to select only compatible columns or to convert the incompatible columns to a compatible type.

The car companies sell lots of things besides cars. Let's suppose we have a table of automobile-related products:

AUTO_PRODUCTS

ITEM_NO	**DESCRIPTION**	**VENDOR**
RB195	Bow tie workout bag	Chevrolet
A1504122	Aladdin travel mug	Dodge
ENA55	Radio flashlight	Jeep

If we want to combine this with one of our other tables—for example, the MODERN_CARS table—we'll need to decide how we're going to map the columns. VENDOR in this table clearly maps to MAKER in the MODERN_CARS table. But if we want to include both ITEM_NO and DESCRIPTION from the AUTO_PRODUCTS table in the combined table, we'll either need to include a dummy column in the select list for the car table—perhaps a literal, such as 'N/A' for "not available"—or we could concatenate ITEM_NO and DESCRIPTION into a single column in the select list for the AUTO_PRODUCTS table.

Let's try the first approach, using a dummy column:

```
SQL> SELECT 'N/A', MODEL, MAKE FROM MODERN_CARS
  2     UNION
  3     SELECT ITEM_NO, DESCRIPTION, VENDOR FROM AUTO_PRODUCTS;

'N/A'        MODEL                MAKE
------------ -------------------- ------------
A1504122     Aladdin travel mug   Dodge
ENA55        Radio flashlight     Jeep
N/A          Cherokee             Jeep
N/A          Corvette             Chevrolet
N/A          Mustang              Ford
RB195        Bow tie workout bag  Chevrolet

6 rows selected.
```

Take a look at the column headings. They are taken from the first SELECT statement and aren't entirely appropriate. We can improve that by using column aliases to supply headings that work for entries from either table. We need to do that only for the first SELECT statement, because that's the only one that matters as far as the column headings go.

Let's try the second approach. Instead of using a dummy column for the MODERN_CAR table, we'll combine the ITEM_NO and DESCRIPTION columns in the AUTO_PRODUCTS table.

```
SQL> SELECT MODEL AS PRODUCT, MAKE AS COMPANY FROM MODERN_CARS
  2  UNION
  3  SELECT DESCRIPTION||' - '||ITEM_NO, VENDOR FROM AUTO_PRODUCTS;

PRODUCT                             COMPANY
----------------------------------- ------------
Aladdin travel mug - A1504122       Dodge
Bow tie workout bag - RB195         Chevrolet
Cherokee                            Jeep
Corvette                            Chevrolet
Mustang                             Ford
Radio flashlight - ENA55            Jeep

6 rows selected.
```

We can now revisit a problem we saw in the previous chapter where we wanted to perform calculations on different groups of data. We had a fruit table and we wanted to give different discounts based on the quantity:

FRUIT

FRUIT	COLOR	QUANTITY	PRICE	PICKED
Apple	Green	12	.5	12-SEP-02
Apple	Red	12	.5	15-SEP-02
Mango	Yellow	10	1.5	22-SEP-02
Mangosteen	Purple	5	2	25-SEP-02
Durian		2	15	
Orange	Orange	10	1	28-AUG-02

Suppose these are the discounts:

```
No discount: QUANTITY < 5
10%:         QUANTITY >= 5 AND QUANTITY < 10
20%:         QUANTITY >= 10 AND QUANTITY < 50
30%:         QUANTITY >= 50
```

We can apply these discounts by using a SELECT statement for each range and combining the results using a union:

```
SQL> SELECT FRUIT, QUANTITY, PRICE,
       PRICE*QUANTITY AS SUBTOTAL, 'No discount' AS DISCOUNT
     FROM FRUITS WHERE QUANTITY<5
   UNION
   SELECT FRUIT, QUANTITY, PRICE,
       PRICE*QUANTITY*.9, '10 Percent'
     FROM FRUITS WHERE QUANTITY >= 5 AND QUANTITY < 10
   UNION
   SELECT FRUIT, QUANTITY, PRICE,
       PRICE*QUANTITY*.8, '20 Percent'
     FROM FRUITS WHERE QUANTITY >= 10 AND QUANTITY < 50
   UNION
   SELECT FRUIT, QUANTITY, PRICE,
       PRICE*QUANTITY*.7, '30 Percent'
     FROM FRUITS WHERE QUANTITY >= 50
   ORDER BY QUANTITY;

FRUIT        QUANTITY      PRICE   SUBTOTAL DISCOUNT
---------- ---------- ---------- ---------- -----------
Durian              2         15         30 No discount
Mangosteen          5          2          9 10 Percent
Mango              10        1.5         12 20 Percent
Orange             10          1          8 20 Percent
Apple              12         .5        4.8 20 Percent
```

Notice that at the end we've added an ORDER BY clause at the end to make the results a little more readable.

Intersect and Minus

The INTERSECT and MINUS operators are not used very often but, together with UNION, they make for a complete set of set operations. INTERSECT is roughly complementary to the UNION operation. Where UNION allowed us to combine the results of two queries, eliminate duplicates, and return the rows that remained, INTERSECT allows us to compare the rows in each table and return any duplicated rows.

INTERSECT is not exactly complementary to UNION because UNION will remove duplicates even if they appear in the same table, but INTERSECT will remove duplicates only if they appear in separate tables.

For example, we saw that our SPORTS_CAR table included some cars that were included in the ANTIQUE_CARS tables. We can find out which cars are in both with this query:

```
SQL> SELECT MODEL, MAKE FROM ANTIQUE_CARS
  2      INTERSECT
  3      SELECT MODEL, MAKE FROM SPORTS_CARS;

MODEL        MAKE
------------ ------------
Bearcat      Stutz
```

The MINUS operator returns the results of the first SELECT statement minus any rows that also appear in the results of the second SELECT statement. We know from the previous intersect query that the Stutz Bearcat is the only car that appears in both ANTIQUE_CARS and SPORTS_CARS, so a MINUS query with these two tables will return all rows in the ANTIQUE_CARS except for the Stutz Bearcat:

```
SQL> SELECT MODEL, MAKE FROM ANTIQUE_CARS
  2  MINUS
  3  SELECT MODEL, MAKE FROM SPORTS_CARS;

MODEL        MAKE
------------ ------------
Firedome     DeSoto
Terraplane   Hudson
```

Notice that UNION and INTERSECT are commutative; we can change the order of the tables without changing the results. MINUS is not commutative. We get different results, depending on which table we put first:

```
SQL> SELECT MODEL, MAKE FROM SPORTS_CARS
  2  MINUS
  3  SELECT MODEL, MAKE FROM ANTIQUE_CARS;

MODEL        MAKE
------------ ------------
Corvette     Chevrolet
Viper        Dodge

SQL>
```

These ask different questions. In English, the first MINUS example asks, "Which antique cars are not sports cars?" The second asks, "Which sports cars are not antiques?"

SUBQUERIES

SQL, as we have seen, has just a few types of DML statements and each of these has several optional clauses. This, I hope you've found, makes it easy to learn the basics. At the same time, the number of combinations of options that are possible can be overwhelming. This is one of the things that make SQL such a powerful and expressive language. One combination is especially formidable: the subquery, which is a SELECT statement within another SQL statement.

Subqueries are important in a relational database for the same reason that joins are. Because we store data in normalized tables, we frequently have to combine data from multiple tables or use data from one table to determine what data to use, change, or delete in another table.

The most important use of subqueries is with SELECT statements. Queries within subqueries are similar to joins and are, in fact, often interchangeable with them. But subqueries aren't just for queries—they're much more versatile than that. They can also be used with CREATE TABLE to create and populate a new table from an existing one, with INSERT and UPDATE to copy data from one table to another and with DELETE to determine which rows in a table to delete.

Single-Value versus Multiple-Value Subqueries

Single-value subqueries are the most common and useful because they can be used almost anywhere that SQL expects a value. Single-value queries are commonly used in a condition, such as in a WHERE clause. The most common type of single-value subquery is one that uses an aggregate function, such as AVG(), MIN(), MAX(). We could use a single-value subquery to find, for example, which students scored higher than the class average.

Multiple-value subqueries are single-column, multiple-row subqueries—essentially lists—and can be compared with a single value, using the list operator IN or a comparison plus either the ANY or ALL operator. For example, if we have a table of people's addresses and a table of zip codes for different cities, we can find which people live in a specific city by using a multiple-value subquery; in this case, the subquery would obtain the list of zipcodes for the selected city and the outer query would compare each person's zipcode to the zipcodes in the list.

Both single-value subqueries and multiple-value subqueries are commonly used in the WHERE clauses of DELETE, UPDATE, and SELECT statements.

Multiple-column, multiple-row subqueries are essentially tables and can be used almost anywhere a table can, particularly in the FROM clause in a SELECT statement. They can also be used in place of the VALUES clause in an INSERT statement.

Correlated versus Noncorrelated Subqueries

The simplest way to use a subquery is to have it simply provide a value, multiple values, or multiple rows to the SQL statement that includes it. This type of subquery that operates entirely independently and unaware of the outer statement is called a *noncorrelated subquery.*

A subquery can also use values from the enclosing SQL statement. This is most common when the outer statement is a SELECT statement, as well, and the subquery compares columns from the table in the outer statement's FROM clause with columns from a table in its own FROM clause. This type of subquery is called a *correlated subquery.* You might think of a correlated subquery as a kind of subroutine. As each row in the outer query is processed, it calls the subquery with a new set of values, which the subquery uses to calculate values that it returns to the outer statement.

Queries with Subqueries: A SELECT within a SELECT

By far, subqueries are most commonly used with SELECT statements, usually as part of a WHERE clause. In Oracle, they can also be used as part of the select list in the FROM clause and in a HAVING clause. We'll see WHERE clauses that use single-value and multiple-value subqueries—some noncorrelated and some correlated.

Single-Value Subqueries

Within a SELECT statement, the most common way to use a subquery is as a single-value subquery in the WHERE clause as part of a comparison. To ensure that the subquery will return a single value, we can either set the appropriate conditions in the subquery's WHERE clause—based on a specific primary key value or our knowledge of the data—or we can use an aggregate function.

We've seen that we can use joins to combine information from multiple tables. We saw the following example when we were looking at joins: The WHERE clause joins the ANTIQUE_CARS and CAR_CLUB tables on the MODEL column. Then we set an additional condition, our query condition—We're looking for the owner of a Stutz:

```
SQL> SELECT C.OWNER, C.MODEL, A.MAKE
  2  FROM ANTIQUE_CARS A JOIN CAR_CLUB C
  3  ON A.MODEL=C.MODEL
  4  WHERE A.MAKE='Stutz';

OWNER        MODEL        MAKE
------------ ------------ ------------
Lou          Bearcat      Stutz
```

This is how we can find out the same information using a single-value query:

```
SQL> SELECT OWNER
  2  FROM CAR_CLUB
  3  WHERE MODEL=(SELECT MODEL
  4               FROM ANTIQUE_CARS
  5               WHERE MAKE='Stutz');

OWNER
------------
Lou
```

There is one important difference between these results, and that is, when we use a join, we have access to information in both of the tables. Presumably, we wanted to know only who the owner of the Stutz is, but if we had wanted to list the MAKE from the ANTIQUE_CARS column in the results, as we did with the join, we couldn't do that with a single subquery like this. Aside from this limitation, a join and a subquery of this type are roughly comparable in terms of efficiency and ease of use. Choosing one form over the other is largely a matter of personal preference.

There are other cases, however, where a subquery is more appropriate to use than a join. This is especially true when we want to use an aggregate function.

Suppose that we wanted to list any fruits in our FRUITS table that cost less than the average. Our first thought might be that we can do this with a simple query, as follows:

```
SQL> SELECT FRUIT, PRICE FROM FRUITS
  2  WHERE PRICE<AVG(PRICE);
WHERE PRICE<AVG(PRICE)
            *
ERROR at line 2:
ORA-00934: group function is not allowed here
```

The problem, in general, is that we can't mix aggregate functions such as AVG() with nonaggregated columns. We can, however, use a subquery (a single-value, noncorrelated subquery) in the WHERE clause to calculate the average:

```
SQL> SELECT FRUIT, PRICE FROM FRUITS
  2  WHERE PRICE < (SELECT AVG(PRICE) FROM FRUITS);

FRUIT           PRICE
---------- ----------
Apple              .5
Apple              .5
Mango             1.5
Mangosteen          2
Orange              1
```

The basic format for a SELECT statement with a single value subquery is:

```
SELECT select_list
FROM table_list
WHERE expression comparison_operator
      (SELECT {aggregate_function(column)}|column
      FROM table_list
      WHERE condition)
[ORDER BY order_list];
```

The subquery should return a single value, either because the WHERE clause in the subquery ensures that only a single row is selected—by referencing the primary key, for example—or because the aggregate function rolls up the values from multiple rows into a single value.

Multiple-Value Subqueries

For some types of queries, we need to use a subquery that returns a list of values: a single-column, multiple-row result. Then we can use a list operator, such as IN, or the combination of a comparison operator and ANY or ALL to compare each row in the outer query with this list.

The basic format for a multiple-value query is:

```
SELECT select_list
FROM table_list
WHERE expression {[NOT] IN}|
                 {comparison_operator ANY|ALL}
      (subquery)
[ORDER BY order_list];
```

Let's take a look at another of the join examples and see how we can accomplish the same thing with a subquery:

```
SQL> SELECT *
  2  FROM ANTIQUE_CARS, CAR_CLUB
  3  WHERE ANTIQUE_CARS.MODEL=CAR_CLUB.MODEL;

MODEL        MAKE         OWNER        MODEL
------------ ------------ ------------ ------------
Bearcat      Stutz        Lou          Bearcat
Terraplane   Hudson       Bob          Terraplane
```

In this example, we joined the ANTIQUE_CARS table with the CAR_CLUB table to find out who in the car club owns an antique car. We can find out the same information by using a multiple-value subquery with the IN list operator. The subquery returns a list of all the entries in the MODEL column in the ANTIQUE_CARS table, and, for each row in the CAR_CLUB table, the outer query attempts to find the MODEL in the subquery list:

```
SQL> SELECT *
  2  FROM CAR_CLUB
  3  WHERE MODEL IN (SELECT MODEL
  4                  FROM ANTIQUE_CARS);

OWNER        MODEL
------------ ------------
Lou          Bearcat
Bob          Terraplane
```

We can also find out which members of the club own cars that are not antiques; we simply add the NOT operator to IN:

```
SQL> SELECT *
  2  FROM CAR_CLUB
  3  WHERE MODEL NOT IN (SELECT MODEL
  4                      FROM ANTIQUE_CARS);

OWNER        MODEL
------------ ------------
Sally        Corvette
Jane         Mustang
```

One advantage of using subqueries is that they are more flexible than joins, and they are easier to understand and modify. If you remember, a join (at least conceptually) starts out with the Cartesian product—every possible combination of rows from the two tables—which the condition filters to the required (and manageable) result. Negating the join condition in the join that is equivalent to this subquery does not produce an equivalent result:

```
SELECT *
FROM ANTIQUE_CARS, CAR_CLUB
      WHERE ANTIQUE_CARS.MODEL!=CAR_CLUB.MODEL;
```

The result of running this is not listed here, because this join does not return the list of club members who do not own antique cars; it returns the Cartesian product, excluding only the two rows where ANTIQUE_CARS.MODEL and CAR_CLUB.MODEL are equal—14 rows of meaningless results.

We can use subqueries with the operators ALL or ANY in combination with a comparison operator. A comparison operator plus ALL or ANY is effectively a list operator, such as IN.

ALL means, in effect, that the comparison is applied to each item in the list and the results are logically combined with AND—the comparison must be true for ALL items:

- **X > ALL(*list*)**: is true if X is greater than every item in *list*; i.e., X is greater than the largest item in the list
- **X >= ALL(*list*)**: X is greater than or equal to the largest item in *list*
- **X < ALL(*list*)**: is true if X is less than every item in *list*; i.e., X is less than the smallest item in the list
- **X <= ALL(*list*)**: X is less than or equal to the smallest item in *list*
- **X = ALL(*list*)**: is true if X is equal to every item in *list* or, stating it conversely, every item in the list is equivalent to X
- **X != ALL(*list*)**: is true if X is not equal to any item in *list*; there is no item in the list equivalent to X

ANY means, in effect, that the comparison is applied to each item in the list and the results are logically combined with OR—the comparison must be true for at least one item. Oracle also has the operator SOME, which is equivalent:

- **X > ANY(*list*)**: is true if X is greater than any (some) item in *list* or, stating it conversely, there is at least one item in the list smaller than X
- **X >= ANY(*list*)**: there is at least one item in the list smaller than or equal to X
- **X < ANY(*list*)**: is true if X is less than any item in *list* or, stating it conversely, there is at least one item in the list larger than X

- **X <= ANY(*list*)**: there is at least one item in the list larger than or equal to X
- **X = ANY(*list*)**: is true if X is equal to any item in *list*; this is equivalent to IN
- **X != ANY(list)**: is true if X is not equal to any item in the list. This means that there is at least one value in the list that is not equal to X.

Correlated Subqueries

In a correlated query, the subquery uses values from the outer query. The most common use of a correlated query is with the EXISTS operator. In its most basic form, it is an alternative to using IN. Here is a query with EXISTS that is equivalent to an example with IN that we saw above:

```
SQL> SELECT OWNER, MODEL
     FROM CAR_CLUB C
     WHERE EXISTS (SELECT *
                   FROM ANTIQUE_CARS
                   WHERE MODEL=C.MODEL);

OWNER        MODEL
------------ ------------
Bob          Terraplane
Lou          Bearcat
```

Notice that we use the asterisk (*) as the select list in the subquery. That is because we aren't returning anything from the subquery to the outer query other than whether or not there is a row that matches the condition in the WHERE clause.

Also notice that in the subquery we need to qualify the columns from the outside query's table. Within the subquery, if there are columns with the same name in both the subquery's table and the outer query's table, the column is assumed to belong to the subquery's table if it isn't qualified as belonging to the outer query's table. We can use the table name or, more conveniently as we do here, an abbreviated alias.

The advantage of using a correlated subquery over an uncorrelated one is that we can use more than one column in our matching condition, and we can match on more complex conditions.

Suppose that we want to find out which fruits in the FRUIT table are ripe—at least, as far as we can tell—using the following FRUIT_COLORS table:

FRUIT_COLORS

FRUIT	**VARIETY**	**RIPE_COLOR**
Apple	Granny Smith	Green
Apple	McIntosh	Red
Orange	Mandarin	Orange
Banana	Cavendish	Yellow

We can do that with a correlated subquery that matches rows in the outer query to rows in the subquery. What we want to know is whether, for each set of FRUIT and COLOR in the FRUIT table, there exists a matching entry in the FRUIT_COLORS table. For example, APPLE and GREEN match, but ORANGE and GREEN do not.

```
SQL> SELECT FRUIT, COLOR
     FROM FRUITS F
     WHERE EXISTS
       (SELECT *
        FROM FRUIT_COLORS
        WHERE F.COLOR=RIPE_COLOR AND F.FRUIT=FRUIT);

FRUIT      COLOR
---------- ----------
Apple      Green
Apple      Red
Orange     Orange
```

We could also use an alias, F, for the FRUITS table to make the statement less cluttered:

```
SELECT FRUIT, COLOR
FROM FRUITS F
WHERE EXISTS
  (SELECT *
   FROM FRUIT_COLORS
   WHERE F.COLOR=RIPE_COLOR AND F.FRUIT=FRUIT);
```

Also notice again that we use (*) for the columns—we aren't interested in any particular column, just whether or not a row matching the WHERE condition exists.

We also could have used a join to get the same information:

```
SQL> SELECT F.FRUIT, F.COLOR
     FROM FRUITS F, FRUIT_COLORS FC
     WHERE F.COLOR=FC.RIPE_COLOR
     AND F.FRUIT=FC.FRUIT;
```

```
FRUIT      COLOR
---------- ----------
Apple      Green
Orange     Orange
Apple      Red
```

The join is more efficient because the subquery is repeated for each row in our query. The join also has another advantage: We can easily use values from the second table in a select list. Once we've matched a fruit and color from one table with a row in the other table, we can identify the variety:

```
SQL> SELECT F.FRUIT, F.COLOR, FC.VARIETY
     FROM FRUITS F, FRUIT_COLORS FC
     WHERE F.COLOR=FC.RIPE_COLOR
     AND F.FRUIT=FC.FRUIT;

FRUIT      COLOR      VARIETY
---------- ---------- ----------------
Apple      Green      Granny Smith
Orange     Orange     Mandarin
Apple      Red        McIntosh
```

It's possible to do this with subqueries, but it's messy. We have to use two separate subqueries—one in the WHERE clause to set the condition and another similar one in the SELECT statement to get the result:

```
SQL> SELECT FRUIT, COLOR,
     (SELECT VARIETY FROM FRUIT_COLORS
         WHERE F.COLOR=RIPE_COLOR AND F.FRUIT=FRUIT)
         AS VARIETY
      FROM FRUITS F
      WHERE EXISTS
        (SELECT *
        FROM FRUIT_COLORS
             WHERE F.COLOR=RIPE_COLOR AND F.FRUIT=FRUIT);

FRUIT      COLOR      VARIETY
---------- ---------- ----------------
Apple      Green      Granny Smith
Apple      Red        McIntosh
Orange     Orange     Mandarin
```

Using Subqueries with CREATE, INSERT, UPDATE, and DELETE

Subqueries within CREATE, INSERT, UPDATE, and DELETE statements aren't as indispensable as they are within SELECT statements. They are sometimes convenient, however, so we'll take a brief look at a few of these uses for subqueries.

CREATE TABLE. You can substitute the column list in a CREATE TABLE statement with AS plus a subquery if you want to duplicate an existing table. The names and types of the columns returned by the subquery determine the names and types of columns in the table. The rows returned by the subquery are inserted into the table after the table is created. The simplest case, creating a copy of a table with the same columns and rows, has this basic format:

```
CREATE TABLE target_table
AS SELECT * from source_table;
```

You can specify a select list if you want to copy only some columns or want to create new columns, using functions and expression. You can add a WHERE clause if you want to copy only certain rows. (If you wanted to copy structure but no rows, you could specify an impossible WHERE clause, such as WHERE 1=2.) This more general format is:

```
CREATE TABLE target_table
AS SELECT select_list
FROM table_list
WHERE condition;
```

Suppose we wanted to create a new car club exclusively for owners of antique cars. While we're at it, we'll include not only the make but also the model in the table—this means we'll use a join in our subquery. We could create a new table like this:

```
SQL> CREATE TABLE ANTIQUE_CAR_CLUB
  2      AS SELECT C.OWNER, C.MODEL, A.MAKE
  3              FROM CAR_CLUB C, ANTIQUE_CARS A
  4              WHERE C.MODEL=A.MODEL;

Table created.
```

Let's take a look at our new, fully furnished table:

```
SQL> SELECT * FROM ANTIQUE_CAR_CLUB;

OWNER        MODEL        MAKE
------------ ------------ ------------
Lou          Bearcat      Stutz
Bob          Terraplane   Hudson
```

An important thing to note, however, is that CREATE TABLE with a subquery copies only the rows and columns of a table. It does not copy any constraints, such as primary or foreign keys, or indexes. Another thing to note is that this statement causes an automatic commit, as is typical for DDL statements; this commit includes the rows that are inserted.

INSERT. Subqueries can be used in INSERT statements to populate one table with data from another table. This is easiest if the tables have the same structure—they must have the same number of columns, compatible by types, column by column—and you want to copy all the rows from one table:

```
INSERT INTO target_table;
SELECT * FROM source_table;
```

As I've warned elsewhere, it isn't a good idea to depend on the columns in a table being in a specific order. Columns sometimes get added or dropped. Although optional, it's best to specify both the column list for the insert table and the select list for the subquery. The general format is:

```
INSERT INTO target_table (column list)
SELECT select_list
FROM table_list
WHERE condition;
```

Let's suppose that we want to create a unified list of cars by combining the ANTIQUE_CARS and MODERN_CARS. First we'll create the table using CREATE TABLE with the subquery we just saw:

```
SQL>    CREATE TABLE ALL_CARS
  2     AS SELECT * FROM ANTIQUE_CARS;

Table created.
```

It already has the cars from the ANTIQUE_CARS, so let's add the cars from MODERN_CARS:

```
SQL> INSERT INTO ALL_CARS (MAKE, MODEL)
  2  SELECT MAKE, MODEL FROM MODERN_CARS;

3 rows created.
```

Now let's see what we've got:

```
SQL> select * from all_cars;

MODEL        MAKE
------------ ------------
Terraplane   Hudson
Firedome     DeSoto
Bearcat      Stutz
Firedome     DeSoto
Mustang      Ford
Corvette     Chevrolet
Cherokee     Jeep

7 rows selected.
```

As we expect, this new table now contains the combined information from the two tables we used to create it.

UPDATE. We can use subqueries in two ways with UPDATE. First, we can use a single-value subquery with a SET clause to obtain values from other tables. Second, we can use a subquery in the WHERE clause to determine which record or records get updated.

Let's look at the first use, updating a field using a value obtained by a subquery. The basic format is:

```
UPDATE table_name
SET column_name1= {value1|subquery1}
   [, column_name2= {value2|subquery2} [,…]]
WHERE condition;
```

Before trying this and any of the remaining examples in UPDATE and DELETE, you may want to COMMIT your changes up until this point so that you can ROLLBACK the changes afterward.

Suppose that a car club member, Bob, sold his Stutz and bought a DeSoto. Assuming that, in this closed universe, the only DeSoto model is the one in the ANTIQUE_CARS table, we can update the CAR_CLUB by obtaining the MODEL from ANTIQUE_CARS using a subquery:

```
SQL> UPDATE CAR_CLUB
     SET MODEL = (SELECT MODEL
                   FROM ANTIQUE_CARS
                   WHERE MAKE='DeSoto')
     WHERE OWNER='Bob';

1 row updated.
```

We can also use a subquery in an UPDATE statement's WHERE clause. Let's double the price of each fruit in the FRUITS table that is ripe, according to the FRUIT_COLORS table. For this, we'll use a correlated subquery:

```
SQL> UPDATE FRUITS F
       SET PRICE=PRICE*2
       WHERE EXISTS (SELECT * FROM FRUIT_COLORS C
                     WHERE F.FRUIT=C.FRUIT
                     AND F.COLOR=C.RIPE_COLOR);

3 rows updated.

SQL> SELECT FRUIT, PRICE FROM  FRUITS;

FRUIT           PRICE
---------- ----------
Apple               1
Apple               1
Mango             1.5
Mangosteen          2
Durian             15
Orange              2

6 rows selected.
```

DELETE. In a DELETE statement, we can use a subquery in the WHERE clause to determine which rows will be deleted. The basic format is:

```
DELETE FROM table_name
WHERE condition(subquery);
```

Let's remove any fruits from the FRUIT_COLORS table that don't appear in the FRUITS table. (Actually, there is only one, banana.)

```
SQL> DELETE FROM FRUIT_COLORS
       WHERE FRUIT NOT IN (SELECT FRUIT
                           FROM FRUITS);

1 row deleted.
```

VIEWS

SELECT statements, as we've seen—particularly in the context of their use as subqueries—can be seen as returning tables. The SQL CREATE VIEW command allows us essentially to "freeze" this table as a view. This view can then be used almost as though it were a full-fledged table.

It is important to note that a view does not capture the results of the query but rather captures the SELECT statement that created it. Changes to the underlying tables will, therefore, be reflected in the view.

Creating and Querying Views

To create a view, we use the following basic format:

```
CREATE VIEW AS subquery
```

The subquery can be simple or arbitrarily complex. It can be used to create a virtual table that contains a subset of data in the actual table, for example; this can be important for security. If we have a table of employee information that includes salary and other sensitive information but we want to make names, offices, and telephone numbers available to all other employees, we can create a view that includes just this information.

Let's take the fruit table as an example and create a view that includes just a few select columns: the fruit name, the quantity, and the price. This is the SELECT statement that gives us that result:

```
SQL> SELECT FRUIT, QUANTITY, PRICE FROM FRUITS;

FRUIT        QUANTITY      PRICE
---------- ---------- ----------
Apple              12         .5
Apple              12         .5
Mango              10        1.5
Mangosteen          5          2
Durian              2         15
Orange             10          1

6 rows selected.
```

We create a view by using this as the subquery:

```
SQL> CREATE VIEW FRUIT_VIEW AS
  2  SELECT FRUIT, QUANTITY, PRICE FROM FRUITS;

View created.
```

Now we can use the view name in place of a table name in a query:

```
SQL> SELECT * FROM FRUIT_VIEW;

FRUIT        QUANTITY      PRICE
---------- ---------- ----------
Apple              12         .5
Apple              12         .5
Mango              10        1.5
Mangosteen          5          2
Durian              2         15
Orange             10          1

6 rows selected.
```

The view is depicted in Figure 4–2.

Another important use arises because of normalization. Information that is commonly used together is often found in separate tables. Rather than denormalizing the data so that it's easy to use, we can use a view to save us the trouble of having to enter complex joins.

We saw this example of a join above:

```
SQL> SELECT C.OWNER, C.MODEL, A.MAKE
  2    FROM ANTIQUE_CARS A, CAR_CLUB C
  3    WHERE A.MODEL=C.MODEL;

OWNER        MODEL        MAKE
------------ ------------ ------------
Lou          Bearcat      Stutz
Bob          Terraplane   Hudson
```

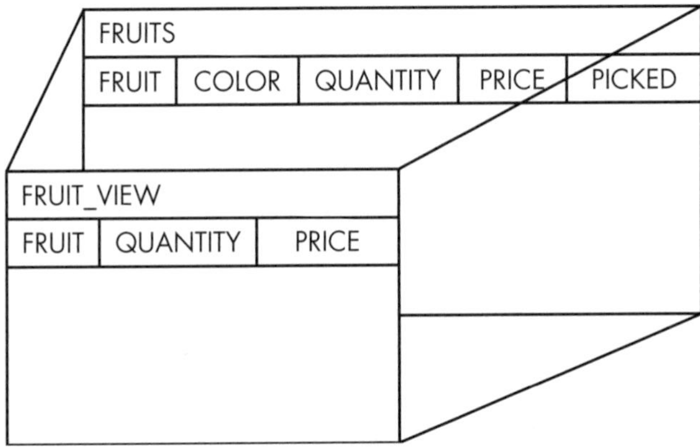

FIGURE 4–2 Creating a view.

We can make this into a view:

```
SQL> CREATE VIEW ANTIQUE_CAR_CLUB_VIEW AS
  2      SELECT C.OWNER, C.MODEL, A.MAKE
  3         FROM ANTIQUE_CARS A, CAR_CLUB C
  4         WHERE A.MODEL=C.MODEL;

View created.
```

Now we can query this view as though it were a table too:

```
SQL> SELECT * FROM ANTIQUE_CAR_CLUB_VIEW;

OWNER        MODEL        MAKE
------------ ------------ ------------
Lou          Bearcat      Stutz
Bob          Terraplane   Hudson
```

Updating Views

Views are not necessarily limited to use in queries. In fact, standard SQL specifies that we should be able to update the underlying tables through a view. Unfortunately, this is not an easy thing to implement and Oracle places some restrictions on using a view to insert, update, or delete rows.

In general, views are updateable only if it is possible to map updates to the underlying table or tables in a straightforward, unambiguous way. This isn't possible if the view contains aggregate functions or GROUP BY clauses, for example. In the case of joins, this is possible only if the join meets certain specific requirements—in particular, one of the join columns must have a unique index. The ANTIQUE_CAR_CLUB_VIEW does not meet this requirement. Even though it seems that it should be unambiguously possible to make this change, Oracle balks:

```
SQL> UPDATE ANTIQUE_CAR_CLUB_VIEW
  2    SET OWNER = 'Ted' WHERE MAKE = 'Hudson';
  SET OWNER = 'Ted' WHERE MAKE = 'Hudson'
      *
ERROR at line 2:
ORA-01779: cannot modify a column which maps to a non key-preserved table
```

Our first view example, using the FRUITS table, isn't disqualified by Oracle's restrictions, however. We can insert a row:

```
SQL> INSERT INTO FRUIT_VIEW VALUES('Tangerine', 10, 1.25);

1 row created.
```

and see that it is added to the underlying table:

```
SQL> SELECT * FROM FRUITS;

FRUIT      COLOR        QUANTITY      PRICE PICKED
---------- ---------- ---------- ---------- ---------
Apple      Green              12         .5 12-SEP-02
Apple      Red                12         .5 15-SEP-02
Mango      Yellow             10        1.5 22-SEP-02
Mangosteen Purple              5          2 25-SEP-02
Durian                         2         15
Orange     Orange             10          1 28-AUG-02
Tangerine                     10       1.25

7 rows selected.
```

Obviously, because our view contains only the FRUIT, QUANTITY, and PRICE columns, it's not possible to insert values for the COLOR and PICKED columns using this view.

Let's delete the row we just added:

```
SQL> DELETE FROM FRUIT_VIEW
  2    WHERE FRUIT='Tangerine';

1 row deleted.
```

Once again, let's take a look at the underlying table to see that it really got updated:

```
SQL> SELECT * FROM FRUITS;

FRUIT      COLOR        QUANTITY      PRICE PICKED
---------- ---------- ---------- ---------- ---------
Apple      Green              12         .5 12-SEP-02
Apple      Red                12         .5 15-SEP-02
Mango      Yellow             10        1.5 22-SEP-02
Mangosteen Purple              5          2 25-SEP-02
Durian                         2         15
Orange     Orange             10          1 28-AUG-02

6 rows selected.
```

To get rid of a view, we use a DROP statement:

```
SQL> DROP VIEW FRUIT_VIEW;

View dropped.
```

Naturally, this only gets rid of the view and has no effect on the underlying table!

Views are an important tool for making a database easier to use. As we saw, queries, subqueries, and joins can be powerful but complicated, hard to use, and hard to debug. (And it can also be hard to prove that the results are actually what you intend.) Views are one way of hiding this difficulty and complexity.

CHAPTER 5

PL/SQL

If you know ADA, Oracle PL/SQL will seem very familiar. If you don't, don't be put off by the comparison with ADA. First of all, PL/SQL is a much smaller language than ADA, and you'll quickly get used to the language features that may make it look strange at first.

What sets PL/SQL apart from other languages, however, is that it is well integrated with Oracle and SQL. In fact, you can generally include SQL statements directly in PL/SQL code. These SQL statements can include PL/SQL variables for either input or output. One important limitation, however, is that SELECT statements returning multiple rows need to be handled differently—as we will see later.

The basic unit of programming in PL/SQL, corresponding to a method in Java, is the block. There are three types of blocks:

- Anonymous blocks—Blocks that we execute immediately, usually interactively from SQL*Plus at an sqlplus prompt. They can also be executed in other contexts (such as from a Java program), but their distinguishing feature is that they are not stored in the database.
- Functions—Blocks that are compiled and stored in the database and can be executed from either the sqlplus prompt or as part of an SQL statement—especially in select lists, WHERE clauses and ORDER BY clauses. Functions differ from procedures in that functions return a value, but procedures don't.
- Procedures—Blocks that are compiled and stored in the database and can be executed from either the sqlplus prompt or other programs. They are similar to functions except they don't return a value. A special type of

procedure is the database trigger which can be executed automatically when a table is changed.

Also in this chapter we will see Java stored procedures. By providing a call specification that maps a Java method's parameters and return type to PL/SQL, we can implement database functions and procedures in Java.

GETTING STARTED WITH PL/SQL

To start, we'll be using anonymous blocks interactively using SQL*Plus. PL/SQL programs can provide output in one of three ways: by writing to the database, by returning a value (either as a return value or through an output parameter), or by writing to a buffer, using the DBMS_OUTPUT utility package. SQL*Plus can redirect the contents of this buffer to the screen, which makes it much easier to write and debug PL/SQL programs.

The DBMS_OUTPUT package is one of a large number of packages that Oracle provides to extend the functionality of the database, SQL, and PL/SQL. These packages are normally installed automatically when an Oracle database is created. Each package contains a number of related procedures or functions. DBMS_OUTPUT provides the following routines for writing to a buffer:

```
PUT(arg);
PUT_LINE(arg);
```

PUT() and PUT_LINE() are similar to the `System.out.print()` and `System.out.println()` methods in Java. The *arg* parameter can be any valid PL/SQL type—PL/SQL will perform the appropriate conversion to text automatically.

PUT() and PUT_LINE() differ from `System.out.print()` and `System.out.println()` in that they do not print to the screen but rather to a memory buffer. To get the text out of the memory buffer, DBMS_OUTPUT provides the complementary routines GET() and GET_LINE(), but we don't need to use them directly. The following command will cause SQL*Plus to display on screen everything sent to the buffer by PUT() and PUT_LINE():

```
SQL> SET SERVEROUTPUT ON SIZE 20000 FORMAT WRAPPED
```

After a PL/SQL block executes, SQL*Plus will automatically use GET_LINE() to retrieve the contents of the buffer and send them to the screen. This SET command also includes options to increase the output buffer size from the default 2,000 bytes to 20,000 and improve the format.

Before diving into the details of PL/SQL, let's write and run a simple program to get familiar with the mechanics that are involved and make sure everything is working right. You can type the code directly in SQL*Plus at the SQL prompt or you can type it in a text editor, such as Notepad or vi, save it as *hello.sql*, then run it from an sqlplus prompt with the START command. We'll take this last approach. Here is the program:

```
/* A first PL/SQL program: hello.sql */
BEGIN
  DBMS_OUTPUT.PUT_LINE('Hello, world!');
END;
```

After saving the program and starting SQL*Plus from a command prompt in the same directory where we saved the program, we can run the program like this:

```
SQL> start hello
  4  /
Hello, world!
PL/SQL procedure successfully completed.
```

Notice that we need to type a slash, (/), followed by Enter, to execute the program.

Basic PL/SQL Language Elements

The raw materials for a PL/SQL program are its lexical elements: comments, identifiers, operators, and functions. We'll briefly examine these individual bits and pieces before seeing how they fit together into a functioning program.

Comments

There are two types of comments in PL/SQL: single-line and multiline comments. Single-line comments begin with two dash marks.

```
-- This is a comment
```

Multiline comments are identical to Java multiline comments. (They are called *multiline* comments because they can span multiple lines, but they can also be limited to a single-line.) They begin with a slash-asterisk (/*) and end with an asterisk-slash (*/):

```
/* This is a multiline
   comment.
 */
```

Comments can begin anywhere on a line, but the single-line comment, obviously, must be the last (or only) text on a line.

Identifiers

The main use of identifiers in PL/SQL is for variable names. These are the rules that an identifier must follow:

- Must begin with a letter, followed by letters, numbers, dollar signs, hash marks, or underscores.
- Not case-sensitive: MYVAR, myvar, and myVar will be interpreted as referring to the same variable.
- An identifier cannot be a PL/SQL-reserved word, such as BEGIN or END.
- Can be enclosed in double quotes, in which case none of the restrictions above apply. For example, the variable `"BEGIN"` is a valid name and is different than `"begin"`. Using quoted identifiers isn't recommended but is sometimes necessary.
- Can be up to 30 characters long.

Identifiers can also be used as labels. These labels can be used with GOTO statements or to label loops. A label is enclosed by double angle brackets and must precede an executable statement. In the following example, we use NULL, which is a valid executable statement that does nothing, to meet this last requirement when the GOTO statement would otherwise be the last executable statement in the PL/SQL block:

```
  /* ... */
  IF USER_INPUT = 'QUIT' THEN GOTO END_PROGRAM;
  /* ... */

<<END_PROGRAM>>
NULL;
```

Operators

The operators in PL/SQL should be familiar, but they are just different enough to cause occasional trouble for someone familiar with Java or C/C++. The two most notable differences are that, in PL/SQL, the assignment operator is (:=) and the equality operator is (=). Consider this example:

```
IF X = Y THEN
  Z := X;
END IF;
```

Fortunately, mistaking one of these for the other or attempting to use (==) will not go unnoticed by the PL/SQL engine.

Assignment Operator

The assignment operator assigns a value to a variable. The value can be either a constant or an expression:

Operator	*Example*
:=	MYVAR := 100;

String Concatenation Operator

Strings can be concatenated in PL/SQL using the concatenation operator.

<table><tr><th>Operator</th><th>Example</th></tr><tr><td>||</td><td>MYSTR := 'ABC' || 'XYZ';</td></tr></table>

Comparison Operators

Comparison operators compare two values and return a Boolean value, TRUE or FALSE, depending on the result of the comparison.

Operator	*Description*
=	Equal
!=, <>, ~=, ^=	Not equal
>	Greater than
>=	Greater than or equal to
<	Less than
<=	Less than or equal to

Notice that we have a choice of inequality operators. It's best to choose one and stick to it.

The result of a comparison can be used immediately as a condition for a control statement, such as IF or WHILE:

```
WHILE X > Y LOOP
  /* program statements */
END LOOP;
```

The value resulting from a comparison can also be assigned to a Boolean variable. For example, assuming MYBOOL was declared as a BOOLEAN, we can make the following assignment:

```
MYBOOL = X > Y;
```

Logical Operators

The logical operators are used with Boolean values. Boolean values, such as those resulting from comparisons, can be combined using the logical operators AND and OR. A Boolean value can be negated using the logical operator NOT.

Operator	*Description*
AND	Logical AND
OR	Logical OR
NOT	Logical NOT

These operators can be used to construct arbitrarily complex conditions. For example, assuming MYFLAG is a Boolean type, we can assign it a TRUE or FALSE value with the following logical expression:

```
MYFLAG =  NOT (STARTCHAR = ENDCHAR) OR CHARSREAD > 0;
```

Note that AND, OR, and NOT correspond to the Java operators (&&), (||), and (!), respectively.

SQL Operators and Functions

PL/SQL also supports the SQL comparison operators, such as the LIKE operator for comparing strings with the wildcard characters (_) and (%). See Chapter 3 for a more detailed description and examples of these operators.

Operator	*Description*
LIKE	String comparison
IS [NOT] NULL	Tests for null value
IN	Test for inclusion in set
BETWEEN...AND	Range test

All SQL functions are also available under PL/SQL, except for aggregate functions such as COUNT() and SUM(). For example, assuming MYSTR is a string (VARCHAR2 or CHAR), we can convert it to all uppercase using the UPPER() function:

```
MYSTR := UPPER(MYSTR);
```

Program Elements

Now that we've seen the basic elements of PL/SQL, we can start to put them together to build programs. Although we will start by writing anonymous blocks, as we'll see later, what we learn here can be easily extended to functions, procedures, and triggers.

An anonymous block has the following format:

```
[DECLARE
  variable declarations]
BEGIN
  executable statements
[EXCEPTION
  exception handlers]
END;
```

The first section, beginning with the keyword DECLARE, is where we declare any variables we will use in our program. The next section, beginning with the word BEGIN, is where we put the statements to be executed normally. The final section is where we provide exception handlers to be executed in case of errors.

Declarations

Before we can use a variable, we must declare it. We must do this (with a few exceptions, such as counters in a FOR...LOOP) in the DECLARE section of a PL/SQL block. Optionally, we can also assign a value to it at the same time. The format for a declaration is

```
identifier [CONSTANT] datatype [ :=  value | DEFAULT value];
```

The *datatype* can be any of the Oracle SQL types, such as NUMBER, VARCHAR2, DATE, or CHAR. In addition, PL/SQL supports a large number of types; examples are BINARY_INTEGER, in which we can store integer values and its subtypes, such as NATURAL, which is restricted to all nonnegative integers, and SIGNTYPE, which is restricted to 1, 0, and –1. We'll restrict ourselves to SQL types, except for the occasional internal use of BOOLEAN, where it makes sense in the program's logic.

A variable can optionally be declared CONSTANT, meaning that its value cannot change. A variable declared CONSTANT must be given a value when declared.

We can also assign a value to a variable when we declare it, using either the assignment operator (:=) or the keyword DEFAULT. The two methods are functionally equivalent, but Oracle recommends using DEFAULT to assign values that have a typical value, such as hours worked per week, and using the assignment operator for values that have no typical value.

We can use previously defined variables in the declarations that follow but forward references are not allowed.

Here are some typical declarations.

```
DECLARE
  MYVAR NUMBER;
  START_DATE DATE := '1-JAN-2002';
  END_DATE DATE := START_DATE + 90;
  COMMISSION NUMBER DEFAULT 0.15;
```

Cursor variables—a special type of buffer or data structure used for holding information from the database—can also be declared in this section. We will learn more about cursors later in this chapter.

Variables can also be defined for user-defined types—these will be covered in the next chapter on Oracle object-relational features.

Program Statements

The main part of a PL/SQL routine, the executable statements, is the BEGIN…END section of a PL/SQL block. These statements can include the usual assignments, calls to other procedures, and so on. But because PL/SQL is Oracle's procedural extension of SQL, it shouldn't surprise us to learn that we can also include SQL statements directly in our PL/SQL code—with some restrictions.

SQL Statements

Most SQL statements don't require that we do anything special in order to use them in PL/SQL and to include PL/SQL variables in our SQL statements. PL/SQL can usually determine by parsing an SQL statement whether an identifier is a PL/SQL variable or a column. Suppose, for example, that we have a table, USER_TABLE, with columns USER_ID, NAME, STREET, and CITY. If we also had PL/SQ variables with the same names, the following statement is legal but ambiguous (at least to us) and confusing:

```
UPDATE USER_TABLE
SET NAME=NAME, STREET=STREET, CITY=CITY
WHERE USER_ID=USER_ID;
```

It's just not a good idea to use the same name for different things. Because cases like this, where we have variables that correspond to column names, are common in PL/SQL, it's good to establish some sort of convention. We can, for example, follow the convention of adding V_ to distinguish between a PL/SQL variable name and its associated column. We might then have the following INSERT statement:

```
INSERT INTO USER TABLE(USER_ID, NAME, STREET, CITY)
  VALUES(V_USER_ID, V_NAME, V_STREET, V_CITY);
```

The one type of SQL statement that we can't always use easily in PL/SQL is the SELECT statement. We'll see later that if our SELECT statement returns multiple rows, we explicitly need to declare a cursor variable to handle those results. In the meantime, we'll use a special form of the SELECT statement—SELECT...INTO—that allows us to query and obtain values for a single row. It has the basic format

```
SELECT select_list
INTO variable_list
FROM table_list
[WHERE condition]
[ORDER BY order_list];
```

Although the WHERE is optional, it's usually necessary in order to ensure that the results are restricted to a single row. Assuming the same USER_TABLE as before, we might have the following query:

```
SELECT NAME, STREET, CITY
INTO V_NAME, V_STREET, V_CITY
WHERE USER_ID=V_USER_ID;
```

Control Flow Structures

Like other procedural languages, such as Java, statements are generally executed sequentially to perform assignments, execute SQL statements, etc. This flow of control can be altered conditionally using the following control structures:

- IF *condition* THEN (optionally with ELSE and ELSIF)
- CASE
- LOOP (usually with EXIT WHEN... *condition*)
- WHILE *condition* LOOP
- FOR *condition* LOOP

These structures each enclose a set of statements which, in turn, can include other nested control structures. Sets of statements are not enclosed using braces, as they are in Java; instead, the end is marked with the keywords END, END IF, or END LOOP.

The normal sequential flow can also be altered unconditionally:

```
GOTO label
```

The use of GOTO is properly discouraged in PL/SQL but in rare instances it can help make code easier to understand.

IF...THEN

The condition in an IF...THEN statement is an expression that evaluates to a Boolean TRUE or FALSE. If the condition is true, any statements after THEN and before END IF are executed.

```
IF X>100 THEN
   X := 100;
END IF;
```

Alternative statements to be executed if the condition is false can be specified using ELSE.

```
IF X>100 THEN
  X := 100;
  Y := 0;
ELSE
  Y := X;
END IF;
```

A sequence of conditions can be tested using ELSIF. An IF statement can have any number of ELSIF statements. Optionally, the sequence can end with ELSE.

```
IF X<= 100 THEN
  Y := 'A';
ELSIF X<=200 THEN
  Y := 'B'
ELSEIF X<=300 THEN
  Y := 'C'
ELSE
  Y := 'Z'
END IF
```

Oracle 9i introduces a CASE statement, which is a more efficient way to implement long IF…ELSIF sequences.

CASE…WHEN

Oracle 9i's CASE is the equivalent of Java's switch control structure. The syntax is

```
CASE selector
  WHEN option THEN
    statement;
    [statement;[…]]
  [WHEN option THEN
    statement;
    [statement;[…]]
  […]]
  [ELSE
    statement;
    [statement;[…]]]
END CASE;
```

The ELSE case at the end is optional, but if you don't provide a default case, an error is raised if the selector does not match any of the WHEN options. This is useful only if you are prepared to handle the exception—we'll take a look at the optional exception handler below.

Oracle's CASE statement is more flexible than Java's because it is not limited to integer types. It can be used with strings, for example:

```
CASE UPPER(USER_INPUT)
  WHEN 'HELLO' THEN
    RESPONSE := 'Hi there!';
  WHEN 'GOODBYE' THEN
    RESPONSE := 'See you later!';
    QUIT_FLAG := TRUE;
  ELSE
    RESPONSE := 'I''m sorry, I don''t understand.';
END CASE;
```

Some caution needs to be exercised when using it with real numbers because they are not exact values—you may need to use the ROUND() or TRUNC() functions to ensure consistent behavior.

There is another form of the CASE statement, the searched CASE statement, that is semantically identical to the IF...ELSIF...ELSE control structure. It has the form:

```
CASE
  WHEN condition THEN
    statement;
    [statement;[…]]
  [WHEN condition THEN
    statement;
    [statement;[…]]
  […]]
  [ELSE
    statement;
    [statement;[…]]]
END CASE;
```

Using a searched CASE statement, we can rewrite the previous example as follows:

```
CASE
  WHEN UPPER(USER_INPUT) = 'HELLO' THEN
    RESPONSE := 'Hi there!';
  WHEN UPPER(USER_INPUT) = 'GOODBYE' THEN
    RESPONSE := 'See you later!';
    QUIT_FLAG := TRUE;
  ELSE
    RESPONSE := 'I''m sorry, I don''t understand.';
END CASE;
```

CASE Expressions

The CASE statement allows us to select statements to execute based on a selector or a set of conditions. But we can also use CASE to form an expression that returns a value based on a selector or set of conditions. The syntax for a CASE expression is:

```
CASE selector
  WHEN option THEN value
  [WHEN option THEN value
  […]]
  [ELSE
    value]
END;
```

Notice that the CASE expression takes END at the end, not END CASE. The following example is nearly identical to the previous examples, except that we are limited to making a single assignment.

```
RESPONSE  :=
  CASE UPPER(USER_INPUT)
    WHEN 'HELLO' THEN 'Hi there!'
    WHEN 'GOODBYE' THEN 'See you later!'
    ELSE 'I''m sorry, I don''t understand.'
  END;
```

Like the CASE statement, the CASE expression also has a form that uses conditions for each option instead of a selector.

```
CASE
  WHEN condition THEN value
  [WHEN condition THEN value
  [...]]
  [ELSE
    value]
END;
```

The previous example, using the searched CASE format, is:

```
RESPONSE  :=
  CASE
    WHEN UPPER(USER_INPUT)='HELLO' THEN 'Hi there!'
    WHEN UPPER(USER_INPUT)='GOODBYE' THEN 'See you later!'
    ELSE 'I''m sorry, I don''t understand.'
  END;
```

LOOP

The LOOP statement lets you create infinite loops. This normally isn't useful by itself but, when used with an EXIT WHEN… statement to end conditionally, the LOOP statement can provide more flexibility than other control structures. PL/SQL, for example, does not have a control structure like Java's do...while, which ensures that the body of a loop is executed at least once, but LOOP with EXIT WHEN… as the last statement in the loop accomplishes the same end.

The syntax for a LOOP is

```
LOOP
  [statements];
  [IF condition THEN EXIT [label]|EXIT [label] WHEN condition];
  [statements];
END LOOP;
```

For example, suppose we have a table, MANAGERS, listing employees in column NAME and their managers in a column MANAGER. If we know the name of an employee, we can work our way up the chain of command from that person like this:

```
LOOP
  DBMS_OUTPUT.PUT_LINE(CURRENT_NAME);
  SELECT MANAGER INTO CURRENT_NAME
    FROM MANAGERS
    WHERE NAME=CURRENT_NAME;
  EXIT WHEN CURRENT_NAME IS NULL;
END LOOP;
```

Each time through the loop, the SELECT statement uses the current employee's name to get the manager's name, making the manager the new current employee. Eventually, we reach the top and come to an employee who has no manager; when the SELECT statement pulls up NULL, we exit the loop.

WHILE...LOOP

The idea of a WHILE...LOOP should be familiar from Java. It repeats as long as a condition is true. The format is:

```
WHILE condition LOOP
  statements;
END LOOP;
```

The following example will print out a string, MYSTR, letter by letter.

```
WHILE LENGTH(MYSTR)>0 LOOP
  DBMS_OUTPUT.PUT_LINE(SUBSTR(MYSTR,1,1));
  MYSTR := SUBSTR(MYSTR,2);
END LOOP;
```

It's worth remarking on two things about the condition in this example's WHILE...LOOP statement. First, like Java (but unlike certain other languages), PL/SQL requires that the condition be a Boolean value so the comparison with zero is necessary. Second, side effects aren't allowed, so we can't store the results of the call to LENGTH() in the condition for use inside the loop. If we needed that value inside the loop, we'd need either to call LENGTH() again or to modify our logic to store it in a variable and then test it—probably by using an unconditional LOOP with an EXIT WHEN... statement, something like this:

```
LOOP
  LEN := LENGTH(MYSTR);
  EXIT WHEN LEN=0;
  /*… */
END LOOP;
```

FOR...LOOP

In PL/SQL, the FOR...LOOP is a relatively simple control structure. It allows iterating through a range of integral values, in either ascending or descending order, incrementing or decrementing by one each time. The format is:

```
FOR counter IN [REVERSE]
  lower_bound expression … upper_bound expression LOOP
  statements;
END LOOP;
```

We can summarize the parts of the FOR...LOOP syntax:

- *counter* is an integer variable that is declared automatically and is valid only within the scope of the loop where it can be used only as a constant.
- *lower_bound_expression* and *upper_bound_expression* can be constants or they can be expressions that are evaluated at runtime; in either case, they must evaluate to numbers. They do not need to be integers; if they are real numbers, they are rounded to the nearest integer. They are evaluated only once, at the beginning.
- By default, without the REVERSE option, the counter iterates from the lower bound to the upper bound, *incrementing by one* each time through the loop. With REVERSE, the counter iterates from the upper bound to the lower bound, *decrementing by one* each time.
- If lower bound and upper bound are equal, the loop will be executed once.
- If the lower bound is greater than the upper bound, the loop will not be executed.

The following example will calculate X factorial for values of X that are positive integers. For example, if X is 5, X factorial is 1*2*3*4*5 = 120. Real positive values of X that are not integers (such as 5.333) are rounded to the nearest integer.

```
X_FACTORIAL := 1;
FOR I IN 2 .. X LOOP
  X_FACTORIAL := X_FACTORIAL * I;
END LOOP;
DBMS_OUTPUT.PUT_LINE(X_FACTORIAL);
```

(Notice that we don't need to start with 1 because if X is 1, the loop will not be executed at all and the initial value of X_FACTORIAL is already the right answer.)

Sometimes we want to increment or decrement by something other than 1. This isn't possible in PL/SQL, but we can usually use a multiplier or some other type of expression within our loop to get the range of values we want. If this isn't possible, it's worth remembering that a FOR...LOOP is really just a WHILE...LOOP with most of the mechanics—counter declaration and initialization, incrementing (or decrementing), etc.—performed automatically. If we need more than that, we need to it ourselves.

Exceptions and Exception Handlers

The final part of a PL/SQL block, optionally, is the EXCEPTION section. Exceptions in PL/SQL are similar in some ways to those in Java. During processing, a warning or error condition occurs, normal execution is stopped, and control is passed to exception handling code.

Perhaps the biggest difference is that catching exceptions is optional in PL/SQL. It often makes sense to ignore them at the PL/SQL level and let them get passed up to the next level, then deal with them there. If we call a PL/SQL function from Java, for example, most JDBC methods already require us to catch SQLException, so it may make sense to handle PL/SQL errors together with all other database exceptions.

We catch exceptions by name. For each error that we want to catch, we need a line such as the following in our exception section:

```
WHEN exception_name THEN
  statements;
```

System Exceptions

The most common system exceptions have predefined names. For example, division by zero has the name DIVISION_BY_ZERO. The following example demonstrates catching a division by zero error and printing its Oracle error code and message.

```
DECLARE
  X NUMBER;
BEGIN
  X := 100/0;
EXCEPTION
 WHEN ZERO_DIVIDE THEN
   DBMS_OUTPUT.PUT('Error caught: ');
```

```
    DBMS_OUTPUT.PUT_LINE(SQLCODE());
    DBMS_OUTPUT.PUT_LINE(SQLERRM(SQLCODE()));
END;
```

Generally, we catch system exceptions because we know something about the circumstances and know that it is safe to ignore the error because we know how to correct the error, or because we need to perform some other action before passing the exception on to the next higher level.

For example, if our system allows users to log in to our application without registering, we may wish to catch the system exception NO_DATA_FOUND when we look up an unregistered user and make a temporary entry in the USERS table:

```
BEGIN
  /* ... */
EXCEPTION
  WHEN NO_DATA_FOUND THEN
    INSERT INTO USERS VALUES(LOGINNAME,'TEMP',SYSDATE);
END;
```

After we've handled an exception, it will not get propagated any further. If we want the next higher level to get the exception so that it can do additional exception processing, we need to re-raise the exception. We do this by using the RAISE statement. In an exception handler, the RAISE statement without any parameters re-raises the current exception:

```
BEGIN
  /* ... */
EXCEPTION
  WHEN NO_DATA_FOUND THEN
    INSERT INTO USERS VALUES(LOGINNAME, 'TEMP',SYSDATE);
    RAISE;
END;
```

Some system exceptions do not have predefined names. If you need to catch an unnamed system exception, it is possible to define your own names for system exceptions, using an exception declaration and a special compiler instruction, EXCEPTION_INIT. But the easiest way to catch an unnamed system exception is to use the catch-all exception name OTHERS, then use the error code to distinguish between the cases you want to deal with specially and the rest.

```
BEGIN
  /* ... */
EXCEPTION
  WHEN OTHERS THEN
    IF SQLCODE=-60 THEN
      /* take special action */
    END IF;
END;
```

Note that all Oracle error codes except NO_DATA_FOUND are negative.

Using a Subblock to Continue after an Exception

When an exception occurs, PL/SQL does not allow us to correct the error in our error handler then go back and pick up where we left off. If there is a situation where we can anticipate that a particular exception is likely to occur and can plan on fixing that error, we can put that code in a subblock with its own exception handler. After handling and correcting the exception, control returns to the enclosing block.

In the following example, we populate a table with the tangent for a consecutive series of degrees. The important point to note about the tangent function is that it is undefined at 90 degrees and 270 degrees—we'd like our table to reflect that fact by setting the tangent to NULL for those values. We'll create our table like this:

```
CREATE TABLE TANGENTS (
  DEGREES NUMBER,
  TANGENT NUMBER);
```

This is our PL/SQL code for populating the table:

```
BEGIN
  DELETE TANGENTS;
  FOR V_DEGREES IN 0..359 LOOP
    BEGIN
      INSERT INTO TANGENTS (DEGREES, TANGENT)
        VALUES (V_DEGREES,TAN(V_DEGREES*ACOS(0)/90));
    EXCEPTION
        WHEN OTHERS THEN
          IF(SQLCODE=-1426) THEN
            INSERT INTO TANGENTS (DEGREES, TANGENT)
              VALUES (V_DEGREES, NULL);
          ELSE
            RAISE;
          END IF;
```

```
    END;
  END LOOP;
  COMMIT;
END;
```

The program loops through the degrees in a circle, from 0 to 359. Within this loop, where we expect that an error will occur, there is a subblock that contains the logic for performing the calculation and doing the insert. Notice that the subblock has access to the variable V_DEGREES, the loop counter from the enclosing block.

The expression to calculate the tangent is a bit complicated because we are using degrees, but the trigonometric functions in Oracle are expecting radians. We can use the following formula to convert from degrees to radians.

```
radians = degrees * 2 π / 360
```

Rather than hardcoding a value for π, we can obtain it from Oracle by using the `ACOS()` function.

```
ACOS(0) = 1/2 π.
```

So the conversion is

```
radians = degrees * 2 * 2 * ACOS(0) / 360 = degrees * ACOS(0) / 90
```

As the loop iterates, all is fine until V_DEGREES hits 90. This causes a numeric overflow ORA-01426. This is not a predefined error, so we can't catch it by name. Instead, we add a catch-all exception handler, OTHERS, and test the SQLCODE to see whether it's –1426. If it is, we insert using NULL for the tangent value. If it's not, we got some other unexpected error; we can re-raise that error and pass it to the enclosing block by calling RAISE.

After running this program, we can select from the TANGENTS table and check the tangent at 90 and 270 degrees to see that it is, in fact, null. We'll include a couple of neighbors for context:

```
SQL> SELECT * FROM TANGENTS
  2  WHERE DEGREES >= 89 AND DEGREES <= 91
  3  ORDER BY DEGREES;

   DEGREES    TANGENT
---------- ----------
        89 57.2899616
        90
        91 -57.289962
```

```
SQL> SELECT * FROM TANGENTS
  2  WHERE DEGREES >= 269 AND DEGREES <= 271
  3  ORDER BY DEGREES;

   DEGREES    TANGENT
---------- ----------
       269 57.2899616
       270
       271 -57.289962
```

User-Defined Exceptions

Sometimes, cases that aren't exceptional to Oracle or to the system may be exceptional to us, and we want to discontinue normal processing and deal with the exception in a different way than the normal course of action. We can do this in one of two ways, depending on whether we want to handle the exception entirely in the PL/SQL block or pass the error back to the calling program.

To handle a user-defined exception in our program, we first need to declare the exception in the declarations section of our PL/SQL block. Once we've done this, we can raise this exception in the code in our program code. This obligates us to provide an exception handler for this exception; otherwise, the calling program will get an unhandled user-defined exception error. The format for defining, raising, and catching an exception is:

```
DECLARE
  [other declarations]
  exception_name EXCEPTION;
  [other declarations]
BEGIN
  [program statements]
  IF exception_condition THEN
    RAISE exception_name;
  END IF;
  [program statements]
EXCEPTION
  [other exception handlers]
  WHEN exception_name THEN
    exception handling code;
  [other exception handlers]
END;
```

An exception handler cannot return a value, so user-defined exceptions aren't useful for functions because the failure to return a value causes an additional error.

Let's consider a procedure to process an order. It will total the values of a customer's line items in an order and compare it with the customer's credit. If there's enough credit, we'll change the status of the line items to SHIP and deduct the total from the customer's credit line. Otherwise, we'll raise an exception, change the status of the order to NO CREDIT, and add a record to an exceptions table.

We'll need several tables for this example. Normally, we would create a table containing general information for the order as a whole, but we'll omit that in this example for the sake of simplicity. We'll include only a table for the order's line items:

```
CREATE TABLE ORDERS (
  ORDER_ID NUMBER,
  CUSTOMER_ID NUMBER,
  ITEM_NUM NUMBER,
  QUANTITY NUMBER,
  PRICE NUMBER,
  STATUS VARCHAR2(12)
);
```

Next, a table for storing information on how much credit the customer has in the system:

```
CREATE TABLE CUSTOMER_CREDITS (
  CUSTOMER_ID NUMBER,
  CREDIT NUMBER
);
```

Finally, a table for logging any exceptions:

```
CREATE TABLE EXCEPTIONS (
  ORDER_ID NUMBER,
  CUSTOMER_ID NUMBER,
  EXCEPTION_NUMBER NUMBER,
  EXCEPTION_MESSAGE VARCHAR2(200)
);
```

And we'll need to populate the tables with some data:

```
INSERT INTO ORDERS VALUES(100, 25, 23001,   1,  3.25,'PENDING');
INSERT INTO ORDERS VALUES(100, 25, 67023,   5,  4.95,'PENDING');
INSERT INTO ORDERS VALUES(100, 25, 33320,   1, 18.00,'PENDING');
INSERT INTO ORDERS VALUES(100, 25, 23102,  10,  9.95,'PENDING');

INSERT INTO CUSTOMER_CREDITS VALUES(25, 100);
```

Notice that the order totals 145.50, but the customer has a credit line of only 100.

We haven't been formally introduced to procedures yet, but for now it will suffice to say that we need to replace the DECLARE statement with a CREATE PROCEDURE statement that defines the procedure's arguments, followed by local declarations, including any exception declarations.

```
CREATE PROCEDURE PROCESS_ORDER (ORDER_NUMBER NUMBER) AS

  CREDIT_EXCEPTION EXCEPTION;
  ORDER_TOTAL NUMBER;
  CUSTOMER NUMBER;
  CREDIT_LIMIT NUMBER;

BEGIN

  SELECT SUM(PRICE*QUANTITY), MAX(CUSTOMER_ID)
    INTO ORDER_TOTAL, CUSTOMER
    FROM ORDERS WHERE ORDER_ID=ORDER_NUMBER
    AND STATUS='PENDING';

  SELECT CREDIT INTO CREDIT_LIMIT
    FROM CUSTOMER_CREDITS WHERE CUSTOMER_ID=CUSTOMER;

  IF ORDER_TOTAL>CREDIT_LIMIT THEN
    RAISE CREDIT_EXCEPTION;
  END IF;

  UPDATE ORDERS SET STATUS='SHIP'
    WHERE ORDER_ID=ORDER_NUMBER AND STATUS='PENDING';
  UPDATE CUSTOMER_CREDITS SET CREDIT=CREDIT-ORDER_TOTAL
    WHERE CUSTOMER_ID=CUSTOMER;
  COMMIT;

EXCEPTION

  WHEN CREDIT_EXCEPTION THEN

        UPDATE ORDERS SET STATUS='NO CREDIT'
        WHERE ORDER_ID=ORDER_NUMBER AND STATUS='PENDING';

        INSERT INTO EXCEPTIONS VALUES(ORDER_NUMBER, CUSTOMER,
          1, 'Order total exceeds credit.');

END;
/
```

We can call this procedure interactively from an SQL*Plus prompt by using a CALL command.

```
SQL> CALL PROCESS_ORDER(100);

Call completed.
```

We can verify the effects of this procedure by selecting from the EXCEPTIONS table.

```
SQL> SELECT * FROM EXCEPTIONS;

ORDER_ID CUSTOMER_ID EXCEPTION_NUMBER EXCEPTION_MESSAGE
-------- ----------- ---------------- --------------------------------
     100          25                1 Order total exceeds credit.
```

We can also see that the ORDERS table has been affected—the STATUS column has been changed.

```
SQL> SELECT * FROM ORDERS;

ORDER_ID CUSTOMER_ID  ITEM_NUM  QUANTITY   PRICE STATUS
-------- ------------ --------- ---------- ----- ----------
100          25       23001         1        3.25 NO CREDIT
100          25       67023         5        4.95 NO CREDIT
100          25       33320         1       18.00 NO CREDIT
100          25       23102        10        9.95 NO CREDIT
```

User-defined exceptions should be used sparingly because they introduce dependencies between code in the database and application code. In general, they should only be used for conditions that should not normally arise; that is, conditions that are truly exceptional. The example here is not very good in this respect because customers are likely to exceed their credit limit fairly as a matter of course.

Returning Error Codes to an Application

If we want to return a user-defined exception to a calling program instead of handling it in our PL/SQL block, we can call the RAISE_APPLICATION_ERROR() procedure. This procedure—part of the DBMS_STANDARD package that is normally installed when a database is created—allows us to select our own error code and message to be returned to the calling application. It accepts either two or three parameters.

```
RAISE_APPLICATION_ERROR(error_number, error_description
[,add_to_stack])
```

The parameters for this procedure are:

- *error_number*—A negative integer between –20,000 and –20,999. This will appear as a positive number in Java.
- *error_message*—An error message up to 2,048 characters long.
- *add_to_stack*—A Boolean determining whether this user error should be added to the error stack (TRUE) or whether the error stack should be cleared and replaced with this error (FALSE). The default, if this parameter is not specified, is FALSE.

Unlike user-defined exceptions declared in the DECLARE section, an exception raised with RAISE_APPLICATION_ERROR() cannot be caught with a handler in the PL/SQL EXCEPTIONS section. Instead, the program stops and the error is immediately returned to the calling application. In Java, this will be caught as an SQLException. The SQLException method getErrorCode() will retrieve the error converted to a positive number.

We can change the previous example to notify the calling program and let the program take whatever action is appropriate—perhaps prompting the user to modify the order or to augment the credit in the system. To do so, we need to remove the declaration of CREDIT_EXCEPTION and the corresponding exception handler. Then we replace the RAISE statement with RAISE_APPLICATION_ERROR(), as follows:

```
CREATE OR REPLACE PROCEDURE PROCESS_ORDER (ORDER_NUMBER NUMBER)
  AS

  ORDER_TOTAL NUMBER;
  CUSTOMER NUMBER;
  CREDIT_LIMIT NUMBER;

BEGIN

  SELECT SUM(PRICE*QUANTITY), MAX(CUSTOMER_ID)
    INTO ORDER_TOTAL, CUSTOMER
    FROM ORDERS WHERE ORDER_ID=ORDER_NUMBER
    AND STATUS='PENDING';

  SELECT CREDIT INTO CREDIT_LIMIT
    FROM CUSTOMER_CREDITS WHERE CUSTOMER_ID=CUSTOMER;

  IF ORDER_TOTAL>CREDIT_LIMIT THEN
    RAISE_APPLICATION_ERROR(-20201,
      'Order total exceeds credit');
  END IF;
```

```
  UPDATE ORDERS SET STATUS='SHIP'
    WHERE ORDER_ID=ORDER_NUMBER AND STATUS='PENDING';
  UPDATE CUSTOMER_CREDITS SET CREDIT=CREDIT-ORDER_TOTAL
    WHERE CUSTOMER_ID=CUSTOMER;
  COMMIT;

END;
/
```

If we call this procedure from Java, it will generate an SQLException exception. We can call the exception's getErrorCode method to obtain the specific error number—in this case, 20201—as shown in this code snippet:

```
try
{
 /* Register JDBC driver,
    get Connection, get Statement stmt …*/

 stmt.executeUpdate("CALL PROCESS_ORDER(" + orderNumber + ")");
}
catch (SQLException e)
{
  if(e.getErrorCode()==20201)
  {
   /* Take appropriate action for insufficient credit */
  }
}
```

Notice that, although we specify a negative number in PL/SQL, –20201, the error code that Java receives is positive, 20201.

Stored Procedures, Functions, and Database Triggers

Anonymous blocks are useful for learning PL/SQL, but except for the occasional utility program, they are rarely useful in building applications. Instead, we generally need to use functions and procedures—programs that are stored inside the database and can be called by SQL statements or by other applications. One special type of procedure, the database trigger, is particularly useful for providing logging or data integrity checks because it is called automatically when a table is changed.

The key difference between functions and procedures is that a function returns a value but a procedure does not. This, in turn, affects how they can be used. Functions are usually called in an SQL statement, for example, in a select list or in a WHERE clause; because of this, they are also subject to certain restrictions. Procedures are usually called from other programs, such as Java programs or database triggers; procedures can also be invoked interactively in SQL*Plus, using the CALL command.

In terms of syntax, procedures and functions differ from anonymous blocks mainly in the header. Instead of DECLARE, we use a CREATE FUNCTION, CREATE PROCEDURE, or CREATE TRIGGER statement to start off the function or procedure. We'll look at each of these separately.

PL/SQL Functions

The format for creating a PL/SQL function is:

```
CREATE [OR REPLACE] FUNCTION function_name [(parameter_list)]
  RETURN return_type
  {AS|IS}
  [local_declarations]
BEGIN
  program_statements
[EXCEPTION
  exception_handlers]
END;
```

Note that:

- The OR REPLACE option is necessary only if the function has already been defined. It's a good policy to leave it off the first time to make certain we aren't accidentally replacing another function with the same name.
- *parameter_list* is necessary if the function takes input parameters. Each parameter takes the form parameter_name data_type. Multiple parameters are separated by commas. All parameters are input parameters by default.
- Parameters' sizes cannot be restricted; that is, we can specify VARCHAR2 but we cannot specify a length. Specifying VARCHAR2(25) will cause an error.
- Parameters can have a default, specified after its datatype, for example, MYVAR VARCHAR2 DEFAULT 'TEMP'.
- There is no difference between using either AS or IS to mark the start of the function body.
- The function must return a value of the type defined by RETURN *data_type*. The datatype can be any Oracle SQL type or user-defined type. (See the next chapter, "Oracle Object-Relational Features," for more information about user-defined types.)

We'll start with a simple example—a function that takes a name and returns a greeting using that name:

```
CREATE FUNCTION GREET (NAME VARCHAR2)
  RETURN VARCHAR2
  AS
 /* no local declarations */
BEGIN
  RETURN 'Hello, '||NAME||'!';
END;
```

Like previous examples, we can either type this at the sqlplus prompt or we can save this in a file—greet.sql, for example—and run it with the START command.

```
SQL> START GREET
  8  /

Function created.
```

Notice that running greet.sql only creates the function. To call it, we can use the select list of an SQL statement querying the dummy table DUAL:

```
SQL> SELECT GREET('Molly') FROM DUAL;

GREET('MOLLY')
------------------------------------------

Hello, Molly!
```

There are a number of rules that a function is required to follow in order to prevent side effects. Principally, these restrictions are:

- A function called from a SELECT statement cannot modify any database tables.
- A function called from an INSERT, UPDATE, or DELETE SQL statement cannot modify or query any of the database tables affected by the SQL statement.
- A function called from a SELECT, INSERT, UPDATE, or DELETE statement cannot call any transaction control statements, either explicity—by calling COMMIT, for example—or implicitly—by calling any DDL statement, such as CREATE TABLE, because DDL statements implicitly call COMMIT.

Let's take a look at another example, a function designed to make it easier to display names from a table in a culturally correct way.

One of the problems we face when designing an application to work in an international context is that different cultures have different rules for names. English speakers sometimes make the assumption that last name, family name, and surname all refer to the same thing. When a name is broken up into different fields in a database, these fields are frequently called FIRST_NAME, MIDDLE_INITIAL, and LAST_NAME (or something equivalent). But in some countries, such as China, the family name is the first name. In Spanish-speaking countries, people usually use both paternal and maternal family names (in that order), and the second-to-last name is the surname. In other countries, such as Indonesia (and particularly in Java), people often do not use family names but go by one or more given names.

To solve this problem, we'll use a table with a given name, surname (which can be one or more family names to solve the problem with multiple last names), and a locale code. (A locale is a two-letter language code from ISO-639 plus, optionally, a country or region code from ISO-3166, and possibly an additional, nonstandard, variant code. We'll use locales, rather than Oracle's NLS parameters because locales are standards-based and because they are what we need to use in Java.) Our table looks like this:

```
CREATE TABLE DIRECTORY (
  GIVEN_NAME VARCHAR2(32),
  SURNAME VARCHAR2(32),
  LOCALE VARCHAR2(8));
```

We'll also have a table that maps a locale to surname order. In addition to locale, this table also has a CHAR(1) that we'll use as Boolean value, 'F' or 'T', to indicate whether the surname is the first name.

```
CREATE TABLE SURNAME_ORDER (
 LOCALE VARCHAR2(8),
 SURNAME_FIRST CHAR(1));
```

Here is some data:

```
INSERT INTO DIRECTORY VALUES('Po', 'Li', 'zh');
INSERT INTO DIRECTORY VALUES('Gabriel', 'García Marquez', 'es');
INSERT INTO DIRECTORY VALUES('Eni Su''aida', NULL, 'id');

INSERT INTO SURNAME_ORDER VALUES('zh', 'T');
INSERT INTO SURNAME_ORDER VALUES('es', 'F');
INSERT INTO SURNAME_ORDER VALUES('id', 'F');
```

Notice that the DIRECTORY table does not represent the way the data is to be displayed; it maintains a distinction only between surname and given name. The display order is determined by the second table, the SURNAME _ORDER table. In those cases where the given name is the only name, it will come first, of course.

The following function, DISPLAY_NAME, uses the SURNAME_ORDER table to determine in which order to concatenate a surname and given name pair, and returns a string with the name in the correct order.

```
CREATE FUNCTION DISPLAY_NAME
  (IN_GIVEN_NAME VARCHAR2,
   IN_SURNAME VARCHAR2,
   IN_LOCALE VARCHAR2)
  RETURN VARCHAR2
  AS
    NAME VARCHAR2(65);
    V_SURNAME_FIRST CHAR(1);
BEGIN

  SELECT SURNAME_FIRST
       INTO V_SURNAME_FIRST
     FROM SURNAME_ORDER
       WHERE LOCALE=IN_LOCALE;

  IF V_SURNAME_FIRST='T' THEN
     NAME := IN_SURNAME||' '||IN_GIVEN_NAME;
  ELSE
     NAME := IN_GIVEN_NAME||' '||IN_SURNAME;
  END IF;

  RETURN NAME;
END;
/
```

We can use this function in a SELECT statement querying the DIRECTORY table as follows:

```
SELECT DISPLAY_NAME(GIVEN_NAME, SURNAME, LOCALE)
FROM DIRECTORY;
```

Notice that this function will fail if a valid locale is not found. One way to ensure that this doesn't happen is to make the LOCALE column in the DIRECTORY table a foreign key that references the SURNAME_ORDER table. We can make data entry easier by providing a default value for the table. To do these two things, we need to make LOCALE a primary key in the

SURNAME_ORDER table, and we need to make LOCALE a foreign key in the DIRECTORY table. To do this, we need to create the tables like this:

```
CREATE TABLE SURNAME_ORDER (
 LOCALE VARCHAR2(8),
 SURNAME_FIRST CHAR(1),
 CONSTRAINT LOCALE_PK PRIMARY KEY (LOCALE)
);

CREATE TABLE DIRECTORY (
  GIVEN_NAME VARCHAR2(32),
  SURNAME VARCHAR2(32),
  LOCALE VARCHAR2(8) DEFAULT 'DEFAULT',
  CONSTRAINT LOCALE_SURNAME_ORDER_FK FOREIGN KEY (LOCALE)
        REFERENCES SURNAME_ORDER(LOCALE)
);
```

Next, we need to make an entry the SURNAME_ORDER table to support this default value.

```
INSERT INTO SURNAME_ORDER VALUES('DEFAULT', 'F');
```

We can also provide a default value programmatically by trapping the NO_DATA_FOUND exception that occurs when we query the SURNAME _ORDER table for a value that doesn't exist by using a subblock for the SELECT statement.

```
 /* ... */
BEGIN

  BEGIN
    SELECT SURNAME_FIRST
         INTO V_SURNAME_FIRST
       FROM SURNAME_ORDER
         WHERE LOCALE=IN_LOCALE;
  EXCEPTION
    WHEN NO_DATA_FOUND THEN
      V_SURNAME_FIRST = 'F'
  END;

  IF V_SURNAME_FIRST='T' THEN
     NAME := IN_SURNAME||' '||IN_GIVEN_NAME;
/* ... */
```

Either method makes it much easier to deal with cases where we don't know what language or country to assign to a name, but because it's easy to omit this data, it's tempting to do so. This leads to problems of data integrity and consistency that we need to solve some other way.

Further, none of this addresses the practical matter that most people do not know the two-letter codes from IS0-639 and ISO-3166. An application that supports internationalization would need to provide a reasonable user interface for selecting language and country—but this is an application design issue that we can't really address here.

Let's take a look at one more function, a function that will assist us in sorting titles. Its primary job is to see whether the first word of a title (a word or a phrase) is an article and, if so, add a comma to the phrase and move the article to the end. "The Doors" becomes "Doors, The", for example.

To support this function, we'll need a table of articles. To provide international support, we'll add a locale column so we can include articles in different languages.

```
CREATE TABLE ARTICLES (
  ARTICLE VARCHAR2(12),
  LOCALE VARCHAR2(8));
```

We'll provide our data in uppercase:

```
INSERT INTO ARTICLES VALUES('THE', 'en');
INSERT INTO ARTICLES VALUES('A', 'en');
INSERT INTO ARTICLES VALUES('EL', 'es');
INSERT INTO ARTICLES VALUES('LA', 'es');
INSERT INTO ARTICLES VALUES('LOS', 'es');
INSERT INTO ARTICLES VALUES('LAS', 'es');
```

For this function, we'll provide a default locale in our parameter list. This lets us call the function with either a title and a locale or with just a title. If it's the latter, the best thing to do would be to default to the locale that corresponds to the NLS_LANGUAGE session parameter (which would require another table mapping Oracle NLS_LANGUAGE parameters to our Java-style locales); but for this example, we'll just default to English:

```
CREATE OR REPLACE FUNCTION PARSE_TITLE
  (IN_TITLE VARCHAR2, IN_LOCALE VARCHAR2 DEFAULT 'en')
  RETURN VARCHAR2
AS

  IS_ARTICLE BOOLEAN;
  WORD_BREAK NUMBER;
  OUT_TITLE VARCHAR2(100);
  ARTICLE_COUNT VARCHAR2(12);
```

```
BEGIN

  WORD_BREAK := INSTR(RTRIM(IN_TITLE), ' ');

  SELECT COUNT(ARTICLE) INTO ARTICLE_COUNT
    FROM ARTICLES
    WHERE ARTICLE=UPPER(SUBSTR(IN_TITLE,1,WORD_BREAK – 1))
    AND LOCALE=IN_LOCALE;

  IF ARTICLE_COUNT = 0 THEN
    IS_ARTICLE := FALSE;
  ELSE
    IS_ARTICLE := TRUE;
  END IF;

  IF IS_ARTICLE AND LENGTH(IN_TITLE) > WORD_BREAK THEN
    OUT_TITLE := SUBSTR(IN_TITLE, WORD_BREAK + 1) || ', '
                 || SUBSTR(IN_TITLE,1, WORD_BREAK –1);
  ELSE
    OUT_TITLE := IN_TITLE;
  END IF;

  RETURN OUT_TITLE;

END;
/
```

Let's try a few tests:

```
SQL> SELECT PARSE_TITLE('The Pixies') FROM DUAL;

PARSE_TITLE('THEPIXIES')
--------------------------------------------------------

Pixies, The

SQL> SELECT PARSE_TITLE('Los Lobos') FROM DUAL;

PARSE_TITLE('LOSLOBOS')
--------------------------------------------------------

Los Lobos

SQL> SELECT PARSE_TITLE('Los Lobos', 'es') FROM DUAL;

PARSE_TITLE('LOSLOBOS','ES')
--------------------------------------------------------

Lobos, Los
```

We'll visit this function again later when we examine database triggers.

PL/SQL Stored Procedures

The format for creating a procedure differs from a function principally in that it has no return value.

```
CREATE [OR REPLACE] PROCEDURE procedure_name [(parameter_list)]
  {AS|IS}
  [local_declarations]
BEGIN
  program_statements
[EXCEPTION
  exception_handlers]
END;
```

By default, the parameters in the parameter list are for input only. They can, however, be used for output, too, to pass a value back to the calling program. (This is true for functions, too, but it's poor practice, particularly because functions are not supposed to have side effects.) The format of a parameter list item is

```
parameter_name [IN|OUT|IN OUT] datatype
```

where IN indicates an input parameter, OUT indicates an output parameter, and IN OUT indicates a parameter used for both input and output.

An IN parameter is the type we are most familiar with. It is a value provided by the calling program that we can use inside our procedure. We are not allowed to change it in our procedure, so it is essentially a constant.

OUT and IN OUT parameters allow the calling program, in effect, to pass a variable by reference. This allows our procedure to change the value of the variable in the calling program. The difference between OUT and IN OUT is that an OUT parameter is initialized to NULL in our procedure, but an IN OUT parameter retains whatever value the calling program set.

Let's take a look at some code that exemplifies this behavior. First we'll create a procedure that takes a variable of each type.

```
CREATE OR REPLACE PROCEDURE CALLEE (INVAR IN VARCHAR2,
  OUTVAR OUT VARCHAR2,
  INOUTVAR IN OUT VARCHAR2)
AS
BEGIN
  DBMS_OUTPUT.PUT_LINE('-  In CALLEE – Before changing variables');
  DBMS_OUTPUT.PUT_LINE('-  INVAR: '||INVAR);
  DBMS_OUTPUT.PUT_LINE('-  OUTVAR: '||OUTVAR);
  DBMS_OUTPUT.PUT_LINE('-  INOUTVAR: '||INOUTVAR);
```

```
  /* INVAR := 'Invar changed';  Not allowed */
  OUTVAR  := 'Outvar changed';
  INOUTVAR := 'Inoutvar changed';

  DBMS_OUTPUT.PUT_LINE('-  In CALLEE — After changing variables');
  DBMS_OUTPUT.PUT_LINE('-  INVAR: '||INVAR);
  DBMS_OUTPUT.PUT_LINE('-  OUTVAR: '||OUTVAR);
  DBMS_OUTPUT.PUT_LINE('-  INOUTVAR: '||INOUTVAR);
END;
/
```

Now we'll create another procedure to call our CALLEE procedure.

```
CREATE OR REPLACE PROCEDURE CALLING_PROCEDURE
AS
  FIRSTVAR VARCHAR2(25) := 'Original first var';
  SECONDVAR VARCHAR2(25) := 'Original second var';
  THIRDVAR VARCHAR2(25) := 'Original third var';
BEGIN
  DBMS_OUTPUT.PUT_LINE('Before calling CALLEE:');
  DBMS_OUTPUT.PUT_LINE('FIRSTVAR: '|| FIRSTVAR);
  DBMS_OUTPUT.PUT_LINE('SECONDVAR: '|| SECONDVAR);
  DBMS_OUTPUT.PUT_LINE('THIRDVAR: '|| THIRDVAR);
  DBMS_OUTPUT.PUT_LINE('---');

  CALLEE(FIRSTVAR, SECONDVAR, THIRDVAR);

  DBMS_OUTPUT.PUT_LINE('---');
  DBMS_OUTPUT.PUT_LINE('After calling CALLEE:');
  DBMS_OUTPUT.PUT_LINE('FIRSTVAR: '|| FIRSTVAR);
  DBMS_OUTPUT.PUT_LINE('SECONDVAR: '|| SECONDVAR);
  DBMS_OUTPUT.PUT_LINE('THIRDVAR: '|| THIRDVAR);
END;
/
```

Here are the results of running the second procedure.

```
SQL> CALL CALLING_PROCEDURE();
Before calling CALLEE:
FIRSTVAR: Original first var
SECONDVAR: Original second var
THIRDVAR: Original third var
---
-  In CALLEE - Before changing variables
-  INVAR: Original first var
-  OUTVAR:
-  INOUTVAR: Original third var
-  In CALLEE - After changing variables
```

```
-  INVAR: Original first var
-  OUTVAR: Outvar changed
-  INOUTVAR: Inoutvar changed
---
After calling CALLEE:
FIRSTVAR: Original first var
SECONDVAR: Outvar changed
THIRDVAR: Inoutvar changed

Call completed.
```

Let's investigate the fates of our three parameters. In CALLING _PROCEDURE, we assigned a value to FIRSTVAR before passing it as an IN parameter to CALLEE. Its value is, indeed, retained when we first print it out in CALLEE. If you try to compile the CALLEE with the assignment to INVAR, you will get an error indicating that INVAR is not allowed as an assignment target, demonstrating that an IN variable is, in fact, a constant we cannot change.

In CALLING_PROCEDURE, we assigned a value to SECONDVAR before passing it as an OUT parameter to CALLEE, but when we first print it out in CALLEE, we see that it has not retained that value—it is initialized to NULL in CALLEE. As expected for an OUT variable, the value we assign it in CALLEE is retained when we return and print it out in CALLING_PROCEDURE.

In CALLING_PROCEDURE, we assigned a value to THIRDVAR before passing it as an IN OUT parameter to CALLEE. In this case, when we first print it out in CALLEE, we see that it still has the value we assigned it in CALLING_PROCEDURE. And, like the OUT variable, when we assign it a value in CALLEE, it retains that value when it is returned to CALLING _PROCEDURE.

We'll see a more detailed example of a procedure when we examine how PL/SQL interacts with SQL and Oracle, using cursors.

Database Triggers

Database triggers are procedures that run automatically when a table is modified. Triggers are associated with INSERT, UPDATE, and DELETE SQL statements affecting a specific table. They can be set to run either before or after the SQL statement. The basic format for a database trigger is:

```
CREATE [OR REPLACE] TRIGGER trigger_name
  {BEFORE|AFTER}
  dml_event_list
  [FOR EACH ROW
    [WHEN condition]]
{CALL procedure}|{pl/sql block};
```

where dml_event_list is one or more of the following, separated by OR:

```
INSERT
UPDATE [OF column_name1[, column_name2 […]]]
DELETE
```

A trigger can be executed either BEFORE or AFTER the SQL statement makes its changes to the table. A BEFORE trigger has the advantage of being able to validate or modify data before it is inserted into a table. An AFTER trigger has the advantage of being able to query or change the table after integrity constraints have been applied and the table is in a consistent state.

Specifying FOR EACH ROW causes the trigger to be executed for each row that is modified by the SQL statement—this is called a *row trigger*. By default, a trigger is a statement trigger and is executed only once for the SQL statement that triggered it.

The WHEN clause specifies a condition that must be satisfied for the trigger to be executed. Because the WHEN clause must be evaluated on a per-row basis, the FOR EACH ROW option must also be specified.

The trigger may call a procedure like those we saw in the previous section or it may include the executable code in a PL/SQL block of its own.

If we include a PL/SQL block in our trigger, we automatically have access to a number of useful variables. First are the *correlation names* that allow you to refer to the old and new values of a row. You can change the correlation names by adding a REFERENCING clause to the CREATE TRIGGER STATEMENT, but by default the names are OLD and NEW.

We can access the old or new values of a column as variables in a BEFORE trigger using this format:

```
:OLD.columnname
:NEW.columnname
```

If we have a BEFORE trigger on a table that has a column named VALUE, we could conceivably have some code in our trigger's body similar to the following that limits the amount by which a column's value can increase.

```
/* ... */
IF :NEW.VALUE > :OLD.VALUE * 1.10 THEN
  :NEW.VALUE := :OLD.VALUE * 1.10;
END IF;
/* ... */
```

In the case of an UPDATE trigger, any :NEW column values not set by the UPDATE statement take their values from the :OLD values.

In an AFTER trigger, we can read only the :OLD values, which, of course, are the table's updated values.

Another useful set of variables available to us in a trigger's PL/SQL block lets us determine why the trigger is being executed. The following are Boolean values we can use in our PL/SQL block.

- INSERTING—TRUE only if trigger is called because of an INSERT statement
- UPDATING—TRUE only if trigger is called because of an UPDATE statement
- DELETING—TRUE only if trigger is called because of a DELETE statement

To take a look at an example of why and how we might use a trigger, let's return once again our CD collection database. One issue that we haven't addressed is how to sort the artists by name. When we first created our tables back in Chapter 2, we didn't consider this issue because a solution would cloud the basic issues we were first learning then.

In brief, there are two problems we face. The first is the internationalization issue that we saw earlier in this chapter: A person's surname is not always his or her last name. The second is the problem that the rules are different for sorting individuals' names, as opposed to groups' names; groups do not have surnames, so they sort by what we could consider to be their given names, but they have the complication that we generally need to ignore articles such as *The*.

Earlier in this chapter we considered these issues and wrote functions to solve them. We can use these two functions in our triggers but we'll need to change our CD_COLLECTION table a bit.

To support different types of names properly we're going to need to:

- Add a surname field
- Add a field to indicate whether it's a group or individual
- Add a field to hold the results of parsing the artist name
- Use a locale instead of a country name

This information is specific to the artist or group, not the CD, so it makes sense to make this a separate table for artist information. We could probably use the SORT_NAME column as a primary key but it's more convenient and efficient to have a numeric key, so we'll add an ARTIST_ID field too.

```
CREATE TABLE ARTISTS (
  ARTIST_ID NUMBER,
  NAME VARCHAR2(50),
  SURNAME VARCHAR2(50),
  IS_GROUP CHAR(1),
  SORT_NAME VARCHAR2(102),
  LOCALE VARCHAR2(8),
  CONSTRAINT ARTIST_PK PRIMARY KEY (ARTIST_ID)
);
```

We'll need a sequence to generate unique ARTIST_ID numbers.

```
CREATE SEQUENCE ARTIST_ID_SEQ;
```

Our trigger will use the BEFORE INSERT option because we need to do some validation and processing of the data before adding it to the ARTISTS table. It will be a row trigger because we need to process individual rows—hence the FOR EACH ROW option.

We will do the following when someone inserts or updates a row in the ARTISTS table:

- If NAME is a group name, as indicated by the IS_GROUP value, and a surname was provided, raise an application error.
- If NAME is a group name, generate SORT_NAME using PARSE_TITLE() function.
- If NAME is an individual name, concatenate SURNAME and NAME to form SORT_NAME. If SURNAME normally comes at the end, separate SURNAME and NAME by a comma. If SURNAME comes first according to the individual's locale, don't include a comma.

Here is the function.

```
CREATE OR REPLACE TRIGGER ARTISTS_TRIGGER
  BEFORE INSERT
    OR UPDATE OF NAME, SURNAME, IS_GROUP, LOCALE
  ON ARTISTS
  FOR EACH ROW
DECLARE
  IS_SURNAME_FIRST CHAR(1);
BEGIN
  DBMS_OUTPUT.PUT_LINE('ARTISTS_TRIGGER ...');
```

```
/* Set default locale */
IF :NEW.LOCALE IS NULL THEN
  :NEW.LOCALE := 'en';
END IF;

/* Group or individual? */
 IF :NEW.IS_GROUP='T' THEN

    DBMS_OUTPUT.PUT('group - ');

    /* A group cannot have a surname */
    IF :NEW.SURNAME IS NOT NULL THEN
      RAISE_APPLICATION_ERROR(-20501,
        'Group cannot have surname');
    ELSE
      SELECT PARSE_TITLE(:NEW.NAME, :NEW.LOCALE)
        INTO :NEW.SORT_NAME
        FROM DUAL;
    END IF;

 ELSE /* Individual */

    DBMS_OUTPUT.PUT('individual - ');

    /* if surname is normally first, don't use comma */
    SELECT SURNAME_FIRST
      INTO IS_SURNAME_FIRST
      FROM SURNAME_ORDER
      WHERE LOCALE=:NEW.LOCALE;

    IF IS_SURNAME_FIRST='T' THEN
      :NEW.SORT_NAME  :=
        :NEW.SURNAME || ' ' || :NEW.NAME;
    ELSE
      :NEW.SORT_NAME  :=
        :NEW.SURNAME || ', ' ||  :NEW.NAME;
     END IF;

 END IF;

 DBMS_OUTPUT.PUT_LINE(:NEW.SORT_NAME);

END;
/
```

We'll insert these values.

```
INSERT INTO  ARTISTS(ARTIST_ID, NAME, SURNAME, IS_GROUP, LOCALE)
  VALUES(ARTIST_ID_SEQ.NEXTVAL,
  'Jian', 'Cui', 'F', 'zh');
INSERT INTO  ARTISTS(ARTIST_ID, NAME, SURNAME, IS_GROUP, LOCALE)
  VALUES(ARTIST_ID_SEQ.NEXTVAL,
  'Laurie', 'Anderson', 'F', 'en');
INSERT INTO  ARTISTS(ARTIST_ID, NAME, SURNAME, IS_GROUP, LOCALE)
  VALUES(ARTIST_ID_SEQ.NEXTVAL,
  'A Perfect Circle', NULL, 'T', 'en');
INSERT INTO  ARTISTS(ARTIST_ID, NAME, SURNAME, IS_GROUP, LOCALE)
  VALUES(ARTIST_ID_SEQ.NEXTVAL,
  'Pearl Jam', NULL, 'T', 'es');
```

We'll select the SORT_NAME column to see what the trigger produced.

```
SQL> SELECT SORT_NAME FROM ARTISTS;

SORT_NAME
------------------------------------

Cui Jian
Anderson, Laurie
Perfect Circle, A
Pearl Jam
```

To display these properly to a user, we would use the DISPLAY_NAME() function we created a few sections ago in the select list and sort by putting the SORT_NAME column in an ORDER BY clause. It doesn't matter with our particular set of data, as it happens, but when we are sorting names in languages other than English, we need to enable linguistic sorting by setting the NLS_SORT session parameter to our preferred language or to a generic linguistic sort, such as WEST_EUROPEAN or, in Oracle 9i, GENERIC_M. (See Chapter 4 for more information about linguistic sorting.) The following command, as you may remember, will accomplish this in SQL*Plus:

```
SQL> ALTER SESSION SET NLS_SORT='WEST_EUROPEAN';

Session altered.
```

Now our data will be displayed in a multiculturally correct order and format.

```
SQL> SELECT DISPLAY_NAME(NAME, SURNAME, LOCALE)
  2  FROM ARTISTS
  3  ORDER BY SORT_NAME;

DISPLAY_NAME(NAME,SURNAME,LOCALE)
-------------------------------------------------

Laurie Anderson
Cui Jian
Pearl Jam
A Perfect Circle
```

Cursors and Cursor Loops

We've seen that the biggest benefit of using PL/SQL to write procedural database programs is that it lets us easily use SQL statements directly in our code. PL/SQL always performs database operations using a memory buffer called a *cursor*. In the statements we've seen so far, PL/SQL has taken care of creating and using this cursor automatically. An automatic cursor of this type is called an *implicit cursor*.

By limiting ourselves to implicit cursors, we've restricted the types of queries we can perform to those that return only a single row. To perform more general queries that can return multiple rows, we can either declare and manage an explicit cursor ourselves, using OPEN, FETCH...INTO, and CLOSE cursor statements or we can use a cursor FOR...LOOP to take care of the details for us. We'll first see how to manage a cursor ourselves.

Declaring and Using a Cursor

A cursor is associated with a specific query. The first step in using one is to declare it in the DECLARE section of our PL/SQL block. The basic format for declaring a cursor is

```
CURSOR cursor_name
  IS select_statement;
```

The cursor_name is an identifier for the cursor—it associates a name with a memory buffer used for performing database operations. The select_statement can be any valid SQL SELECT statement.

Suppose we want to retrieve the artists listed in the ARTISTS table from the last example. We can declare a cursor like this:

```
DECLARE
    CURSOR C_ARTISTS IS SELECT *
      FROM ARTISTS
      ORDER BY SORT_NAME;
```

Attributes

In PL/SQL objects such as rows, columns, cursors, and variables have one or more properties, or attributes, associated with them. For example, a row has a set of columns with specific names and datatypes, and a column has a datatype. We can obtain these properties by appending the *attribute indicator* (%) plus the name of the attribute to the name of the object. There are three attributes that are especially useful for managing cursors: %TYPE, %ROWTYPE, and %NOTFOUND.

%TYPE

One way that we can use attributes is in variable declarations. %TYPE is used to obtain the datatype of columns in a table or cursor. We can use it, for example, to declare variables of the same types as the columns in the ARTISTS table. Notice that we use dot notation with a table name plus a column name.

```
DECLARE
  V_ARTIST_ID TABLE.ARTIST_ID%TYPE;
  V_NAME TABLE.NAME%TYPE;
  /* etc. */
```

Using this technique, rather than specifying an SQL type explicitly, improves the maintainability of the code because changes to the types of the columns in the table will automatically be reflected in the PL/SQL code.

%ROWTYPE

We can use the %ROWTYPE attribute of a table to declare a row object—also known as a *record*—based on a table or a cursor. For example, we can declare a row object, based on the ARTISTS table, in this way:

```
DECLARE
  ARTISTS_REC ARTISTS%ROWTYPE;
```

Once we've populated this record, using a cursor (or a SELECT...INTO statement), we can retrieve the fields from ARTISTS_REC using dot notation: ARTISTS_REC.ARTIST_ID, ARTISTS_REC.NAME, etc.

%FOUND, %NOTFOUND

These are two of several attributes unique to cursors. The %FOUND attribute of a cursor is TRUE when a cursor FETCH succeeds in retrieving a row. The %NOTFOUND is TRUE when the FETCH fails. These are useful for processing a cursor's result set, as we will see.

Declaring a cursor does not actually execute the query. To execute the query, we must use an OPEN statement in the BEGIN section of our PL/SQL block using the following format:

```
OPEN cursor_name;
```

Once the cursor is open, we can begin retrieving data from it, row by row, using the FETCH...INTO statement. The FETCH...INTO statement requires us to provide a variable or variables to store the values retrieved.

```
FETCH cursor_name INTO variable_list;
```

When we are finished using a cursor, we need to close the cursor using the CLOSE statement.

```
CLOSE cursor_name;
```

Let's use the cursor we previously declared to retrieve a row from the ARTISTS table. We'll declare variables of the appropriate type, using the %TYPE attribute of the columns in the ARTISTS table.

```
DECLARE

 CURSOR C_ARTISTS IS SELECT *
   FROM ARTISTS
   ORDER BY SORT_NAME;

   V_ARTIST_ID  ARTISTS.ARTIST_ID%TYPE;
   V_NAME       ARTISTS.NAME%TYPE;
   V_SURNAME    ARTISTS.SURNAME%TYPE;
   V_IS_GROUP   ARTISTS.IS_GROUP%TYPE;
   V_SORT_NAME  ARTISTS.SORT_NAME%TYPE;
   V_LOCALE     ARTISTS.LOCALE%TYPE;

BEGIN

  OPEN C_ARTISTS;
  FETCH C_ARTISTS INTO
    V_ARTIST_ID, V_NAME, V_SURNAME, V_IS_GROUP,
    V_SORT_NAME, V_LOCALE;

  DBMS_OUTPUT.PUT_LINE(V_SORT_NAME);

END;
/
```

We can use functions or expressions in our select list, too, but we need to assign them aliases. Here, we'll use the cursor's %ROWTYPE to define a record. We'll include the DISPLAY_NAME() function with the alias DISPLAY_NAME in a cursor's select list so that we can access it using dot notation like a column.

```
DECLARE
  CURSOR C_ARTISTS IS SELECT
    DISPLAY_NAME(NAME, SURNAME, LOCALE) AS DISPLAY_NAME
    FROM ARTISTS
    ORDER BY SORT_NAME;
  C_ARTISTS_REC C_ARTISTS%ROWTYPE;
BEGIN
  OPEN C_ARTISTS;
    FETCH C_ARTISTS INTO C_ARTISTS_REC;
    DBMS_OUTPUT.PUT_LINE(C_ARTISTS_REC.DISPLAY_NAME);
  CLOSE C_ARTISTS;
END;
/
```

There's little point in using a cursor that returns multiple rows if we fetch only one. Although we could use multiple FETCH statements, it's obviously better to use a loop to process multiple rows. We have at our disposal two cursor attributes that can help—%FOUND and %NOTFOUND. We can use these in the following way:

```
LOOP
  FETCH cursor_name INTO variable_list;
  IF cursor_name%FOUND THEN
    /* process rows */
  ELSE
    EXIT;
  ENDIF;
END LOOP;
```

Or, better:

```
LOOP
  FETCH cursor_name INTO variable_list;
  IF cursor_name%NOTFOUND THEN
    EXIT;
  END IF;
  /* process rows */
END LOOP;
```

We can display the complete list of artists with the following:

```
DECLARE
  CURSOR C_ARTISTS IS SELECT
    DISPLAY_NAME(NAME, SURNAME, LOCALE) AS DISPLAY_NAME
    FROM ARTISTS
    ORDER BY SORT_NAME;
  C_ARTISTS_REC C_ARTISTS%ROWTYPE;
```

```
BEGIN
  OPEN C_ARTISTS;
  LOOP
    FETCH C_ARTISTS INTO C_ARTISTS_REC;
    IF C_ARTISTS%NOTFOUND THEN
      EXIT;
    END IF;
    DBMS_OUTPUT.PUT_LINE(C_ARTISTS_REC.DISPLAY_NAME);
  END LOOP;
  CLOSE C_ARTISTS;
END;
/
```

Cursor Parameters and Return Values

Cursors have two other options that we've omitted from the basic format we saw above. They can accept parameters and they can return a value. The complete format for declaring a cursor is

```
CURSOR cursor_name [(parameter_list)]
   [RETURN return_type]
  IS select_statement;
```

The return_type is used in creating cursor specifications for inclusion in a package; we will not cover that here.

The parameter_list is similar to the parameter list for a function or procedure. Multiple parameters are separated by commas. Each parameter has the format

```
parameter_name datatype [{DEFAULT|  := } default_value]
```

We can use a parameter_name in the cursor's query in the same way that we can use PL/SQL variables in SQL statements that use an implicit cursor. The parameters are passed when the cursor is opened, like this:

```
OPEN cursor_name(parameters);
```

For example, we could alter the last example to display a range of names by passing the cursor start and end parameters and using them in a WHERE clause.

```
DECLARE
  CURSOR C_ARTISTS
    (START_NAME VARCHAR2, END_NAME VARCHAR2)
    IS SELECT
      DISPLAY_NAME(NAME, SURNAME, LOCALE) AS DISPLAY_NAME
      FROM ARTISTS
```

```
        WHERE SORT_NAME>= START_NAME AND SORT_NAME<= END_NAME
         ORDER BY SORT_NAME;
  C_ARTISTS_REC C_ARTISTS%ROWTYPE;
BEGIN
  OPEN C_ARTISTS('A', 'M');
  /* ... */
```

Normally, of course, the START_NAME and END_NAME parameters would not be hard-coded but would've been passed in as the arguments to the function or procedure, for example.

Cursor FOR...LOOP

PL/SQL offers an easier alternative to opening, fetching, testing, and closing a cursor ourselves—the cursor FOR...LOOP. This is similar to the standard FOR...LOOP we've already seen. The format for a FOR...LOOP is

```
FOR record_name IN {cursor_name|query} LOOP
  /* process record */
END LOOP;
```

In place of a simple counter variable, like that in a regular FOR...LOOP, we have an implicitly declared row object, or record. This record is equivalent to a record declared using the %ROWTYPE attribute of the FOR...LOOP's cursor. The fields of a record, as we've seen previously, can be accessed using dot notation. The scope of the record is limited to the loop body.

There are two basic options for a cursor FOR...LOOP: We can use an explicitly declared cursor with the query specified in a cursor declaration or we can use an implicitly declared cursor by specifying the query in the FOR...LOOP statement instead of using an already declared cursor. These two examples are equivalent.

```
/* Explicitly declared cursor */
DECLARE
  CURSOR C_ARTISTS IS
    SELECT ARTIST_ID, SORT_NAME FROM ARTISTS
      ORDER BY SORT_NAME;
BEGIN
  FOR C_ARTISTS_REC IN C_ARTISTS LOOP
    DBMS_OUTPUT.PUT_LINE(C_ARTISTS_REC.SORT_NAME);
  END LOOP;
END;


/* Cursor implicitly declared by query */
BEGIN
```

```
    FOR C_ARTISTS_REC IN
        (SELECT ARTIST_ID, SORT_NAME FROM ARTISTS
          ORDER BY SORT_NAME)
      LOOP
      DBMS_OUTPUT.PUT_LINE(C_ARTISTS_REC.SORT_NAME);
    END LOOP;
  END;
```

The second format, using the query directly in the FOR…LOOP, is more concise.

If we want to use a cursor with parameters we need to use the first format, with an explicit cursor. This isn't an important advantage because we can accomplish the same thing in a FOR…LOOP query by including variables in the query.

This next example shows how we can use a cursor's parameters in the query's WHERE clause.

```
/* Explicitly declared cursor
 * with parameters
 */
DECLARE
  CURSOR C_ARTISTS(START_NAME VARCHAR2, END_NAME VARCHAR2)
    IS
    SELECT ARTIST_ID, SORT_NAME FROM ARTISTS
      WHERE SORT_NAME >= START_NAME AND SORT_NAME <= END_NAME
      ORDER BY SORT_NAME;
  BEGIN_RANGE VARCHAR2(1) := 'A';
  END_RANGE VARCHAR2(1) := 'M';

BEGIN
  FOR C_ARTISTS_REC IN C_ARTISTS(BEGIN_RANGE, END_RANGE) LOOP
    DBMS_OUTPUT.PUT_LINE(C_ARTISTS_REC.SORT_NAME);
  END LOOP;
END;
```

This next example shows how we can accomplish the same thing by using PL/SQL variables in the FOR…LOOP query.

```
/* Cursor implicitly declared by query
 * using PL/SQL variables
 */
DECLARE

  BEGIN_RANGE VARCHAR2(1) := 'A';
  END_RANGE VARCHAR2(1) := 'M';
```

```
BEGIN
  FOR C_ARTISTS_REC IN
      (SELECT ARTIST_ID, SORT_NAME FROM ARTISTS
        WHERE SORT_NAME >= BEGIN_RANGE AND SORT_NAME <= END_RANGE
        ORDER BY SORT_NAME)
    LOOP
    DBMS_OUTPUT.PUT_LINE(C_ARTISTS_REC.SORT_NAME);
  END LOOP;
END;
```

Java Stored Procedures

Since Oracle 8i, Oracle has included a Java Virtual Machine (JVM) inside the database. In Oracle 9i Release 2, the JVM supports JDK 1.3 and conforms fully to the Java Language Specification. Having a JVM inside the database allows Java methods to run inside the database. To do this, we need to write a PL/SQL function or procedure call specification that, instead of including an implementation in PL/SQL, includes a LANGUAGE JAVA clause that maps a Java method's parameters and return types to PL/SQL types.

There are few restrictions on what a Java method can do when it runs inside the database—the most obvious one being that we can't have a user interface. For example, standard input (from the keyboard) and standard output (to the screen) are not available. Because these calls are ignored by the Oracle JVM, we can use calls to System.out.println() for debugging outside the database and simply leave them in our code when we load it into the database.

Java stored procedures offer the advantage of speed when compared with Java programs that run outside the database, especially those that involve a lot of interaction with the database. Java stored procedures offer nearly the same performance as PL/SQL stored procedures. If speed is critical, Java stored procedures can be compiled to native executable code using Oracle's ncomp utility. The advantage that Java stored procedures have over PL/SQL is that they are portable.

Depending on the application design and performance requirements, a Java program can be deployed in a client application, in a middle tier, or inside the database. This flexibility can make development much easier. Further, assuming that no proprietary extensions are used, a Java stored procedure might even be portable to other vendor's databases—Java is quickly becoming the de facto standard language for database stored procedures.

The Java Class and Stored Procedure Method

A Java stored procedure is a method, but one of the requirements of Java is that everything must belong to a class. For our example, we'll create a class, `Procedures`, to contain our method, `myMethod()`. If we were to create other Java stored procedures, we could implement them as in methods in this class too. We can also include a `main()` method, which will allow us to run the stored procedures outside the database for testing and debugging purposes.

To interact with the database, a Java method needs to obtain a connection. When the method is running inside the database as a stored procedure, there are two ways to do this. The first is to call the `DriverManager`'s `defaultConnection()` method:

```
DriverManager.defaultConnection();
```

The second is to call the `getConnection()` method:

```
DriverManager.getConnection("jdbc:default:connection:");
```

These differ in that the first one always returns the same `Connection` object, but the second returns a new object each time. Unless you have a specific reason for wanting a new object each time, Oracle recommends using the `defaultConnection()` method.

Regardless of which way you get a connection, because it is associated with an implicit connection, you should not close it.To test and debug Java stored procedures outside the database, as a standalone program, you can obtain a connection in the `main()` method using the Oracle JDBC driver and store it in a class variable. (We'll disregard the details of this for now.) The `main()` method can then call the stored procedure method `myMethod()`.

If `myMethod()` is called by `main()` it will already have a connection provided by `main()`. If it doesn't have a connection, it will know that it is running as a stored procedure inside the database and that it should obtain the server-side connection instead.

In addition to the code for obtaining a connection, `myMethod()` uses JDBC to query the database. JDBC will be formally introduced in Chapter 8, "Introduction to JDBC." Here, we'll just point out some of the highlights.

`myMethod()` creates an SQL statement by concatenating a fixed string with the method's `name` parameter.

```
String sql = "SELECT LAST_NAME FROM NAMES WHERE FIRST_NAME = '"
        + name + "'";
```

This SQL statement is executed by calling a `Statement` object's `executeQuery()` method, which returns a `ResultSet` object.

```
ResultSet rs = stmt.executeQuery(sql);
```

After locating the first row by calling the `ResultSet`'s `next()` method, we retrieve a `String` value from a `ResultSet` with the `ResultSet`'s `getString()` method. The parameter in this call to `getString()` refers to the first column in the `ResultSet`:

```
fullname = name + " " + rs.getString(1);
```

Here is the complete class, which can be compiled and run at a command prompt or loaded into the database so `myMethod()` can be used as a Java stored procedure.

```
import java.sql.*;
import oracle.jdbc.*;

public class Procedures {
  static Connection conn = null;

  public static void main(String [] args)
  {
    try
    {
       DriverManager.registerDriver(
       new oracle.jdbc.OracleDriver());
       conn = DriverManager.getConnection(
              "jdbc:oracle:thin:@noizmaker:1521:osiris",
              "david", "bigcat");
       String [] sa = new String [1];
       System.out.println("procedure returned: "
         + myMethod("John"));
       conn.close();
    }
    catch(SQLException e)
    {
       System.out.println("Caught " + e);
    }
  }

  public static String myMethod(String name)
  throws SQLException
  {
    String fullname = "Unknown";
```

```
        try
        {
           if(conn==null)
           {
             conn = DriverManager.getConnection(
                "jdbc:default:connection:");
           }
           else
           {
              System.out.println("Executing at command prompt...");
           }

           Statement stmt = conn.createStatement();
           String sql = "SELECT LAST_NAME FROM NAMES WHERE FIRST_NAME = '"
                         + name + "'";
           System.out.println(sql);
           ResultSet rs = stmt.executeQuery(sql);
           if(rs.next())
           {
             fullname = name + " " + rs.getString(1);
           }
       }
       catch(SQLException e)
       {
           System.out.println("Caught " + e);
       }
       return "Hello " + fullname;
    }
}
```

The other important thing to notice is that, in order to be used as a stored procedure or function, a Java method must be static—inside the database there is no enclosing context available that is able to instantiate an object.

Loading and Publishing a Java Stored Procedure

Oracle provides a command line utility, loadjava, that will load a Java source, class, or .jar (or .zip) file into the database. If we load a source file, by default, it will not be compiled until the first time it is called at runtime—which can cause, at best, a delay and, at worst, an error, should compilation fail. Perhaps the best option is to load the source file and use the -resolve option to compile it immediately; this has the advantage that it will load the source code into the database where it will remain available for future maintenance.

We can take the sample program above and, once we're sure it compiles and runs as expected at a command prompt, we can load and compile it with the following command, which includes the -resolve option, username and password, and Java source file:

```
loadjava -resolve -user david/bigcat Procedures.java
```

With the loadjava utility, no news means good news: It normally only produces output if there are errors.

Publishing the Stored Procedure

To use the stored procedure we need to publish it by creating a call specification that maps its parameters and return type to PL/SQL types. This is similar to how we define PL/SQL functions and procedures except that, instead of providing a body that includes PL/SQL executable code, we substitute a LANGUAGE JAVA clause.

The basic syntax for a function is

```
CREATE [OR REPLACE] FUNCTION function_name [(parameter_list)]
  RETURN sql_type {AS|IS}
LANGUAGE JAVA
  NAME 'class_name.method_name([full_java_type [,…]])
  return full_java_type';
```

The basic syntax for a procedure is

```
CREATE [OR REPLACE] PROCEDURE procedure_name [(parameter_list)]
  {AS|IS}
LANGUAGE JAVA
  NAME 'class_name.method_name([full_java_type [,…]])';
```

A parameter in the optional parameter list has the following format:

```
parameter_name [IN | OUT | IN OUT] sql_type
```

We can publish the method `myMethod()` in the example above as a function with the following command in SQL*Plus:

```
SQL> CREATE FUNCTION HELLO(NAME VARCHAR2)
  2    RETURN VARCHAR2 AS
  3  LANGUAGE JAVA
  4    NAME 'Procedures.myMethod(java.lang.String)
  5    return java.lang.String';
  6  /

Function created.
```

To try out the function, we'll need to create a NAMES table and insert a couple of rows if it doesn't exist already from a previous example.

```
CREATE TABLE NAMES(FIRST_NAME VARCHAR2(25),
  LAST_NAME VARCHAR2(25));
INSERT INTO NAMES VALUES('John', 'Smith');
INSERT INTO NAMES VALUES('Maria', 'Garcia');
```

We can call the function from an SQL statement. For example, we can include it in the select list with a literal and query the dummy table DUAL.

```
SQL> SELECT HELLO('John') FROM DUAL;

HELLO('JOHN')
------------------------------------

Hello John Smith
```

IN and IN OUT Parameters

The call specification allows us to specify whether a parameter is for input, output, or both—IN, OUT, or IN OUT. If not specified, the default is IN. Although it is allowed, it is considered poor practice for a function to have OUT or IN OUT parameters. In Java, OUT or IN OUT parameters must be array types—typically, a single element array of the appropriate type.

Let's add a method to our Procedures class that returns a string, using a parameter. We'll overload the existing `myMethod()` and create a new one that returns the results in a parameter instead of as a return value.

```
public static void myMethod(String name, String [] retval)
throws SQLException
{
   retval[0] = myMethod(name);
}
```

We'll publish it as a procedure as follows:

```
SQL> CREATE PROCEDURE HELLO_PROC(NAME VARCHAR2, RETVAL OUT VARCHAR2)
       AS
     LANGUAGE JAVA
       NAME 'Procedures.myMethod(java.lang.String,
               java.lang.String[])';

     /

Procedure created.
```

We can test this interactively in PL/SQL. We'll need to create the OUT variable.

```
SQL> VARIABLE OUTVAR VARCHAR2(25);
```

We call the procedure with the CALL command. Notice that we need to prefix the host variable with a semicolon.

```
SQL> CALL HELLO_PROC('Maria', :OUTVAR);
```

We print the output variable with a PRINT command.

```
SQL> PRINT OUTVAR

OUTVAR
--------------------------------
Maria Garcia
```

For More Information on Java Stored Procedures...

Java stored procedures are a sort of hybrid of PL/SQL and Java. The emphasis in this chapter on PL/SQL has been on using call specifications to make Java methods appear like PL/SQL procedures and functions to the database. Apart from a few restrictions described earlier (including, in particular, the fact that they must be static methods), there is nothing special about the Java methods used as stored procedures. To learn more about writing Java stored procedures you'll need to learn more about JDBC, which Chapters 8 and 9 cover in much more depth than what's been touched on here. Although the emphasis there is on using JDBC in standalone applications, the lessons learned there also apply to developing Java stored procedures.

CHAPTER 6

Oracle Object-Relational Features

Oracle introduced most of its object-relational features in Oracle 8i. Of these features, object types are the most fundamental. Object types are user-defined types that correspond to classes in Java. They allow us to model data in the database the same way we do in our programs, using a set of attributes and methods for each object.

Designing a database to use object techniques is dramatically different from taking a relational approach. The most common technique in object-oriented design is composition, including classes within other classes, like Russian dolls, which is exactly the opposite approach for relational databases. The first step toward normalization is to "un-nest" the data and put aggregate or repeating types in separate tables.

Consider the design of the CD collection database. To conform to the first normal form, we made one table to hold information about each CD as a whole and another separate table. If we were to design a Java program that worked with our CD collection, we would likely have two classes, a CD class and a Song class, but they wouldn't be completely separate. The CD class would be related to the SONG class by aggregation: We'd probably include an array (or Vector) of type Song in our CD class.

Using Oracle's object-relational features, we can create a similar object in the database. We can create an object type that includes the songs for each CD in a nested table; each row in the CD table would include a table with the songs on that CD.

If we are writing an application in an object-oriented language such as Java and we are using the database to store our objects' data, it seems reasonable to mimic the structure of our objects in the database. This obviates the need for a separate layer to perform object-relational mapping. We'll see how this works in practice when we explore using JDBC together with Oracle's object-relational features.

The case for implementing methods, as opposed to data, in the database is not as compelling, however—at least not when most of our code is already in Java classes on the client side. Nonetheless, there are cases when we might consider using this feature of Oracle's object types, so we'll examine methods, too.

Oracle introduced a few new object-relational features in Oracle 9i, most notably, inheritance. We'll examine these features briefly at the end of this chapter, but everything else in this chapter—except for one or two instances, duly noted—is applicable to both Oracle 8i and 9i.

Object Types

Object types in Oracle are the equivalent of classes in Java. Like Java classes, they have attributes and methods. An object type can be used as the datatype in a table column; as an attribute in another object; and as an argument, variable, or return value for a method.

In Oracle, attributes correspond to the columns in a table. In the same way that attributes in Java can be of either primitive types, such as `int` and `float`, or other classes, such as `String` and `FileWriter`, attributes in Oracle can be either standard SQL datatypes, such as NUMBER and VARCHAR2, or other object types, including nested tables and arrays.

In Oracle, methods are functions or procedures written in PL/SQL, Java, or C/C++. We'll take a look at methods later; for now, we'll consider simple object types without methods.

Creating Object Types

Creating an object type resembles creating a table but does not actually allocate any space for storing data. This is the basic format used to define a simple object type without any methods:

```
CREATE TYPE type_name AS OBJECT (
  column_name1 column_type1
  [, column_name2 column_type2[,…]]
);
```

This does not create an object—it only defines the type. It assigns a name to the type and assigns names and types to each of its attributes. We can create a type, POINT_TYPE, which has two attributes, X and Y, like this:

```
SQL> CREATE TYPE POINT_TYPE AS OBJECT (
  2     X,
  3     Y
  6   )
  7   /

Type created.
```

Notice that, as we did for PL/SQL, we need to type a slash at the end, rather than a semicolon, in order to execute this command. If there had been errors in compilation, we would've typed SHOW ERROR to get SQL*Plus to list them.

Now when we create a table, we can use this object type as the type for a column, just as we would any other datatype. Here is an example of how we might use the POINT_TYPE object in a relational table.

```
SQL> CREATE TABLE CIRCLES (
  2      RADIUS  NUMBER,
  3      CENTER  POINT_TYPE
  4   );

Table created.
```

Assuming that the table has some data—we'll see how to perform inserts into an object type in a moment—we can query a table that includes object types in the same way that we do other tables.

```
SQL> select radius, center from circles;

    RADIUS CENTER(X, Y)
---------- -------------------------------------------
         3 POINT_TYPE(2, 2)
```

Notice that the column CENTER is returned as a POINT_TYPE. If we want the values *X* and *Y* returned individually, we need to include and fully qualify the object's X and Y attributes in the SELECT statement with an alias for the table and the object's column name as follows:

```
SELECT RADIUS, C.CENTER.X, C.CENTER.X FROM CIRCLES C;
```

This provides a result in a more familiar format:

```
SQL> SELECT RADIUS, C.CENTER.X, C.CENTER.X FROM CIRCLES C;

    RADIUS   CENTER.X   CENTER.X
---------- ---------- ----------
         3          2          2
```

Which format we use depends in large part on our application and whether it is prepared to accept objects in addition to standard SQL types.

Object Tables

We can also create a table where every row is an object. This type of table is called an *object table*, and it has the interesting characteristic that you can use it in two ways: either as a table with a single column of that object type or as a standard relational table that has the same column definitions as the object type. The format for creating an object table is:

```
CREATE TABLE table_name OF object_type;
```

Suppose we wanted to keep track of a number of points, perhaps to create a scattergram to test how well two variables are correlated—for example, inches of rain in April and number of flowers in May. We might create a table:

```
SQL> CREATE TABLE BLOOM_DATA OF POINT_TYPE;

Table created.
```

There are two advantages to using object tables. The first advantage is that object tables simplify the use of objects somewhat. Because an object table's column types coincide with the object type, we don't need to qualify the object attributes with the object name. We can insert data into an object table just as we would into a relational table.

```
SQL> INSERT INTO BLOOM_DATA VALUES(2,3);

1 row created.
```

Querying the attributes of an object in an object table is easier than querying a multicolumn table with objects.

```
SQL> SELECT X,Y FROM BLOOM_DATA;

         X          Y
---------- ----------
         2          3
```

The second advantage is that object tables can be a convenient way of using object types as templates for creating tables, ensuring that multiple tables have the same structure. For example, we can create an address book type and use it as a template for separate but identical tables for business, school, and personal contacts—although it may be preferable to have a single table and add a column identifying the type of contact.

Methods

Although we haven't explicitly included any methods in our object definition above, our objects already include one automatically: the default *constructor*. We need a constructor in order to create objects, particularly when we use INSERT or UPDATE to add data to our tables.

The constructor has the same name as the object type and it takes one argument for every attribute in the object type. The POINT_TYPE object that we defined above, for example, has the two attributes, X and Y. To insert a row into our CIRCLES table, we use the following INSERT statement with the POINT_TYPE(x, y) constructor:

```
SQL> INSERT INTO CIRCLES VALUES (
  2              3,
  3              POINT_TYPE(5,5)
  4  );

1 row created.
```

Using a constructor to create and insert an object into an object table is optional. For example, we can insert a row into our BLOOM_DATA table, as follows:

```
INSERT INTO BLOOM_DATA(POINT_TYPE(2, 12));
```

But because of the object table's dual nature, we can also treat it as an ordinary relational table with columns corresponding to those of the object type.

```
INSERT INTO BLOOM_DATA VALUES(3, 15);
```

User-Defined Methods

Constructors are necessary and, fortunately, they are provided for free by the system. In addition, we may also wish to have other methods associated with our object types to provide behavior that we want available anywhere we might want to use that object.

Encapsulating the behavior of objects together with their attributes makes objects easier to understand, maintain, and reuse. If we change the underlying representation of our data, for example, any code that needs to change to correspond to those changes is in the same place.

To define our own methods, we first need to declare them when we define the object type. This part is the same, regardless of what language, (PL/SQL, Java, or C/C++), we will use to implement them. Methods can be either procedures or functions. As you may remember, the difference between the two is that functions return a value. Functions are more useful than procedures because we can use them in such places as select list items, WHERE clauses, and ORDER BY clauses. Because of this, our examples will be limited to functions.

```
CREATE TYPE type_name AS OBJECT (
    column_name1 column_type1
    [, column_name2 column_type2[,…]] ,
    MEMBER FUNCTION method_name [(argument_list)]
        RETURN datatype
    [, additional methods …]
);
```

For each defined method, this specifies the method's name, its argument list (optionally), and its return type. If the method is implemented in PL/SQL, we need to perform one more step, creating the *type body*.

```
CREATE TYPE BODY  type_name AS

  MEMBER FUNCTION method_name RETURN datatype {AS|IS}
    variable declarations …
    BEGIN
      method code …
      RETURN return value;
    END;
  END;

  [additional functions or procedures]

END;
```

Notice that each function or procedure block is preceded by either of the keywords AS or IS—it doesn't make any difference which. We'll use AS.

Let's create a new object type, LINE_TYPE, that contains two points, a starting point and an end point. We'll include a method to calculate length, GETLENGTH(), which takes no parameters and returns a NUMBER.

```
SQL> CREATE TYPE LINE_TYPE AS OBJECT (
       START_POINT POINT_TYPE,
       END_POINT   POINT_TYPE,
       MEMBER FUNCTION GETLENGTH RETURN NUMBER
     );
     /

Type created.
```

As mentioned above, we can create methods using PL/SQL, Java, or C/C++. Java and PL/SQL are preferable for short procedures or procedures that interact a lot with the database. C/C++ procedures, because they are compiled into native machine code, can execute more quickly but they incur a lot of overhead because they are executed as external processes outside the database. C/C++ is preferable for long, complicated routines that do not interact much with the database. The following is the implementation of the GETLENGTH() method in PL/SQL:

```
SQL> CREATE OR REPLACE TYPE BODY LINE_TYPE AS

       MEMBER FUNCTION GETLENGTH RETURN NUMBER AS
         BEGIN
           RETURN SQRT(
               POWER(START_POINT.X-END_POINT.X,2)
              +POWER(START_POINT.Y-END_POINT.Y,2)
           );
         END;

     END;
     /

Type body created.
```

The code in this function consists of this one statement:

```
RETURN SQRT(
    POWER(START_POINT.X-END_POINT.X,2)
    +POWER(START_POINT.Y-END_POINT.Y,2)
```

The important thing to notice is that we automatically have access to the object's START_POINT and END_POINT and their attributes. This is because, even though we did not define any parameters for our function, we get one for free: SELF. This parameter refers to the current instance of the object that the method belongs to, in this case, LINE_TYPE. It is Oracle's equivalent of Java's *this*. Because no other object is specified, START_POINT and END_POINT are assumed to refer to the SELF object. The following code, where we explicitly use SELF, means exactly the same thing as the code above.

```
RETURN SQRT(
    POWER(SELF.START_POINT.X-SELF.END_POINT.X,2)
    +POWER(SELF.START_POINT.Y-SELF.END_POINT.Y,2)
```

If we create a table that includes a LINE_TYPE and call this GETLENGTH() function in a SELECT statement that queries that table, Oracle will iterate through every row selected, passing each row's LINE_TYPE object to this function.

Let's create an object table of LINE_TYPE to test our method.

```
SQL> CREATE TABLE LINES OF LINE_TYPE;

Table created.
```

We'll insert a line of data.

```
SQL> INSERT INTO LINES VALUES(POINT_TYPE(1,1), POINT_TYPE(4,5));

1 row created.
```

Notice that, because LINES is an object table, we don't have to use the LINE_TYPE constructor to insert LINE_TYPE objects into it, but because each LINE_TYPE contains POINT_TYPE objects, we do need to use the POINT_TYPE constructor to insert the starting point and end point—we get only one free layer with our object table.

We can call the GETLENGTH() method as follows:

```
SQL> SELECT L.GETLENGTH() FROM LINES L;

L.GETLENGTH()
-------------
            5
```

Notice that in the call to GETLENGTH(), we need to qualify the method name with an alias for the table name.

It's pretty common for functions, such as GETLENGTH(), not to take any arguments. When a function or procedures takes no arguments, we omit the parentheses and argument list in the CREATE TYPE and CREATE TYPE BODY statements, but we still need to include an empty pair when we call it in a SELECT statement. Note that this is inconsistent with regular SQL functions, which do not take parenthesis if they do not have arguments.

Let's take a look at a couple more examples. First we'll take a look at a method that takes an argument. Arguments can be of any SQL type, e.g., VARCHAR2, NUMBER, or user-defined types, including object types. We can also optionally specify whether it is an input variable, an output variable, or both, using the keywords IN, OUT, and INOUT but only IN makes sense for functions, and because this is the default mode, we usually just omit it.

For this example, we'll define yet another type, RECTANGLE, with two methods, a CONTAINS method, which takes an argument of POINT_TYPE; and GETAREA, which is a special type of method—a *map method*—that we'll explain later. First we create the type.

```
SQL> CREATE TYPE RECTANGLE_TYPE AS OBJECT (
       TOP_LEFT POINT_TYPE,
       WIDTH    NUMBER,
       HEIGHT   NUMBER,
       MAP MEMBER FUNCTION GETAREA RETURN NUMBER,
       MEMBER FUNCTION CONTAINS (PT IN POINT_TYPE) RETURN NUMBER
     )
     /

Type created.
```

Next we create the type body for the PL/SQL code.

```
SQL> CREATE OR REPLACE TYPE BODY RECTANGLE_TYPE AS

       MAP MEMBER FUNCTION GETAREA RETURN NUMBER AS
               BEGIN
                       RETURN WIDTH*HEIGHT;
               END;

       MEMBER FUNCTION CONTAINS
         (PT IN POINT_TYPE) RETURN NUMBER AS
                       IS_INSIDE NUMBER := 0;
               BEGIN
                       IF(  PT.X > TOP_LEFT.X
                          AND PT.X < TOP_LEFT.X + WIDTH
                          AND PT.Y > TOP_LEFT.Y
                          AND PT.Y < TOP_LEFT.Y + HEIGHT
                       )
                       THEN
                          IS_INSIDE := 1;
                       END IF;
```

```
                           RETURN IS_INSIDE;
                   END;
    END;
    /

Type body created.
```

We'll create a table that uses this type:

```
SQL>     CREATE TABLE RECTANGLES (
           LABEL VARCHAR2(25),
           RECTANGLE RECTANGLE_TYPE
         );

Table created.
```

And insert some data.

```
SQL> INSERT INTO RECTANGLES VALUES('One',
       RECTANGLE_TYPE(POINT_TYPE(10,50), 40, 20));

1 row created.

SQL> INSERT INTO RECTANGLES VALUES('Two',
       RECTANGLE_TYPE(POINT_TYPE( 0, 0), 10, 10));

1 row created.
```

Notice that we need to use two constructors, one nested within the other, because we've nested a POINT_TYPE inside a RECTANGLE_TYPE inside a regular multicolumn table. (In the previous example, we didn't need to use a constructor for highest level object, LINE_TYPE, because it was an object table of LINE_TYPE.)

The first method we'll test is the CONTAINS() method. It determines whether a point that is passed in as an argument is inside the rectangle defined in the RECTANGLE_TYPE object. Oracle does not support a Boolean type, so we use 0 to represent false and 1 to represent true.

```
SQL> SELECT LABEL, R.RECTANGLE.CONTAINS(POINT_TYPE(20,60))
       AS CONTAINS
     FROM RECTANGLES R;

LABEL                       CONTAINS
------------------------- ----------
One                                1
Two                                0
```

```
SQL> SELECT LABEL, R.RECTANGLE.CONTAINS(POINT_TYPE( 5, 5))
       AS CONTAINS
     FROM RECTANGLES R;

LABEL                       CONTAINS
------------------------- ----------
One                                0
Two                                1
```

Comparison Methods

The second method we included in the object type and object type body above is one of two types of comparison methods—a map method. A map method is a type of comparison method that takes no arguments and returns a standard scalar Oracle SQL type, such as NUMBER or VARCHAR2, that Oracle will use implicitly to perform comparisons. Suppose that we have a number of rectangles and want to put them in order—on what basis do we do that? Perhaps arbitrarily, our map method for RECTANGLE_TYPE (as suggested by its name, GETAREA()), returns the area of the rectangle.

We can call our map method, GETAREA(), directly, like the other methods we've seen so far.

```
SQL> SELECT LABEL, R.RECTANGLE.GETAREA()
     FROM RECTANGLES R;

LABEL                     R.RECTANGLE.GETAREA()
------------------------- ---------------------
One                                         800
Two                                         100
```

However, the important characteristic of this map method is that Oracle will use it implicitly when we use a RECTANGLE_TYPE object in a comparison, such as in a WHERE clause or an ORDER BY clause. If we order the RECTANGLES table by RECTANGLE, for example, we should see our rectangles in ascending order (the default order) by area.

```
SQL> SELECT LABEL, R.RECTANGLE.GETAREA()
     FROM RECTANGLES R
     ORDER BY RECTANGLE;

LABEL                     R.RECTANGLE.GETAREA()
------------------------- ---------------------
Two                                         100
One                                         800
```

We can also see the indirect results of the GETAREA() method when we compare RECTANGLE_TYPE objects. In the following example, we'll create a RECTANGLE_TYPE object directly in our SELECT statement, with an area of 200 to use for comparison in a WHERE clause.

```
SQL> SELECT LABEL, R.RECTANGLE.GETAREA()
  2  FROM RECTANGLES R
  3  WHERE RECTANGLE > RECTANGLE_TYPE(NULL, 10, 20);

LABEL                     R.RECTANGLE.GETAREA()
------------------------- ---------------------
One                                         800
```

Notice that this comparison works only because both objects being compared are of the RECTANGLE_TYPE type and we have a map method for that type. Even though what ultimately gets compared is a NUMBER representing the area, we can't provide a NUMBER directly; a WHERE clause like this does not work.

```
SQL> SELECT LABEL, R.RECTANGLE.GETAREA()
  2  FROM RECTANGLES R
  3  WHERE RECTANGLE > 200;
WHERE RECTANGLE > 200
                  *
ERROR at line 3:
ORA-00932: inconsistent datatypes
```

There is one other type of comparison method, an *order method.* An object type's order method takes one argument, of the same object type, to which it compares the SELF object. If the object whose method is called, SELF, is smaller than the object that is passed in as an argument, the value returned must be negative. If the objects are equal, the value returned must be zero, and if SELF is larger than the object passed in, a positive value must be returned. How this result is determined is entirely up to the order method.

This is how we could have used an order method in our example. First, the type definition:

```
CREATE TYPE RECTANGLE_TYPE AS OBJECT (
  TOP_LEFT POINT_TYPE,
  WIDTH            NUMBER,
  HEIGHT   NUMBER,
  ORDER MEMBER FUNCTION GETAREA
    (RECT IN RECTANGLE_TYPE)
    RETURN NUMBER,
  /* ... */
)
/
```

And the type body:

```
CREATE OR REPLACE TYPE BODY RECTANGLE_TYPE AS

     ORDER MEMBER FUNCTION GETAREA
       (RECT IN RECTANGLE_TYPE)
       RETURN NUMBER AS
            BEGIN
               RETURN (WIDTH*HEIGHT)-(RECT.WIDTH*RECT.HEIGHT);
            END;
       /* ... */

END;
/
```

A map method has the advantage of efficiency because it associates each object with a single scalar value. An order method has the advantage of flexibility because it can perform an arbitrarily complex comparison between two objects, which might not necessarily be possible by reducing each object to a single value. However, an order method is a user-defined function that is called for each pair of objects to be compared—making it slower than using a map method, especially for sorts, where it may need to be called many times.

Implementing Methods in Java

For Java programmers who are unfamiliar with PL/SQL, implementing methods in Java may seem a promising option. Unfortunately, there are quite a few steps required to do this. If the methods are fairly simple, you may find it more worth your while to master just enough PL/SQL to get the job done. If the methods are not simple or you really don't want to code in PL/SQL, you may wish to consider implementing the object methods outside the database—use the database to hold only object attributes and implement methods in client-side Java classes that map to the server-side database objects.

Nonetheless, there are some advantages to implementing methods in the database in Java if the methods are substantial enough to justify the overhead. Methods that run inside the database are much faster, especially if they are database-intensive. Compared with PL/SQL, the flexibility, power, and expressiveness of the Java language (not to mention its familiarity) are pretty compelling when faced with a daunting programming task that is performance-critical. Portability may clinch the case for implementing important code in Java: Should you later decide to move functionality out of the database and into a client application written in Java (or into a middle-tier), you won't need to rewrite the code. In fact, you may wish to develop the method outside the database first, then move it into the database only once it is has been fully debugged and tested, using your familiar development tools.

There is an important restriction for methods implemented in Java: They can be only static methods because they are not passed a SELF value. In other words, they do not have an object instance available. If you wish to implement a function that operates on object instances—for example, every row in the SELECT statement's result set—you will need to pass the object into the function or a value that will allow the method to get the object for itself as one of the parameters.

The steps necessary to implement an object method in Java are:

- Define the method in the object type specification.
- Create a call specification for the method and include it in the type body. (If there are no methods that need to be implemented in the type body, the call specification can be included in the type specification, instead.)
- Create a Java class that includes the static method.
- Load the class in the database.

For this example, we'll create an object type for triangles. The object composition is shown in Figure 6–1.

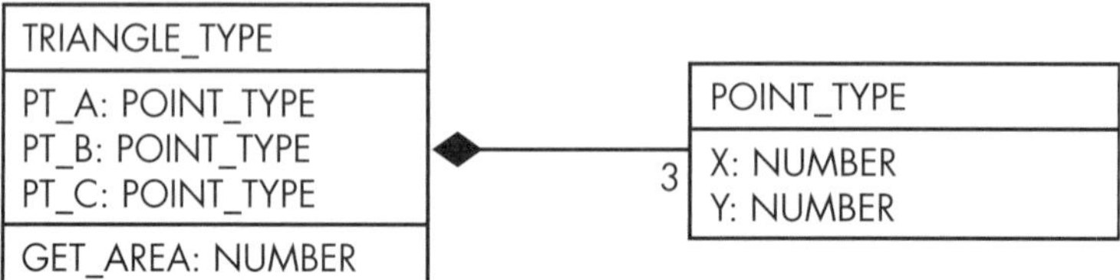

FIGURE 6–1 Object composition.

We could use a type specification and separate type body, like we did before.

```
CREATE TYPE TRIANGLE_TYPE AS OBJECT (
  PT_A POINT_TYPE,
  PT_B POINT_TYPE,
  PT_C POINT_TYPE,
  STATIC FUNCTION GETAREA(LAB IN VARCHAR2)
    RETURN NUMBER
)
/
```

```
CREATE TYPE BODY TRIANGLE_TYPE AS

  STATIC FUNCTION GETAREA(LAB in VARCHAR2)
    RETURN NUMBER
  AS LANGUAGE JAVA
  NAME 'Triangle.getArea(java.lang.String)return double';

END;
/
```

In this case, however, we don't have any code in our body type, so we can include the call specification in the type specification, instead. We'll execute this all-in-one statement in place of the two separate statements above:

```
SQL> CREATE TYPE TRIANGLE_TYPE AS OBJECT (
       PT_A POINT_TYPE,
       PT_B POINT_TYPE,
       PT_C POINT_TYPE,

       STATIC FUNCTION GETAREA(LAB in VARCHAR2)
         RETURN NUMBER
       AS LANGUAGE JAVA
       NAME 'Triangle.getArea(java.lang.String)return double'
     )
     /

Type created.
```

Now we can create a table using the TRIANGLE_TYPE.

```
SQL> CREATE TABLE TRIANGLES (
       LABEL VARCHAR2(25),
       TRIANGLE TRIANGLE_TYPE,
       CONSTRAINT TRIANGLE_PK
         PRIMARY KEY(LABEL)
     );

Table created.
```

In the interest of simplicity, we've been lax in identifying primary keys in previous examples, but in this case, because we are going to use the LABEL column as the identifier in our method, we need to ensure that it is unique.

Next, we'll populate the table with some data.

```
SQL> INSERT INTO TRIANGLES
  2    VALUES('One',
  3      TRIANGLE_TYPE(POINT_TYPE(1,2),POINT_TYPE(5,6),
POINT_TYPE(3,2)));

1 row created.

SQL> INSERT INTO TRIANGLES
  2    VALUES('Two',
  3      TRIANGLE_TYPE(POINT_TYPE(0,0),POINT_TYPE(0,4),
POINT_TYPE(4,0)));

1 row created.

SQL> COMMIT;

Commit complete.
```

To create the Java class and load it into the database, we'll follow most of the same steps we did when we created Java stored procedures in the previous chapters. As before, we won't examine the JDBC code in depth here—that's coming up in the next chapter.

Because it's easiest to code and debug outside the database, we'll write our code to work both outside and inside the database. The biggest difference between running inside and outside the database is that, inside, we have a default connection, and outside, we need to obtain our own connection. Cleanup is also a little different because we shouldn't close the default connection. To facilitate this, our class `Triangle` will include a `main()` to get a connection before calling our method `getArea()` and will set a flag so that we can clean up appropriately.

```
import java.sql.*;

public class Triangle {
static Connection conn = null;
static String testval="One";
boolean isLocal = false;

  public static void main(String [] args)
  {
    try
    {
DriverManager.registerDriver(
       new oracle.jdbc.OracleDriver());
      conn = DriverManager.getConnection(
```

```
                    "jdbc:oracle:thin:@noizmaker:1521:osiris",
                    "david", "bigcat");
          isLocal = true;
          getArea(testval);
        }
        catch(SQLException e)
        {
          System.out.println("Caught " + e);
        }
      }
```

Because the `getArea()` method doesn't automatically have an object instance to work with, we need to either provide the object or pass it a value so that it can obtain the information from it on its own. In the sample implementation here, we'll pass it the value for LABEL so that our method can obtain the corresponding TRIANGLE object from the TRIANGLES table. (A better implementation would not need to be tied to a specific table. The right way to do it would be for `getArea()` to take an argument of type TRIANGLE_TYPE, but interpreting an object—which we could pass to Java as java.sql.Struct—is beyond the scope of what we're doing here.) We use a SELECT statement to obtain the X and Y coordinates of each of the three points in TRIANGLE as double, using LABEL in the WHERE clause.

```
public static double getArea(String label)
{
  double area = 0;
  try
  {
    if(conn==null)
    {
     conn =
         DriverManager.getConnection("jdbc:default:connection:");
      }
      Statement stmt = conn.createStatement();
      String sql = "SELECT " +
                  "T.TRIANGLE.PT_A.X, T.TRIANGLE.PT_A.Y," +
              "T.TRIANGLE.PT_B.X, T.TRIANGLE.PT_B.Y," +
              "T.TRIANGLE.PT_C.X, T.TRIANGLE.PT_C.Y " +
                  "FROM TRIANGLES T WHERE LABEL ='" +
                  label +"'";

      ResultSet rs = stmt.executeQuery(sql);
```

To calculate the triangle's area, we'll use Heron's formula. According to this formula, given the lengths of the three sides of a triangle, a, b, and c, the area A is

$$s = (a + b + c)/2$$

$$A = sqrt(s\ (s - a)\ (s - b)(s - c))$$

Because our SELECT statement obtains only the x and y coordinates, we use a helper method, `getLength()`, to calculate the lengths `a`, `b`, and `c`, and from that, the `area`.

```
if(rs.next())
{
  double ax, ay, bx, by, cx, cy;
  double a, b, c;

  ax = rs.getDouble(1);
  ay = rs.getDouble(2);
  bx = rs.getDouble(3);
  by = rs.getDouble(4);
  cx = rs.getDouble(5);
  cy = rs.getDouble(6);

  a = getLength(ax, ay, bx, by);
  b = getLength(bx, by, cx, cy);
  c = getLength(cx, cy, ax, ay);

  /* Calculate area using Heron's  formula */
  double s = (a + b +c)/2; // perimeter/2
  area = Math.sqrt(s * (s - a) * (s - b) * (s - c));
}
```

Finally, we do some cleanup; close the resources we used (except the default connection!) and return the area that we calculated.

```
catch(SQLException e)
{
   System.out.println("Caught " + e);
}
finally
{
  rs.close();
  stmt.close();
  if(isLocal)
  {
```

```
          conn.close(0); // don't close default connection!
        }
      }
      return area;
    }
```

This is the helper method for calculating the distance between two points, ax, ay, and bx, by:

```
  static double getLength(double ax, double ay, double bx, double by)
  {
   return Math.sqrt(Math.pow((ax-bx),2) + Math.pow((ay-by),2));
  }

}
```

One of the benefits of object-oriented programming is that it makes it easier to reuse code. One of the new object-relational features in Oracle 9i, the ability to create transient objects to use in SELECT statements, can help us do this. In a previous example, we created a LINE_TYPE object that had a method for calculating the length of a line. If our code doesn't need to support Oracle 8i we can reuse the GETLENGTH() method in the LINE_TYPE object type and replace the Java code for calculating length. We could use the following query to obtain the lengths a, b, and c from Oracle:

```
// Oracle 9i version:
String sql = "SELECT " +
  "LINE_TYPE(T.TRIANGLE.PT_A,T.TRIANGLE.PT_B).GETLENGTH(), "
+
  "LINE_TYPE(T.TRIANGLE.PT_B,T.TRIANGLE.PT_C).GETLENGTH(), "
+
   "LINE_TYPE(T.TRIANGLE.PT_C,T.TRIANGLE.PT_A).GETLENGTH()  "
+
  "FROM TRIANGLES T WHERE LABEL ='" + label +"'";

ResultSet rs = stmt.executeQuery(sql);
double a, b, c;
if(rs.next())
{
  a = rs.getDouble(1);
  b = rs.getDouble(2);
  c = rs.getDouble(3);

  /* Calculate area using Heron's  formula */
  double s = (a + b +c)/2; // perimeter/2
  area = Math.sqrt(s * (s - a) * (s - b) * (s - c));
}
```

After we've compiled and tested this code, we can load the class into the database by using the Oracle loadjava utility. At the command prompt, we enter:

```
C:\myjava>loadjava -v -u david/bigcat Triangle.class
```

This command produces the following output:

```
arguments: '-v' '-u' 'david/bigcat' 'Triangle.class'
creating : class Triangle
loading  : class Triangle
```

Now we can query the table, using our method. Because GETAREA() is a static method, it is not associated with any instance, and we need to qualify it with the *type* name, TRIANGLE_CLASS, not the instance name or the column name in the TRIANGLES table, TRIANGLE. We need to pass LABEL as an argument to the method so that it can retrieve the proper row and calculate the area (essentially using a subquery) for each row in the result set.

```
SQL> SELECT LABEL, TRIANGLE_TYPE.GETAREA(LABEL) FROM TRIANGLES;

LABEL                    TRIANGLE_TYPE.GETAREA(LABEL)
------------------------ ----------------------------
One                                                 4
Two                                                 8
```

Troubleshooting Java Methods

Implementing methods in Java may seem to be a lot of trouble. If you are experimenting with your own code and are experiencing problems, you should be aware that this is common; troubleshooting can be a tedious and sometimes frustrating experience. A good approach is to take it one step at a time and simplify each step as much as possible.

For example, to make sure that the method is being called correctly—that it is being passed the right parameters and is returning the expected value—you might try replacing the Java code with something simple at first. It may, for example, be easier to get this version of the `getArea()` method working before the real Java method.

```
public double getArea(String label)
{
   return label.length();
}
```

This bypasses any problems that the JDBC and SQL code might cause and lets us concentrate on making sure the call specification and loadjava are working as expected.

Another troubleshooting technique is to eliminate possible problems with the object type and object type body by publishing the method as a standalone stored procedure or function—this won't interfere with the same method being called as an object method. After using loadjava to upload the `Triangle` class into the database, you can publish the `getArea()` method as follows:

```
SQL> CREATE OR REPLACE FUNCTION GETTRIANGLEAREA(LABEL VARCHAR2)
         RETURN NUMBER
         AS LANGUAGE JAVA
         NAME 'Triangle.getArea(java.lang.String)return double';
     /

Function created.
```

Now you can test this function independently of the object type mechanism.

```
SQL> SELECT GETTRIANGLEAREA('One') FROM DUAL;

GETTRIANGLEAREA('ONE')
----------------------
                     4
```

Note that, although we don't need to use the TRIANGLES table explicitly in our query if we already know a valid value for LABEL, it still must be present because our method uses it implicitly.

Finally, in the course of testing, debugging, and troubleshooting, you will need to drop object types, type bodies, and tables, perhaps repeatedly. The commands you need to do this and the order you need execute them are:

```
DROP TABLE tablename;
DROP TYPE BODY object_type_name;
DROP OBJECT TYPE object_type_name;
```

Given all that, you may wonder whether implementing object methods in Java is worth all the trouble. If it makes sense from a design point of view and seems warranted by performance considerations, you may wish first to try to build a prototype or a pilot project before committing to Java object methods.

Nested Collections

In some of the examples above, we've seen that we can nest single objects within other objects. For example, our CIRCLE_TYPE included a POINT _TYPE for the center. We are not limited to including single objects within other objects; we can also include objects with multiple values called *collections*. There are two collection types in Oracle, nested tables and VARRAYs. They are similar in the type of data they can store because they both can include objects. The differences are:

- Nested tables
  - Can be of unlimited size.
  - Are essentially unordered, like relational tables.
- VARRAYS
  - Must be of a fixed size, one size for all instances.
  - Can be retrieved as an ordered array in a procedural language, but inside Oracle, are treated as a single indivisible unit.
  - Are stored efficiently.

In Oracle 8i, only a single level of nesting is supported. Oracle 9i allows multiple levels of nesting. Except as noted, most of the examples in this section will work with either version of Oracle.

Nested Tables

As you might expect, nested tables are tables that are stored as part of another table. We use them much like we use other object types: We define a table type just as we did an object type and we can use a table type, like an object type, as the datatype in a table column, as an attribute in another object, and as an argument, variable, or return value for a method.

This is the general format for creating a table type:

```
CREATE TYPE table_type_name AS TABLE OF {object_type|datatype}
/
```

Suppose we want to keep track of the daily high temperature for a group of cities for an indefinite period of time. We can create a nested table of NUMBER to hold daily highs for each city. First, we create the table type:

```
SQL> CREATE TYPE NUMBER_TABLE AS TABLE OF NUMBER
  2  /

Type created.
```

Now we can use NUMBER_TYPE almost anywhere that we would use a standard SQL datatype, including as the column type of a relation table. The format for creating a table that contains a nested table is almost the same as creating any other table, except that we need to provide one more piece of information: where to store the information for the nested tables. This storage clause specifies the name of a table it is to create and use to hold the information for all of the nested tables in our main table. (Apart from creating it, we won't ever need to refer to this storage table again—set it and forget it.) The format is:

```
CREATE TABLE (
  column_name1 {data_type|object_type|table_type}
    [,column_name2 {data_type|object_type|table_type}[,…]]
    [additional create table options]
)
NESTED TABLE column_name STORE AS storage_table_name;
```

Let's create our table of cities, including state and country, and a table of temperatures for each.

```
SQL> CREATE TABLE DAILY_HIGHS(
  2     CITY        VARCHAR2(32),
  3     STATE       VARCHAR2(32),
  4     COUNTRY     VARCHAR(32),
  5     TEMPS       NUMBER_TABLE
  6   )
  7   NESTED TABLE TEMPS STORE AS DAILY_HIGHS_TEMPS_STORAGE;

Table created.
```

We insert data into a table that contains a nested table in much the same way that we insert into a table that contains an object: by using a constructor. A table constructor has the same name as the table type and it accepts multiple rows separated by commas.

```
type_name([value[, value[,…]]]);
```

We can include as many values as we like to insert multiple rows. (If we want to insert an empty table, we can use the constructor with no values.) To insert a city, Houston, for example, with the list of temperatures 98, 97, and 95, we can use the following statement:

```
SQL> INSERT INTO DAILY_HIGHS
  2    VALUES('Houston', 'TX', 'USA',
  3      NUMBER_TABLE(98,97, 95));

1 row created.
```

In general, we can address a nested table like we would any other table by using a TABLE subquery. The subquery must have a WHERE clause that restricts the selection to the single row containing the table we want to update. This is the general format of a TABLE subquery:

```
TABLE(SELECT nested_table_name
    FROM table_name
    WHERE single_row_condition)
```

To continue inserting rows into a table that's already been created using a table constructor, we can use the familiar INSERT statement, replacing the table name with a table subquery:

```
INSERT INTO TABLE(SELECT nested_table_name
  FROM table_name
  WHERE single_row_condition) VALUES (value);
```

We can insert a new row into our DAILY_HIGHS table as follows:

```
SQL> INSERT INTO
      TABLE(SELECT TEMPS
         FROM DAILY_HIGHS
         WHERE CITY='Houston')
     VALUES(90);

1 row created.
```

To drop a nested table, we don't use a DROP statement. We instead simply set the nested table entry to NULL.

```
SQL> UPDATE DAILY_HIGHS SET TEMPS=NULL
      WHERE CITY='Houston';

1 row updated.
```

If we try to insert into this row's table now, we get an error.

```
SQL> INSERT INTO
      TABLE(SELECT TEMPS
           FROM DAILY_HIGHS
           WHERE CITY='Houston')
          VALUES(90);
INSERT INTO
*
ERROR at line 1:
ORA-22908: reference to NULL table value
```

We can add a table to an existing row using an UPDATE statement with the table constructor. Once again, we can add as many rows as we like at the same time. The following statement adds an empty table:

```
SQL> UPDATE DAILY_HIGHS SET TEMPS=NUMBER_TABLE()
  2     WHERE CITY='Houston';

1 row updated.
```

The nested table in the preceding examples has been a single column of NUMBER. The other option we can use for a nested table is an object type. Let's continue with a similar example but extend it to include highs, lows, and dates for each city. First we need to create the object type.

```
SQL> CREATE TYPE TEMP_RECORD_TYPE AS OBJECT (
  2     DAY  DATE,
  3     HIGH NUMBER,
  4     LOW NUMBER
  5  )
  6  /

Type created.
```

Next we create a table type of this object type.

```
SQL> CREATE TYPE TEMP_RECORD_TABLE AS
  2     TABLE OF TEMP_RECORD_TYPE
  3  /

Type created.
```

Now we can create a table that includes this nested table of objects.

```
SQL> CREATE TABLE DAILY_TEMPS(
  2     CITY          VARCHAR2(32),
  3     STATE         VARCHAR2(32),
  4     COUNTRY       VARCHAR(32),
  5     TEMPS         TEMP_RECORD_TABLE
  6  )
  7  NESTED TABLE TEMPS STORE AS DAILY_TEMPS_TEMPS_STORAGE;

Table created.
```

To insert dates, highs, and lows into this table, we need to use the table constructor, of course. But because the nested table contains objects, we also need to use the object constructor. Once again, we can insert multiple rows at once with the table constructor; this time using multiple object constructors separated by commas, as follows:

```
SQL> INSERT INTO DAILY_TEMPS
       VALUES('Reno', 'NV', 'USA',
         TEMP_RECORD_TABLE(
            TEMP_RECORD_TYPE('18-APR-2002',61,31),
            TEMP_RECORD_TYPE('29-APR-2002',53,36),
            TEMP_RECORD_TYPE('30-APR-2002',51,30)
         )
     );

1 row created.
```

Let's next take a brief look at querying tables. We'll insert some more data to make things more interesting.

```
SQL> INSERT INTO DAILY_TEMPS
       VALUES('Anchorage', 'AK', 'USA',
         TEMP_RECORD_TABLE(
            TEMP_RECORD_TYPE('18-APR-2002',46,35),
            TEMP_RECORD_TYPE('29-APR-2002',50,39),
            TEMP_RECORD_TYPE('30-APR-2002',51,39)
         )
     );

1 row created.
```

If we use a simple SELECT on a nested table, we get the nested information identified by type within parentheses, like this:

```
SQL> SELECT CITY, TEMPS FROM DAILY_TEMPS;

CITY
--------------------------------
TEMPS(DAY, HIGH, LOW)
------------------------------------------------------------

Reno
TEMP_RECORD_TABLE(TEMP_RECORD_TYPE('18-APR-02', 61, 31),
TEMP_RECORD_TYPE('29-APR-02', 53, 36), TEMP_RECORD_TYPE('30-APR-02',
51, 30))

Anchorage
TEMP_RECORD_TABLE(TEMP_RECORD_TYPE('18-APR-02', 46, 35),
TEMP_RECORD_TYPE('29-APR-02', 50, 39), TEMP_RECORD_TYPE('30-APR-02',
51, 39))
```

Using SQL*Plus, this is hard to read. In a programming environment, such as Java with JDBC, this is tedious to process. We could use nested cursors to deal with it, but another alternative is to un-nest, or *flatten*, the table, using a TABLE expression in the query. What we will do, in effect, is perform a join of the outer table with the inner table.

```
SQL> SELECT CITY, T.*
  2  FROM DAILY_TEMPS D, TABLE(D.TEMPS) T;

CITY                             DAY            HIGH       LOW
-------------------------------- --------- ---------- -----
Reno                             18-APR-02        61     31
Reno                             29-APR-02        53     36
Reno                             30-APR-02        51     30
Anchorage                        18-APR-02        46     35
Anchorage                        29-APR-02        50     39
Anchorage                        30-APR-02        51     39

6 rows selected.
```

Notice that we assign an alias D to the outer table and that we use this alias in the TABLE expression to select the nested table. Then we assign an alias T to the nested table to use in our select list.

As a final example, we add a WHERE clause to this query.

```
SQL> SELECT CITY, T.*
  2  FROM DAILY_TEMPS D, TABLE(D.TEMPS) T
  3  WHERE T.LOW <= 32;

CITY                                    DAY             HIGH   LOW
-------------------------------- --------------- ------ ---
Reno                                 18-APR-02        61     31
Reno                                 30-APR-02        51     30
```

This by no means exhausts the options and possibilities of using nested tables, but we hope it's enough for you to understand them, evaluate them, and possibly start using them.

VARRAYS

VARRAYS are much like nested tables, but rather than being of unlimited size, we must specify their size when we declare them—like an array in Java. The advantage that they have over nested tables is that they store collections much more efficiently. The disadvantage is that VARRAYs can be manipulated only as a whole. They are *opaque* to Oracle—it doesn't know anything about what's inside them. It can't query them or change them. In order to manipulate individual elements, we must retrieve the VARRAY into an array type in a procedural language, such as Java, where we can address and alter individual elements, using indexes. When we are through updating the array, we must insert it back into the database as a single chunk of data.

The basic format for declaring a VARRAY is

```
CREATE TYPE type_name AS VARRAY(n) OF {data_type|object_type)
/
```

Instead of creating a TRIANGLE_TYPE with three separate points, for example, we could have used a VARRAY(3) of POINT_TYPE.

```
SQL> CREATE TYPE TRIANGLE_VARRAY AS VARRAY(3) OF POINT_TYPE
  2  /

Type created.
```

To include methods, however, we would then need to create an object type that uses this VARRAY.

```
CREATE TYPE VTRIANGLE_TYPE AS OBJECT (
    POINTS TRIANGLE_VARRAY,
   STATIC FUNCTION GETAREA(LAB in VARCHAR2)
      RETURN NUMBER
   AS LANGUAGE JAVA
     NAME 'Triangle.getArea(java.lang.String)return double'
 )
 /
```

We would next need to update our Java Triangle class to use VARRAY instead of the individual points, create a new table, etc., as we did before.

Let's take another example. Suppose we have a Web server application and we want to track the last 100 visitors to each page on our site. One way to do this is to use a circular buffer.

Conceptually, a circular buffer is like a list, but the end of the list loops back around to the beginning. We can implement this with an array by using two pointers, one to tell us what the first entry in the buffer is and one to tell us what the last (most recent) entry is. Eventually, when the list fills up, the pointer to the last entry wraps back to the beginning, and from then on, the two pointers advance together.

First we'll create the VARRAY to use as the buffer for each Web page.

```
SQL> CREATE TYPE VISITOR_VARRAY AS VARRAY(100) OF VARCHAR2(25)
  2     /

Type created.
```

Now we create the table with the page name, the starting index, the index of the end of the buffer, and the VARRAY for each page. This step is a little simpler than including nested tables because by default, Oracle takes care of deciding how to store the VARRAY.

```
CREATE TABLE VISITORS (
   PAGE_NAME  VARCHAR2(25),
   START_INDEX NUMBER,
   END_INDEX NUMBER,
   USERNAME   VISITOR_VARRAY
);
Table created.
```

We'll initialize a page with two sample entries.

```
INSERT INTO VISITORS
  VALUES('INDEX.HTML',0,1,
         VISITOR_VARRAY('TestUser1','TestUser2'));
```

Querying tables with VARRAYs is similar to querying tables with nested tables.

```
SQL> SELECT PAGE_NAME, U.*
  2     FROM VISITORS V, TABLE(V.USERNAME) U;

PAGE_NAME                 COLUMN_VALUE
------------------------- -------------------------
INDEX.HTML                TestUser1
INDEX.HTML                TestUser2
```

Proceeding further requires a procedural language, but in summary, this is what we will need to do to add a username to this list:

- Query the VISITORS for the page we are interested in, retrieving START_INDEX and END_INDEX into int types and the USERNAME VARRAY into an array.
- Find the index of the next available entry by incrementing END_INDEX—in this case, to 2—and insert the new username at that position in the array.

- Update START_INDEX if necessary.
- Update the USERNAME column for this page with the entire updated array.

In addition to the brief steps outlined above, our code will, of course, need to deal with two special cases, wrapping the indexes to 0 when they get to the end of the array and advancing the start index when the end index catches up to it.

INHERITANCE AND OBJECT EVOLUTION IN ORACLE 9i

One of the fundamental features of most object-oriented languages is inheritance. It is of prime importance in Java, for example, in that everything (except primitives) ultimately is a subclass of, or inherits from, objects. Much of the criticism of the object-relational features in Oracle 8i has centered on the lack of support for inheritance. Inheritance, however, is only one way that a class can be reused. Composition, which is supported by Oracle 8i, is at least as important. Nonetheless, inheritance is often considered a hallmark of object-orientation, and it is the most significant new feature in Oracle 9i.

Object evolution, the ability to alter existing objects, is another important feature in Oracle 9i. As we will see, much of the need for object evolution—which, from a user point of view, is nothing more than using the ALTER TYPE statement—is due to the additional maintenance that object types require when we use inheritance.

Inheritance

One of the main goals of object-oriented programming is to increase the reuse of code. One way to do this with objects is by identifying the characteristics that they have in common—attributes and methods—and encapsulating those characteristics into a class, a *superclass*, that other classes, *subclasses*, can share. In Oracle 9i, these are called *supertypes* and *subtypes*.

The textbook example of a superclass and its subclasses is a hierarchy beginning with Person as the superclass and Employee and Student as its subclasses. To model this in Oracle, we can create a Person object type. The syntax is the same as we saw before, except that we need to add one new option: NOT FINAL. By default, an object type is FINAL, meaning that it cannot be subclassed:

```
SQL> CREATE TYPE PERSON_TYPE AS OBJECT (
  2    NAME     VARCHAR2(32),
  3    DOB      DATE,
  4    SEX      CHAR(1),
```

```
    MEMBER FUNCTION GETAGE RETURN NUMBER
  ) NOT FINAL
  /

Type created.
```

To create an employee subtype, we use a CREATE TYPE statement with UNDER plus the name of the supertype:

```
SQL> CREATE TYPE EMPLOYEE_TYPE UNDER PERSON_TYPE (
    COMPANY     VARCHAR2(25),
    DEPARTMENT  VARCHAR2(25),
    SALARY      NUMBER,
    JOB_TITLE   VARCHAR2(25),
    HIRE_DATE   DATE,
    MEMBER FUNCTION GETSENIORITY RETURN NUMBER
  )
  /

Type created.
```

We can use the SQL*Plus DESC command to examine the structure of the employee type and see that EMPLOYEE has not only the attributes and methods we declared in the CREATE TYPE EMPLOYEE statement but those that it inherits from PERSON as well (Figure 6–2):

```
SQL> DESC EMPLOYEE_TYPE
 EMPLOYEE_TYPE extends SCOTT.PERSON_TYPE
 Name                                   Null?    Type
 -------------------------------------- -------- -------- ----

 NAME                                            VARCHAR2(32)
 DOB                                             DATE
 SEX                                             CHAR(1)
 COMPANY                                         VARCHAR2(25)
 DEPARTMENT                                      VARCHAR2(25)
 SALARY                                          NUMBER
 JOB_TITLE                                       VARCHAR2(25)
 HIRE_DATE                                       DATE

METHOD
------
 MEMBER FUNCTION GETAGE RETURNS NUMBER

METHOD
------
 MEMBER FUNCTION GETSENIORITY RETURNS NUMBER
```

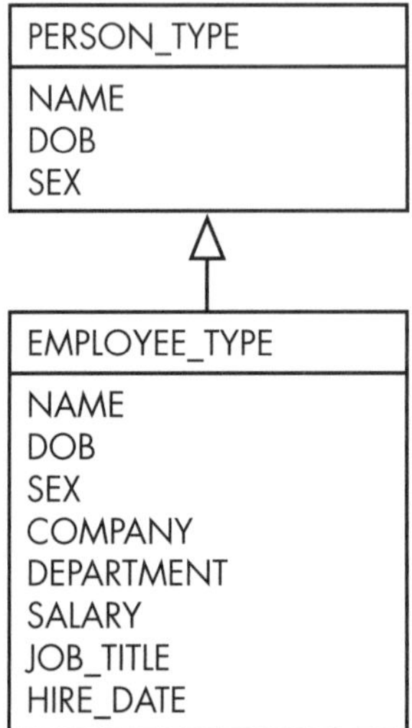

FIGURE 6–2 Object inheritance.

NOT INSTANTIABLE: Abstract Types and Methods

Oracle 9i supports many of the features that we are familiar with from Java. For example, we can create an abstract type: a type that cannot be instantiated. To create an abstract type, we add the option NOT INSTANTIABLE to our type specification. To use this type, we must first create a subtype that inherits from it.

If a type is NOT INSTANTIABLE, any or all of its methods can also be declared NOT INSTANTIABLE. This is a way to force subtypes to implement methods: If a subtype does not implement a superclass's NOT INSTANTIABLE method, the subtype itself must be declared NOT INSTANTIABLE.

Let's consider building a graphics library. We could start by defining a supertype SHAPE. It will contain the characteristics and behaviors we wish all our shapes to have in common, such as color and area. It will be abstract, or not instantiable, because any real shape must also include attributes that determine its geometry, based on lines, curves, points or some combination. We can declare the supertype like this:

```
SQL> CREATE TYPE SHAPE_TYPE AS OBJECT (
       COLOR          VARCHAR2(12),
       OUTLINE_STYLE VARCHAR2(12),
      NOT INSTANTIABLE MEMBER FUNCTION GETAREA RETURN NUMBER
     ) NOT INSTANTIABLE NOT FINAL
     /

Type created.
```

We want to be able to get a shape's area, but because there is no general way to calculate that, we don't implement it here. Instead, to make it a requirement that subtypes provide a way to calculate their area, we declare a noninstantiable GETAREA function.

Let's create a subtype ELLIPSE_TYPE. Because we plan on instantiating this type, we need to include the GETAREA() member function, which we'll implement in the type body. Because a GETAREA function is already declared in the supertype (even though it is NOT INSTANTIABLE), we must use the OVERRIDING option here.

```
SQL> CREATE TYPE ELLIPSE_TYPE UNDER SHAPE_TYPE (
       MINOR_AXIS  NUMBER,
       MAJOR_AXIS  NUMBER,
       CENTER      POINT_TYPE,
       OVERRIDING MEMBER FUNCTION GETAREA RETURN NUMBER
     )
     /
```

We must also include the OVERRIDING keyword when we create the type body.

```
SQL> CREATE TYPE BODY ELLIPSE_TYPE AS

       OVERRIDING MEMBER FUNCTION GETAREA
           RETURN NUMBER AS
           BEGIN
               RETURN MINOR_AXIS*MAJOR_AXIS*3.1415927;
           END;

     END;
     /
```

Now we can create a table that includes ELLIPSE_TYPE and insert some data. Notice that the ELLIPSE_TYPE constructor takes as its arguments the attributes for both the supertype and the subtype, in that order; there is no separate constructor for the supertype.

```
SQL> CREATE TABLE ELLIPSES (
       LABEL    VARCHAR2(12),
       ELLIPSE  ELLIPSE_TYPE
     );

Table created.
```

```
SQL> INSERT INTO ELLIPSES
       VALUES ('One',
         ELLIPSE_TYPE('Red','Bold',10,20,
           POINT_TYPE(5,5)));

1 row created.
```

We can query this the same as any other table with an object type. A simple query returns nested objects.

```
SQL> SELECT * FROM ELLIPSES;

LABEL
------------
ELLIPSE(COLOR, OUTLINE_STYLE, MINOR_AXIS, MAJOR_AXIS, CENTER(X, Y))
---------------------------------------------------------------------

One
ELLIPSE_TYPE('Red', 'Bold', 10, 20, POINT_TYPE(5, 5))
```

As before, if we want to un-nest the objects, we need to use an alias for the table and qualify each column with dot notation.

```
SQL> SELECT LABEL,
       E.ELLIPSE.COLOR AS COLOR,
       E.ELLIPSE.MAJOR_AXIS AS A,
       E.ELLIPSE.MINOR_AXIS AS B,
       E.ELLIPSE.CENTER.X AS X,
       E.ELLIPSE.CENTER.Y AS Y
     FROM ELLIPSES E;

LABEL    COLOR                A          B    X           Y
-------- -------- ------------- ---------- ---- -----------
One      Red                 20         10    5           5
```

Overriding isn't limited to NOT INSTANTIATED methods; a subtype can override any supertype method unless the method is declared FINAL in the supertype.

Oracle also supports overloaded functions—methods that have the same name but take different arguments. For example, the SHAPE object type may have two methods called STRETCH() for increasing the size of a shape, one that takes a single parameter that increases the overall shape of an object, and one that takes two parameters that will increase the X and Y dimensions independently. Overloaded methods can be defined in a single type (such as these two STRETCH() methods in the SHAPE type) or in a subtype. If we were to create a subtype of SHAPE for three-dimensional shape (say SHAPE3D), we might want to add yet another STRETCH() method that allows us to stretch a shape in the Z-dimension.

Object Evolution

The addition of support for inheritance in Oracle 9i introduced a lot of new options, so adding support for object evolution makes managing object types somewhat easier. For example, the default for a type is FINAL, which means that we cannot subclass it. If it turns out in the course of development that we should have allowed something to be subclassed that we hadn't considered before, it is fairly easy to change it. If we wanted to allow ELLIPSE_TYPE to be subclassed, we can do that with the statement

```
SQL> ALTER TYPE ELLIPSE_TYPE NOT FINAL CASCADE;

Type altered.
```

In addition to NOT FINAL, we need to include CASCADE in this case because the ELLIPSE_TYPE has a dependent object: the ELLIPSES table.

When we use Oracle's object-relational features, we introduce a lot of dependencies between types and tables. To deal with that, the ALTER TYPE statement has a number of options, such as CASCADE, that specify what should be done about dependents and their data. Failing to get this right can leave objects in an invalid state, and they won't work until they are fixed. Object evolution should be approached carefully. The best thing to do is to get it right the first time. In a development environment, we usually have the luxury of being able to drop everything—types, tables, and data—and start over; this is the next best thing.

CHAPTER 7

SQLJ

By now you've learned a number of SQL commands and worked with a database a bit, creating tables, entering data, and performing queries. All of this has been interactive at an SQL prompt in SQL*Plus—great for learning but not very useful for a programmer. You've also learned how to program using PL/SQL—which is great for discrete procedures and functions but not for building complete applications that a user can interact with. That is a task for a higher-level host language such as Java. In this and the remaining chapters, we'll learn how to write Java programs that interact with the database procedurally.

We start with SQLJ because it is the most direct approach. SQLJ allows you to imbed SQL statements directly in your Java code—this is the easiest way to access a database from Java, especially for a programmer new to working with databases.

A translator (or precompiler) does the hard work for you by interpreting the SQLJ statements and converting them into standard Java and JDBC. The amount of code necessary to process result sets is much less with SQLJ than it is if we use JDBC directly.

Another advantage to SQLJ is that SQL statements are interpreted at compile time, so the precompiler can not only check their syntax but optionally, if the database is accessible, can also check to be sure they are consistent with the database schema.

The principal drawback to SQLJ is that it allows only static SQL statements. Because most of the SQL statements in an application are usually static, this is not too serious a shortcoming. It is possible to mix SQLJ and JDBC. Use SQLJ wherever possible and resort to JDBC whenever necessary. This can be somewhat messy, however, and it's best to stick to one or the other.

Another consideration that should be made is whether it is wise to introduce an additional tool (and dependency) in the development process. Depending on the size of the project and the amount of database programming required, the benefit of using SQLJ over JDBC may be outweighed by the added complexity of the environment, especially if JDBC is being used directly, as well.

In summary, SQLJ is the best and fastest way of adding simple database support to a program, especially if you do not have much experience with JDBC. If your needs are more demanding or you think you will need to use JDBC eventually, anyway, you probably should bite the bullet and go directly to JDBC from the start.

SQLJ Statements and the SQLJ Translator

To use SQLJ, we embed SQLJ statements directly in our Java code. SQLJ statements are not valid Java source code, however, so we need to distinguish between SQLJ files and Java files. We do this by naming our SQLJ files with a .sqlj suffix. Then, instead of compiling them with the javac compiler, we need to process them with the SQLJ translator.

Normally, the SQLJ compiler does two things for you: It interprets the SQLJ file and creates a valid Java source file—a .java file—from it, then compiles the Java source file into an executable class file. The process is illustrated in Figure 7–1.

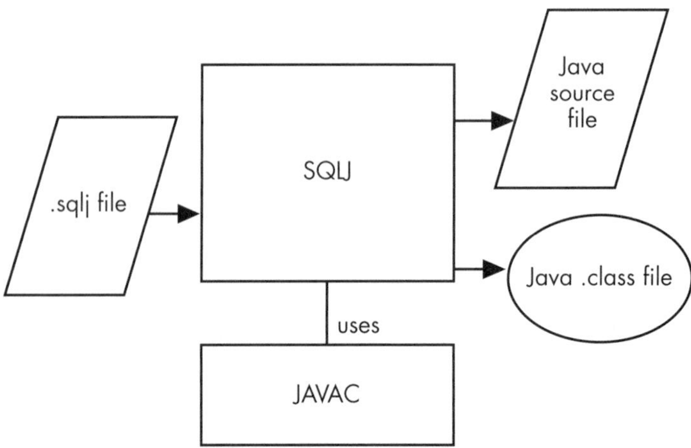

FIGURE 7–1 SQLJ compilation.

Connecting with SQLJ

Two things are required for a program to connect to a database using SQLJ. First, you must make sure that your CLASSPATH includes the SQLJ classes. If, for example, Oracle is installed in C:\oracle\orac90, the CLASSPATH must include

```
.;C:\oracle\ora90\jdbc\lib\classes12.jar;c:\oracle\ora90\sqlj\li
b\runtime12.zip;c:\oracle\ora90\sqlj\lib\translator.zip
```

Second, you must determine the database uniform resource locator (URL), which you will need to use in the Oracle.connect() method—the method you need to call in your Java program to connect to the database. The URL specifies:

- Which JDBC driver to use—OCI or thin
- The database name (or SID) and, optionally, the server name
- Username and password

To use the OCI driver with the database OSIRIS, username SCOTT, and the password TIGER, the URL is

```
jdbc:oracle:oci:scott/tiger@osiris
```

The OCI driver is the native Oracle driver, and it relies on the Oracle client software being installed on the system. If you have successfully tested your ability to connect to the database using SQL*Plus, this should work as well. The other available JDBC driver, the pure Java thin driver, has the advantage of not requiring the installation of the Oracle client software, so code that uses that driver is more portable. For now, we will stick to the OCI driver, because it is easier to use and troubleshoot.

The last part of the URL is the logon string and should work essentially as it does when you include it as part of the command line for SQL*Plus. The only difference is that if you wish to use the default database, you must still include the @ sign in the URL. If your program fails to connect, try the following at a command prompt:

```
C:\sqlplus scott/tiger@osiris
```

If this is successful, make sure that your CLASSPATH is correct for the version of Java you are using and that everything is typed correctly.

More details on using the JDBC drivers are available in Chapters 7 and 8.

Let's start with this short example that logs us into the Oracle sample account, SCOTT, with the password TIGER:

```
// SimpleExample.sqlj

import java.sql.*;
import sqlj.runtime.ref.DefaultContext;
import oracle.sqlj.runtime.Oracle;
```

```
public class SimpleExample
{
   public static void main (String [] args)
   {
     try
     {
       Oracle.connect("jdbc:oracle:oci:scott/tiger@osiris");
       String name;
       #sql {SELECT ENAME INTO :name FROM EMP WHERE EMPNO=7900};
       System.out.println("Found: " + name);
     }
     catch (SQLException e)
     {
       System.out.println("Caught: " + e);
     }

   }
}
```

First, notice the import statements at the top: We import the SQL package and a couple of classes specific to SQLJ.

Because our code deals with SQL, we need to catch `SQLExceptions`. In this simple example, we don't do anything but print out the result, should a problem occur. In a real program, we need to be more discerning than this. We can anticipate certain exceptions and provide an appropriate response.

Next, notice the `Oracle.connect()` method. This contains a string, the database URL, that must be modified to include the name of your database. This actually will load one of two JDBC drivers and make it available as the default connection context for the SQLJ statements in the program.

Once we've imported those SQL and SQLJ classes and gotten connected, we can start embedding SQL statements in our code.

This example has just one SQLJ statement that queries the Oracle sample table, EMP:

```
#sql {SELECT ENAME INTO :name FROM EMP WHERE EMPNO=7900};
```

SQL statements in SQLJ are always preceded with `#sql`. This can be followed by a number of options, including Java class modifiers such as public and static, and an assignment. Because this is a simple example, we haven't included any of these. Next is an opening brace: This is where we can actually start using SQL—but not just standard SQL. SQLJ extends SQL to make it easier to integrate with Java.

There are two notable things about the statement in this example. The query includes the syntax, SELECT...INTO. This is an SQLJ (and PL/SQL) extension of the standard SQL SELECT that makes it easier to obtain single-row results. We'll learn more about single row queries later in this chapter. For now, we'll just note the general features of this statement. Like a standard SQL select statement, SELECT is followed by a select list, in this case, a single column. SQLJ also introduces the INTO syntax, which allows us to specify a Java host variable where the value returned by the SQLJ statement is to be stored.

Finally, we close the SQLJ statement with a brace and semicolon. Note that we do not terminate the SQL statement itself with a semicolon. The database connectivity layer, JDBC, which is working behind the scenes for us, is responsible for properly terminating SQL queries.

After this SQLJ statement is executed, we will find the query's result in the Java variable `name` and, if everything was successful, we print it out.

Having typed this program into a file called SimpleExample.sqlj, we are prepared to compile it. We use the sqlj command at a command prompt to do this. The easiest way is simply:

```
C:\sqlj SimpleExample.sqlj
```

But we can also provide a connection string so that the SQLJ translator can connect to the database to do additional checking for us.

```
C:\sqlj -user=scott/tiger SimpleExample.sqlj
```

The `-user=scott/tiger` option causes the SQLJ translator to connect to the database at compile time and validate the SQL statements against the database.

If our path and CLASSPATH are set up correctly and there are no other errors in the code, SQLJ will do its job silently—no news is good news. If you want feedback, you can add the `-status` flag to the command line.

The SQLJ translator creates a number of different files. First, it converts the embedded SQLJ statements into calls to the SQLJ runtime, which is a thin wrapper for the JDBC driver, and saves this as a Java source file, SimpleExample.java. By default, it also compiles it into SimpleExample.class.

This isn't all, however; it also creates Java objects containing detailed information about each SQL statement in our program. By default, these Java objects are serialized—converted to a form that can be saved and retrieved as a file—but there is an SQLJ translator option that allows them to be saved as .class files, instead.We can run the SimpleExample.class file like any other Java program.

```
C:\java SimpleExample
```

If all goes well, it will print out:

```
Found: JAMES
```

Simple Embedded SQL Statements

The easiest SQLJ statements to code are DDL statements, such as CREATE TABLE, ALTER TABLE, and DROP TABLE. This is the general format:

```
#sql { SQL statement };
```

The following code sample fragment creates a table:

```
#sql { CREATE TABLE  EXAMPLE(
     COL1NUMBER,
     COL2VARCHAR2(10))};
```

DML statements such as INSERT, UPDATE, and DELETE are easy, too. Typically, they are used to insert, change, or delete data, based on values determined at runtime by the Java code. To facilitate this, SQLJ allows Java variables and expressions within the SQL statement. Note that, although SQL statements, including column names are case-insensitive, Java host variables and expressions are sensitive. Java variables embedded in SQL are called *host variables* or *bind variables* and are distinguished by being preceded by a colon.

```
:name
```

There are three types of host variables which have the modes IN, OUT, and INOUT. IN variables provide input values from the SQL point of view and are used, for example, to add data to the database in INSERT statements and to set criteria in WHERE clauses. OUT variables must be l-values—that is, they must be assignable, or valid to use on the left side of an equal sign; OUT variables, we shall see, are used principally for returning results from queries. INOUT variables are used when calling procedures that have parameters that are used for both input and output. We can specify the mode by adding it after the colon and separating it from the variable name by whitespace.

```
:IN name
```

In general, however, the host variables default to the appropriate mode, IN or OUT, based on the SQL statement. (We won't be using procedures in this chapter, so we don't need to be concerned about INOUT for now.)

DDL statements expect IN variables. In addition to variables, we can also use other types of Java expressions in place of IN variables. If we are using a Java expression that consists of more than just a variable name, however, the expression needs to be enclosed within parentheses; otherwise, the SQLJ translator will try to interpret the first token alone as a variable. Assuming that the variables have been previously declared and initialized, here are some examples of valid host variables and expressions:

```
:name
:(names[i])
:(firstname + " " + lastname)
:IN (mystring.substring(2,3))
:IN (i + 100)
```

Suppose we want to populate the table created above, EXAMPLE, with three rows like these:

COL1	*COL2*
1	A
2	B
3	C

The following code sample will do this:

```
int i;
for(i=1; i<=3; i++)
{
    #sql {INSERT INTO EXAMPLE VALUES
    (:i, :(Character.toString((char)('A' + i - 1))))};
}
```

Notice that we use a static method, `Character.toString()`, as the host expression. It converts a character value, calculated from the int variable `i`, into a `String`, so that we can generate the sequence of letters.

There is one final statement that we must include after inserting this data: COMMIT. Unless we commit the transaction, the changes we made to the database will be discarded when the program ends because, by default; SQLJ does not automatically commit our changes. This following statement should be added after the `for` loop above:

```
    #sql {COMMIT};
```

It's also possible to commit automatically so that changes to the database are immediately made permanent. This is a property of our connection, and the easiest way to change it is by using an alternate form of the `Oracle.connect()` method that takes an additional parameter, a flag that controls auto-commit.

```
Oracle.connect("jdbc:oracle:oci:scott/tiger@osiris", true);
```

By default, this flag is set to false by the SQLJ compiler. (As we will see, this is the opposite of the behavior for JDBC, where auto-commit is on by default.) There are advantages to both, but the difference is basically that auto-commit is slightly more convenient to use, whereas manual-commit allows better control over transactions because it allows us to back out of a transaction completely when a portion of it fails.

Single-Row Queries

Our example above used the special single-row SELECT…INTO statement which, as you will see, is far easier to use than any other way of querying a database. The drawback is that you must somehow ensure that the query will return only a single row; otherwise, an SQLException will result at runtime. The surest way to ensure this is to restrict using SELECT…INTO statements to queries that have a WHERE clause that uses the table's primary key.

The general format of a single-row query in SQLJ is

```
SELECT expression1[, expression2[, …]]
  INTO :hostexpression1[,:hostexpression2[,…]]
  FROM table
  [optional SQL clause]
```

- *expression1, expression2*, etc. are columns or any other expressions valid in a SELECT statement column list, including functions and calculations—anything that is valid in a standard SQL SELECT list.
- *hostexpression1, hostexpression2*, etc. are Java host variables, fields, or array elements that will accept assignment. There must be one host expression for every expression in the select list. The type of each host expression must also be appropriate for the corresponding select list item.
- The optional SQL clause can be a WHERE clause, a subquery, or anything that is valid in a standard SQL SELECT statement.

In our simple example, we obtained the name of an employee, given by an employee number. Let's take a look at an example that uses several columns of several types. Taking a look at the EMP table, we see

```
SQL> desc emp;
 Name                                      Null?    Type
 ----------------------------------------- -------- -------

 EMPNO                                     NOT NULL NUMBER(4)
 ENAME                                              VARCHAR2(10)
 JOB                                                VARCHAR2(9)
 MGR                                                NUMBER(4)
 HIREDATE                                           DATE
 SAL                                                NUMBER(7,2)
 COMM                                               NUMBER(7,2)
 DEPTNO                                             NUMBER(2)
```

We'll pick just a few columns for our SELECT statement: ENAME, JOB, SAL, and HIREDATE. It's good practice to first try our SQL statement in SQL*Plus.

```
SQL> SELECT ENAME, JOB, SAL, HIREDATE
  2  FROM EMP
  3  WHERE EMPNO=7900;

ENAME      JOB              SAL HIREDATE
---------- --------- ---------- ---------
JAMES      CLERK            950 03-DEC-81
```

In our Java code, we'll create the host variables:

```
String name, job;
int salary;
Date hiredate;
```

Then we'll embed our SQL statement, adding the INTO clause to transfer the values from the SELECT into our Java host variables.

```
    #sql {SELECT ENAME, JOB, SAL, HIREDATE
      INTO :name, : job, :salary, :hiredate
      FROM EMP
      WHERE EMPNO=7900};
```

Finally, we print out the values.

```
System.out.println("Name: " + name + ", Job: " + job,
   ", Salary: " + salary + ", Hire date: " + hiredate);
```

This is the output, if all's gone well:

```
Name: JAMES, Job: CLERK, Salary: 950, Hire date: 1981-12-03
```

In one final example, we'll use a join and combine values from two different tables. We'll include the employee's name and city, and calculate length of employment based on hire date. The name and date of hire are in the EMP table. We can calculate the length of employment by subtracting the date of hire from the current date. In Oracle, the current date is available as the pseudo-column SYSDATE.

We can find out the employee's location based on the department table. This requires a join between the EMP and the DEPT table; joining the two on the DEPTNO column to obtain the LOC.

We can first run the following SQL statement in SQL*Plus to verify that this works and that it gives us what we want.

```
SQL> SELECT ENAME, LOC, TRUNC((SYSDATE-HIREDATE)/365.25,0)
  2  FROM EMP, DEPT
  3  WHERE EMP.DEPTNO=DEPT.DEPTNO AND EMP.EMPNO=7900;

ENAME      LOC           TRUNC((SYSDATE-HIREDATE)/365.25,0)
---------- ------------- ----------------------------------
JAMES      CHICAGO                                       20
```

(Notice that we need to identify the table for each column in the WHERE statement, but in the select list, this isn't necessary because the columns we are selecting are unambiguous.)

To use this SQL statement in an SQLJ single-row query, we need to add the INTO clause to transfer the results to the Java host variables.

```
String name, city;
int years;
#sql { SELECT ENAME, LOC,TRUNC((SYSDATE-HIREDATE)/365.25,0)
       INTO :name, :city, :years
       FROM EMP, DEPT
       WHERE EMP.DEPTNO=DEPT.DEPTNO AND EMP.EMPNO=7900 };
System.out.println("Name: " + name +", City: " + city +
                   ", Years: " + years);
```

Multiple-Row Queries

Although the single-row query is convenient, the more frequent case is that a query returns (or can return) multiple rows. There is no way around the fact that this is significantly more complicated to code. The only consolation is that using SQLJ to process multiple-row result sets is easier and less error-prone than using JDBC.

There are two ways to process multiple-row queries: named iterators and positional iterators. In both cases, we declare an iterator class that we will use to iterate through the result set, row by row. The iterator class has a parameter list that defines the host variables it accepts. The host variables parameter list must match the select list of the SELECT statement by either name or type. As you might guess, in a named iterator, the host variable parameters are associated by name with the select list items. In a positional iterator, they are associated by the position of the select list items.

An important feature of both types of iterators is that they are strongly typed—the number and types of the host variables are specified at compile time in the class's parameter list.

In general, the steps required for creating and using an iterator, named or positional, are the same:

- Declare the iterator class.
- Declare the iterator instance variable.
- Instantiate and populate the iterator with an SQL statement.
- Iterate to access each row.
- Close the iterator.

The difference is in the details, as we shall see.

Named Iterators

In a named iterator, the iterator's parameters are associated with the items in the select list by name—this requirement for explicit identification between a named iterator and its corresponding SELECT statement makes for a stronger and less error-prone association than that of a positional iterator.

Named iterators provide an additional convenience. Because the parameters have names, the SQLJ translator is able to provide us with accessor methods, based on those names.

Declaring a Named Iterator. The declaration for a named iterator looks more like a method declaration than a class declaration, mostly because it has a list of parameters with a type and a name for each—but it is nonetheless a class declaration. This is the basic format:

```
#sql <modifiers> iterator classname(
     hosttype1 hostname1[, hosttype2 hostname2,…]);
```

- *modifiers* are any Java class modifiers, such as `public`, `private`, `protected`, and `static`.
- *classname* is the class that will be created.

- *hosttypen* is the Java type of the host variable for column *n*.
- *hostnamen* is the name of the Java host variable and must match the name of an item in the select list—the column name or a column alias. The match between the Java variable and the column name or alias is not case-sensitive, so the column in the SELECT statement may be specified as ENAME but the Java variable may be named `ename`.

This class declaration can appear anywhere that a standard Java class declaration can appear, because the SQLJ translator will, in fact, turn it into a full-fledged class in place, complete with member variables and methods.

Declaring the iterator outside the scope of any class is probably the easiest thing to do. The main limitation is that if it is declared public, it will need to be in a file of its own—but it's not a good idea to make iterators public, anyway. If functionality of this type needs to be exposed to other classes, it should be done indirectly through a wrapper or an accessor class. This is an example of a declaration outside the class:

```
// EmployeeExample.sql

import java.sql.*;
import sqlj.runtime.ref.DefaultContext;
import oracle.sqlj.runtime.Oracle;

#sql iterator EmployeeIter(String ename, Long sal, String job);

public class EmployeeExample
{
   // etc.
```

There are advantages to declaring the iterator inside a class—as an inner class—but this can cause problems if we try to instantiate the iterator in a static method such as factory method.

Iterators as Inner Classes

For the sake of simplicity, the iterator class examples we have seen have been declared as top-level classes, outside the scope of the class that uses them. From an object-oriented design point of view, however, it's best to declare the iterator inside the scope of the class where it will be used—as an inner class. Inner classes are nice because they encapsulate behavior within the class that requires them—it makes for neater code.

The only drawback to declaring an iterator as an inner class is that you can't instantiate the iterator inside a static method. This is legal Java but the code to do it is somewhat convoluted, and the SQLJ translator doesn't know how to produce it.

For example, the following generates an error when the Java compiler tries to compile the code produced by the SQLJ translator:

```
public class EmpExample
{
  #sql iterator EmpIter(String emp, String job, long sal);

  public static main(String []args)
        {

  try
  {
    Oracle.connect("jdbc:oracle:oci:scott/tiger@osiris");
   EmpIter empiter;

   // sqlj botches this:
   #sql empiter = {SELECT ENAME, JOB, SAL FROM EMP};}
   // ...
```

The problem is that the SQLJ translator generates code like this in EmpExample.java to instantiate `EmpIter`:

```
EmpIter empiter = new EmpIter(); // doesn't work!
```

The necessary code to instantiate the inner class inside a static method is this:

```
EmpExample.EmpIter empiter = new EmpExample().new EmpIter();
```

One way around this is to declare the iterator class static.

```
// EmpExample.sql

public class EmpExample
{
    #sql static iterator EmpIter(
          String emp, String job, long sal);

   public static main(String []args)
   {

   try
   {
     Oracle.connect("jdbc:oracle:oci:scott/tiger@osiris");

   // Now this works:
   #sql empiter = {SELECT ENAME, JOB, SAL FROM EMP};
   // ...
```

This works because a static inner class, although semantically a member of the enclosing class, is really a top-level class from the compiler's point of view—it doesn't need an instance of its enclosing class to be instantiated itself.

Another solution is to instantiate the outer class in the static method, then have the static method call a nonstatic method in the outer class instance. This nonstatic method is then able to instantiate the iterator.

```
public class EmpExample
{
    #sql iterator EmpIter(String emp, String job, long sal);

    public static void main(String []args)
    {
         EmpExample example = new EmpExample();
         Example.execSQL;
    }

    void execSQL()
    {
     try
     {
     Oracle.connect("jdbc:oracle:oci:scott/tiger@osiris");
    #sql empiter = {SELECT ENAME, JOB, SAL FROM EMP};
```

Declaring the Named Iterator Instance Variable. Before we can instantiate and populate an iterator, we first need to declare an instance variable for the iterator class, as follows:

```
EmployeeIter empiter;
```

Instantiating and Populating a Named Iterator. Now that we have an instance variable for our iterator class, we can use SQLJ to instantiate it and populate the iterator for us. We do it with this statement:

```
#sql empiter = {SELECT ENAME, JOB, SAL FROM EMP};
```

SQLJ translates this into code that instantiates the iterator class, executes the SQL statement using JDBC, and populates the iterator with the result set. Each item in the SQL statement's select list is matched by name to a host variable, as declared in the iterator class's parameter list. It doesn't matter if the select list items appear in the same order as the host variables parameter list. There must be at least as many items in the select list as there are host variables. Extra items in the select list are ignored.

Sometimes, columns have cryptic names, and it may be out of our power to change them. We can assign an alias in the SELECT statement using the AS keyword; in this example we change SAL to SALARY:

```
#sql empiter = {SELECT ENAME, JOB, SAL AS SALARY FROM EMP};
```

Column aliases are especially useful when we perform calculations or include function calls in our select list. For example, in the single-query example, we calculated the number of years from an employee's hire date. To include this in a query using a named iterator, we need to use an alias, as follows:

```
SELECT ENAME, TRUNC((SYSDATE-HIREDATE)/365.25,0) AS YEARS
FROM EMP
```

Accessing the Rows in a Named Iterator. In order for us to move to the first row and to move from row to row after that, the iterator class that SQLJ generates for us provides a `next()` method. The `next()` method returns true if there is a next row, false if there are no more rows. The logic to iterate through a result set is

```
while(empiter.next())
{
  // access and process this row…
}
```

To access the columns in each row, the iterator class provides us with a set of accessor methods, one accessor method for each host variable we listed in the named iterator's declaration. The methods each have the same name and type as the variables. For this declaration:

```
#sql iterator EmployeeIter(String ename, long sal, String job);
```

SQLJ will produce the following accessor methods:

- `String ename()`
- `long sal()`
- `String job()`

Although it is common in Java for accessor methods to be named by capitalizing the first letter of the variable and adding the prefix *get,* SQLJ is an exception: The accessor methods have exactly the same name as the variables they access.

Closing the Iterator. The last step after we have finished using the iterator is to free the resources that it is using by calling its `close()` method. Failing to do this can cause a resource leak, which can eventually cause the program—or more mysteriously, other people's programs on other systems—to fail when the database resources necessary to perform a query or other operations are exhausted.

Named Iterators Sample Programs. This small sample program goes through the steps necessary for using a named iterator to perform a multiple-row query: declaring the named iterator, declaring an instance variable for the iterator, instantiating and populating the iterator variable with an SQL call, accessing the rows, and closing the iterator when we're finished.

```
// EmpQuery.sql

import java.sql.*;
import sqlj.runtime.ref.DefaultContext;
import oracle.sqlj.runtime.Oracle;

 #sql iterator EmployeeIter(String ename, Long sal, String job);

public class EmpQuery
{
   public static void main(String []args)
   {
    try
    {
      Oracle.connect("jdbc:oracle:oci:scott/tiger@osiris");
      EmployeeIter empiter;
     #sql empiter = {SELECT JOB, SAL, ENAME FROM EMP ORDER BY SAL DESC};
      while(empiter.next())
      {
        System.out.println("Name: " + empiter.ename() + ", Job:
                    " + empiter.job() + ", Salary: " + empiter.sal());
      }
      empiter.close();
    }
    catch (SQLException e)
    {
          System.out.println("Caught: " + e);
      }
     }
}
```

Here is another example that uses columns aliases and performs a join on two tables. It is similar to the second example we saw for single queries, except that we don't restrict the query to a single employee.

```
// EmpAliasQuery.sql

import java.sql.*;
import sqlj.runtime.ref.DefaultContext;
import oracle.sqlj.runtime.Oracle;

#sql iterator EmployeeIter(String name, String city, int years);

public class EmpAliasQuery
{
```

```
    public static void main(String []args)
    {
     try
     {
       Oracle.connect("jdbc:oracle:oci:scott/tiger@osiris");
       EmployeeIter empiter;

         #sql empiter = {SELECT ENAME AS NAME, LOC AS CITY,
                 TRUNC((SYSDATE-HIREDATE)/365.25,0)AS YEARS
                 FROM EMP, DEPT WHERE EMP.DEPTNO=DEPT.DEPTNO};
         while(empiter.next())
         {
           System.out.println("Name: "+empiter.name()
                             + ", City: "+empiter.city()
                             + ", Years: " + empiter.years());
         }
         empiter.close();
          }
       catch (SQLException e)
       {
         System.out.println("Caught: " + e);
       }
    }
}
```

Positional Iterators

Positional iterators are an alternative to named iterators. Because they are similar to the way embedded SQL queries are used in other languages (in particular, Oracle's Pro*C precompiler for C/C++), many experienced developers find them more familiar and comfortable to use.

For those unfamiliar with Pro*C, however, they are somewhat more complicated and less flexible to code than are named iterators. Because they associate the iterator's parameters with items in the select list anonymously, the only check performed at runtime is to ensure that the types of each are compatible; extra care needs to be taken to prevent errors.

Declaring Positional Iterators. In a positional iterator, the iterator's parameters are associated with items in the SQL select list by position, not name. Because the SQLJ positional iterator declaration includes an anonymous list of parameter types, it doesn't look quite like either a method or class declaration. This is the basic format:

```
#sql <modifiers> iterator classname(
      hosttype1 [, hosttype2 ,…]);
```

- *modifiers* are any Java class modifiers, such as public, private, protected, and static.
- *classname* is the class that will be created.
- *hosttypen* is the Java type of the host variable for column *n*.

This declaration can appear anywhere that a standard Java class declaration can appear.

The order of the host types in the parameter list must correspond to the SQL SELECT statement. Suppose we want to process the results returned by the query:

```
SELECT ENAME, JOB, SAL FROM EMP;
```

The corresponding Java type for ENAME and JOB is `String`. We have several suitable variable types for SAL, but we'll go with `long`, just to keep it simple and safe. The positional iterator declaration then would be

```
#sql iterator EmployeeIter(String, String, long);
```

The easiest way to use this is as a top-level class, by declaring it in the same file but outside the scope of the class that uses it. We'll see an example shortly.

Declaring the Positional Iterator Instance Variable and Host Variables. Exactly as with a named iterator, we need to declare an instance variable for the iterator before we can instantiate and populate it. However, in addition to the iterator instance variable, we also need to declare and initialize host variables for each of the iterator's parameters. These names don't need to match the select list item names, of course, but it's helpful if the names are at least similar, so that the relationship is clear. We also need to initialize them, to either 0 in the case of primitives or `null` in the case of classes such as `String` or `Date`.

```
// Declare Iterator instance variable
EmployeeIter empiter;

// Declare and initialize iterator host variables
String empName = null;
String empJob = null;
long empSalary = 0L;
```

Instantiating and Populating a Named Iterator. The positional iterator is instantiated and populated by an SQLJ statement, the same as a named iterator.

```
#sql empiter = {SELECT ENAME, JOB, SAL FROM EMP};
```

This instantiates the instance variable, executes the SQL statement, and populates the iterator with the result set.

Accessing the Rows in a Positional Iterator. Positional iterators provide us with a way to move from row to row and to access the columns, like named iterators, but the technique is quite different.

To access the rows in a positional iterator, we need to use a special SQLJ statement, FETCH...INTO, which transfers the results of each row from the iterator to our host variables. It looks like (but isn't) a standard SQL statement.

```
#sql {FETCH :iterator INTO :hostvariable1, : hostvariable2, … };
```

When we first call this statement it advances to the first row of the iterator's result set. Thereafter, it moves to the next row. If this move is successful, it then populates the host variables. We can then test to see whether the call to FETCH...INTO was successful by calling the method `endFetch()`. If `endFetch()` returns true, it means that the FETCH...INTO was unsuccessful and that we have exhausted our result set. If `endFetch()` returns false, it means that FETCH...INTO was successful and a new row has been read into our host variables.

This might suggest, incorrectly, that we might be able to use a `while` loop as follows:

```
// This loop doesn't work
while(!empiter.endFetch())
{
   #sql {FETCH :empiter INTO :empName, :empJob, :empSalary);
   // process empName, empJob, emp Salary here?
}
```

There are two problems with this loop. First, `endFetch()` returns true if it is called before FETCH...INTO, so we would never enter this loop in the first place. We could fix that by using a `do…while` loop, which guarantees that the loop executes at least once, but we're still left with the problem that we don't know whether valid values were returned by FETCH...INTO until after we call `endFetch()`, so at the end, we process a row of bogus values. (Because we are guaranteed that the last call to FETCH...INTO is invalid, we could use a `do…while` loop as long as we discard the last set of results. This is possible if the host variables are members of an array or if we are inserting the returned values into a dynamic structure, such as a vector or linked list, for example, that we can fix up after the loop.)

A better approach, however, is to test `endFetch()` immediately after the FETCH...INTO statement and use it to set a flag for the `while` loop and, at the same time, to decide whether to process the host variables.

```
boolean done = false;
while(!done)
{
  #sql {FETCH :empiter INTO :empName, :empJob, :empSalary};
  if(!(done = empiter.endFetch())
  {
    System.out.println("Name:  " + empName +
                       ", Job:  " + empJob +
                       ", Salary:  " + empSalary);
  }
}
```

Another way to accomplish the same thing is to use an infinite loop and break out of it when `endFetch()` returns true:

```
while(true)
{
  #sql {FETCH :empiter INTO :empName, :empJob, :empSalary};
  if(empiter.endFetch())
{
break;
}

  System.out.println("Name:  " + empName +
                     ", Job:  " + empJob +
                     ", Salary:  " + empSalary);

}
```

Note that because the assignment of the host variables is conditionally executed, the Java compiler will complain if they are not initialized outside the loop. This is why we initialize them to 0 or null when we declared them.

CHAPTER 8

Introduction to JDBC

JDBC is the Java database connectivity API. It is the foundation of all database features in Java. We can avoid using JDBC directly, for example, by using SQLJ to embed SQL statements in our Java code, but this code needs to be processed by an SQLJ preprocessor, which translates our SQLJ statements into JDBC. There are other database technologies for Java, EJB (Enterprise JavaBeans) and JDO (Java Data Objects), which hide JDBC behind the scenes for us and allow us to concentrate on objects, but they require additional software and learning a new way to program.

JDBC is not difficult to program, though it can be somewhat tedious because of the number of classes and methods involved and, especially, the number of steps required to process a query.

One drawback of using JDBC directly—as opposed to using a mapping layer, such as EJB or JDO, which can hide database details—is that it introduces dependencies between the Java code and the database but this can be ameliorated by careful design. It is usually best to encapsulate JDBC code in a data access layer comprising a limited number of classes.

CONNECTING TO THE DATABASE

The hardest thing about using JDBC is usually getting the JDBC drivers to connect to the database in the first place. The principle difficulty is because we need to get three different things working together: our Oracle database, our Java development environment, and the JDBC drivers to connect the Oracle database and our Java programs.

There are numerous options and alternatives for connecting, many of which we'll explore in the next chapter, but for now we'll start with the basics. These are the steps required to connect to the database:

- Setting up the Oracle, Java, and JDBC environment
- Importing the JDBC classes we need
- Loading and registering the JDBC driver
- Getting a `Connection` object from the driver

Setting up the Oracle, Java, and JDBC Environment

Before trying to get JDBC working, you should make sure that you have an Oracle database running and basic connectivity working. You should be able to start SQL*Plus, log into a database, and do a simple query. See Chapter 2 (or your database administrator) for more information if necessary.

You should also make sure that you have installed the Java software development kit. The latest version, Java 2 Platform, Standard Edition Version 1.4, is recommended. You should be able to create a Java source file, compile it, and run it.

Finally, you should set your CLASSPATH environment variable to include the Oracle JDBC driver. This is provided by Oracle in the [ORACLE_HOME]\jdbc\lib directory. If you are using Java 1.1, you should use classes11.zip. If you are using Java 1.2 or above (including 1.4 as recommended), you should use classes12.zip. For the sake of simplicity, we'll assume that you are using classes12.zip.

If you are using Windows 98, you can set your CLASSPATH by including the following line in the C:\AUTOEXEC.BAT file:

```
SET CLASSPATH=.;[ORACLE_HOME]\jdbc\lib\classes12.zip.
```

Notice that we have actually added two entries to the CLASSPATH variables, [ORACLE_HOME]\jdbc\lib\classes12.zip and a single period, separated by a semicolon. A single period, you may already know, indicates the current directory in the Unix and Windows operating system. If no CLASSPATH is defined, by default it will look in the current directory and the Java Virtual Machine (JVM) directory for classes. If CLASSPATH is defined, it will look only in the directories specified in CLASSPATH and the JVM directory. It will no longer look in the current directory unless the current directory is explicitly included in the CLASSPATH.

If you are using Windows NT/2000/XP, you can set CLASSPATH using the System applet in the Control Panel. Details differ slightly for NT and XP, but in Windows 2000, select the Advanced tab in the System applet then click the Environment Variables button.

If a CLASSPATH variable does not already exist, start by choosing New. Type in CLASSPATH as the variable name and .;\[ORACLE_HOME]\jdbc\lib\classes12.zip as the variable value.

If a CLASSPATH has already been defined, highlight it and select Edit. If there is already an entry for classes12.zip or classes11.zip, make a note of it and remove it if it's different than the path and file you plan to use. Otherwise, add \[ORACLE_HOME]\jdbc\lib\classes12.zip to what is already there. In either case, make sure it starts with a period and semicolon (.;).

Importing the JDBC Classes

The Java compiler needs to import the JDBC classes we will be using. At the top of our Java source file, we need to include the following import statements:

```
import java.sql.*;
import oracle.jdbc.driver.*;
```

If the CLASSPATH hasn't been set correctly, the second import above will generate a complaint from the compiler, claiming that the package `oracle.jdbc.driver` does not exist.

Loading and Registering the JDBC Driver

To load the JDBC driver requires two steps: loading the class and registering it with the `DriverManager`. As it turns out, though, we need to do only one of these, and the other will happen automatically. If we load the driver by name, using the static `Class.forName()` method, the driver, as part of its initialization, will register itself with the `DriverManager`. We'll take the alternate approach, however, and register it explicitly with this line of code:

```
DriverManager.registerDriver(new oracle.jdbc.OracleDriver());
```

The `DriverManager` will automatically load the driver for us.

Getting a Connection

The `DriverManager` is responsible for connecting us to resources. When we want to use a resource, such as a database, we construct a Uniform Resource Locater (URL) and use it to request a `Connection` object from the `Driver-`

Manager. The DriverManager will search the registered drivers for one that can accept our URL.

Oracle provides two JDBC drivers, an OCI driver and a pure-Java thin driver; each of these accepts several different types of URLs. We will use the thin driver with a URL of the following format:

```
"jdbc:oracle:thin:@<host>:<port>:<sid>"
```

My database server is named *noizmaker*, I use the default port 1521, and my database's system identifier (SID) is *osiris*, so my URL is:

```
"jdbc:oracle:thin:@noizmaker:1521:osiris"
```

DriverManager has a number of different getConnection() static methods available, but we will use one that lets us specify username and password as separate parameters. The call looks like this:

```
Connection conn = DriverManager.getConnection(
                  "jdbc:oracle:thin:@noizmaker:1521:osiris"
                           "scott", "tiger");
```

Factory Methods

The getConnection() method is one of many static methods in the Java API that are often referred to as *factory methods*. A factory method is a method that creates objects. It typically belongs to the abstract class or interface and returns an instance of a concrete class that implements an abstract class or interface. Because all we really care about is that it implements the Connection interface, this allows the implementation to hide irrelevant details from us, such as the precise type of the concrete class and the way it is initialized. This increases the portability and flexibility of the implementation because the factory can then have the freedom to give us different concrete classes with different features initialized in different ways, depending on the situation or environment.

Sample Connection Program

The following sample program puts all the above together:

```
// TestConnection.java – Load JDBC and connect to database

import java.sql.*;
import oracle.jdbc.driver.*;

public class TestConnection {
```

```
public static void main(String [] vars)
{
  Connection conn;
  try
  {
DriverManager.registerDriver(new
  oracle.jdbc.OracleDriver());

// The following needs to be edited with
// your database specifics:
      conn = DriverManager.getConnection(
    "jdbc:oracle:thin:@noizmaker:1521:osiris",
        "scott", "tiger");
 }
 catch (SQLException e)
 {
   System.out.println("Caught: " + e);
   System.exit(1);
 }
}
}
```

After editing the URL to include the proper parameters for your database, you should be able to compile and run this program. If the program runs without printing an error message, you can assume it connected to the database correctly. We'll expand this example to provide output in the next section when we add code to execute an SQL statement.

EXECUTING SQL STATEMENTS

The easiest kind of SQL statements to use are DDL statements, including CREATE TABLE, ALTER TABLE, and DROP TABLE, and the DML statements INSERT, UPDATE, and DELETE—that is, everything except SELECT. SELECT, because it returns data—and sometimes a lot of data—will be covered in a later section.

To execute an SQL statement, we will first obtain a `Statement` object from our `Connection` object. `Statement` has a number of methods that let us execute an SQL statement. The easiest method to use for nonquery SQL statements is `executeUpdate()`. The following code, which assumes we have a valid `Connection` object, `conn`, demonstrates how we can create and populate a table with a row of data.

```
Statement stmt = conn.createStatement();
stmt.executeUpdate("CREATE TABLE EXAMPLE" +
                   "(COL1 VARCHAR2(30)," +
                   " COL2 VARCHAR2(30)," +
                   "NUM1 NUMBER)");
int rows;
rows = stmt.executeUpdate("INSERT INTO EXAMPLE VALUES" +
                          "('Column 1', 'Column 2', 1)");
    System.out.println("Rows updated: " + rows);
```

The `executeUpdate()` method returns an `int`, indicating how many rows were updated by the SQL statement. In the case of a DDL, however, such as our CREATE TABLE statement, it always returns 0, so we can ignore the return value in that case.

Notice in the examples, also, that the SQL statement is not terminated with a semicolon. It is the responsibility of the JDBC driver to provide the proper termination.

The easiest way to include variables in SQL statements when using JDBC is to generate the SQL statement dynamically. Suppose that we wish to add another row to our table above and that we have the values in Java variables. We can compose the SQL statement and execute it as follows:

```
String column1 = "ABC";
String column2 = "XYZ";
int i = 120;

String sql = "INSERT INTO EXAMPLE VALUES ('" +
    column1 + "', '" + column2 + "', " + i + ")";
  rows = stmt.executeUpdate(sql);
System.out.println("Updated: " + rows);
```

This approach is straightforward but coding is somewhat tedious, and composing the strings requires careful attention to delimiters, especially because the strings will get parsed twice, according to two different sets of rules. The first thing to consider is how the Java compiler will interpret the string. Literal double quotes that are to be included as part of the SQL statement need to be escaped with a slash (\), for example. Let's suppose that we want to insert the string: He said "Here's Johnny!"

Java requires that we escape the double quotes like this:

```
String s = "He said \"Here's Johnny!\""
```

The next thing to consider is that SQL expects a string to be delimited by single quotes and requires that a literal single quote (or apostrophe) within the constant be escaped by another single quote, like this:

```
INSERT INTO EXAMPLE (COL1) VALUES ('He said "Here''s Johnny!"');
```

Writing this as a JDBC query means we need to take both sets of rules into account.

```
rows = stmt.executeUpdate("INSERT INTO EXAMPLE (COL1) VALUES ('He said
\"Here''s Johnny!\"')");
```

Needless to say, this makes for strings that are hard to compose and interpret. One thing that can help is a helper method that will escape single quotes for SQL.

```
public static String escSingleQuote(String sql)
{
  int start= 0;
  int end = sql.indexOf('\'');
  if(end<0)
  {
     return sql; // short-circuit
  }
  StringBuffer sb = new StringBuffer();
  while(end>=0)
  {
    sb.append(sql.substring(start,end));
    sb.append('\'');
    start = end;
    end = sql.indexOf("'", start + 1);
  }
  sb.append(sql.substring(start,sql.length()));
  return sb.toString();
}
```

Notice that this method uses a `StringBuffer` to construct the new string. This is because a regular `String` object is immutable. There are no methods that allow us to change it. If we are going to perform repeated concatenations on a string, it is better to use a `StringBuffer`, which is not immutable, and call the `toString()` method at the end.

Concatenating Strings Efficiently

When `String` objects in Java are joined using the "+" operator, the Java compiler creates a temporary `StringBuffer` object and calls the `String-Buffer's append()` method to perform the concatenation for each string being joined. At the end, it calls the `Stringbuffer's toString()` method to get back a `String` object. Consider the following code:

```
String sql = "INSERT INTO EXAMPLE VALUES (";
sql = sql + "'ABC', ";
sql = sql + "'XYZ',";
sql = sql + 123 + ")";
```

Though it is clear and easy to follow, it is inefficient because the Java compiler turns it into the equivalent of the following code:

```
String sql = "INSERT INTO EXAMPLE VALUES (";
sql = new StringBuffer(sql).append("'ABC', ").toString();
sql = new StringBuffer(sql).append("'XYZ',").toString();
sql = new StringBuffer(sql).append(123).append(")").toString();
```

It is more efficient to do the concatenation in as few statements as possible.

```
String sql = "INSERT INTO EXAMPLE VALUES (" +
        + "'ABC', ";
        + "'XYZ',";
        + 123 + ")";
```

Alternatively, we can use a `StringBuffer` ourselves to construct the string in parts.

```
StringBuffer sqlBuffer = "INSERT INTO EXAMPLE VALUES (";
SqlBuffer.append("'ABC', ");
SqlBuffer.append(+ "'XYZ',");
SqlBuffer.append(123 + ")");
String sql = ssqlBuffer.toString();
```

This latter example isn't as efficient as the all-in-one statement, but if we need to construct an SQL statement piecemeal, based on intermediate results from other methods or queries, this is an adequate approach—it's still an improvement over simply concatenating strings.

PreparedStatement

Yet another alternative to using a `Statement` object that includes variables by concatenating strings is to use a `PreparedStatement` instead. A `PreparedStatement` allows us to embed placeholders for variables in the SQL statement.

The placeholders for variables in a `PreparedStatement` are called *bind variables* and are similar to the host variables we used in SQLJ, but instead of specifying the Java host variable directly in the SQL statement, we use a question mark (?) for each variable, then call set methods to set the value of each one, using an index. This is called a *parameterized* SQL statement.

We define the parameterized SQL statement at the time we create the `PreparedStatement`, not when we execute it, as with `Statement`. So although a `Statement` object can be used repeatedly to execute arbitrary, different SQL statements, a `PreparedStatement` can be used to execute only a single SQL statement. Because the prepared SQL statement contains bind variables, it can be executed multiple times with different values.

```
PreparedStatement ps = conn.prepareStatement(
   "INSERT INTO EXAMPLE  VALUES( ?, ?, ?)");
```

To set the variables in the statement, there are a large number of set methods, of the form `setXXX()`, where `XXX` is a Java primitive type or class, such as `int` or `String`. Each set method takes a first parameter, an integer, that indicates which bind variable is to be set—where the first bind variable is 1—and a second parameter, the value. Set methods include `setInt()`, `setLong()`, `setFloat()`, `setDouble()`, `setString()`, `setDate()`, and `setTime()`.

Depending on the types of the columns in the EXAMPLE table, we might be able to set the three bind variables in the PreparedStatement above as follows:

```
ps.setString(1, "Henry");
ps.setString(2, "Cow");
ps.setInt(3, 1968);
```

Once all the variables are bound, the prepared statement can be executed.

```
ps.executeUpdate();
```

Bind variables aren't used only for values to be inserted; they can also be used anywhere a text or numeric constant is valid in an SQL statement, such as in a WHERE clause:

```
PreparedStatement ps = conn.prepareStatement(
   "UPDATE EXAMPLE SET COL1=? WHERE COL2=?");
ps.setString(1,"Don''t have a");
ps.setString(2,"Cow");
ps.executeUpdate();
```

Statement versus PreparedStatement

`Statement` and `PreparedStatement` both have advantages. In general, `Statement` is simple, efficient, and is to be preferred, with the following exceptions:

When many variables are involved, `PreparedStatement` offers an advantage over `Statement`, because using a series of set methods is a better structured, less error-prone, and more efficient approach than converting everything to a string and concatenating strings. Because of this, `PreparedStatements` are most commonly used with nonquery statements such as INSERT and UPDATE.

When the same SQL statement can be reused many times by using bind variables, `PreparedStatement` offers a performance advantage, because the database needs to parse the SQL statement only once. (On the other hand, if a statement will be called only once or twice, `Statement` is more efficient because of the higher overhead associated with a `PreparedStatement`.)

In any case, do not let performance be the single guiding force in your choice. If performance is critical, you should test to ensure that the difference is enough to justify using an approach that isn't as good from a design, testing, or maintainability point of view.

CallableStatements

A `CallableStatement` is similar to a `PreparedStatement`, but it is used for calling functions and stored procedures in the database, rather than standard SQL DDL or DML statements. You may remember that both functions and stored procedures may have input parameters, output parameters, or parameters that are used for both input and output. (It is bad practice, however, to use output or input/output parameters with functions.) The difference between the two is that a function has a return value but a procedure does not. To allow the use of both input and output parameters, `CallableStatement` not only has methods for setting parameters in the SQL statement, such as a `PreparedStatement`, but it also has methods for registering and obtaining output variables.

The Oracle `CallableStatement` implementation accepts two types of syntax: Oracle-specific PL/SQL block syntax and the standard SQL-92 call syntax. Assuming that we want to call a function, func, that takes one parameter, the Oracle PL/SQL block syntax looks like this:

```
"begin ? := func(?); end;"
```

The notable features are that it begins with the keyword `begin`, followed by the assignment and function call, a semicolon, and the keyword `end`. Input and output parameters are indicated with question marks.

The SQL-92 call syntax for the same function looks like this:

```
"{? = call func(?)}"
```

The notable features about this syntax are that the entire statement is enclosed by braces and that the function name is immediately preceded by the keyword `call`. Parameters are indicated with question marks, as with the PL/SQL syntax.

In the examples that follow, we'll use the standard SQL-92 syntax.

Calling a Procedure. Suppose we want a procedure that looks up someone's first name if we provide the last name. Further suppose that we want to know the first name only if it is unambiguous—if there is only one person with that last name. We'll define a PL/SQL stored procedure with three parameters, one input parameter so that we can provide the last name and two output parameters: one for the first name (if unique) and one for the count of people having the last name we provided. To create the procedure, enter the following at an SQL prompt:

```
CREATE OR REPLACE PROCEDURE GET_FIRST_NAME(
                            IN_LNAME   IN  VARCHAR2,
                            OUT_FNAME  OUT VARCHAR2,
                            OUT_COUNT OUT NUMBER)
AS
BEGIN
  SELECT COUNT(*) INTO OUT_COUNT FROM NAMES
        WHERE LAST_NAME LIKE IN_LNAME;
  IF (OUT_COUNT = 1) THEN
    SELECT FIRST_NAME INTO OUT_FNAME FROM NAMES
        WHERE LAST_NAME LIKE IN_LNAME;
  END IF;
END;
/
```

To call this procedure from Java, we first create a `CallableStatement` object as follows using the SQL-92 syntax:

```
CallableStatement cs = conn.prepareCall(
      "{call GET_FIRST_NAME(?, ?, ?)}");
```

We set the first parameter, which is an input parameter.

```
cs.setString(1, "Smith");
```

To set the output parameters, we use the `registerOutputParameter()` method. This takes two parameters, the position of the output parameter and the type of the output parameter. The types are defined in the `java.sql.Types` class. For the `name` variable, because Oracle's VARCHAR2 is not a standard SQL type, we'll use `Types.CHAR`.

```
cs.registerOutParameter(2, Types.CHAR);
```

We'll register the `count` variable as `Types.INTEGER`.

```
cs.registerOutParameter(3, Types.INTEGER);
```

Now we're prepared to call the procedure by calling the `execute()` method.

```
cs.execute();
```

To allow us to obtain the values of the output parameters and function call return values, the CallableStatement has a large number of `getXXX()`, where `XXX` represents the type, such as `String` or `int`. Here is how we obtain the count of matches that the procedure returned and the name, if a single unique match was found.

```
int count = cs.getInt(3);
System.out.println("Count: " + count);
String name=null;
if(count==1)
{
  name = cs.getString(2);
}
System.out.println("name: " + name);
```

Finally, at the end we close the `CallableStatement` and the connection.

```
cs.close();
```

Calling a Function. The steps for calling a function are the same as for calling a procedure. We create the `CallableStatement`, using either the PL/SQL block syntax or the SQL-92 call syntax, set the input parameters with the appropriate `getXXX()` methods, and register the function's return variable, using the `registerOutputParameter()` method. Here we'll call an existing SQL function, SOUNDEX(), which, for a given name, returns a character string representing a phonetic approximation of the name (represented by a letter followed by a three-digit number). This is often used, for example, to look up a name in an electronic directory when the exact spelling is unknown.

```
cs=conn.prepareCall("{? = call SOUNDEX(?)}");
cs.registerOutParameter(1, Types.CHAR);
cs.setString(2,"HELLO");
```

```
cs.execute();
String soundex=cs.getString(1);
System.out.println("Soundex=" + soundex);
cs.close();
```

When to Use CallableStatements. `CallableStatements` have a significant overhead beyond that of straight SQL calls—not to mention the added complexity of developing and maintaining a stored procedure or function in the database. They should generally be used only if the operation they perform requires multiple SQL statements or if the operation is one that is to be shared with other database client applications. See Chapter 5, "PL/SQL," for more information about creating and using stored procedures and Java stored procedures.

EXECUTING SQL QUERIES

The most commonly used SQL statement is the SELECT statement. We can execute SELECT statements using either a `Statement` or a `PreparedStatement` object. Both `Statement` and `PreparedStatement` have a method, `executeQuery()`, that executes an SQL SELECT command and returns a `ResultSet` containing the results of the query in the form of a table. Consider this query using `Statement`:

```
Statement stmt = new conn.getStatement();
ResultSet rs = stmt.executeQuery(
   "SELECT ENAME, JOB, SAL FROM EMP");
```

The `ResultSet` that this example returns contains three columns, ENAME, JOB, and SAL, as specified in the select list. Assuming the database hasn't been altered since Oracle was installed, it will contain 14 rows.

Navigating a ResultSet

We access the `ResultSet` one row at a time, starting at the first row and advancing one row forward at a time. (By default, this is the only way to move through a `ResultSet`—we'll see other options in Chapter 9, "Advanced JDBC Features.") Associated with the `ResultSet` is a cursor, a kind of pointer, which is initially set to point before the first row. To advance it to the first row and every row after that, we need to call the `ResultSet`'s `next()` method. The `next()` method returns a Boolean value: true if it was successful in advancing to the next row, false if there are no more rows. This is the usual way to iterate through a `ResultSet`:

```
while(rs.next())
{
  // Process current row, column by column
}
```

Once we have positioned the cursor at a valid row by calling the `next()` method, we use the `ResultSet`'s `getXXX` methods to access the columns in the row. Each of the row's columns can be addressed in one of two ways: by the column's name or by its index, starting at 1. In general, it is most efficient to retrieve data from columns by index, in order. Like the set methods for `PreparedStatement`, `ResultSet` has many `get` methods. (Actually, there are about twice as many `get` methods because of the two ways of addressing a column.) The most commonly used are those for basic Java types and classes, such as `getInt()`, `getLong()`, `getFloat()`, `getDouble()`, `getString()`, `getDate()`, and `getTime()`. For each column, we need to choose the most appropriate type.

Our sample SQL statement returned three columns, which we know hold an employee's name, job, and salary. The most appropriate method for retrieving name and job is pretty obviously `getString()`, because they're both variable-length character fields.

It's not as obvious which get method we should use for salary. Most of the numeric types will work, but `getLong()` is the best and safest choice, because we know the values are integer values, and we don't want to limit anyone's earning potential unduly.

Another option for retrieving a number from a `ResultSet`, if we intend to display only a number and don't need to do anything with the value, is to use `getString()`. In general, JDBC is fairly forgiving and will perform any necessary conversions, if possible.

Here is a more complete query example:

```
Statement stmt = new conn.getStatement();
ResultSet rs = stmt.executeQuery(
   "SELECT ENAME, JOB, SAL FROM EMP");
String name=null, job=null;
long salary=0L;

while(rs.next())
{
  name = rs.getString(1);
  job = rs.getString(2);
  salary = rs.getLong(3);
```

```
    System.out.println("Name: " + name +
                       ", Job: " + job +
                       ", Salary:" + salary);
}
```

In some cases, we may want to let the database perform formatting for us—most notably, for dates and times—and we need to accept a string in those cases, rather than an underlying numerical value. For example, we can obtain year as an apostrophe followed by two digits like this:

```
rs = stmt.executeQuery(
   "SELECT TO_CHAR(SYSDATE, '''YY') FROM DUAL");
System.out.println("Year: " + rs.getString(
```

Which, in 2003, prints out

```
Year: '03
```

In many cases, we have a choice about using Oracle or Java to perform formatting. As in this case, it is often easier to use Oracle. Java, on the other hand, is more flexible and has greater support for internationalization, such as for culturally dependent date and time formats. The important thing is to be consistent—you'll want to choose one or the other, based on the needs of your application.

Using Column Names

In the examples we have seen so far, we have retrieved values for each column by using the column's index. We can also use each column's name—that is necessary if we have a query such as this:

```
ResultSet rs = stmt.executeQuery("SELECT * FROM EMP");
```

(We shouldn't really write queries like this, because it could return unexpected results, should the table change in the future, and because it could return information we don't need, which is wasteful and inefficient). We don't necessarily know in what order the columns are returned. Even if we did, we shouldn't depend on that order, because it could change. Consequently, we need to get the values by using the names of the columns. We can get the name from ENAME, the job from JOB, and the salary from SAL, like this:

```
String name=null, job=null;
long salary=0L;

while(rs.next())
{
   name = rs.getString("ENAME");
   job = rs.getString("JOB");
   salary = rs.getLong("SAL");

   System.out.println("Name:  " + name +
                      ", Job:  " + job +
                      ", Salary:" + salary);
}
```

Using PreparedStatement for Queries

The previous examples used `Statement` for executing queries, but a `PreparedStatement` can be used, too, and has the same benefits and drawbacks it has for other types of SQL statements that we saw above. If we will be executing an SQL statement repeatedly with different values, it may be preferable to use a `PreparedStatement` so that it is parsed only once by the database. The bind variables in a query are most commonly used in a WHERE clause. Here is a query for an employee selected by employee number:

```
PreparedStatement ps = conn.prepareStatement(
   "SELECT ENAME, JOB, SAL FROM EMP WHERE EMPNO=?");
ps.setInt(1, 7900);
String name=null, job=null;
long salary=0L;

ResultSet rs = ps.executeQuery();
while(rs.next())
{
   name = rs.getString(1);
   job = rs.getString(2);
   salary = rs.getLong(3);

   System.out.println("Name:  " + name +
                      ", Job:  " + job +
                      ", Salary:" + salary);
}
```

Bind variables are not limited to WHERE clauses; they can be used anywhere in an SQL statement that a text or numeric constant can be used, as well, such as in a select list expression. This is useful if we want to supply a value for an SQL function, for example. Suppose we want to list each employee's year of hire; we can supply the format string using a bind variable, in case we want to be able to change it based on user input.

```
PreparedStatement ps = conn.prepareStatement(
   "SELECT ENAME, TO_CHAR(HIREDATE,?) FROM EMP");
ps.setString(1,"YYYY");
String name=null, hireyear=null;

ResultSet rs = ps.executeQuery();
while(rs.next())
{
   name = rs.getString(1);
   hireyear = rs.getString(2);

   System.out.println("Name: " + name +
                      ", Year: " + hireyear);
}
```

ResultSetMetaData

`ResultSetMetaData` is a class that we can use, as the name indicates, to obtain information about a `ResultSet` itself. This information includes number, names, and properties of the columns in the `ResultSet`, and the name of the table and schema of each column.

We obtain the `ResultSetMetaData` from a `ResultSet`, using the `getMetaData()` method. Assuming that we have obtained a `PreparedStatement` object, `ps`, we can obtain a `ResultSet` and its associated `ResultSetMetaData` like this:

```
ResultSet rs = ps.executeQuery();
ResultSetMetaData rmd = rs.getMetaData();
```

Since the columns in this query all belong to the single table we can get the table name from any of the columns.

```
System.out.println("Tablename: " + rmd.getTableName(1));
```

We can get the column count and iterate through the columns to obtain information about them.

```
int count = rmd.getColumnCount();
for(int i=1; i<=count; i++)
{
  System.out.println("Name: " + rmd.getColumnLabel(i) +
                     "  Type: " + rmd.getColumnTypeName(i));
}
```

`ResultSetMetaData` is useful for getting table and column information when displaying database information in a table format, and is preferable to using hard-coded headings, which require greater diligence to make sure they remain correct when the database or queries are changed.

Large Objects—BLOBs and CLOBs

The SQL types we've used so far in this and previous chapters—NUMBER, VARCHAR2, and DATE—correspond more or less to basic Java types, such as `int`, `long double`, `Date`, and `String`. To allow maximum flexibility, SQL also supports untyped objects, which—unlike the other SQL types—are virtually unlimited (up to 4 gigabytes) in size. These are called *large objects* (LOBs) and come in two varieties, character large objects (CLOBs) and binary large objects (BLOBs). The latter are especially well named because they are, in effect, just blobs to the database—undifferentiated stuff with no meaning, as far as the database is concerned.

One way to think of the difference between BLOBs and CLOBs is by analogy to the difference between text files and binary files in some operating systems. Text files, like CLOBs, are associated with a character set and are plain text, without formatting information; typical examples are HTML, XML, and plain text documents. Binary files, like BLOBs, can contain anything at all; typical examples are: executable files, image files, sound files, and documents produced by word processing programs.

The comparison between LOBs and operating system files is not entirely spurious. LOBs are most commonly used to store and retrieve operating system files in a database. They are not limited to this, of course; data generated in memory (such as byte arrays or strings, for example) could also be stored in a LOB. Also, serialized Java objects could be stored in a BLOB—which presents interesting possibilities for roll-your-own object persistence.

An important thing to note is that the LOB data (except for small objects) is not saved in the database table itself. Instead, a locator is stored in the table. This locator introduces a layer of indirection that can make LOBs somewhat complicated to work with.

Reading and Writing BLOBs and CLOBs

There are two ways to write LOB data to the database. The first, and most straightforward, is to use the `PreparedStatement`'s `setBinaryStream()` or the `setCharacterStream()` methods to insert the data. This works only with the OCI JDBC driver in Oracle versions 8.1.6 and greater. The other way is to obtain a binary or character stream from the LOB locator. The following examples use BLOBs, but they are identical to using CLOBs.

Writing a BLOB Using the PreparedStatement setBinaryStream() Method

Assuming that we are using the OCI driver and have a valid `Connection` object, `conn`, we can insert an MP3 file as a BLOB in the database like this:

```
// write blob using PreparedStatement setBinaryStream
PreparedStatement ps = conn.prepareStatement(
        "INSERT INTO MP3S (ID, FILENAME, MP3) " +
        "VALUES(?, ? , ?)" );

ps.setLong(1, 199);
ps.setString(2, "Elevation.mp3");

File file = new File ("C:\\MyTunes\\Television\\Elevation.mp3");
FileInputStream fileStream = new FileInputStream(file);
ps.setBinaryStream(3, fileStream, (int) file.length());
ps.executeUpdate();
ps.close();
rs.close();
fileStream.close();
```

The `setBinaryStream()` method conveniently takes an input stream and its length as its parameters and takes care of the details of reading the file for us.

Writing a BLOB Using a Locator

If we are using the thin driver, the `PreparedStatement` class does not support the method `setBinaryStream()` above. Instead, we need to obtain the output stream for the BLOB from the BLOB locator. This means that we must create an empty BLOB first before we can write data to it. We cannot create a BLOB in Java; the database must create the BLOB for us. To create a BLOB, we insert a row using the function EMPTY_BLOB() to provide the BLOB value in the insert value list (in addition to any other non-BLOB information).

```
// write blob using locator
//  - step 1: insert with empty BLOB
PreparedStatement ps = conn.prepareStatement(
        "INSERT INTO MP3S (ID, FILENAME, MP3) " +
        "VALUES(?, ? , EMPTY_BLOB())" );
ps.setLong(1, 199);
File file = new File("C:\\MyTunes\\Television\\Elevation.mp3");
ps.setString(2, "Elevation.mp3");
ps.executeUpdate();
ps.close();
```

Next, we query the table to obtain the locator created by EMPTY_BLOB(), use the locator to obtain the binary stream, and write the data to the stream. These steps must all be part of a single transaction. To do this, we must make sure auto-commit is false and lock the row by using the SQL command SELECT…FOR UPDATE for the query. This is the code required to obtain the binary stream:

```
// Get BLOB locator
conn.setAutoCommit(false);
ps = conn.prepareStatement("SELECT MP3 FROM MP3S "
                            + "WHERE ID = ? FOR UPDATE");
ps.setLong(1, 199);
rs = ps.executeQuery();
BLOB blob = null;
if(rs.next())
{
   blob = ((OracleResultSet)rs).getBLOB(1);
}

// Standard JDBC Blob method not supported by Oracle API:
// OutputStream outStream = blob.setBinaryStream();

// This is Oracle's version:
OutputStream outStream = blob.getBinaryOutputStream(0);
```

Note that there are a few Oracle-specific features here. First, we need to use Oracle's `BLOB`, rather than the JDBC standard `Blob`. `ResultSet` is an interface defined by JDBC, but the actual implementation is an `OracleResultSet`, so we can cast `rs` to `OracleResultSet` to call the Oracle-specific `getBLOB()` method (rather than the JDBC standard `getBlob()` method), which returns a `BLOB` instead of a `Blob`. Finally, we call the `BLOB`'s `getBinaryOutputStream()` method to obtain the stream.

Now we are finally prepared to write to the stream. In the previous example, the `PreparedStatement`'s `setBinaryStream()` method took care of reading from one stream and writing to the other for us. Here, we must do this job ourselves, and to do this, we need a temporary buffer. This is the code for opening the file stream, reading from it, and writing to the output stream, a buffer's worth of data at a time:

```
// use buffer to write from file to db
int size = blob.getBufferSize();
byte [] buffer = new byte[size];
int length = -1;
while ((length = inStream.read(buffer)) != -1)
```

```
{
  outStream.write(buffer, 0, length);
}
inStream.close();
outStream.close();
conn.commit();

ps.close();
rs.close();
```

This, using the BLOB locator, is obviously a great deal more trouble than writing the BLOB directly as a binary stream, but if you write a general-purpose BLOB class, you'll have to do it only once.

Reading BLOBs and CLOBs

As was the case with writing BLOBs and CLOBs, there are two ways to read them. The most straightforward way is to use the `PreparedStatement`'s `getBinaryStream()` or `getCharacterStream()` classes. The more complicated way is to use the `getCLOB()` or `getBLOB()` methods to obtain the locator and use that to obtain an input stream. Fortunately, support for the first method is consistent in the JDBC drivers and that is the method used in the following example. As in the previous section, BLOBs are used in the examples but the use of CLOBs is identical:

```
// Read BLOB into file
String sql = "SELECT FILENAME, MP3 FROM MP3S " +
             "WHERE ID = ?";
PreparedStatement ps = conn.prepareStatement(sql);
ps.setLong(1, id);
ResultSet rs = ps.executeQuery();
if(rs.next())
{
    filename = "C:\\TEMP\\" + rs.getString(1);
    File file = new File(filename);
    FileOutputStream outStream = new FileOutputStream (file);
    InputStream inStream = rs.getBinaryStream(2);

    // set up buffer for transfer
    byte [] buffer = new byte[BUFFERSIZE]; //BUFFERSIZE==2048
    int length = -1;

    // Read and write, buffer by buffer
    while((length = inStream.read(buffer)) != -1)
    {
       outStream.write(buffer, 0, length);
```

```
        }
        inStream.close();
        outStream.close();

    }
    rs.close();
    ps.close();
```

Notice that we need to set up a buffer to transfer data from the input stream to the output stream. Had we used the BLOB locator to obtain the input stream (as in the previous example), we could have called the `BLOB`'s `getBufferSize()` method to obtain the optimal size for the buffer. Here, we're using an arbitrarily sized 2K buffer—this could probably be adjusted for better performance. On my system, `getBufferSize()` returns 32288.

CHAPTER 9

Advanced JDBC Features

In the previous chapter, we covered the essential features of JDBC, most of which were introduced in the JDBC 1.0 specification, the version of JDBC included in JDK 1.1. In this chapter, we will learn additional JDBC 1.0 options, but we will also cover new features introduced in JDBC 2.0 and 3.0.

First, we will consider the different ways we can connect to a database. We will cover:

- Different types of JDBC drivers
- Different ways of supplying the connection information, such as the database URL, username, and password
- The `DataSource` class, new in JDBC 3.0, that Sun recommends we use

Next, we will consider some additional `ResultSet` options that were introduced in JDBC 2.0:

- Scrollability—the ability to navigate the `ResultSet` backward and forward, as well as moving to specific records
- Sensitivity—the ability to see changes made to the database by others without re-executing the query
- Updateability—the ability to change values in the `ResultSet` and store those changes in the database

We will also look at another new JDBC 3.0 feature, `RowSets`. `RowSets` are an extension of `ResultSets` that adds a JavaBean interface. We will look in particular at Oracle's implementation of two types of `RowSets`:

- `Cached RowSet`—caches a `ResultSet` so we can use it even if we are not connected to a database. `Cached RowSets` are serializable, so they can be saved in files and transmitted to remote users. Because they have the full functionality of a `ResultSet`, they can be browsed and updated. Changes can later be applied to the database by reconnecting.
- JDBC `RowSet`—provides a thin wrapper around a `ResultSet`. This is useful principally if we want to take advantage of `RowSet` as a JavaBean component.

In Chapter 6, we covered Oracle's object-relational features. Here, we will see how to work with those features in JDBC. We examine two approaches:

- Weakly typed objects—use a generic object, `Struct` (or Oracle's extension, `STRUCT`), that we can use to hold an Oracle database object.
- Strongly typed objects—use a custom class that implements the `SQLData` interface (or Oracle's extension, `ORAData`) to hold Oracle database objects and can be integrated as a first-class object in our Java architecture.

Connection Options

To connect to a database, we are faced with a confusing number of alternatives. To begin with, we have to, at a minimum, decide between the two drivers Oracle provides. This is important because the JDBC API consists entirely of interfaces—nothing is implemented in the Java JDK. Choosing a JDBC driver is choosing the JDBC implementation.

The next complication is the fact that each JDBC driver has its own way of specifying connection information. The database URL, username, and password options vary from one to another.

Finally, Sun has suggested that the traditional way of getting a database connection, by loading and registering the driver, may be deprecated in the future. Instead, as of JDBC 3.0, we should be using the `DataSource` class. This is part of the overall goal of bringing JDBC 3.0 in line with other J2EE technologies, such as JNDI.

The important thing, at this point, is to understand what the options are and to choose the one that is most suitable for your environment.

JDBC DRIVER TYPES

Oracle, as mentioned in the last chapter, provides us with two JDBC drivers—an OCI driver and a pure-Java thin driver. These are, respectively, type 2 and type 4 drivers. There are, more generally, four types of drivers available.

Type 1: Bridge driver. The purpose of a JDBC driver is to connect Java code to a database. In many cases, the most expedient way of doing this is to connect Java to an existing driver that uses another comparable technology, such as Microsoft's Open Database Connectivity (ODBC). In fact, the most common driver of this type is a JDBC-ODBC bridge, which maps JDBC calls to ODBC calls and allows a Java program to use databases supporting ODBC.

Type 2: Native API driver. This type of driver, of which the Oracle OCI driver is an example, uses the Java Native Interface (JNI) to allow Java code to connect to the database client API—software written for a specific platform and database. In the case of the Oracle OCI driver, it requires that the standard Oracle client software be installed and properly configured. Java, through JNI, calls the Oracle Call Interface binaries.

Type 3: Middleware driver. This is a pure-Java driver (at least on the client side) that connects to a middleware layer, such as BEA's Weblogic. This middleware generally runs on a server of its own and provides the ability to connect to one or more databases, possibly from different vendors. This type of driver is provided by the middleware vendor and is the most flexible because of the additional layer of abstraction that the middleware provides.

Type 4: Pure-Java driver. This is a pure-Java driver that connects directly to the database, using the database's network protocol directly. No additional software or configuration is required on the client.

Oracle recommends using its OCI type 2 driver for best performance, but others have reported a conflicting experience and instead recommend the pure-Java driver. This difference is likely to be application-specific. In any case, if you have serious performance requirements, you should perform your own testing with your own application to decide which to use. The JDBC examples in this book will generally use the thin driver because of its greater portability.

URL Format Options

In addition to the URL format that was used in the last chapter, there are quite a few more that the Oracle drivers accept. I'll describe a few, not just in the interest of thoroughness, but because this may provide a clearer understanding of how the drivers locate and connect to a database.

The Oracle OCI driver and thin driver both accept URLs having the same basic format.

```
"jdbc:oracle:driver:@database"
```

The *driver* option can be either *thin* or *oci*.

The *database* option generally differs depending on whether the thin driver or the OCI driver is used. For the OCI driver, the Oracle database's System Identifier (SID) is sufficient. For the thin drive, the database's hostname and port must also be specified in the following format:

```
host:port:sid
```

This is how we can connect using the thin driver using this format:

```
// Thin driver connection:
Connection conn = DriverManager.getConnection(
    "jdbc:oracle:oci:@noizmaker:1521:osiris",
    "scott", "tiger");
```

The OCI driver uses the Oracle client software installed on the client machine so it can use the database's SID to find the database in the same way that other Oracle client software, such as SQL*Plus does—using the keyword=value entries in the TNSNAMES.ORA file to identify the hostname and port. If you used the Oracle Universal Installer to set up the connection to your database, this file will have been created for you in the [ORACLE_HOME]\network\admin directory. Mine has the following entry:

```
OSIRIS =
  (DESCRIPTION =
    (ADDRESS_LIST =
      (ADDRESS = (PROTOCOL = TCP)(HOST = noizmaker)(PORT = 1521))
    )
    (CONNECT_DATA =
      (SERVICE_NAME = OSIRIS)
    )
  )
```

Using the name *osiris* for the <database> entry is sufficient to connect using the OCI driver.

```
//OCI driver connection
Connection conn = DriverManager.getConnection(
      "jdbc:oracle:oci:@osiris", "scott", "tiger");
```

In addition, either driver will accept a string of keyword=value pairs as the database identifier, like those in tnsnames.ora.

```
// OCI driver connection with keyword=value pairs
Connection conn = DriverManager.getConnection(
  "jdbc:oracle:oci:"
  +"@(description=(address=(host= noizmaker)"
  +"(protocol=tcp)(port=1521))(connect_data=(sid=osiris)))",
   "scott",
   "tiger");

//Thin driver connection with keyword=value pairs
Connection conn = DriverManager.getConnection(
  "jdbc:oracle:thin:"
  +"@(description=(address=(host= noizmaker)"
  +"(protocol=tcp)(port=1521))(connect_data=(sid=osiris)))",
   "scott",
   "tiger");
```

Including Username and Password in the URL

In addition to the methods calls shown above, which include the username and password as separate parameters, it is also possible to include username and password as part of the URL. We saw above that all URLs include a database identifier which is preceded by an @ sign. This can be preceded by an optional login parameter.

```
login@database
```

The login parameter has the following format:

```
username/password
```

Using this option, a call to get a connection might look like this:

```
"jdbc:oracle:thin:scott/tiger@noizmaker:1521:osiris");
```

USING DATASOURCE INSTEAD OF DRIVERMANAGER

`DriverManager` has one significant drawback: It requires hard-coding vendor options and details about the database and server configurations. To use the code on another system, to change the database, or to change username or password, etc., we may need to edit the source code, recompile, and retest.

There are several approaches that we can take to minimize this problem. One option is to put these specifics in a properties file or a configuration file that is read at startup time, perhaps using XML or a Java `ResourceBundle`. These minimize but don't solve the problem.

In JDBC 2.0, Sun introduced an alternative with a more far-reaching approach, the `DataSource` class. `DataSource` allows our code to locate and connect to a resource, such as a database, by using a logical name. This can make our code more portable and easier to maintain. It also allows us to encapsulate some of the connection details at a higher-level—using a datasource is necessary, in fact, if we want to use the connection pooling and distributed transactions that application servers can provide.

The mapping of the logical name to a specific resource is intended to be managed at the higher level, outside of the application, by a naming service such as Java Naming and Directory Interface (JDNI). Using `DataSource` with JNDI is simple, assuming that you have a naming service set up already. (This may be provided by an application server, for example.) The naming service will allow you to associate a database URL with a logical name, using the following steps:

```
Context ctx = new InitialContext();
DataSource ds = (DataSource)ctx.lookup("jdbc/logical_database_name");
Connection con = ds.getConnection(username, password);
```

It is also possible to use `DataSource` without JNDI and set the `DataSource` properties in our code. This is essentially equivalent to using `DriverManager`. We lose the advantages of portability and maintainability, and gain verbosity. Nonetheless, because Sun may deprecate `DriverManager` at some time in the future, it's worth at least considering using `DataSource` anyway, especially if we are writing an application that will eventually use JNDI.

Here are three steps we need to use `DataSource` without JNDI:

- Import the `OracleDataSource` class
- Create a `DataSource` object
- Set the `DataSource` properties
- Get a `Connection` from the `DataSource`

Importing and Using DataSource Class

The first two steps are straightforward. At the top of the file, we import the class.

```
import oracle.jdbc.pool.OracleDataSource;
```

In the body of the code, we instantiate the class.

```
OracleDataSource ods = new OracleDataSource();
```

Setting DataSource Properties

`DataSource` has getter/setter methods to manage properties, which follow the convention used for JavaBeans. For any property `xyz`, the method to get its current value is called `getXyz()`, and the method to set it is called `setXyz()`. The properties we need to set in order to log into an Oracle database are.

- `driverType`
- `serverName`
- `networkProtocol`
- `databaseName`
- `portNumber`
- `user`
- `password`

Here is the code to set them:

```
ods.setDriverType("thin");
ods.setServerName("noizmaker");
ods.setNetworkProtocol("tcp");
ods.setDatabaseName("osiris");
ods.setPortNumber(1521);
ods.setUser("scott");
ods.setPassword("tiger");
```

Here is a sample program for connecting, using `DataSource` without JNDI:

```
// TestDataSource.java – Load JDBC and connect to database

import java.sql.*;
import oracle.jdbc.driver.*;
import oracle.jdbc.pool.OracleDataSource;

public class TestDataSource {

public static void main(String [] vars)
{
 Connection conn;
 try
 {
     OracleDataSource ods = new OracleDataSource();
```

```
      ods.setDriverType("thin");
      ods.setServerName("noizmaker");
      ods.setNetworkProtocol("tcp");
      ods.setDatabaseName("osiris");
      ods.setPortNumber(1521);
      ods.setUser("david");
      ods.setPassword("bigcat");
      conn = ods.getConnection(); catch (SQLException e)
  }
  catch(SQLException e)
  {
    System.out.println("Caught: " + e);
    System.exit(1);
  }
}
}
```

In the remainder of this chapter we'll use the `DataSource` method to connect using the thin driver.

SCROLLABLE, SENSITIVE, UPDATEABLE RESULTSETS

In the past, it was possible to retrieve records from a result set only in order, one by one, primarily because databases like Oracle retrieved data piece-wise into a buffer of fixed size, and this limitation allowed for a more efficient implementation.

This limitation is reflected in the implementation of the JDBC 1.0 `ResultSet` class, which had a single method for navigating through a `ResultSet`, `next()`. But, like other limitations, this has been overcome, and new releases of Oracle and JDBC feature scrollable `ResultSets`. Scrollability lets you traverse a result set forward and backward. This is furthermore associated with random access of a result set—the ability to access a row by absolute or relative position.

In addition to being scrollable, JDBC 2.0 `ResultSets` can be sensitive, which means that they can reflect changes made to the database while the `ResultSet` is open; `ResultSets` can also be updateable, which means that rows in the `ResultSet` can be changed, added, or deleted.

These features, particularly sensitivity, need to be used with caution, however. The underlying mechanism for obtaining results sets by groups of rows has not changed—navigating between a few widely scattered rows can cause the database to fetch many rows behind the scenes, severely impairing performance.

Scrolling through ResultSets

By default, a ResultSet is not scrollable, and the only way to navigate between rows is to start at the beginning and continue one at a time with the next() method. Sometimes, such as when a user is browsing information interactively, it's useful to be able to reverse direction or to skip forward or backward. To create a scrollable ResultSet, we need to specify this when we call Connection's createStatement()—or createPreparedStatement()—method to get a Statement. It's Statement or PreparedStatement that returns ResultSets to us, after all, when we call the executeQuery() method.

We can't just specify scrollability, however. If you specify one of the new ResultSet features, you must specify them all. The default createStatement() and createPreparedStatement() methods have no parameters. The simplest methods that we can use to specify scrollability have two parameters.

```
createStatement(int resultSetType,
                int resultSetConcurreny)

createPreparedStatement(int resultSetType,
                        int resultSetConcurreny)
```

(There are two more methods that have, in addition, a third parameter to specify holdability which we won't use here.)

The first parameter, resultSetType, actually controls two settings: scrollability and sensitivity. It can take one of the following three values:

```
ResultSet.TYPE_FORWARD_ONLY
ResultSet.TYPE_SCROLL_INSENSITIVE
ResultSet.TYPE_SCROLL_SENSITIVE
```

TYPE_FORWARD_ONLY is the default no-scrolling option we get when we use no parameters; INSENSITIVE is implied. The next two allow our ResultSets to be scrollable and let us select whether they are sensitive or not, as well.

The second parameter, resultSetConcurrency, lets us select whether our ResultSet is updateable. The two options are:

```
ResultSet.CONCUR_READ_ONLY
ResultSet.CONCUR_UPDATABLE
```

Assuming that we've already got a Connection, conn, and we want a Statement, we can select scrollable, insensitive, read-only ResultSets like this:

```
Statement stmt = createStatement(
                        ResultSet.TYPE_SCROLL_INSENSITIVE,
                        ResultSet.CONCUR_READ_ONLY);
```

Now, when we execute a query, we'll be able to navigate it in many different ways. Methods available are:

Sequential	
next()	Moves cursor to next record
previous()	Moves cursor to previous record
Random access	
first()	Moves cursor to first record of ResultSet
last()	Moves cursor to last record of ResultSet
beforeFirst()	Moves cursor before first record of ResultSet
afterLast()	Moves cursor after last record of ResultSet
absolute(int row)	Moves cursor to specified row; counting from the beginning of the ResultSet if positive, from the end if negative
relative(int rows)	Moves cursor specified number of rows, forward if positive, backward if negative
Location information	
lng getRow()	Returns current row number, 0 if no current row
isFirst()	True if cursor is on first row, false otherwise
isLast()	True if cursor is on last row, false otherwise
isBeforeFirst()	True if cursor is before first row, false otherwise
isAfterLast()	True if cursor is after last row, false otherwise

We can easily imagine an application where a user can submit a query and get a window full of results. The user then may have the option to scroll up or down a line or a page at a time (within the limits of the results). The query might be:

```
ResultSet rs = stmt.executeQuery(
  "SELECT NAME, DESCRIPTION, MODEL, PRICE " +
  "FROM PRODUCTS " +
  "WHERE TYPE=' "+ prod_type + "' AND PRICE <= " + price);
```

We'll probably need to tell the user how many pages of results were retrieved. To do that, we need to find out how many rows were returned and divide that number by the number of rows we can display per page, plus one if there is a partial page at the end. There is no direct way to find out the number of rows in a `ResultSet`. We need to move to the last record and call `getRow()`, which returns the current row's number. We'll assume that `ROWS_PER_PAGE` is a symbolic constant set to the number of rows per page and that `rowCount` is a class attribute.

```
rs.last();
int rowCount = rs.getRow();
int pages = rowCount/ROWS_PER_PAGE;
if(pages * ROWS_PER_PAGE < rowCount)
{
  pages++;
}
```

Let's assume that we cache a page's worth of rows locally in a vector as strings. For the query above, we could store each row as a string array of four elements, one for each column in the query. Even though the PRICE column is likely a NUMBER column, calling `getString()` will provide the necessary conversion and is perfectly adequate for display purposes (although we might want to do something about the format in our SQL query). Perhaps we would pass this vector to a display function that formats it as an HTML table for output to a browser. We'll get the number of columns like this:

```
ResultSetMetaData rsmd = rs.getMetaData();
int columnCount = rsmd.getColumnCount();
```

We'll create two methods for updating the vector. One will add a row at the beginning or end, then adjust the vector size back to `ROWS_PER_PAGE`. Another will refresh all the rows in the vector. Both of these methods will start retrieving data from the current row—they are not responsible for navigation. In fact, these low-level methods are responsible for leaving the cursor where they found it so that the higher level method isn't confused.

First, here's our method for reading a row from the database into an array of strings; both of the methods that update the vector will call it.

```
private String [] readRow()
throws SQLException
{
  String [] sArray = new String [columnCount];

  for(int i=1; i<=columnCount; i++)
  {
    sArray[i - 1] = rs.getString(i);
  }
  return sArray;
}
```

Next is our method for filling in the vector with the next ROWS_PER_PAGE rows (or until the next() method stops returning rows). Notice that, because we want to start at the current row but use next() in the loop, we must first move back one row by calling previous().

```
private void fillVector()
throws SQLException
{
  v.clear();
  int startRow = rs.getRow();
  rs.previous();

  for(int i=0; i < ROWS_PER_PAGE && rs.next(); i++)
  {
    v.add(readRow());
  }
  rs.absolute(startRow);
}
```

Our other method for updating the vector will "scroll" it up or down by inserting a row at the beginning and removing one at the end, or by adding a row at the end and removing the row at the beginning. We'll define symbolic constants to indicate the direction of the scroll.

```
private static final int SCROLLUP   = -1;
private static final int SCROLLDOWN =  1;
```

This method will get a row of data, add it, and adjust the vector appropriately.

```
private void scrollVector(int scrollDirection)
  throws SQLException
  {
    System.out.println("scrolling: " + scrollDirection);
    String [] sArray;
    if((sArray = readRow())!=null);
    {
      switch(scrollDirection)
      {
        case SCROLLUP:    if((sArray = readRow())!=null)
                          {
                            v.removeElementAt(v.size()-1);
                            v.insertElementAt(sArray, 0);
                          }
                          break;
```

```
            case SCROLLDOWN: int startRow = rs.getRow();
                             rs.relative(ROWS_PER_PAGE - 1);
                             if((sArray = readRow())!=null)
                             {
                               v.removeElementAt(0);
                               v.add(sArray);
                             }
                             rs.absolute(startRow);
                             break;
          }
        }
      }
```

To navigate the vector in response to the user, we need to move the cursor to the appropriate row and call `fillVector()` if we are displaying a new page as a result of PageUp, PageDown, Home, or End, or call `scrollVector()` if we are moving one row up or down. First, we'll define some symbolic constants to indicate direction. The calling class will provide one of these as a result of user input:

```
public static final int PAGEUP =    1;
public static final int PAGEDOWN =  2;
public static final int HOME =      3;
public static final int END =       4;
public static final int UP =        5;
public static final int DOWN =      6;
```

To navigate the `ResultSet`, we need to move the cursor by translating these into the appropriate call: `previous()` or `next()` for `UP` and `DOWN`; `relative()` for `PAGEUP` or `PAGEDOWN`; and `absolute()` for `HOME` and `END`. We also need to determine the parameters correctly, based on the direction of the move and boundary conditions.

The following public method responds to the navigation request and returns the updated vector:

```
public Vector getDataVector(int move)
  throws SQLException
  {
     /* Note: Only REFRESH is valid if the query
      * returned too few results
      */
    if(pages==1)
    {
       move = REFRESH;
    }
```

```
    int startRow = rs.getRow();
    switch(move)
    {
      case PAGEUP:   if(startRow >= ROWS_PER_PAGE)
                     {
                       rs.relative(-ROWS_PER_PAGE);
                     }
                     break;
      case PAGEDOWN: if(startRow < (rowCount-(ROWS_PER_PAGE*2)))
                     {
                       rs.relative(ROWS_PER_PAGE);
                     }
                     else
                     {
                       rs.absolute(-ROWS_PER_PAGE);
                     }
                     break;
      case HOME:     rs.first();
                     break;
      case END:      rs.absolute(-ROWS_PER_PAGE);
                     break;
      case UP:       if(startRow > 1)
                     {
                       rs.previous();
                     }
                     break;

      case DOWN:     if(startRow <= rowCount - ROWS_PER_PAGE)
                     {
                       rs.next();
                     }
                     break;
      case REFRESH:  startRow = -1;
                     break;
    }

    switch(rs.getRow() - startRow)
    {
      case  0: break; // no move, no action
      case -1: scrollVector(SCROLLUP);
               break;
      case  1: scrollVector(SCROLLDOWN);
               break;
      default: fillVector();
               break;
    }
    return v;
  }
```

To use these methods in an application, we'd put them in a class—for example, `ScrollWindow`. Depending on whether the application wants to manage the database connection and whether the class knows how to determine the database URL, we could have the following constructors:

- `ScrollWindow(String query)`
- `ScrollWindow(ResultSet rs)`
- `ScrollWindow(String username, String password, String query)`

In addition, we'd want to have some public get methods for obtaining `rowCount`, as well as pages. We might also want a set method to allow the user to set the number of rows per page.

Sensitive ResultSets

Our last example was not sensitive to changes in the data. Once the user submits the query, the entire ResultSet is effectively cached. If we want to be able to see changes as they are made by others, we can create our `Statement` object with the `ResultSet.TYPE_SCROLL_SENSITIVE` option. The database will provide the updated record, if it's been changed, when we move to a new row.

```
Statement stmt = createStatement(
                    ResultSet.TYPE_SCROLL_INSENSITIVE,
                          ResultSet.CONCUR_READ_ONLY);
```

In addition, in order for our `ResultSet` to be scroll-sensitive, we must observe the following restrictions on our queries:

- We can select from only a single table.
- We cannot use an ORDER BY clause.
- We cannot use SELECT *. (But, interestingly, we can use "*" with a table alias, such as SELECT T.* FROM *tablename* T.)

If we don't comply with these restrictions, the `ResultSet` will be automatically and silently downgraded to scroll-insensitive. If we attempt to perform operations that are specific to scroll-sensitive results sets, such as `refreshRow()`, we will get an error indicating that the feature is not supported.

Suppose that the following query retrieves a hundred rows, which we display to the user:

```
ResultSet rs = executeQuery("SELECT COL1 FROM TEST");
While(rs.next())
{
   System.out.println(rs.getString(1));
}
```

If someone elsewhere changes a row and we retrieve the hundred rows by moving back to the beginning of the result set and displaying them again, the change will appear.

```
rs.first();
While(rs.next())
{
   System.out.println(rs.getString(1));
}
```

Updates are not always immediately visible, however. By default, Oracle's JDBC driver fetches 10 rows of data at a time. The fetch obtains the most recent data for those 10 rows at that time. As long as we navigate within these 10 rows, Oracle will not perform another fetch; hence, no updates to those rows will be visible. Not until we navigate to a row outside these 10 prefetched rows will Oracle perform another fetch. At that time, Oracle will once again fetch 10 more rows, including any updates, starting with the new current row. We can also update the data by calling the `refreshRow()` method, which will fetch 10 rows, starting with the current row.We can also change the fetch size by calling `setFetchSize()` with the number of rows we want fetched at a time. There is no maximum fetch size, but Oracle recommends 10 as the most effective setting. Poor use of either of the `refreshRow()` or `setFetchSize()` methods can cause serious performance problems, due to either an increased number of round trips to the database or unnecessarily large amounts of data being returned from the database.

Let's take a look at an example of a sensitive `ResultSet`. We'll open two `ResultSets` from two different `Statements`, one sensitive, one not. Using a third `Statement`, we'll change the data and see whether the changes can be seen in the other two.

```
import java.sql.*;

public class Sensitive {

public static void main(String [] vars)
{
 Connection conn;
 String sql;
```

```
try
{
   OracleDataSource ods = new OracleDataSource();
   ods.setDriverType("thin");
   ods.setServerName("noizmaker");
   ods.setNetworkProtocol("tcp");
   ods.setDatabaseName("osiris");
   ods.setPortNumber(1521);
   ods.setUser("david");
   ods.setPassword("bigcat");

   Statement stmtWrite = conn.createStatement();
   Statement stmtInsensitive = conn.createStatement(
                           ResultSet.TYPE_SCROLL_INSENSITIVE,
                           ResultSet.CONCUR_READ_ONLY);
   Statement stmtSensitive = conn.createStatement(
                           ResultSet.TYPE_SCROLL_SENSITIVE,
                           ResultSet.CONCUR_READ_ONLY);

   // Create and populate a table
   stmtWrite.executeUpdate("CREATE TABLE TEST (COL1 NUMBER)");
   for(int i=0; i<20; i++)
   {
     sql = "INSERT INTO TEST VALUES( " + i +")";
     stmtWrite.executeUpdate(sql);
   }

   // Query: get sensitive and insensitive ResultSets
   sql = "SELECT COL1 FROM TEST";
   ResultSet rsInsensitive = stmtInsensitive.executeQuery(sql);
   ResultSet rsSensitive = stmtSensitive.executeQuery(sql);

   // Change table after query
   sql = "UPDATE TEST SET COL1 = COL1 * 10";
   stmtWrite.executeUpdate(sql);

   // Now print out result sets
   System.out.println("Insensitive Sensitive");
   while(rsInsensitive.next()&&rsSensitive.next())
   {
     System.out.print(rsInsensitive.getString(1));
     System.out.print("             ");
     System.out.println(rsSensitive.getString(1));
   }
   rsSensitive.close();
   rsInsensitive.close();
   stmtWrite.close();
```

```
      stmtInsensitive.close();
      stmtSensitive.close();
      conn.close();
    }
    catch (SQLException e)
    {
      System.out.println("Caught:" + e);
    }
  }
}
```

The output from this program is

```
Insensitive Sensitive
0           0
1           1
2           2
3           3
4           4
5           5
6           6
7           7
8           8
9           9
10            100
11            110
12            120
13            130
14            140
15            150
16            160
17            170
18            180
19            190
```

The sequence of events was:

- Create table and data.
- Query table and obtain result set.
- Change table data.
- Retrieve data from result set.

The first column, the results from the insensitive `ResultSet`, are what we expected. They are the values the table held when we queried it.

The second column is not what we might naively expect. The first 10 values are the old values, and the last 10 are the new values. But we know, of course, that 10 values were fetched at the time of the query—the default fetch size—and a new fetch wasn't triggered until we requested a row that wasn't in the first 10 rows.

One experiment you may wish to try is changing the fetch size, to 2 for example, prior to the query to see that only the first two rows keep their stale values.

```
stmtSensitive.setFetchSize(2);
ResultSet rsSensitive = stmtSensitive.executeQuery(sql);
```

You might also try to reverse the order in which you retrieve the rows.

```
rsSensitive.afterLast();
rsInsensitive.afterLast();
while(rsInsensitive.previous()&&rsSensitive.previous())
{
        System.out.print(rsInsensitive.getString(1)+"
");
        System.out.println(rsSensitive.getString(1));
}
```

In this case, because the database doesn't know any better, it fetches the first 10 rows, but right at the start we ask for the last row, so it immediately needs to fetch again, and all the values are the latest.

Updateable ResultSets

A user interface that uses a scrollable `ResultSet` invites the user to browse through the data interactively; depending on the type of application, we may want to allow the user to change the data.

Perhaps we have an on-line store that allows users to place orders. When a user is reviewing an existing order and wants to change it, it's much easier to update the database by changing the row in the `ResultSet` rather than identifying the row, then creating and executing a separate UPDATE statement.

In addition to updating existing rows, updateable `ResultSets` also allow us to delete rows and to insert new rows. It's not required that an updateable `ResultSet` be scrollable, as well, but generally it's easier to manage updates if you can scroll too.

As with scroll-sensitive `ResultSets`, there are important restrictions on the types of queries that are allowed for updateable `ResultSets`.

- We can select from only a single table.
- We cannot use an ORDER BY clause.

- We cannot use SELECT *. (But we can use "*" with a table alias, such as SELECT T.* FROM *tablename* T.)
- Our SELECT statement can include only columns from the table, not expressions or functions.

The `ResultSet` will be automatically downgraded if our query doesn't meet these restrictions and will cause an error when we attempt to perform an update, insert, or delete.

In addition to these general restrictions, we will be able to perform inserts only if we meet the following condition:

- Our SELECT statement must include any columns that are necessary for the insert, such as key and non-nullable columns.

The first step in updating a row is to position the cursor on it by using the `next()` method—or if we're using a scrollable `ResultSet`, using any of the methods, such as `previous()`, `absolute()`, or `relative()`. Next, we set the new value by calling one of the many `updateXXX()` methods, according to the type of column we want to update. The `updateXXX()` methods correspond to the `setXXX()` methods that we use for `PreparedStatements`, and as with the `setXXX()` methods, we can address a column by either its index or its column name. These methods include:

```
updateInt(int columnIndex, int value)
updateInt(String columnName, int value)

updateLong(int columnIndex, long value)
updateLong(String columnName, long value)

updateFloat(int columnIndex, float value)
updateFloat(String columnName, float value)

updateDouble(int columnIndex, double value)
updateDouble(String columnName, double value)

updateString(int columnIndex, String value)
updateString(String columnName, String value)

updateDate(int columnIndex, Date value)
updateDate(String columnName, Date value)

updateTime(int columnIndex, Time value)
updateTime(String columnName, Time value)
```

Once we've updated a column or columns in a `ResultSet` row, we update the database by calling the `updateRow()` method. Assuming that we have a valid connection, we can create a `Statement`, query to obtain a `ResultSet`, and change a value in a row as follows:

```
Statement stmt = conn.createStatement(
                        ResultSet.TYPE_SCROLL_INSENSITIVE,
                        ResultSet.CONCUR_UPDATABLE);
stmt.executeUpdate(
  "CREATE TABLE UPDATE_TEST(COL1 VARCHAR2(25))");
stmt.executeUpdate("INSERT INTO UPDATE_TEST VALUES('Hello')");
stmt.executeUpdate("INSERT INTO UPDATE_TEST VALUES('Goodbye')");

ResultSet rs = stmt.executeQuery("SELECT COL1 FROM UPDATE_TEST");

if(rs.next())
{
    System.out.println(rs.getString(1));
}

rs.updateString(1, "Howdy");
rs.updateRow();
rs.first();
System.out.println(rs.getString(1));
```

To delete an existing row, we position the cursor on the row and call `deleteRow()`. Assuming that we're still on the first row, we can delete the second row as follows:

```
rs.next();
rs.deleteRow();
```

After the delete, the cursor moves to the previous row. (If the cursor was on the first row, it will end up before the first row.) If the `ResultSet` is scrollable, the row numbers of the rows after the deleted row will be adjusted to reflect the deletion.

In addition to changing and deleting existing rows, an updateable `ResultSet` also allows us to insert new rows. In this case, of course, it makes no sense to move to an existing row first. Instead, JDBC provides a special insert row and a method, `moveToInsertRow()`, to move there. Once there, we can call any of the `updateXXX()` methods to set the columns, then at the end call `insertRow()` to perform the actual insert into the database. Suppose that we've already obtained an updateable `ResultSet`, as in the example above. We can insert a row like this:

```
rs.moveToInsertRow();
rs.updateString(1, "This is a test");
rs.insertRow();
```

To move back to the row we were on before moving to the insert row, we can call:

```
rs.moveToCurrentRow();
```

Inserted rows are not visible in the `ResultSet`.

Updating a row and inserting a row, you may have noticed, require two steps: first updating the values in the row, then updating the database by calling either `updateRow()` or `insertRow()`, as appropriate. If you move to another row before calling `updateRow()` or `insertRow()`, the changes are discarded. You can also discard the changes explicitly by calling `cancelRowUpdates()`.

Deleting a row takes just one step: calling `deleteRow()`. This immediately causes the row to be deleted from the database.

All three cases—updating, inserting, and deleting rows—are subject to the normal rules for transactions. It can still be rolled back if it has not been committed—but remember that, by default in JDBC, auto-commit is set to true, so as soon as `updateRow()`, `insertRow()`, or `deleteRow()` are called, the operation is committed.

RowSets

At the heart of every `RowSet` is a `ResultSet`. A `RowSet` can do everything that a `ResultSet` can and more, because the `RowSet` interface extends the `ResultSet` interface. One of the extensions is that a `RowSet` is a JavaBean component; this has important benefits. We can use `RowSets` together with visual JavaBean development tools to develop database applications without needing to do much (or any) coding directly with JDBC. We can also register listeners, such as windows, with a `RowSet` so they are notified to update themselves whenever data changes.

There are two general types of `RowSets`. Three specific implementations have been proposed for these so far:

- Connected RowSets: `JDBCRowSet`
- Disconnected RowSets: `CachedRowSet`, `WebRowSet`

A JDBC `RowSet` is a connected `RowSet`. It is connected at all times in the same way that a `ResultSet` is because it is, in effect, just a thin wrapper on `ResultSet` that provides JavaBean functionality. It is not serializable.

A cached RowSet is a *disconnected* RowSet. A cached RowSet connects initially to obtain its data but then disconnects. The ResultSet data is cached in memory. Changes can be made to the RowSet in memory, using the same update method that we used for updateable ResultSets. When we apply the changes to the database, the RowSet will reconnect to the database.

A cached RowSet is also serializable, which means that we can save it in a file or send it to another computer. We can browse it and change the RowSet using the same interface as a ResultSet, even though we no longer have access to a JDBC driver or the database. After we're finished making changes, we can serialize it again and send it back to a computer with access to the database in order to apply the changes we made off-line.

A WebRowSet is an extension of a CachedRowSet that can present its data as an XML document.

At the time of this writing, Sun has only Early Access implementations of each proposed type of RowSet; they are described as experimental and unsupported technology.

Oracle 9i includes an implementation of two types: a JDBC RowSet, OracleJDBCRowSet; and a cached RowSet, OracleCachedRowSet.

We will examine only the two Oracle implementations here.

RowSet Setup

To use Oracle's RowSet implementations we first need to add another entry to our CLASSPATH.

```
CLASSPATH=current_entries;{ORACLE_HOME}/ jdbc/lib/ocrs12.zip
```

In our source code we need to add two or three imports. To be able to access the Oracle RowSet implementations we need to add

```
import oracle.jdbc.rowset.*;
```

The RowSet interface is defined in the javax.sql package, so we'll need to add that too.

```
import javax.sql.*;
```

If we are going to be serializing RowSets to files, we'll also need to add

```
import java.io.*;
```

What we do next depends on which RowSet we'll be using. We'll take a look at both cached and JDBC RowSet examples.

Using a Cached RowSet

Assuming that our environment is set up and our source code imports the appropriate packages, the next step in using a `RowSet` is instantiating it. We instantiate Oracle's cached `RowSet` implementation, `OracleCachedRowSet`, like any other class, using the default constructor.

```
OracleCachedRowSet rowset = new OracleCachedRowSet();
```

We can populate the `RowSet` in two ways. We can use an existing `ResultSet` and call the `populate()` method. Assuming that we have a `ResultSet rs`, we could call populate like this:

```
rowset.populate(rs);
```

More typically, however, we provide the `RowSet` with the information it needs to connect to the database and the SQL query we want it to use. Because `RowSet` is a JavaBeans component, we provide it with information by calling setter methods. In particular, we need to set the database URL, username, and password. According to JavaBeans conventions, these methods start with `set`, followed by the property name, with the first letter of each property capitalized. Username and password each count as single words; the query goes into a property called `command`.

```
rowset.setUrl ("jdbc:oracle:thin:@noizmaker:1521:osiris");
rowset.setUsername ("david");
rowset.setPassword ("bigcat");
rowset.setCommand ("SELECT COL1 FROM TEST");
```

To connect and populate the `RowSet`, we call the `execute()` method.

```
rowset.execute();
```

Once we've done this, we can navigate the rowset exactly as though it were a `ResultSet`.

```
while(rowset.next())
{
   System.out.println(rowset.getInt(1));
}
```

In addition (or instead), we can serialize it and send it over the network, write it to a file and email it to a remote user, or download it to a handheld computer. The `RowSet` can be deserialized—turned back into an object—and used, even if there is no access to the database or JDBC. After making changes, a remote user could reserialize the updated RowSet and send it back so that the changes can be applied to the database.

To serialize a RowSet and write it to a file, we need to wrap FileOutputStream with the ObjectOutputStream class and call the ObjectOutputStream's writeObject() method.

```
String filename = "test.ser";
FileOutputStream outStream = new FileOutputStream(filename);
ObjectOutputStream objOut = new ObjectOutputStream(outStream);
objOut.writeObject(rowset);
objOut.close();
```

To deserialize a RowSet—read a serialized RowSet into an object for use in a program—we use FileInputStream and ObjectInputStream and call the ObjectInputStream's readObect() method.

```
FileInputStream inStream = new FileInputStream(filename);
ObjectInputStream objIn = new ObjectInputStream(inStream);
RowSet newrowset = (RowSet) objIn.readObject();
objIn.close();
```

Here, we've read the RowSet into a new object, newrowset. We can navigate this just like the original RowSet we've effectively cloned. Note that it preserves the state of the RowSet at the time we serialized; if we read through the original RowSet and left the cursor pointing after the last row, we'll need to move it back to the beginning by calling the RowSet's beforeFirst() method if we want to read it from beginning to end again.

```
newrowset.beforeFirst();
for(int i = 0; newrowset.next(); i++)
{
   System.out.println("row " + i +": " + newrowset.getInt(1));
}
```

Updating through a Cached RowSet

By default, a RowSet is scrollable but is set to read-only. To be able to update, we need to set the readOnly property to false. (There is also a concurrency property that we can set to ResultSet.CONCUR_UPDATABLE, but this has no effect in OracleCachedRowSet.) Notice that we can do this even with a RowSet that was previously serialized.

```
newrowset.setReadOnly(false);
```

Now we can perform an update exactly as we did with an updateable `ResultSet`, position the cursor, update the column (or columns), then update the row.

```
newrowset.last();
newrowset.updateInt(1,9999);
newrowset.updateRow();
```

We need to do one more thing to actually connect and store the changes in the database, call the `OracleCachedRowSet`'s `acceptChanges()` method.

```
newrowset.acceptChanges();
```

To execute this method, our program will once again need to use a JDBC driver and make a connection to the database. (Presumably our program would have different startup options that determine whether or not it should try to connect to the database.) After calling `acceptChanges()`, the database will no longer be serializable. If you need to update and serialize a number of times, you should call `acceptChanges()` only once, at the end.

In order for `RowSets` to be updateable they must comply with the same restrictions that apply to updateable `ResultSets`:

- We can select from only a single table.
- We cannot use an ORDER BY clause.
- We cannot use SELECT *. (But we can use a table alias, such as SELECT T.* FROM *tablename* T.)
- Our SELECT statement can include only columns from the table, not expressions or functions.

If we want to be able to perform inserts, we must also ensure that we meet the following condition:

- Our SELECT statement must include any columns that are necessary for the insert, such as key and non-nullable columns.

Finally, we also must remain attentive to the fact that cached `RowSets` are held in memory and make sure that they are not too large, especially if they are to be used in small devices, such as PDAs or handheld PCs with limited memory.

JDBC RowSets

A JDBC `RowSet`, like any `RowSet`, extends a `ResultSet` to provide a JavaBean interface. Unlike a `CachedRowSet`, however, it does not store the

ResultSet in memory but instead keeps open a JDBC connection to the database for the life of the RowSet.

A JDBCRowSet is best suited for building applications that use Swing/AWT and other JavaBean components. A JDBCRowSet can potentially allow us to build a live data view. Not only can the user change the data in a JTable view (which is already possible with a ResultSet), but the view can also be notified of changes in the database so that it can update the view.

As a JavaBean, a JDBCRowSet is more conveniently implemented using a visual builder tool, with a minimum amount of handwritten code.

Applications that include a graphical user interface (GUI) that presents data to a user and allows the user to manipulate it are commonly designed using the Model-View-Controller (MVC) pattern. In this pattern, the Model is a class that represents the data, the View is a class that displays the data, and the Controller is a class the provides the user with a means of manipulating the data by interacting with the display, keyboard, and mouse. Here, we are interested in the interaction of the Model and the View.

Java's toolkit for building graphical interfaces has a class for representing tabular data, JTable, that is well suited to displaying data from a database. The important thing to note about a JTable is that Java's designers intend for it to be used as the view: It does not contain any data. It expects a companion class, a model, to hold the data.

In order for the JTable to be able to obtain data from the model, the model needs to implement an interface, TableModel, that specifies the methods that the table will use to get information from the model. These include such things as: getColumnCount(), getRowCount(), getColumnClass(), getValueAt(int row, int col), and setValueAt(Object value, int row, int col). Our model will include a JDBCRowSet that it will use to implement each of these calls. Here is the beginning of the class, including the constructor. Note that we cache a few values, such as the number of rows, ahead of time:

```
public class RowSetModel extends AbstractTableModel {

int rows;
String[] columnNames = {};
OracleJDBCRowSet rowset = new OracleJDBCRowSet ();
ResultSetMetaData  metaData;

    public RowSetModel()
    {
          try
          {
  rowset.setUrl(
```

```
              "jdbc:oracle:thin:@noizmaker:1521:osiris");
            rowset.setUsername("david");
            rowset.setPassword("bigcat");
            rowset.setType(ResultSet.TYPE_SCROLL_SENSITIVE);
            rowset.setConcurrency(ResultSet.CONCUR_UPDATABLE);
            rowset.setCommand(
             "SELECT NAME, DESCRIPTION, PRICE FROM PRODUCTS");
            rowset.execute();
            metaData = rowset.getMetaData();
            int numberOfColumns =  metaData.getColumnCount();
            columnNames = new String[numberOfColumns];
            for(int column = 0;
                   column < numberOfColumns; column++)
            {
                columnNames[column] =
                       metaData.getColumnLabel(column+1);
            }
            rowset.last();
            rows = rowset.getRow();
            fireTableChanged(null);
        }
        catch (SQLException e)
        {
            System.err.println("Caught: " + e);
        }
    }
```

Because we want our view to be live, we set type to `TYPE_SCROLL_SENSITIVE`. And because we want to be able to update values, we need to set the concurrency to `CONCUR_UPDATABLE`.

Here are the methods we're required to implement. We use strings for all columns—this isn't necessarily recommended, but it works here, thanks to automatic conversions.

```
public String getColumnName(int column)
{
    if (columnNames[column] != null) {
        return columnNames[column];
    } else {
        return "";
    }
}

public Class getColumnClass(int column)
{
        return String.class;
```

```
    }

    public boolean isCellEditable(int row, int column)
    {
        try {
            return metaData.isWritable(column+1);
        }
        catch (SQLException e) {
            return false;
        }
    }

    public int getColumnCount()
    {
        return columnNames.length;
    }

    public int getRowCount() {
        return rows;
        }

        public Object getValueAt(int aRow, int aColumn)
        {
        String s = null;
        try
        {
        rowset.absolute(aRow+1);
        s = rowset.getString(aColumn+1);
        System.out.println("retrieved: " + s);
        }
        catch (SQLException e)
        {
        System.out.println("Caught: " + e);
        }
        return s;
        }

    public void setValueAt(Object value, int row, int column)
    {
        try
        {
         rowset.absolute(row+1);
         rowset.updateString(column + 1, (String) value);
         rowset.updateRow();
        }
        catch (SQLException e)
        {
```

```
            //     e.printStackTrace()**;
            System.err.println("Update failed: " + e);
        }
    }
```

To create a `JTable`, our View class will first instantiate the `RowSetModel`, then will pass this model to the `JTable` constructor.

```
public class RowSetView implements RowSetListener {

    public RowSetView ()
    {
        JFrame frame = new JFrame("Table");
        frame.addWindowListener(new WindowAdapter() {
            public void windowClosing(WindowEvent e)
                                {System.exit(0);}});

        RowSetModel rsm = new RowSetModel();

        // Create the table
        JTable tableView = new JTable(rsm);
        rsm.addRowSetListener((RowSetListener)this);

        JScrollPane scrollpane = new JScrollPane(tableView);
        scrollpane.setPreferredSize(new Dimension(700, 300));

        frame.getContentPane().add(scrollpane);
        frame.pack();
        frame.setVisible(true);
    }
```

So far, our example will update values in the database if we change them in our data window. The values in the data window will also change when we scroll through them with the cursor if they've changed in the database.

It is possible to register a listener with the `RowSet` so that we can update our view automatically. First, we need to create a listener.

```
class MyListener implements RowSetListener {

  public void cursorMoved(RowSetEvent event)
  {
  }
  public void rowChanged(RowSetEvent event)
  {
  }

  public void rowSetChanged(RowSetEvent event)
```

```
    {
        fireTableDataChanged();
    }

}
```

Then we need to register the listener in the constructor.

```
MyListener rowsetListener =  new MyListener ();
           rowset.addRowSetListener (rowsetListener);
```

There are still a number of user interface issues that need to be solved in order to fully implement this, however, and we won't consider this further except to note again that there are JavaBean development tools that facilitate building applications from components such as `RowSets`.

Using Oracle Object-Relational Features with JDBC

So far, we've seen in this chapter and in the previous one how we can use Java with relational data. We've recommended putting JDBC and SQL functionality in their own classes as a separate layer to isolate the rest of the application from the details of how data is stored. But the rest of the application still has to deal with the fact that the data is not represented as objects.

We've also seen that Oracle will allow us to define our own object types. If we're using objects in Oracle, it's easy to "flatten" them to look like standard relational objects by using the appropriate SQL queries, but this is really defeating the purpose of Oracle's object-relational features—though there may be situations where this is expedient.

It would be really convenient to store and retrieve Oracle objects and use them as objects in Java. There are, in fact, two ways to do this. The first is to use the weakly typed default Java class for a database object, `Struct`. The second is to create strongly typed custom classes in Java for Oracle objects.

Weakly Typed Objects

`Structs` are more efficient than are custom classes and are far easier to set up; their disadvantage is that they can't be fully integrated into your application architecture because they are defined dynamically—you might think of them as second-class classes.

Selecting Structs

Retrieving an Oracle object as a weakly typed `Struct` is as simple as using the `ResultSet`'s `getObject()` method and assigning it either the standard JDBC `Struct` type or Oracle's `STRUCT` type.

Our first example shows the steps necessary for retrieving an object using the standard Java `Struct`. First, we'll create an object type using SQL*Plus.

```
SQL> CREATE TYPE ELEMENT_TYPE AS OBJECT (
       ATOMIC_NUMBER NUMBER, --  can't name a column NUMBER
       SYMBOL VARCHAR2(2),
       NAME   VARCHAR2(20),
       MASS   NUMBER
     );
     /

Type created.
```

We'll create a table that includes the object type.

```
SQL> CREATE TABLE PERIODIC_TABLE (
       PERIOD          NUMBER,
       COLUMN_GROUP    NUMBER,   -- can't name a column GROUP
       ELEMENT ELEMENT_TYPE
     );

Table created.
```

And we'll insert some data.

```
SQL> INSERT INTO PERIODIC_TABLE
      VALUES (1,1, ELEMENT_TYPE(1, 'H', 'Hydrogen', 1.008));

1 row created.

SQL> INSERT INTO PERIODIC_TABLE
      VALUES (1,8, ELEMENT_TYPE(2, 'He', 'Helium', 4.003));

1 row created.

SQL> INSERT INTO PERIODIC_TABLE
      VALUES (2,1, ELEMENT_TYPE(3, 'Li', 'Lithium', 6.941));

1 row created.
```

Back in Java, assuming we have valid `Statement` object, `stmt`, we can query the table like this:

```
ResultSet rs = stmt.executeQuery(
  "SELECT SELECT PERIOD, COLUMN_GROUP, ELEMENT" +
  "FROM PERIODIC_TABLE");
```

We can retrieve the first two columns, which are a standard SQL type, using `getInt()`.

```
int period = rs.getInt(1);
int group = rs.getInt(2);
```

The third column, which is the ELEMENT_TYPE, we retrieve using `getObject()`, but we need to cast it to a `STRUCT` (or `Struct`) and assign it to a `STRUCT` object.

```
STRUCT elementStruct = (STRUCT) rs.getObject(3);
```

We can retrieve the object attributes—also known as the *fields* or *properties* of the object—from a `STRUCT` in the form of an `Object` array by calling the `Struct` `getAttributes()` method.

```
Object elementAttr[] = elementStruct.getAttributes();
```

The `getAttributes()` method effectively retrieves each of the object's attributes and maps it to an appropriate Java type, as defined by the connection's type map table, if it has one; otherwise, the default SQL to Java mappings are used. When we read an attribute from the `Object` array, we need to cast the attribute to its actual type. Table 9–1 lists the essential type mappings.

TABLE 9–1 Basic SQL to Java Type Mappings

Oracle SQL type	*Java type*
VARCHAR2,CHAR	String
NUMBER	BigDecimal
DATE	Date

The NUMBER type mapping to `BigDecimal` is necessary to hold any possible value of NUMBER, but it's rarely the most appropriate Java type. We usually have to perform a conversion, based on our knowledge of the data, by calling one of `BigDecimal`'s `xxxValue()` methods, such as `intValue()` or `doubleValue()`, to get an appropriate Java primitive type.

The first attribute, atomic weight, is a NUMBER in the database. We can call `BigDecimal`'s `intValue()` method to convert it to `int`—the most appropriate Java type for atomic weight.

```
int atomic_number = ((BigDecimal)elementAttr[0]).intValue();
```

The second and third attributes, atomic symbol and name, are both VARCHAR2, so they will automatically be Strings.

```
String symbol =  (String) elementAttr[1];
String name =    (String) elementAttr[2];
```

If a String is retrieved from an object array by casting an element to a string and it looks like hexadecimal gibberish—when you print it out, for example—you probably need to add [ORACLE_HOME]/jdbc/lib/nls_charset12.zip to your CLASSPATH.

The fourth parameter, atomic mass, is also an SQL NUMBER, which we'll get as a `BigDecimal`. The most appropriate Java type is `float`, so we'll use the `BigDecimal floatValue()` method.

```
float mass = ((BigDecimal) elementAttr[3]).floatValue();
```

An alternative to using the `getAttributes()` method is to use the `getOracleAttributes()` method. This returns the attributes as Oracle JDBC datatypes, such as `NUMBER` and `CHAR`. These have conversion methods to standard Java types.

```
Object elementAttr[] = elementStruct.getOracleAttributes();
int atomic_number = ((NUMBER) elementAttr[0]).intValue();
String symbol =     ((CHAR)   elementAttr[1]).toString();
String name =       ((CHAR)   elementAttr[2]).toString();
float mass =        ((NUMBER) elementAttr[3]).floatValue();
```

Performing the conversion from Oracle JDBC types to Java types ourselves has the advantage that we avoid unnecessary intermediate conversions.

Inserting and Updating Object Types

Unfortunately, the standard Java `Struct` doesn't provide a way to create a new `Struct`—we can obtain one only by selecting an object type from the database. Fortunately, Oracle's `STRUCT` has additional functionality, including a means of creating a new `STRUCT` that we can insert into the database. Because we're working closely with Oracle-specific object-relational features anyway, there's little benefit to be gained by choosing the standard option and lots of benefit to be gained from Oracle's extensions, so we'll use only the Oracle `STRUCT` in these examples.

When we retrieve an object type from the database into a STRUCT, the JDBC driver obtains the information it needs to create the STRUCT and the attributes array from the database, behind the scenes. If we want to create a STRUCT object from scratch and insert it into the database, we need to obtain the same information about the object type from the database ourselves—this information comes in the form of an object called a StructDescriptor, which is unique to Oracle's implementation.

To use STRUCT and the StructDescriptor classes, we need to import the Oracle JDBC classes at the top of our source file.

```
import oracle.sql.*;
```

To get a StructDescriptor, we call a static method, createDescriptor(), with the name of the object type and a valid connection to the database. Here is how we obtain the descriptor for our ELEMENT_TYPE:

```
String elemTypeName = "ELEMENT_TYPE";
StructDescriptor elemDesc =
   StructDescriptor.createDescriptor(elemTypeName, conn);
```

StructDescriptor has a number of interesting methods. One of these, getMetaData(), returns metadata about the object type in the form of a ResultSetMetaData object.

```
ResultSetMetaData elemMetaData = elemDesc.getMetaData();
```

We can obtain information about the object's attributes by calling ResultMetaData methods, such as getColumnCount(), getColumnName(), getColumnType(), and getColumnTypeName().

```
int columns = elemMetaData.getColumnCount();
System.out.println("Number of attributes: " + columns);
System.out.println("Attributes: ");
for(int i = 1; i <= columns; i++)
{
   System.out.print(elemMetaData.getColumnName(i)+"     ");
   System.out.println(elemMetaData.getColumnTypeName(i));
}
```

Unlike the standard Java Struct, Oracle's STRUCT has a public constructor that we can call. It requires a StructDescriptor, a Connection, and an array of objects for the attributes. First, we'll create and populate an attributes array.

```
Object [] elemAttr = new Object [4];
elemAttr[0] = new BigDecimal(4);     // Atomic number
elemAttr[1] = "Be";                  // symbol
```

```
elemAttr[2] = "Beryllium";           // name
elemAttr[3] = new BigDecimal(9.012);// mass
```

Now we have all the parts we need to call the `STRUCT` constructor.

```
STRUCT elemStruct = new STRUCT(elemDesc, conn, elemAttr);
```

We can use this `STRUCT` to perform an INSERT into the PERIODIC _TABLE table in two ways. We can use it with `PreparedStatement`.

```
PreparedStatement ps = conn.prepareStatement(
    "INSERT INTO PERIODIC_TABLE VALUES(?, ?, ?)");
ps.setInt(1, 2); // period
ps.setInt(2, 2); // group
ps.setObject(3, elemStruct);
int rows = ps.executeUpdate();
```

Alternatively, if we have an updateable result set, we can use that to perform an insert. We'll add another record this way. To obtain an updateable result set, you may remember we need to set type and concurrency when we create our `Statement`.

```
Statement stmt = conn.createStatement(
  ResultSet.TYPE_SCROLL_INSENSITIVE,
  ResultSet.CONCUR_UPDATABLE);
ResultSet rs = stmt.executeQuery(
  "SELECT SELECT PERIOD, COLUMN_GROUP, ELEMENT" +
  "FROM PERIODIC_TABLE");
```

We'll need to create a new `STRUCT` but because the `StructDescriptor` is associated with the object type and not any particular table or object, we can reuse it. We'll keep the same attributes array, but we'll assign new values to it.

```
elemAttr[0] = new BigDecimal(5);    // Atomic number
elemAttr[1] = "B";                  // symbol
elemAttr[2] = "Boron";              // name
elemAttr[3] = new BigDecimal(10.81);// mass
elemStruct = new STRUCT(elemDesc, conn, elemAttr);
```

To perform the insert using the `ResultSet`, we move to the insert row, update each of the fields using the appropriate `updateXXX()` method—`updateObject()` is the one we need for our `STRUCT`—then we call `insertRow()`.

```
rs.moveToInsertRow();
rs.updateInt(1,2);  // period
rs.updateInt(2,13); // group
rs.updateObject(3, elemStruct);
rs.insertRow();
```

Strongly Typed Objects

`STRUCT` is a one-size-fits-all, easy-to-use class that will accommodate any Oracle object type. But if you want a strongly typed class of your own design that fits into your application's design, you can do that, too, by implementing either the `SQLData` or the `ORAData` interface in the class definition. Once we register our `SQLData` or `ORAData` class with the JDBC driver's type map, we can read and write objects of this class automatically, using standard JDBC calls.

Implementing Custom Classes with the SQLData Interface

We'll take a look at the Java standard `SQLData` interface first. The `SQLData` interface requires that we implement three methods:

```
getSQLTypeName();
readSQL(SQLInput stream, String typeName);
writeSQL(SQLOutput stream);
```

In addition, we need to provide a public, parameterless constructor that the JDBC driver can call.

```
public classname()
{
}
```

For this example, we'll use the ELEMENT_TYPE object type we created above. Each row of the table must correspond to an object in Java; to do this we need to make a table with a single column of type ELEMENT_TYPE—an object table won't work, interestingly enough, because it appears to be a relational table with columns corresponding to the object attributes.

```
SQL> CREATE TABLE ELEMENTS (ELEMENT ELEMENT_TYPE);

Table created.
```

Let's create a Java class, `Element`, to correspond to the Oracle ELEMENT_TYPE. We'll include the Oracle typename, as well as private instance variables to hold the object's attributes.

```
public class Element implements SQLData {
  private static final String typeName="ELEMENT_TYPE";
  private int    number;
  private String symbol;
  private String name;
  private float  weight;
```

The first SQLData method that we'll implement, getSQLTypeName(), is trivial. Because we associate our class with the Oracle object by hard-coding the object's SQL type name, we just need to return that string.

```
public String getSQLTypeName()
{
  return typeName;
}
```

The next method that we'll implement, readSQL(), requires us to read a stream from the database, calling the appropriate readXXX() method for each attribute of ELEMENT_TYPE, in the order of their appearance in the object type, to populate our instance variables.

```
public void readSQL(SQLInput inStream, String typeName)
throws SQLException
{
 number = inStream.readInt();
 symbol = inStream.readString();
 name   = inStream.readString();
 weight = inStream.readFloat();
}
```

The last method we need to implement, writeSQL(), is similar to readSQL()—it requires us to write to a stream, calling the appropriate writeXXX() method for each attribute of ELEMENT_TYPE in the proper order.

```
public void writeSQL(SQLOutput outStream)
throws SQLException
{
  outStream.writeInt(number);
  outStream.writeString(symbol);
  outStream.writeString(name);
  outStream.writeFloat(weight);
}
```

Finally, we need to provide this constructor:

```
public Element()
{
}
```

That is all that's required to create the custom class, but as we'll see, we may want to create another constructor and other methods to make it easier to use the `Element` class and to hide some of the database details from client classes.

In order for it to use our class, we need to let the JDBC driver know that it exists and that it corresponds to the Oracle ELEMENT_TYPE. By default, when we retrieve an object from a `ResultSet`, it will map it to a `STRUCT`. To get ELEMENT_TYPE objects mapped to the `Element` class, we need to create or extend the JDBC connection's type map.

Updating the SQL-Java Type Map

The JDBC type map is an implementation of the `Map` interface. It maps a key—in this case, an SQL typename—to a value—in this case, a Java class. There is a type map automatically associated with a connection. We can retrieve it like this:

```
Map typeMap = conn.getTypeMap();
```

As long as it implements the `Map` interface, the actual class of the type map isn't important, but as it happens, it is a `Hashtable`. (And, until we add something to it, it is initially empty.) To add the mapping for ELEMENT _TYPE, we call the `Map put()` method with the typename and the Java class; we get the Java class by calling the `Class.forName()` method.

```
typeMap.put("ELEMENT_TYPE", Class.forName("Element");
```

This map entry causes the JDBC driver to map the Oracle object type ELEMENT_TYPE to the Java `Element` type when we retrieve the object from the database.

Using Custom Classes

Once we've mapped our class to the corresponding object type, we can retrieve an object from the `ResultSet` using the `getObject()` method. The JDBC driver will create a class object by calling our parameterless constructor and will populate it by calling our `readSQL()` class. In this example, we use a `PreparedStatement` to select a particular element by atomic number.

```
PreparedStatement ps = conn.prepareStatement(
      "SELECT * FROM ELEMENTS E " +
      "WHERE E.ELEMENT.ATOMIC_NUMBER = ?");
ps.setInt(1, number);
```

```
ResultSet rs = executePSQuery(ps);
ResultSet rs = ps.executeQuery();
Element e = null;
if(rs.next())
{
      e = (Element) rs.getObject(1);
}
```

To insert an `Element` object into the database, we first need to create it. We could call the default constructor, then set the attributes, but we'll create another constructor, for convenience, instead.

```
public Element(String typeName, int number, String symbol,
     String name, float weight)
throws SQLException
{
    // this.typeName = typeName;
    this.number = number;
    this.symbol = symbol;
    this.name = name;
    this.weight = weight;
}
```

In the following example, we'll call this constructor, then insert it by using a `PreparedStatement`:

```
e = new Element("ELEMENT_TYPE",
    number, symbol, name, weight);
getConnection();
PreparedStatement ps = conn.prepareStatement(
  "INSERT INTO ELEMENTS VALUES (?)");
ps.setObject(1, e);
ps.executeQuery();
ps.close();
```

In this case, the JDBC driver calls our `getSQLTypeName()` method to determine the Oracle type, then calls our `writeSQL()` to get our class's attributes.

The examples above may suggest that the client class accesses the database to read and write `Element` objects—that is one possible implementation. Below is a more complete example that encapsulates all the database access in the `Element` class itself. A client application is expected to create and get an `Element` object using the static factory methods `getElement()` and `createElement()`. However, there is nothing except good manners to prevent it from calling the default constructor, which must be public—though this will allow it to insert only an empty object.

```
// Element.java
import java.sql.*;
import oracle.jdbc.pool.OracleDataSource;
import oracle.jdbc.driver.*;
import oracle.sql.*;
import java.math.BigDecimal;
import java.util.*;

public class Element implements SQLData {
  private static Connection conn = null;
  private static boolean typeMapSet = false;
  private static final String typeName="DAVID.ELEMENT_TYPE";
  private int    number;
  private String symbol;
  private String name;
  private float  weight;

  /* Constructors */
  public Element()
  {
  }

  private Element(int number, String symbol,
     String name, float weight)
  throws SQLException
  {
     // this.typeName = typeName;
     this.number = number;
     this.symbol = symbol;
     this.name = name;
     this.weight = weight;
   }

   // Interface implementation ...
    public String getSQLTypeName()
    {
      return typeName;
    }

      public void readSQL(SQLInput inStream, String typeName)
      throws SQLException
      {
      // typeName = typeName; already set
      number = inStream.readInt();
      symbol = inStream.readString();
      name   = inStream.readString();
      weight = inStream.readFloat();
      }
```

```
public void writeSQL(SQLOutput outStream)
throws SQLException
{
  outStream.writeInt(number);
  outStream.writeString(symbol);
  outStream.writeString(name);
  outStream.writeFloat(weight);
}

// utility methods
public static Connection getConnection()
throws SQLException
{
  if(conn==null)
  {
    OracleDataSource ods = new OracleDataSource();
    ods.setDriverType("thin");
    ods.setServerName("noizmaker");
    ods.setNetworkProtocol("tcp");
    ods.setDatabaseName("osiris");
    ods.setPortNumber(1521);
    ods.setUser("david");
    ods.setPassword("bigcat");
    conn = ods.getConnection();
  }
  setTypeMap();
  return conn;
}

private static void setTypeMap()
 throws SQLException
{
  if(!typeMapSet)
  {
    Map typeMap = conn.getTypeMap();
    try
    {
       typeMap.put(typeName, Class.forName("Element"));
       typeMapSet = true;
    }
    catch (ClassNotFoundException e)
    {
      System.out.println("Caught: " + e);
    }
  }
}

 // Access methods
    // Create new Element
```

```
public static Element createElement(int number, String symbol,
  String name, float weight)
throws SQLException
{
  getConnection();
  Element e = null;
  if((e = getElement(number)) == null)
  {
    e = new Element(number, symbol, name, weight);
    PreparedStatement ps = conn.prepareStatement(
      "INSERT INTO ELEMENTS VALUES (?)");
    ps.setObject(1, e);
    ps.executeQuery();
    ps.close();
  }
  return e;
}

public static Element getElement(int number)
throws SQLException
{
  getConnection();
  PreparedStatement ps = conn.prepareStatement(
        "SELECT * FROM ELEMENTS E " +
        "WHERE E.ELEMENT.ATOMIC_NUMBER = ?");
  ps.setInt(1, number);
  return executePSQuery(ps);
}

public static Element getElement(String symbol)
throws SQLException
{
  getConnection();
  PreparedStatement ps = conn.prepareStatement(
        "SELECT * FROM ELEMENTS E " +
        "WHERE E.ELEMENT.SYMBOL = ?");
  ps.setString(1, symbol);
  return executePSQuery(ps);
}

private static Element executePSQuery(PreparedStatement ps)
throws SQLException
{
  Element e = null;
  ResultSet rs = ps.executeQuery();
  while(rs.next())
  {
    e = (Element) rs.getObject(1);
  }
```

```
      rs.close();
      ps.close();
      return e;
    }

    int getNumber()
    {
      return number;
    }

    String getSymbol()
    {
      return symbol;
    }

    String getName()
    {
      return name;
    }

    float getWeight()
    {
      return weight;
    }

    int getNeutrons()
    {
      return Math.round(weight) - number;
    }
}
```

This is a trivial example of how a client application could use the `Element` class:

```
// Molecule.java - uses Element
import java.sql.*;

public class Molecule {

  public static void main(String [] args)
  {
    try
    {
     Element.createElement(
        1, "H", "Hydrogen", 1.008F);

      Element.createElement(
        8, "O", "Oxygen", 15.999F);

      Element hydrogen = Element.getElement("H");
```

```
        Element oxygen   = Element.getElement("O");

        System.out.println("Elem: " + oxygen.getName());
        System.out.println("  Neutrons (avg): "
           + oxygen.getNeutrons());
        System.out.println("Elem: " + hydrogen.getName());
        System.out.println("  Neutrons (avg): "
           + hydrogen.getNeutrons());
      }
      catch (SQLException e)
      {
        System.out.println("Caught: " + e);
      }
    }
  }
```

Implementing Custom Classes with the ORAData Interface

Oracle's proprietary `ORAData` interface offers performance advantages over the `SQLData` interface because it does not automatically perform conversions from SQL types to Java types.

Another advantage is that we do not have to update the connection's type map, because the object is passed to and from our class as an Oracle `STRUCT`. (The method signatures actually specify `Datum`, but that is a superclass of `STRUCT`.) Our class is responsible for conversion of the `STRUCT`'s attributes to and from Java types. An alternative is to keep the attributes in their SQL format and let the client class perform the conversion, if the client class is database-savvy. If calculations need to be performed on the attributes, it may be more efficient and accurate to defer conversion.

Creating a custom class using the `ORAData` interface actually requires that we implement two interfaces: `ORAData` and `ORADataFactory`. Each of these requires that we implement one method. The `ORADataFactory` interface requires that we implement a `create()` method that takes a `Datum` and returns a populated instance of our class.

```
public ORAData create(Datum d, int sqlType) throws SQLException
{
  if(d==null)
  {
    return null;
  }
  Object [] attributes = ((STRUCT) d).getOracleAttributes();
  System.out.println("Datum is" + d.getClass().getName());
  return new OraDataElement(
     ((NUMBER) attributes[0]).intValue(),
```

```
    ((CHAR)attributes[1]).toString(),
    ((CHAR)attributes[2]).toString(),
    ((NUMBER) attributes[3]).floatValue());
}
```

Converting the `Datum` is identical to what we did when we used `STRUCT`s directly as weakly typed classes. After casting the `Datum` to a `STRUCT`, we obtain the attributes in an object array by calling the `getAttributes()` or `getOracleAttributes()` method, depending on whether we want Java types or Oracle JDBC datatypes.

The `ORAData` interface requires that we implement a `toDatum()` method that converts the attributes of our class and returns them as a `STRUCT`. Creating a `STRUCT`, you may remember, requires us to get a `StructDescriptor` and stuff our attributes into an object array.

```
public Datum toDatum(Connection conn) throws SQLException
  {
    StructDescriptor sd =
      StructDescriptor.createDescriptor("ELEMENT_TYPE", conn);
      Object [] attributes = {
        new NUMBER(number),
        new CHAR(symbol, CHAR.DEFAULT_CHARSET),
        new CHAR(name, CHAR.DEFAULT_CHARSET),
        new NUMBER(weight)};
      return new STRUCT(sd, conn, attributes);
  }
```

It doesn't matter in this case whether we provide Oracle JDBC types or Java types, like we did before—i.e., `BigDecimal` in place of NUMBER and `String` in place of CHAR—the driver will determine and perform the appropriate conversion in either case.

In addition to these interface requirements, we also must provide a way for the client application to obtain an instance of our class that implements the `ORADataFactory` class. (This can be a separate class from our `ORAData` class, but here, our custom class implements both interfaces.) This is commonly done by having a static instance in our class and providing a method to return it.

```
static final OraDataElement oraDataElementFactory =
    new OraDataElement();

public static ORADataFactory getFactory()
{
   return oraDataElementFactory;
}
```

To facilitate creating an object to insert into the database, we'll provide a constructor that a client application can use.

```
public OraDataElement (int number, String symbol,
    String name, float weight)
  {
    this.number = number;
    this.symbol = symbol;
    this.name = name;
    this.weight = weight;
  }
```

To use the `ORAData` class to insert an object, we create the object by calling the constructor, then use an `OraclePreparedStatement` (not just a `PreparedStatement`) to insert it.

```
OraDataElement ee = new OraDataElement(16,"S","Sulfur", 32.06F);
OraclePreparedStatement ps = (OraclePreparedStatement)
   conn.prepareStatement("INSERT INTO ELEMENTS VALUES(?)");
ps.setORAData(1, ee);
ps.execute();
ps.close();
```

To use the `ORAData` class to read objects, we select into an `OracleResultSet` (not just a `ResultSet`) and call the `getORAData()` method. Notice that the `getORAData()` method requires the `getFactory()` method that we defined above.

```
Statement stmt = conn.createStatement();
OracleResultSet rs = (OracleResultSet) stmt.executeQuery(
     "SELECT * FROM ELEMENTS");
while(rs.next())
{
    OraDataElement e = (OraDataElement) rs.getORAData(1,
    OraDataElement.getFactory());
    System.out.println("Name:" + e.name);
}
```

Finally, just as we did with the `SQLData` example, we could encapsulate all the database functionality in the `ORAData` class to hide it from the client class.

CHAPTER 10

Introduction to J2EE and Persistence

Java 2 Enterprise Edition (J2EE) represents Sun's vision of a unified platform for building distributed enterprise applications. As such, it contains a broad range of technologies, including support for transactions, security, messaging, authentication, and resource pooling. Most applications will require just a few of these technologies. However, one technology that most applications will require is J2EE's support for persistence—the ability to store and retrieve information. The fundamental Java technology for database access, as we have seen, is JDBC. We know that JDBC can be used directly, but it also plays an important part in other technologies, such as Enterprise JavaBeans (EJB).

The primary goal of this chapter is to understand the place of JDBC and Java database development as part of the J2EE platform and to develop an overview of the roles that databases can play in a distributed application. We will examine general design issues and several common solutions. In working with the examples, we'll also learn to use Oracle's J2EE server, Oracle Containers for Java (OC4J), and Oracle's integrated development environment, JDeveloper.

A J2EE OVERVIEW

The pieces that make up the J2EE architecture can be divided into three categories, as can be seen in Figure 10–1.

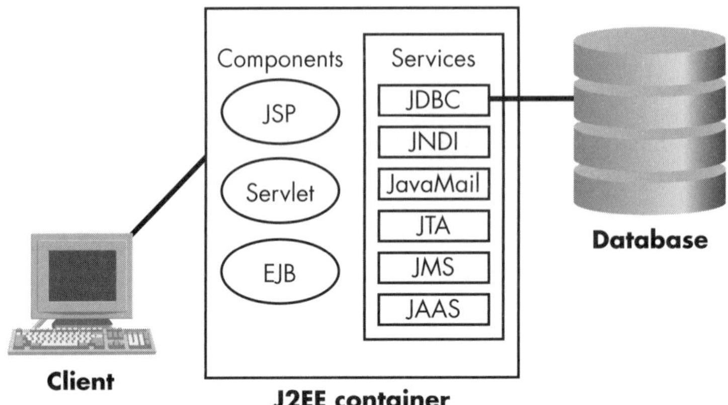

FIGURE 10–1 J2EE components, containers, and services.

These are:

- Components: Reusable, encapsulated program elements.
- Containers: The runtime environments for components that mediates between the components and connectors.
- Services: Providers of access to external services via standard APIs.

Components

There are three types of components defined in the J2EE model. These are:

- Servlets
- Java Server Pages (JSPs)
- Enterprise JavaBeans (EJBs)

Servlets and JSPs are components designed specifically for building Web-based applications and for simplifying the task of programming in an HTTP environment. These two technologies are more than adequate for developing many Web applications.

EJBs are distributed objects that can be used to build multitier distributed applications. These applications can be either client-server applications or, in conjunction with servlets and JSPs, powerful, scalable Web applications. Because they encourage a component-based design, EJB applications can also be made flexible enough to accommodate multiple types of clients in addition to or instead of Web applications.

Servlets

Servlets are Java classes that are associated with a URL—when a user types a specific Web address into a browser, the servlet class is called with any parameters that the user may have provided. These parameters could be information that the user provided in an HTTP form or information provided in the URL itself. In response to the user request, a servlet generally either generates a new HTML page dynamically or passes control to another component, such as a JSP.

JSPs

JSPs are essentially HTML documents with embedded programming. This programming is similar to JavaScript with the important distinction that JavaScript is processed by the client browser, whereas JSPs are processed by the server. In fact, JSPs are converted into servlets. The client browser never sees the JSP (or servlet) code, only the HTML that is generated as a result of processing it.

JSPs and servlets are largely interchangeable, but as we shall see, JSPs are best for designing Web pages with HTML and should include a bare minimum of code, whereas servlets are best for programming the logic of the Web site and the business in Java.

EJBs

EJBs are objects that can be invoked remotely and for this reason are a key J2EE component for building distributed, multitier applications. There are three different kinds of EJBs—session beans, entity beans, and message (or message-driven) beans. In brief:

- Session beans are general-purpose beans and are used to implement business logic.
- Entity beans are persistent objects and usually represent data stored in a database.
- Message-driven beans are objects that are invoked asynchronously when a client sends a message via a messaging service.

Session beans and entity beans are both used for database access, often in combination. In this chapter, we'll see an example of how a particular type of entity bean, a container-managed persistent entity bean, can simplify database access by delegating all database tasks—creating retrieving, updating, and deleting records—to the EJB container. In the next chapter, we'll take a more complete look at how session beans, entity beans, and databases can be used together.

Message-driven beans are an interesting new feature in EJB (as of EJB 2.0), but they don't typically interact with a database and won't be covered here.

Containers

J2EE containers are programs that run on a server in order to provide a runtime environment for components. Containers manage the life cycles of components in response to client applications and mediate between components and the services they provide.

There are two types of containers:

- Web containers support servlets and JSPs.
- EJB containers support EJBs.

Typically, a program called an *application server* will perform these two roles. Even when that is the case, it is useful to consider these roles separately. Because one of the key goals of Java is portability—not just between platforms but also between vendors—Web applications and EJB applications developed for one application server, such as Oracle 9iApplication Server (AS), will usually run unchanged on another, such as BEA WebLogic, provided that you avoid proprietary features.

Services

To be compliant with the J2EE specification, a container must provide a number of different services. These services are largely implementations of interfaces defined by the J2EE specification that permit a component to use a legacy system or technology, using a standard API. These include:

- JDBC: Database access
- JNDI: Java Naming and Directory Interface
- JavaMail
- JTA: Java Transaction API
- JMS: Java Messaging
- JAAS: Java Authentication and Authorization Service

Even though most applications will use just a few of these services, the requirement that they all be supported helps ensure portability of J2EE applications across different vendors' application servers. The down side of this is that even if you use only a subset of this functionality, you may end up having to purchase and support an application server that is more complicated and expensive than you need.

Designing a J2EE Application

J2EE applications generally fall into two general categories: Web applications and client-server applications. The difference, obviously, is that in a Web application, the client interface uses a Web browser, whereas in a client-server application, the client interface is a standard application written using Java or another programming language.

This distinction between Web applications and client-server applications is not strict, however, because a well-designed multitier J2EE application can be flexible enough that the presentation layer—the portion of the application that interacts with the client interface—can be replaced with no change to the business logic or any other back-end components, such as a database. This is an important benefit, because it means that an application can be quickly extended in the face of emerging business needs, such as the need to support Web services.

The most commonly used design for building multitier applications is called the *Model View Controller* (MVC) design (Figure 10–2).

This design breaks an application into three parts with the following responsibilities:

- Model: Represents the data and the underlying business logic.
- View: Presents the data.
- Controller: Mediates between the View and Model and allows the user to interact with the data.

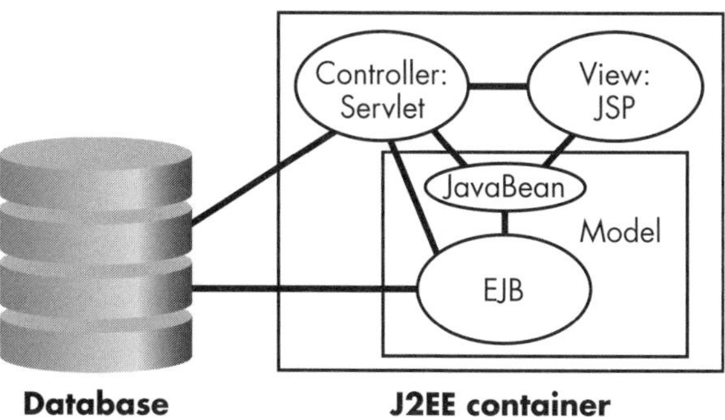

FIGURE 10–2 MVC architecture in J2EE.

There are a number of ways to implement this design using J2EE components, depending on the type of application. Assuming that it is a critical design requirement to use a database for storage, Table 10–1 lists some possible implementations.

TABLE 10–1 Some Possible Implementations of the MVC Design

	Web application 1	*Web application 2*	*Client-server application*
Model	JavaBeans/JDBC	EJB	EJB
View	JSP	JSP	Java application
Controller	Servlet/Java classes	Servlet/Java classes	EJB/Java classes

The first application, Web application 1, is not strictly a J2EE application because it uses only Web components and does not use EJB. It uses JavaBeans as its Model classes and uses JDBC to access the database. This design is relatively simple to develop and is the one most commonly followed.

The second Web application, the EJB model (Figure 10–3), uses Web components for the Controller and View, but it uses EJB (or possibly, EJB plus JavaBeans) to access the database. This design is significantly more complex to develop than is the non-EJB version, largely because of issues introduced by the use of EJBs.

The third application is a client-server application that is fundamentally based on EJB. If the requirements demand a distributed application—especially if the requirements include transaction support, authentication, or access to legacy systems—EJBs can hide many of the details and much of the complexity from the developer.

In this chapter, we will use Oracle 9i AS OC4J to develop examples that demonstrate the use of servlets and JSPs. Apart from the details of deployment and configuration, nothing will be Oracle-specific and should work on any other application server. We will also take a brief look at using Oracle's

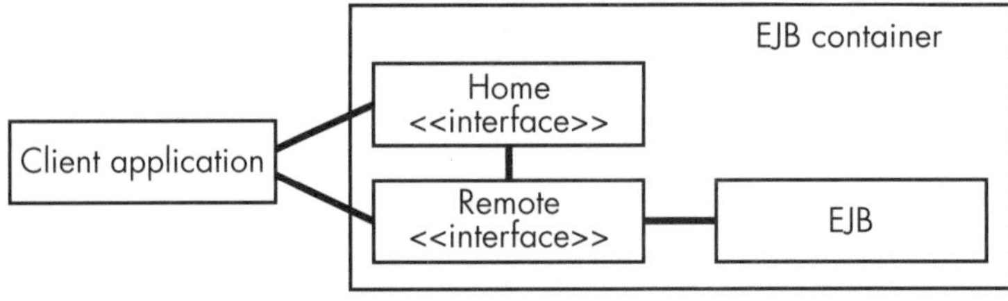

FIGURE 10–3 The EJB model.

JDeveloper to develop a container-managed persistent entity bean as means of providing easy access to the database. In the next chapter, we'll explore EJBs in general and in more detail.

Persistence in a Java Web Application

The sample Web application we'll examine here will provide a simple Web view for the CD collection database that we've been developing off and on in previous chapters. It will allow searching for CDs based on artist or title.

The principal design goal is to divide the logic of the application into distinct areas of responsibility. In particular, with a Web application, it is important to keep the code for page design separate from the application logic because typically, different developers or development teams are responsible for each. Not only do these tasks require different skill sets, but appearance of a Web site also may change more frequently than the underlying logic.

A similar consideration applies between the general application logic and the database access logic; this is particularly true in a larger application that integrates with a database that is used for other applications. The application's code will change more frequently than the underlying database. But even if the same developer or developers are responsible for the general application and the database access logic, it is easier to maintain and reuse components if the database components are independent of other components.

Applications sometimes use separate servlets to perform different actions, but this example will use a single servlet as the only entry point into the application. The servlet will do little more that obtain an instance of another class, a helper class that will actually process the request. We can consider this combination of a servlet and its helper classes depicted in Figure 10–4, to be the controller in the MVC model.

There are two main benefits to using a single servlet with plain old Java classes as the controller. First, it allows us to simplify overall logic because a single class delegates to the appropriate helper class based on the request. Second, it simplifies the issue of multi-threading. Because servlets are only instantiated once, then shared by all requests, we need to make sure that everything we do in them is thread-safe. For example, instance variables that are modified by one thread could affect another adversely and yield unexpected results. Off-loading most of the logic to controller classes, which are instantiated for each thread individually, minimizes these concerns.

The job of the controller helper classes is to obtain whatever data is necessary to fulfill the request and to send it to a JSP page that is responsible for

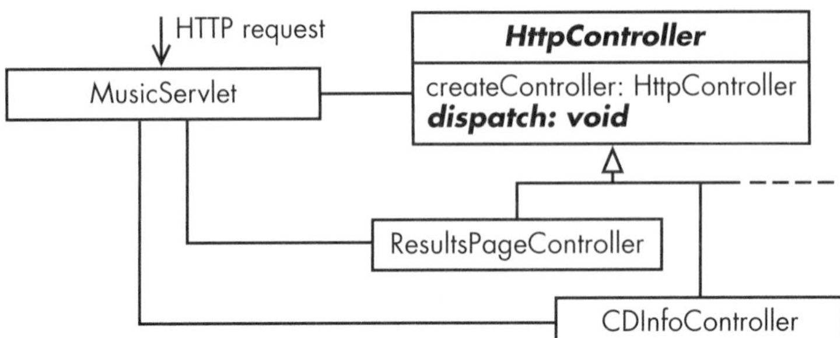

FIGURE 10–4 The servlet and helper classes.

displaying it. As we shall see, JavaBeans are the ideal vehicle for transporting this data from the servlet/controller classes to the JSP page.

We'll next look at each of these parts in more depth.

Controller: Servlet and Helper Classes

When the Web server gets a request for a URL that is mapped to a servlet by the container, it instantiates the servlet class (if it hasn't been instantiated already) then calls several methods. These methods are implemented in the `HttpServlet` superclass, so by virtue of the fact that our servlet extends `HttpServlet`, we don't have to implement them—unless we want our servlet to actually do something! Because that is always the case, we need to override at least one of these methods—usually either `doGet()`, `doPost()`, or both.

When a browser requests a Web page, it usually sends either an HTTP GET or an HTTP PUT request. These differ in the way they pass information to the Web server but they have the same net effect. (GET sends the information all as a single line as part of the GET request; POST sends the information as separate lines following the POST request.) Depending on which one was used to invoke our servlet, the Web container will call either `doGet()` or `doPost()`. We'll always use POST when we set up forms but if a user types our servlet's URL into the browser, that will send a GET request, so we need to implement both. We could have `doGet()` call `doPost()` or vice versa or (for the sake of symmetry) we can have them both call another method. Here we take the latter route and use a method called `doAction()`. This is the start of the `MusicServlet` class:

```
import java.io.*;
import javax.servlet.*;
import javax.servlet.http.*;

public class MusicServlet extends HttpServlet {

  public final static String pageParamName = "REQUESTPAGE";
  public final static String defaultPage = "/StartPage.jsp";

      public void doGet(HttpServletRequest request,
        HttpServletResponse response)
  {
    doAction(request, response);
  }

      public void doPost(HttpServletRequest request,
        HttpServletResponse response)
  {
    doAction(request, response);
  }
```

Both methods, `doGet()` and `doPost()`, take the same arguments, `HttpServletRequest` and `HttpServletResponse`, that we pass on to the `doAction()` method. The `HttpServletRequest` object contains (among other things) any information that came with the request. This information is stored as name-value pairs, which are called *parameters* (or *attributes*).

We define one parameter, `REQUESTPAGE`, for internal use by our application. As we'll see later, it tells us what page to go to next. If `REQUESTPAGE` is set, we use its value as a key to determine which controller class to instantiate to service this request. Our controller class has a method, `dispatch()`, that we call to hand off the request.

When a user first types in the URL for our servlet, however, `REQUESTPAGE` is not set. In this case, we want to go to our default or home page, StartPage.jsp. We also go to this default page if we are unable to instantiate a controller class based on the `REQUESTPAGE` value.

```
public void doAction(HttpServletRequest request, HttpServletResponse
response)
  {
    try
    {
      String page = request.getParameter(pageParamName);
      HttpController controller;
      if(page==null
```

```
          || (controller=
              HttpController.createController(page))==null)
        {
          RequestDispatcher dispatcher =
            getServletContext().getRequestDispatcher(defaultPage);
                dispatcher.forward(request, response);
        }
        else
        {
          controller.dispatch(request, response,
                getServletContext());
        }
      }
      catch(Exception e)
      {
        System.out.println("Caught: " + e);
      }
    }
  }
```

The StartPage.jsp page is actually just a plain HTML form. One limitation of the `RequestDispatcher.forward()` method is that we can't forward HTTP POST requests to a static HTML page—and we'll be doing that a lot. The solution is simply to name the HTML file with the .jsp extension. StartPage.jsp is the first thing the user will see when starting the application. It has fields for artist and title, as well as a Search button.

```
<!DOCTYPE HTML PUBLIC "-//W3C//DTD 4.0 Transitional//EN">
<HTML>
<HEAD>
<TITLE>CD Collection Search</TITLE>
</HEAD>
<BODY>
<FORM ACTION="/servlet/MusicServlet" METHOD="POST">
<TABLE>
  <TR><TD COLSPAN=2 ALIGN=CENTER>
         <H2>CD Collection Search</H2>
      </TD></TR>
  <TR>
    <TD>Artist:</TD><TD><INPUT TYPE="TEXT" NAME="ARTISTNAME"></TD>
  </TR>
  <TR>
    <TD>CD Title:</TD><TD><INPUT TYPE="TEXT" NAME="CDTITLE"></TD>
  </TR>
  <TR><TD COLSPAN=2 ALIGN=CENTER>
       <INPUT TYPE="SUBMIT" NAME="SEARCH" VALUE="Search collection">
```

```
      </TD>
   </TR>
</TABLE>
<INPUT TYPE="HIDDEN" NAME="REQUESTPAGE" VALUE="RESULTSPAGE">
</FORM>
</BODY>
</HTML>
```

Once the user has filled in the form and pressed Submit, it will be posted to the URL listed as the ACTION attribute in the FORM tag near the top of the file: /servlet/MusicServlet. This is the same URL that starts the application, but the difference is that this form has this hidden input field near the bottom to set the `REQUESTPAGE`:

```
<INPUT TYPE="HIDDEN" NAME="REQUESTPAGE" VALUE="RESULTSPAGE">
```

When we return to the servlet from this page, the value of the `REQUESTPAGE` parameter—in this case, `RESULTPAGE`—can be obtained as follows:

```
String page = request.getParameter(pageParamName);
```

The `HttpController` `createController()` method is called with this value so that it can determine which concrete controller class to instantiate:

```
controller= HttpController.createController(page)
```

The mapping between valid `REQUESTPAGE` values (the *page* argument in the call above) and the concrete controller classes are in a .properties file. There are only two controller classes implemented in this example, as shown in the following file, PageClasses.properties:

```
# PageClasses.properties
# These are the page name to controller class mappings

RESULTSPAGE = ResultsPageController
CDINFO = CDInfoController
```

The `HttpController` class factory method, `createController()`, reads the properties, (using a helper method), looks up the requested page value to obtain the classname, then instantiates the class by name.

```
import java.io.*;
import java.util.*;
import javax.servlet.*;
import javax.servlet.http.*;
```

```
public abstract class HttpController
{

       private final static String propertiesFileName =
         "config\\PageClasses.properties";
       private static Properties properties = null;

  public static HttpController createController(String pageName)
  {
    HttpController controller = null;
    if(properties==null)
    {
      readProperties();
    }
    if(properties!=null)
    {
      String className = properties.getProperty(pageName);
      if(className!=null)
      {
        try
        {
          controller = (HttpController)
            Class.forName(className).newInstance();
        }
        catch(Exception e)
        {
          System.out.println("Caught " + e);
        }
      }
    }
    return controller;
  }

   private static void readProperties()
  {
    try
    {
      properties = new Properties();
      FileInputStream is = new
          FileInputStream(propertiesFileName);
      properties.load(is);
    }
    catch (IOException e)
    {
      System.out.println("Caught: " + e);
    }
  }
```

The controller class that is instantiated, which is a concrete subclass of HttpController, is required to implement one method, as declared in HttpController.

```
public abstract void dispatch(HttpServletRequest request,
                              HttpServletResponse response,
                              ServletContext servletContext)
        throws ServletException, IOException;
}
```

As a result of the user pressing the Search button, the servlet is invoked with REQUESTPAGE set to RESULTPAGE, causing HttpServlet to instantiate the ResultsPageController class. The ResultsPageController class has a single method, dispatch(), as required by its superclass, HttpClass.

```
import java.io.*;
import java.util.*;
import javax.servlet.*;
import javax.servlet.http.*;

public class ResultsPageController extends HttpController {

  private static final String jspPageName = "/MusicSearch.jsp";
  private static final String artistParamName = "ARTISTNAME";
  private static final String titleParamName  = "CDTITLE";

  public void dispatch(HttpServletRequest request,
                       HttpServletResponse response,
                       ServletContext servletContext)
   throws ServletException, IOException
  {
    String artistName = request.getParameter(artistParamName);
    String cdTitle    = request.getParameter(titleParamName);
    MusicResults results = new MusicResults(artistName, cdTitle);
            request.setAttribute("MusicResults", results);
    RequestDispatcher dispatcher =
        servletContext.getRequestDispatcher(jspPageName);
    dispatcher.forward(request, response);
  }
}
```

This method does several things: First, it obtains the search parameters that the user specified, using the HTML form above, by calling getParameter(). (These are in the request parameters named ARTISTNAME and CDTITLE.) Second, it uses these parameters to create a JavaBean: an object of type MusicResults that holds the results of the search (as we'll soon see). Finally, it adds the

`MusicResults` object to the `HttpServletRequest`, using the `setAttribute()` method, and forwards the request to the JSP page that will display it.

Model: JavaBeans

JavaBeans, as we use the term here, are really nothing special. (JavaBeans used in other contexts can be more complex, particularly those used to build graphical user interfaces [GUIs].) They are just a convention for building classes that are primarily designed for holding data and, in this context, are also called *value objects*. Most (and often all) of their methods are getter and setter methods—methods to allow other classes to store information in them and pull information out of them.

The conventions that we use for JavaBeans are:

- Attributes are stored as private instance variables. The first letter of the attribute is lowercase; other words in the variable name are capitalized. For example, an attribute may be named `myVariable`.
- Methods are provided to obtain the value of each attribute. These `getter` methods are named `get` plus the name of the attribute. The first letter of the attribute is uppercase, in this case, so the name of the method to get myVariable would be `getMyVariable()`. Getter methods take no parameters.
- Methods are provided to set the value of each attribute. These `setter` methods are named `set` plus the name of the attribute with first letter uppercase, as with the getter methods. The name of the method to set myVariable would be `setMyVariable()`. Setter methods take one parameter, the attribute value.
- The JavaBean class must have a no-argument constructor.

When we use JavaBeans to hold data from a database, we can take two approaches: we can use lightweight JavaBeans that have no database access logic or we can use heavyweight JavaBeans that know how to retrieve and store themselves in the database.

The benefit of using lightweight JavaBeans is that they are smaller, and we can potentially encapsulate all database access logic in another single, separate class—a data access object. The benefit of using heavyweight JavaBeans is that, although they are larger and have some code that is duplicated in other JavaBeans, they are completely self-contained and hide the database completely from the rest of the application. Furthermore, most of the code that is redundant could be implemented in a JavaBean superclass.

In this example, the `MusicResults` class is a heavyweight JavaBean, mainly to keep the number of classes in this sample application to a minimum. Given the search parameters that the user specified, `MusicResults` knows how to populate itself from the database and will fill several vectors with the results of a query constructed using the search parameters.

```
import java.sql.*;
import java.util.Vector;

public class MusicResults
{
  Connection connection = null;
  private Vector artist = new Vector();
  private Vector title = new Vector();
  private Vector artistId = new Vector();
  private Vector cdId = new Vector();
  private int size = 0;
  private static final int MAXRESULTS = 25;

  public MusicResults()
  throws SQLException
  {
    connect();
    executeQuery(null, null);
  }

  MusicResults(String artistName, String cdTitle)
  {
    try
    {
      connect();
      executeQuery(artistName, cdTitle);
    }
    catch(SQLException e)
    {
      System.out.println("Caught: " + e);
    }
    finally
    {
      try
      {
        if(connection!=null)
        {
          connection.close();
        }
      }
```

```
      catch
      {
        // ignore error closing connection
      }
    }
  }

  private void executeQuery(String artistName, String cdTitle)
  throws SQLException
  {
    StringBuffer sql = new StringBuffer(
          "SELECT DISPLAY_NAME(A.NAME, A.SURNAME, A.LOCALE), " +
          "C.ALBUM_TITLE, A.ARTIST_ID, C.CD_ID " +
          "FROM ARTISTS A, CD_COLLECTION C " +
          "WHERE C.ARTIST_ID = A.ARTIST_ID ");

    if(artistName!=null && !artistName.equals(""))
    {
      sql.append(
         "AND UPPER(DISPLAY_NAME(A.NAME, A.SURNAME, A.LOCALE)) " +
         "LIKE UPPER('%" +
         artistName + "%') ");
    }

    if(cdTitle!=null && !cdTitle.equals(""))
    {
      sql.append("AND UPPER(C.ALBUM_TITLE) LIKE UPPER('%" + cdTitle +
        "%') ");
    }
    sql.append("ORDER BY A.SORT_NAME, C.ALBUM_TITLE");

    Statement stmt = connection.createStatement();
    ResultSet rs = stmt.executeQuery(sql.toString());
    int i = 0;

    while(rs.next() && i++ < MAXRESULTS)
    {
      artist.add(rs.getString(1));
      title.add(rs.getString(2));
      artistId.add(new Integer(rs.getInt(3)));
      cdId.add(new Integer(rs.getInt(4)));
    }
    size = artist.size();
    rs.close();
    stmt.close();
  }

  private void connect()
  throws SQLException
```

```
{
      DriverManager.registerDriver(
      new oracle.jdbc.OracleDriver());
      connection = DriverManager.getConnection(
            "jdbc:oracle:thin:@noizmaker:1521:osiris",
            "david", "bigcat");
}
```

We'll consider several aspects of this code separately: how it connects to the database, the query that it makes, and its characteristics as a JavaBean.

The Database Connection

Obtaining a database connection is computationally costly. In this example, we've kept the code simple but if it were a real application that we expect would see significant traffic, we would likely consider finding a way to reuse connections, rather than using a new one for each request. One possible way is to reuse the connection on a per-session basis by storing it in the session scope with `request.setAttribute()`. Another way that might be more complicated to set up initially but has a better performance payoff is to use a JDBC 2.0 connection pool.

The Database Query

One of the database tables we are querying is the ARTISTS table, for which we developed a number of different PL/SQL stored procedures and a trigger to make it easier to display artist's names—individuals and groups—in a linguistically correct way. We will use this in a join, together with the CD_COLLECTION table.

The CD_COLLECTION table, which we last saw in Chapter 3, needs to be updated to use the ARTISTS table we created in Chapter 5, however. Specifically, we need to remove the artist information from CD_COLLECTION table and replace it with a foreign key that references ARTIST_ID, the primary key in the ARTISTS table. This is how we redefine CD_COLLECTION:

```
DROP TABLE CD_COLLECTION;
CREATE TABLE CD_COLLECTION (
  ALBUM_TITLE VARCHAR2(100),
  RELEASE_DATE DATE,
  LABEL VARCHAR2(25),
  ARTIST_ID NUMBER,
  CD_ID NUMBER,
  FOREIGN KEY (ARTIST_ID) REFERENCES ARTISTS(ARTIST_ID),
  PRIMARY KEY (CD_ID)
);
```

We'll also add some records for each of the artists in the ARTISTS table.

```
INSERT INTO CD_COLLECTION VALUES(
  'Mer de Noms', '1-JAN-2000', 'Virgin', 24,
  CD_ID_SEQUENCE.NEXTVAL);
INSERT INTO CD_COLLECTION VALUES(
  'Big Science', '1-JAN-1982', 'Warner', 29,
  CD_ID_SEQUENCE.NEXTVAL);
INSERT INTO CD_COLLECTION VALUES(
  'Mister Heartbreak','1-JAN-1984','Warner',29,
  CD_ID_SEQUENCE.NEXTVAL);
INSERT INTO CD_COLLECTION VALUES(
  'Nothing to My Name', '1-JAN-1989', 'EMI Hong Kong', 22,
  CD_ID_SEQUENCE.NEXTVAL);
INSERT INTO CD_COLLECTION VALUES(
  'Power of the Powerless', '1-JAN-1999', 'World Beat', 22,
  CD_ID_SEQUENCE.NEXTVAL);
INSERT INTO CD_COLLECTION VALUES(
  'Ten', '1-JAN-1991', 'Epic', 25,
  CD_ID_SEQUENCE.NEXTVAL);
INSERT INTO CD_COLLECTION VALUES(
  'Vitalogy', '1-JAN-1994', 'Epic', 25,
  CD_ID_SEQUENCE.NEXTVAL);
```

The SQL to query these two tables is generated dynamically by our code, based on whether the user typed any search criteria into the Artist or Title boxes. The first part of the query is constant and sets up a join between the ARTISTS table and the CD_COLLECTION tables. This is the SQL:

```
SELECT DISPLAY_NAME(A.NAME, A.SURNAME, A.LOCALE),
  C.ALBUM_TITLE, A.ARTIST_ID, C.CD_ID
  FROM ARTISTS A, CD_COLLECTION C
  WHERE C.ARTIST_ID = A.ARTIST_ID
```

The select list, you'll note, uses the user-defined function DISPLAY_NAME() (from Chapter 5) to put the name together in a culturally correct way, based on the artist's locale. For example, in Chinese names, the surname comes first, followed by the given name, whereas in English, it's the reverse.

The next part varies, depending on whether the user entered text for artist and title. If there is text for artist, the following is appended:

```
AND UPPER(DISPLAY_NAME(A.NAME, A.SURNAME, A.LOCALE))
        LIKE UPPER('%artistName%')
```

If there is a title, the following is appended:

```
AND UPPER(C.ALBUM_TITLE) LIKE UPPER('%cdTitle%')
```

It is important to recognize that comparisons such as this can cause performance problems. Normally, this query would require the database to use the DISPLAY_NAME() and UPPER() functions for every row in the database to perform the comparison. If there are a lot of records in the table, this can take a long time and performance could easily be degraded to unacceptable levels.

One solution available in Oracle 9i is to use function-based indexes. This will store the results of a function in an index. Another solution is to store the results of these calculations in separate columns each time a row is inserted or updated, using a trigger as we did for the SORT_NAME column and to create an index on these columns. For a large production system, issues such as this need to be considered carefully by an experienced database administrator or consultant.

The JavaBean Class

Because the query can return multiple rows of results which we store in vectors, our value class, `MusicResults`, is not a totally compliant JavaBean because the getter methods take a parameter specifying the index of the attribute.

```
  public String getArtistAt(int i)
  {
    return (String) artist.elementAt(i);
  }

  public String getTitleAt(int i)
  {
    return (String) title.elementAt(i);
  }

  public int getArtisIdAt(int i)
  {
    return ((Integer)artistId.elementAt(i)).intValue();
  }

  public int getCdIdAt(int i)
  {
    return ((Integer)cdId.elementAt(i)).intValue();
  }

  public int getSize()
  {
    return size;
  }
}
```

The fact that this is not a pure JavaBean means that we'll be able to load it as a JavaBean in our JSP page but we won't be able to take advantage of some of the special automatic support that JSP has for JavaBeans. We'll need to call the getter methods explicitly using embedded Java code.

View: The JSP Page

JSP, as noted above, is a server-side scripting language that is embedded within HTML. It is comparable to other server-side scripting products, such as ASP and ColdFusion. JSP has the advantage that it is based on Java, so it is platform and vendor-neutral and works well with other Java technologies.

Assuming that a Web server supports JSP, a JSP page can be placed anywhere in the server's directory structure that a regular HTML page can be placed, and it will automatically be translated into a Java servlet class, compiled, and run the first time it is requested.

It's beyond the scope of this book to teach JSP but before delving into the JSP page used to display the search results, we'll briefly look at four common scripting elements: scriptlets, expressions, actions, and custom tags.

JSP Scriptlets

Scriptlets are bits of Java code that are embedded within the HTML code. A scriplet has the basic format

```
<% Java code %>
```

The Java code in a scriptlet can be multiple statements or even just part of a statement. (What's important is that the Java code, if spread across various scriplets, must be valid as a whole.) The following example declares and initializes a variable to the number of milliseconds since 12:00 a.m. GMT on 1 January 1970:

```
<%  long secs = (new java.util.Date()).getTime(); %>
```

We can create a loop.

```
<% for(int i=0; i<10; i++)
   {
     // do something
   }
%>
```

What can we do inside the loop? We can do the usual Java things but we can also break the loop into two separate scriplets and put some HTML in the middle.

```
<% for(int i=0; i<10; i++)
   {
%>

<H2> I'm thinking! </H2>

<%
   }
%>
```

This will print out "I'm thinking!" 10 times.

JSP Expressions

JSP expressions allow us to embed a Java expression in HTML code. Its basic format is

```
<%= Java expression %>
```

At runtime, the value of the Java expression is calculated, converted to a string, and included in the HTML page that is sent to the user's browser. For example, we can print out the value of the `startTime` variable that we declared and initialized above like this:

```
<%= secs %>
```

This will convert the long value to a string and print it out as part of the pages HTML code in essentially the same way that using `System.out.print()` would.

Besides being useful for creating user-visible text, JSP expressions can also be used to generate HTML tags and JavaScript dynamically. Tags and JavaScript, after all, are just text to the Web server—they are interpreted only when they reach a user's browser.

JSP Actions

JSP actions (or tags) are XML tags that invoke Java code. For example, to use a JavaBean, we use a `useBean` tag with the following syntax:

```
<jsp:useBean id="name" class="classname" scope="scope" />
```

The `id` attribute indicates the variable name that is associated with the bean. The `class` attribute refers to the JavaBean's class name. The `scope` attribute refers to whether the bean belongs to the current request (by setting it to either "`page`" or "`request`"), the current session (by setting it to "`session`"), or the entire application for the duration of the servlet's lifetime (by setting it to "`application`").

When JSP processes this tag, it first checks to see whether a bean that matches the `id` attribute has already been instantiated in the specified scope. If there is, it uses that bean. If not, it instantiates a new bean of the specified class. To access the `MusicResults` bean that we created using our controller class, we use the following tag:

```
<jsp:useBean id="musicResults"
             class="MusicResults" scope="request" />
```

Note that the `id` attribute, `musicResults`, is the name we gave the bean when we called `request.setAttribute()` in our controller class. The class attribute, `MusicResults`, is the name of the Java class that `musicResults` is an instance of. The scope is the request because we associated the bean with the session's request parameter by calling `request.setAttribute()`.

Another JSP action is the `getProperty` tag that we can use to obtain values from a bean. It has the following attributes:

```
<jsp:getProperty name="name" property="propertyname"/>
```

The name here corresponds to the `id` with which we associated the bean in the `useBean` tag. The property must correspond to a standard (i.e., parameterless) getter method in the bean class. As it happens, our `MusicResults` class has only one such method, `getSize()`, which returns the value of the private instance variable `size`. We can get this property as follows:

```
<jsp:getProperty name="musicResults" property="size"/>
```

This is equivalent to the following JSP expression which uses an explicit Java method call:

```
<%= musicResults.getSize() %>
```

Custom Tags

It bears mentioning, if only in passing, that a feature introduced in JSP 1.1, custom tags, can be invaluable in reducing the amount of Java code in a JSP page.

Custom tags are grouped into custom tag libraries, which are groups of Java classes that are mapped to tag names, using an XML file called a *tag library descriptor file* (TLD). They are used on the JSP page in exactly the same way that standard JSP actions are used.

In our example, the amount of Java code that we need to include in our JSP page is already fairly small, so we won't use custom tags. Custom tags would, in this case, increase the complexity while doing little to reduce the coding that is necessary on the JSP page.

The Search Results JSP

Now that we've seen the basics of JSP, let's take a look at the JSP that will display our search results. First is a standard HTML header.

```
<!DOCTYPE HTML PUBLIC "-//W3C//DTD 4.0 Transitional//EN">
<HTML>
<HEAD>
<TITLE>CD Collection Search Results</TITLE>
</HEAD>

<BODY>
<H2>CD Collection Search Results</H2>
<P>
```

Next is the useBean tag.

```
<jsp:useBean id="musicResults"
             class="MusicResults"
             scope="request" />
```

A FORM tag indicates that when the user presses a Submit button, the form information should be posted to the `MusicServlet`.

```
<FORM ACTION="/servlet/MusicServlet" METHOD="POST">
```

The next section displays the search results in a table, looping through the bean's values using Java code embedded as JSP scriplets and expressions.

```
<TABLE BORDER=2>
<TR><TH>Select</TH><TH>Artist</TH><TH>Title</TH><TR>

<%  for(int i= 0; i<musicResults.getSize() ;i++)
    {
%>
     <TR>
```

One column in the table contains a button that the user can press to see information about a specific CD. Its value is set to the CD's CD_ID; when we process the form information in a controller, we can obtain its value by using the CDSELECTED parameter.

```
<TD>
  <INPUT TYPE="SUBMIT" VALUE=" > " NAME=
         "CDSELECTED=<%=MusicResults.getCdIdAt(i)%>;
          ARTISTNAME=<%=MusicResults.getArtistAt(i)%>">
</TD>
```

Note that the NAME attribute, beginning with CDSELECTED, has been broken into two lines and indented for clarity; it should be a single line that concatenates the selected CD_ID and the artist's name. The reason for this is that, depending on which Submit button is pressed, we want to pass both of these values to our servlet, but a Submit button allows passing only one value. A second issue you may notice is that we don't pass these values in the VALUE attribute but instead convert them to name-value pairs that we pass as the NAME attribute. This is because there is no foolproof way in HTML to display something other than the VALUE in the Submit button, and we don't want our internal CD ID and the artist's name displayed in each of the Submit buttons, so we set the VALUE to something appropriate for display. We'll see how to retrieve these values later.

The next lines call the bean's getter methods to obtain the artist name and CD title.

```
  <TD><%= musicResults.getArtistAt(i) %></TD>
  <TD><%= musicResults.getTitleAt(i) %></TD>
  </TR>

<%  } %>
```

A button at the bottom will return us to the search page indirectly by setting the CDSELECTED value to "New search".

```
<TR><TD COLSPAN=3 ALIGN=CENTER>
  <INPUT TYPE="SUBMIT" NAME="CDSELECTED" VALUE="New search">
</TD></TR>
```

The next line is a hidden field that indicates the page that the `MusicServlet` should use next.

```
<INPUT TYPE="HIDDEN" NAME="REQUESTPAGE" VALUE="CDINFO">
```

Whether the user selects a CD or selected a new search, the `MusicServlet` will invoke the controller class corresponding to CDINFO. If the CDSELECTED value is "New search", the controller will return to the default search instead of performing the search.

Finally, we close the remaining open tags.

```
</FORM>
</TABLE>
</BODY>
</HTML>
```

In the next section, we'll see how to deploy and run what we have so far using the Oracle's Containers for J2EE.

The Oracle Containers for J2EE, OC4J

The Oracle Containers for J2EE, OC4J, is a key component of Oracle 9i AS. Oracle 9i AS is a comprehensive package of components for building robust, scaleable Web and multitier applications, but OC4J is, in itself, what is normally referred to as an *application server.* (OC4J is, in fact, the Orion application server, which Oracle has licensed and re-branded.) It is the only component needed for developing and testing EJB, servlets, and JSPs.

You should not need to download and install the entire Oracle 9i AS suite to obtain OC4J. Not only can OC4J be downloaded and installed individually, but it also comes bundled with the Oracle 9i database and with Oracle JDeveloper. Because the EJB examples in this chapter and the next will use JDeveloper, it is recommended that you use the version of OC4J that comes with JDeveloper.

Installing JDeveloper

After downloading the JDeveloper zip files from Oracle, installation is as simple as unzipping it into the directory of your choice, such as c:\jdev. There is no installation or setup program to run. The OC4J standalone server's home directory will be

```
c:\jdev\j2ee\home
```

This OC4J directory is separate from the OC4J server embedded in JDeveloper, so we won't have to worry that making changes will cause problems with JDeveloper. It provides us with a separate, standalone test environment to which we can deploy J2EE applications after debugging in the integrated JDeveloper environment.

Installing the OC4J Standalone Server. If you choose not to use JDeveloper, you should instead download the standalone version of OC4J because it is likely to be more recent than the version bundled with Oracle database. It's a relatively small and painless download and installation.

Like JDeveloper, there is no installation program to run; simply unzip it to a directory such as c:\OC4J. The OC4J home directory in this case will be

```
c:\OC4J\j2ee\home
```

Running OC4J

Before starting OC4J for the first time, you will need to set the administrative password. In the OC4J home directory, verify that there is a file called oc4j.jar and type

```
java -jar oc4j.jar -install
```

You will be prompted to enter an admin password, ("adminpwd", for example), twice. To start OC4J, enter the following command:

```
java -jar oc4j.jar
```

You can verify that OC4J is running by opening a browser and entering http://localhost:8888 in the browser's URL address box. (The reason for this URL is that, because we are using the same machine as client and server, we can refer to the server as *localhost*. By default, the Web server built into OC4J uses port 8888 for HTTP, so as not to conflict with any other Web servers on the machine. Because the standard default HTTP port is 80, we need explicitly to specify the port :8888 as part of our URL.) You should get a Web page welcoming you to Oracle9i AS Containers for J2EE.

DEPLOYING THE WEB APPLICATION

Normally, when deploying a Web application that uses servlets, it's common practice to put all the necessary Java classes into a .jar file, put them in a specific directory, and modify a configuration file so that the Web container recognizes it.

This is not necessary for OC4J—at least for development purposes. It is necessary only to put the Java source files in the default servlet directory and the JSP, HTML and any other resource files (.gif or .jpg, if we have any) go in the default-web-app directory. OC4J will automatically compile not only the JSPs but also the Java source files.

To deploy the application we've built so far:

- Copy MusicServlet.java, HttpController.java, ResultsPage.controller.java, MusicResults.java, CDInfoController.java, and MessengerBean.java to

  ```
  default-web-app\WEB-INF\classes
  ```

- Copy StartPage.jsp, MusicSearch.jsp, and NotImplemented.jsp to

  ```
  default-web-app
  ```

- Copy the PageClasses.properties file to

  ```
  config
  ```

- In the config directory, open the global-web-application.xml file with a text editor and change the value of the development attribute orion-web-app tag to true. It should appear as follows:

  ```
  <orion-web-app
  jsp-cache-directory="./persistence"
  servlet-webdir="/servlet"
  development="true"
  >
  ```

Changing the development attribute in the global-web-application.xml file will cause OC4J automatically to recompile servlets when they are updated. But beware that OC4J does not notice changes to classes that are not servlets. To get the helper classes to recompile, it may be necessary to delete the .class files, then stop and restart the server.

Assuming that all the files are in the right place and OC4J is running (and that the Oracle database is running too, of course), we can try running the MusicServlet application.

Running the MusicServlet Web Application

After deploying the application as described above, entering the following address in your browser should start the application:

```
http://localhost:8888/servlet/MusicServlet
```

The servlet directory is necessary because this was specified as the default servlet in the orion-web-app tag in the global-web-application.xml file that we saw above. `MusicServlet`, of course, is the name of the servlet we want to run.

The first time we run the `MusicServlet` application, it will take a while to load, because the container needs to compile the servlet and JSP files. It will be much faster thereafter.

One thing that should be pointed out is that standard output from the servlets and Java classes are sent to the console. This allows us to use System.out.println() for debugging, in lieu of a more interactive development environment, such as JDeveloper.

Stopping the OC4J Server

To stop the OC4J server, open another command prompt window and enter the following command in the OC4J home directory:

```
java -jar admin.jar ormi://localhost admin adminpwd -shutdown
```

EJBs and Web Applications

EJBs have two important but distinct characteristics:

- They are distributed components.
- They provide access to the services of the EJB container.

These topics will be considered more extensively in the next chapter, but in the context of Web applications, the second characteristic is the most attractive. One type of EJB is particularly alluring: container-managed persistent entity beans. Because the EJB container automatically takes care of storing and retrieving a CMP bean's data, CMP beans can completely free a developer from having to write database access code.

EJBs, and particularly CMP entity beans, bear a superficial resemblance to standard JavaBeans; after obtaining a bean (using a few mysterious lines of code), we use getter and setter methods to obtain and change the information in it. The container takes care of the rest.

The benefit of having database access taken care of automatically by using CMP entity beans comes at a significant cost. This cost includes:

- Increased overhead of configuring and administering the EJB container
- Decreased performance
- Increased complexity of developing and deploying the application

Most of these costs are incurred because EJB is principally a technology for building distributed components. The mechanism for invoking an object method remotely introduces several layers of indirection between a call from an application to an EJB. Although some significant optimizations can be made, this is true even when EJBs are actually local and use a local interface instead of the remote interface.

Some of the development costs can be mitigated to a degree by using an IDE, such as Oracle JDeveloper. Wizards in JDeveloper allow you to create and deploy a CMP bean, based either on an existing database table or a table that it creates for you, almost effortlessly. It can be argued, however, that this is a pretty extreme way to avoid writing database access code, especially if you look behind the scenes and see what's really going on and how many class files are generated to implement a single entity bean.

Although you will need to consider carefully whether CMP beans are appropriate for a production application, you may nonetheless find that using an automated tool to generate an EJB from an existing table can be a convenient way to prototype code.

Creating a Container-Managed Persistent Entity Bean Using JDeveloper

In this section, we will extend the Web application we began earlier in this chapter by using an EJB to obtain the track information for a selected CD. Normally, we wouldn't mix data access techniques; this is just a demonstration for comparing the different techniques.

Starting JDeveloper

Because JDeveloper does not provide an installation program, it is not available from the start menu or an icon on your desktop. Instead, after downloading and unzipping JDeveloper, you will need to locate the jdev\bin directory and run the executable jdevw.exe manually. You can do this at a DOS prompt by navigating to it using the Windows Explorer or by selecting Run from the Start menu. If you've installed JDeveloper in a directory c:\JDeveloper, the full path would be

```
c:\JDeveloper\jdev\bin\jdevw.exe
```

A more convenient alternative to starting JDeveloper manually is to create a shortcut for JDeveloper on your desktop. Do this by right-clicking on an empty area of your desktop, selecting New | Shortcut, and entering the full path and filename for jdevw.exe (or press Browse and locate it that way). You can then start JDeveloper by double clicking on this shortcut.

Create a Workspace and Project

After JDeveloper starts, the System Navigator will appear in the top left pane of the main window. To create a workspace and project for developing the EJB:

- Right-click on the root entry, Workspaces.
- Click on New Workspace.
- In the dialog box that appears, change the last part of the directory name to ejbExamples. (The full path, if JDeveloper were installed in c:\JDeveloper, would be c:\JDeveloper\jdev\mywork\ejbExamples). Change the filename to ejbExamples.jws. Leave the box labeled "Add a New Empty Project" checked. Press OK.
- In the next dialog box, change the last part of the directory name to CDBean. Change the filename to CDBean.jpr. Press OK.

Create a Connection to the Database

We will be creating an EJB based on an existing table, the CD_COLLECTION table. To enable JDeveloper to connect to the database and locate this table, we will need to ensure that JDeveloper has a working database connection. At the bottom of the System Navigator tree:

- Locate and right-click on Connections.
- From the popup menu, select New Database Connection.
- On the next box, Welcome to the Connection Wizard, press Next.
- Enter the database name as the name of the connection, for example, Osiris. Ensure that Connection Type is Oracle (JDBC). Press Next.
- Enter username and password, leave Role empty, and check the Deploy Password box. Press Next.
- Verify the entries for Driver, Hostname, and JDBC Port. These should be "thin", "localhost" (or the machine name), and "1521."
- Enter the SID for the database, for example, OSIRIS. Press Next.
- In the next box, press the Test Connection button. This should display "Success!" in the Status box. If it does not, press Back, review your entries, and verify that they agree with your database settings. You may

also want to verify independently that the database is running by connecting using SQL*Plus.

- Once the test is successful, press Finish.

Create the CMP Entity Bean

We will use a wizard to create the EJB. As you will see, we need only to indicate the type of bean, CMP based on a table, and identify the table. JDeveloper will do the rest. In the System Navigator:

- Right-click on the project name, CDBean.jpr.
- Select New… from the popup menu.
- In the box that appears, select Enterprise JavaBeans from the left side, then select Container-managed Entity Beans from Tables. Press OK.
- In the next box, for JDBC Connection, select the connection you created for the database in the last step, e.g., Osiris.
- In the list of tables that appears in the Available Tables list, locate the CD_COLLECTION table. (You can enter *CD* in the Table Name Pattern box to find it more quickly.) Highlight CD_COLLECTION and press the single right arrowhead to select it. Press Next.
- Accept the defaults in the next box and press Finish.

Test the Entity Bean Using the Embedded OC4J

JDeveloper can automatically create a sample application to test the EJB. We'll first test it using the OC4J container embedded in the JDeveloper IDE. First, start the bean:

- Right-click on the Cd_collection bean.
- Select Run Cd_collection.

The log window will show that the embedded OC4J server has been started and that the bean has been deployed. Next, we'll create a test application.

- Right-click on the Cd_collection bean.
- Select Create Sample Java Client.
- Ensure that the button labeled *Connect to OC4J Embedded in JDeveloper* is selected and press OK.

This will create a small class that will include a `main()` method to exercise the Cd_collection bean. To run the sample application:

- Right-click on Cd_collectionClient.java.
- Select Run Cd_collectionClient.java

The output, listing all the records in the CD_COLLECTION table, will display in the log window.

Create a Connection for the Standalone OC4J Instance

To test the application and bean on an application server—in this case, on a standalone instance of OC4J—we first need to create a connection for the application server:

- Right-click on the Connections, select New Application Server Connection.
- Press Next on the welcome screen.
- Enter a name for the connection, such as OC4J.
- Accept the default of Oracle9i Application Server and press Next.
- Leave username *admin*. For the password, enter the admin password (if OC4J was set up as described earlier in this chapter, this will be *adminpwd*), and check the box labeled Deploy Password. Press Next.
- In the next box, accept the default settings and press Next.
- In the next box, press Test Connection. If you do not get the "Success!" message, use the Back button to review your settings.
- Once the test is successful, press Finish.

Deploying the EJB

The first step in deploying an EJB is to create a deployment profile that establishes some basic settings:

- Right-click on the CDBean project, CDBean.jpr.
- Select New.
- In the box that appears, select Deployment Profiles on the left side, then select EJB Jar File - J2EE EJB Module on the right. Press OK.
- Change the filename of the deployment profile to CDBean.deploy in the next box and press Save.

- In the next box, accept the default filenames for the .jar file, the .ear file, and the Enterprise Application Name. Press OK.

Once we've created the deployment profile, we can deploy the bean as follows:

- Right click on the newly created deployment profile, CDBean.deploy.
- Select Deploy to => OC4J.
- The log window will show the progress of the deployment, including the creation of the .jar and .ear files, as well as invocation of the OC4J admin tool. Eventually, it will indicate that Deployment is finished.

Testing the EJB on the Standalone OC4J Server

To test the EJB on the standalone server, we can generate another test application:

- Right-click on the Cd_collection bean.
- In the box that appears, select Connect to Remote App Server. Ensure that the J2EE application name is CDBean and that the Oracle9i AS Connection name is OC4J. Press OK.

This creates a new client application, Cd_collectionClient1.java. Locate this under the CDBean project in the System Navigator.

- Right-click on Cd_collection1.java.
- Select Run Cd_collection1.java from the popup menu.

This sample application should produce the same results as the first one, listing all the records in the CD_COLLECTION table. In the next section, we'll use some of the code produced to access the EJB from our Servlet/JSP application.

Using a CMP Entity Bean in a Web Application

There are several ways that a CMP entity bean can be incorporated into a Web application.

- JSP Scriptlets: It's possible to include code to access it directly in a JSP, but it takes a lot of code and, as discussed earlier, it's not good practice to include a lot of code in a JSP.

- JSP Custom tags: A slightly better way to use EJBs in a JSP application is to write a set of custom tags that allow the JSP to use the EJB; this would be a good choice if the application was primarily JSP-based and most Java code was already implemented using a custom tag library.
- Servlets/Java classes/JavaBeans: Because it takes a fair amount of Java code to use an EJB, it's generally best to use a more sophisticated method than just JSP or JSP and custom tags. As discussed earlier, the MVC design pattern, using JSP for presentation, servlets, and helper classes as the controller and EJBs (or EJBs and JavaBeans) as the model has advantages in terms of flexibility and maintainability.

Of these alternatives, the third is clearly the most appropriate for our CD Web application.

In the example so far, we've created one JavaBean, a heavyweight one that has the logic in it to access the database and populate itself. Similarly here, we could create a heavyweight JavaBean that calls the EJB and populates itself. In a real application, we would want to be consistent in our choice. Here, to provide variety in the examples, we'll use a lightweight JavaBean. The controller class will call the EJB and populate the JavaBean before forwarding the request to a JSP, which will display the information contained in the JavaBean.

The CDInfoController

The `CDInfoController` class contains the logic for obtaining a CMP bean containing the CD information we want. First are the imports, some constants, and instance variables.

```
import java.io.*;
import java.util.*;
import javax.servlet.*;
import javax.servlet.http.*;
import java.util.Hashtable;
import javax.naming.Context;
import javax.naming.InitialContext;
import mypackage1.Cd_collection;
import mypackage1.Cd_collectionHome;
import mypackage1.Cd_collectionPK;
import java.util.Collection;
import java.util.Iterator;
import java.lang.Long;

public class CDInfoController extends HttpController {
```

```
private static final String CD_SELECTED   = "CDSELECTED";
private static final String ARTIST_NAME   = "ARTISTNAME";
private static final String CD_BEAN   = "CDBean";
private static final String JSP_PAGE = "/CDInfo.jsp";
private static final String ERROR_PAGE = "/NotFound.jsp";

private String artistName;
private long cdid;

public void dispatch(HttpServletRequest request,
                     HttpServletResponse response,
                     ServletContext servletContext)
 throws ServletException, IOException
{

  Cd_collection cdBean = null;
  CDInfoBean cdinfo = new CDInfoBean();
  parseCDSelected(request);
```

The literal constants are the names of the JPS files and the names of the attributes that we use to communicate with them. We also instantiate the JavaBean (CDInfoBean—not shown here) that we will use to store the CD information.

The variables `artistName` and `cdid` are the information that we need to obtain from the attribute that was set when the user pressed the Submit button for a particular CD. Remember that these two values were concatenated into a single string and set as the NAME attribute of a session parameter because of limitations in the way an HTML Submit button is implemented in certain browsers.

The logic for obtaining information from the `CDSELECTED` attribute is not straightforward because we don't know the precise name of the attribute. We only know that it begins with `CDSELECTED`, as in the following example:

```
CDSELECTED=112;ARTISTNAME=Richard Thompson
```

The helper method, `parseCDSelected()`, looks through the session's attributes, locates this string and parses it, and sets the class's `cdid` and `artistName` variables. We interrupt the presentation of the `dispatch()` method to present the code for this helper method.

```
void parseCDSelected(HttpServletRequest request)
{
  Enumeration paramNames = request.getParameterNames();

  while(paramNames.hasMoreElements())
  {
```

```
      String paramName = (String) paramNames.nextElement();
      System.out.println("-- " + paramName);
      if(paramName.startsWith(CD_SELECTED))
      {
        StringTokenizer st= new StringTokenizer(paramName, ";=", true);
        if(st.countTokens()>=7)
        {
          if(     st.nextToken().equals(CD_SELECTED)
              && st.nextToken().equals("="))
          {
            cdid=Long.parseLong(st.nextToken().trim());
          }

          if(    st.nextToken().equals(";")
             && st.nextToken().equals(ARTIST_NAME)
             && st.nextToken().equals("=")
            )
          {
             artistName=st.nextToken().trim();
          }
        }
      }
    }
  }
```

Note that this method is fairly strict in enforcing the format of the attributes; this is useful for debugging purposes. Normally, it would be sufficient simply to ensure that the right number of tokens are present and retrieve the desired ones, throwing the rest away.

Calling the EJB

To use an EJB, we need to obtain two objects:

- The home object. This object serves as an EJB factory and manages the life cycle of the EJB object.
- The EJB object. This is the object that we interact with in the same way we would with a standard JavaBean. It's different from a JavaBean, in that it is actually only a stub that delegates our calls to the real bean implementation.

To find the home object, we use JNDI, the Java API for naming and directory services. The following code, lifted straight out of the sample client application Cd_collection1.java that JDeveloper created for us, sets a number of parameters to obtain an initial context for the JNDI search. (It uses a hashtable that it builds dynamically, but this is equivalent to using a properties file, which is what we would do in a production environment.) The code then uses JNDI to obtain the home object for our EJB, `Cd_collection`. Here, we are once again looking at the code for the `dispatch()` method:

```
try
{
  // source from sample application code
  Hashtable env = new Hashtable();
  env.put(Context.INITIAL_CONTEXT_FACTORY,
   "com.evermind.server.rmi.RMIInitialContextFactory");
  env.put(Context.SECURITY_PRINCIPAL, "admin");
  env.put(Context.SECURITY_CREDENTIALS, "adminpwd");
  env.put(Context.PROVIDER_URL, "ormi://noizmaker/CDBean");
  Context ctx = new InitialContext(env);
  Cd_collectionHome cd_collectionHome =
      (Cd_collectionHome)ctx.lookup("Cd_collection");
  // end source from sample code
```

Once we have the home object, we can obtain our EJB object by using the CDID and the `findByPrimaryKey()` finder method that obtains the corresponding bean. To do this, we need to create a primary key. In theory, we can use a Java wrapper class as the primary key (and need to use a custom Java class only if it is something more complex, such as a combination of columns) but JDeveloper by default creates a custom primary key class. In this case, it wraps the `long` value representing the CDID. To use the primary key class it has created, `Cd_collectionPK()`, we instantiate it by calling its constructor, which takes a long value. We then use this key and call the finder method that obtains the corresponding bean.

```
Cd_collectionPK pk = new Cd_collectionPK(cdid);
cd_collection = cd_collectionHome.findByPrimaryKey(pk);
```

We can now use this bean by calling its getter and setter methods. Here, we only use it to obtain information to populate a JavaBean, `CDBeanInfo`:

```
    // fill JavaBean
    cdinfo.setAlbumTitle(cdBean.getAlbum_title());
    cdinfo.setReleaseDate(cdBean.getRelease_date());
    cdinfo.setLabel(cdBean.getLabel());
    cdinfo.setArtistID(cdBean.getArtist_id());
    cdinfo.setCDID(cdBean.getCd_id());
 }
catch(Exception e)
{
  System.out.println("Caught: " + e);
}
```

Once we've successfully put the information in a JavaBean, we can set this bean and the artist's name as request attributes. We then obtain and call a request dispatcher; note that we call an error page instead of the regular JSP if we are unable to obtain the CD information.

```
RequestDispatcher dispatcher=null;
if(cd_collection!=null)
{
  request.setAttribute(ARTIST_NAME, artistName);
          request.setAttribute(CD_BEAN, cdinfo);
  dispatcher = servletContext.getRequestDispatcher(JSP_PAGE);
}
else
{
  dispatcher = servletContext.getRequestDispatcher(ERROR_PAGE);
}
dispatcher.forward(request, response);
```

This is the JSP file for displaying the CD information:

```
<!DOCTYPE HTML PUBLIC "-//W3C//DTD 4.0 Transitional//EN">
<HTML>
<HEAD>
<TITLE>CD Info</TITLE>
</HEAD>

<BODY>
<H2>CD Info:</H2>

<jsp:useBean id="CDBean"  class="CDInfoBean" scope="request" />
Album title: <%= CDBean.getAlbumTitle() %><BR>
Artist name: <%= request.getAttribute("ARTISTNAME") %> <BR>
Label: <%= CDBean.getLabel() %><BR>
Release date: <%= CDBean.getReleaseDate() %><BR>

<FORM ACTION="/servlet/MusicServlet" METHOD="POST">
<INPUT TYPE="SUBMIT" NAME="PROCEED" VALUE="Continue">
<INPUT TYPE="HIDDEN" NAME="REQUESTPAGE" VALUE="STARTPAGE">
</FORM>

</BODY>
</HTML>
```

Add the CDInfoController.java and CDInfoBean.java files to the default-web-app\WEB-INF\classes directory and the JSP file to the default-web-app directory, and run the MusicResults application again. This time, when we select a CD, the information for the selected CD will appear in the new CD Info page.

CHAPTER 11

A Quick Tour of EJB

Traditionally, distributed applications were built using protocols, most notably TCP/IP, designed to allow autonomous processes on separate machines to exchange data. A typical client-server application, for example, might comprise a client application that does the processing and display of data and a database server that does nothing but provide the data. The reverse situation is also possible; the client application may be responsible only for the presentation of the data with all processing done on the server.

Modern distributed applications, however, often do not just transfer data but in addition allow one machine to invoke procedures on a remote machine. A popular standard for remote procedure calls (RPC) was developed in the 1980s. The Common Object Request Broker Architecture (CORBA) extended this procedural approach to an object-oriented one by specifying an infrastructure and protocol for distributed objects; this standard allows programs running on different types of hardware and written using different programming languages, to interoperate. EJB, the J2EE distributed object model, is based on CORBA (as well as Java's Remote Method Invocation technology) and is, to some degree, interoperable with CORBA.

In addition to benefits such as better sharing of resources and security, remote object architectures such as CORBA and EJB enable us to build reusable software components that can interoperate with other software components without regard to their location on the network. EJB, because it is based on Java, improves the portability of distributed components across application servers and hardware platforms.

The EJB Distributed Object Model

Enterprise JavaBeans are not JavaBeans; they simply have a similar name because, like JavaBeans, they are components. But EJBs are not merely components—they are distributed components that interoperate by means of proxies. This means that they are not called directly like JavaBeans, but indirectly, through a somewhat complicated mechanism, in order to provide *location transparency*. Location transparency means that a client does not need to know or explicitly determine the location of a remote object.

From the point of view of the client application, the following steps are required to call an EJB method:

- Make a call to JNDI to obtain a home object.
- Call the home object to obtain the EJB object.
- Call the EJB object's method.

Behind the scenes, the client application doesn't actually call the EJB object directly; instead, it calls a local stub that serializes the parameters—called *marshalling* the data—and sends them to the EJB object on the server. The EJB object *unmarshalls* the data, converting it back into Java objects and primitives. This is the first layer of indirection, and it is the key to achieving location transparency.

The EJB object is responsible for managing transactions, security, and resources—everything but the business methods that we define in our bean implementation. Once any necessary services, such as authentication, have been performed, the EJB object ultimately calls the bean implementation to perform the business logic. This is the second layer of indirection, and it allows the EJB container to intercept and intercede in method calls in order to provide services.

To enable this process to work, we (possibly with the aid of a software tool) need to write four pieces of code:

- The home interface
- The remote interface
- The bean implementation class
- The deployment descriptor

Notice that, of these, only the bean implementation is an actual class that is compiled into executable code. The other three files are essentially declarative—the application server and its deployment tools use these interfaces to create the glue-code, including a number of wrapper classes, to support our bean implementation as a distributed component.

Once an EJB is deployed to an application server, the application server manages the life cycle of the bean. Depending on the type of bean and other factors (such as load), the application server may instantiate the bean, populate it with data from the database, save it to disk temporarily, update the database, or destroy the bean, as different calls are made by a client application.

As mentioned previously, there are three kinds of beans:

- Session beans
- Entity beans
- Message-driven beans

We'll next take a brief look at each of these.

Session Beans

Session beans are typically used to implement business methods. They are associated with actions and processes, and are sometimes described as verbs. There are two types of session beans:

- Stateless session beans
- Stateful session beans

Stateless Session Beans

Stateless session beans are used when it is not necessary for the bean to maintain information about the client between method calls. A stateless session bean might be used to build a data analysis component, for example, that accepts input data, processes it, and returns a result of some sort. Another example might be a pricing component that accepts a bill of materials as input and returns the calculated cost that takes into account factors such volume discounts; in this case, the session bean may, in fact, be a façade bean that works in conjunction with other beans to retrieve prices from a database or other systems.

Stateful Session Beans

Stateful session beans are used when the bean must maintain information—often called *conversational state*—about the client between method calls. This is usually the case for beans that support an interactive application. A common example is the ubiquitous shopping cart used by Web applications to allow a user to browse a catalog and add or remove items to an order.

Session Beans and Persistence

Session beans are not persistent objects. This means that, once the client closes the session (or the EJB container is shut down or crashes), the information that it stored is not saved. The principal difference between session beans and standard Java objects is that session beans are distributed objects. Like standard Java objects, any data they contain is lost as soon as they cease to exist.

Even though session beans are not persistent objects, it doesn't mean that they cannot use persistent data. They are entirely capable of using a database to store or retrieve data. Session beans are sometimes more efficient than entity beans for accessing data from a database, especially for providing read-only access.

Session beans are often used to provide a wrapper, or façade, for one or more entity beans. When multiple entity beans are used, a session bean façade can provide greater control and flexibility in setting transaction boundaries.

Entity Beans

The primary characteristic of entity beans is that they represent persistent information about people, places, or things. They are sometimes called nouns. Persistent in this case means that the information in an entity bean is saved, even if the client application closes its session or the EJB container is shut down or crashes—this is an assurance that the vendor of an application server must provide. This persistence could, in theory, be implemented in many ways, such as writing to operating system files, but in practice, a database is used—usually a standard relational database, such as Oracle.

There are two types of entity beans:

- Container-managed persistent (CMP) entity beans
- Bean-managed persistent (BMP) entity beans

CMP Beans

In the previous chapter, we saw an example of a CMP entity bean. Each bean was mapped to a row in a database table, and the EJB container managed all database access behind the scenes. We only used the CMP bean to retrieve data in that example, but the EJB can also automatically update the database behind the scenes as we create, update, and destroy CMP beans.

When we used a wizard in JDeveloper to create the CMP from a database table in the last chapter, the only option it provided was to map the bean to a single row of a table or view. Based on our selection, it created the EJB deployment descriptor, an XML file that describes this mapping. If we need more flexibility than that offered by the JDeveloper wizard, we can create or modify this file ourselves. Not only can we be more selective about mapping columns, but by using a special query language, EJB-QL, we can also define the SQL that the container will use, as well.

BMP Beans

In a BMP entity bean, we write the persistence code ourselves. To do this, we need to implement a set of methods specified by the EntityBean interface, usually using JDBC, that create, delete, retrieve, and update the database table or tables corresponding to our bean.

Choosing Between CMP and BMP Beans

Choosing between CMP and BMP is not always easy. Here are some considerations:

- CMP pros:
  - Rapid application development
  - Potentially better performance
  - Better portability between databases
- CMP cons:
  - Hard to debug
  - Dependent on vendor tools—or XML and EJB-QL—for mapping
- BMP pros:
  - Greater control and flexibility
  - Easier to understand and debug
  - Requires two calls to the database to load an object
- BMP cons:
  - Database code is tedious to write and error-prone

Both actually have a lot going for them and present no serious disadvantages. Given that CMP is easiest to use and excellent for prototyping, the best approach may simply be to use CMP at first and move beans to BMP if it proves necessary later as you gain better understanding of the problem and greater experience with EJB.

Using Session Beans Instead of Entity Beans

A more important question is whether to use entity beans at all. Sometimes, a session bean with JDBC may be easier to develop and may perform better than an entity bean, because entity beans have much more overhead. On the other hand, attempting to code a complex relationship in a session bean using JDBC could become unwieldy, and entity beans may be better suited to this type of task. Answering this question will ultimately depend on your (and possibly your teammates') experience and the application requirements.

Message-Driven Beans

Message-driven beans are fundamentally different from session and entity beans in that they do not use a remote execution protocol. Message beans are invoked asynchronously using a messaging service; because there is no guarantee that the message will be delivered in a timely manner, the client does not wait for a reply. The system may be set up so that the client will hear back from the message bean later via email. The issues involved in developing message-driven beans are not typically database-related and we won't consider them here any further.

Introduction to Bean Building: A Stateless Session Bean

In the previous chapter, we used JDeveloper to create a container-managed persistent entity bean automatically for us. At that time, we merely used the bean as a sort of magic data access object and didn't examine it in detail. For bean types other than CMP, JDeveloper produces some common boilerplate code, but by itself, this code has no functionality and we'll need to add some code of our own in order to complete the bean.

To become familiar with the details of EJBs and the process of developing, packaging, and deploying them—and before moving on to the issues of persistence—we'll start with a simple Hello, world example, using a stateless session bean.

First we'll add a new project, HelloWorld, to the JDeveloper workspace we created in the last chapter:

- Right-click on the workspace ejbExamples.
- Select New Project.
- Select Projects on the left side of the box that appears and Empty on the right.
- Change the directory name to HelloWorld.
- Change the filename to HelloWorld.jpr and press OK.

Now, we'll create the stateless session bean:

- Right-click on the new project, HelloWorld.jpr.
- Select New…
- Click on Enterpise JavaBeans on the left side of the box and Stateless Session bean on the right. Press OK.
- On the Enterprise JavaBean Wizard welcome screen, press Next.
- Change the EJB name to HelloWorld; press Next.
- Accept the defaults in the next screen, and press Finish.

This will create four files, the essential parts of the EJB:

- HelloWorldHome.java—The home interface, extends EJBHome.
- HelloWorldBean.java—The bean implementation, implements sessionBean.
- HelloWorld.java—The remote interface, extends EJBObject.
- Deployment descriptor—An XML file.

The Home Interface—HelloWorldHome.java

The home interface allows us to obtain a reference to the bean. This is the home interface that JDeveloper created for us:

```
package mypackage2;
import javax.ejb.EJBHome;
import java.rmi.RemoteException;
import javax.ejb.CreateException;

public interface HelloWorldHome extends EJBHome
{
  HelloWorld create() throws RemoteException, CreateException;
}
```

This is fine just the way it is. Typically, we don't need to do anything special in the home interface of a session bean.

The Bean Implementation—HelloWorldBean.java

As it stands, our bean won't do much. We need to add a method to the bean implementation that returns a *Hello, world* message. This is what the bean implementation looks like before we touch it:

```
package mypackage2.impl;
import javax.ejb.SessionBean;
import javax.ejb.SessionContext;

public class HelloWorldBean implements SessionBean
{
  public void ejbCreate()
  {
  }

  public void ejbActivate()
  {
  }

  public void ejbPassivate()
  {
  }

  public void ejbRemove()
  {
  }

  public void setSessionContext(SessionContext ctx)
  {
  }
}
```

Notice that JDeveloper has created a number of methods that begin with `ejb`. These are required methods that the application server will call during the life cycle of the bean. We can add code to these if we want the bean to do something special—immediately after it's created or before it's destroyed, for example. Otherwise, we can just leave them empty, as we will here.

The `setSessionContext()` gives us the opportunity to save a reference to the context that the bean is running in. We could create a class attribute, `SessionContext ctx`, and set it using a line of code like this:

```
this.ctx=ctx;
```

This can be used for obtaining session information and information about the bean itself. This is important in some cases, but we won't need it for this example.

The only change we'll make is to add this method after the `setSessionContext()`, for example:

```
public String getMessage()
{
  return "Hello, world";
}
```

The Remote Interface—HelloWorld.java

The bean implementation isn't the only code we need to change. Client programs interact with our bean only indirectly. What clients actually see is the remote interface. For every method in our bean implementation that we want a client to able to call, we need to add the method's signature to the remote interface. Here is what the interface looks like as initially created by JDeveloper:

```
package mypackage2;
import javax.ejb.EJBObject;

public interface HelloWorld extends EJBObject
{
}
```

We'll add the following line to the HelloWorld class:

```
public String getMessage() throws java.rmi.RemoteException;
```

Notice that, because this is the remote interface, it is possible that an error may occur while calling it, due to network problems, for example, so we must indicate that it can throw a RemoteException.

The Deployment Descriptor—ejb-jar.xml

JDeveloper also creates the deployment descriptor: an XML file that describes an EJB (or EJBs, if we have more than one in a project). The descriptor for a stateless session bean is fairly simple, as deployment descriptors go, but it's still nice not to have to type it in by hand.

```
<?xml version = '1.0' encoding = 'windows-1252'?>
<!DOCTYPE ejb-jar PUBLIC "-//Sun Microsystems, Inc.//DTD Enterprise
JavaBeans 1.1//EN" "http://java.sun.com/j2ee/dtds/ejb-jar_1_1.dtd">
<ejb-jar>
   <enterprise-beans>
      <session>
         <description>Session Bean ( Stateless )</description>
         <display-name>HelloWorld</display-name>
         <ejb-name>HelloWorld</ejb-name>
         <home>mypackage2.HelloWorldHome</home>
         <remote>mypackage2.HelloWorld</remote>
         <ejb-class>mypackage2.impl.HelloWorldBean</ejb-class>
         <session-type>Stateless</session-type>
         <transaction-type>Container</transaction-type>
      </session>
   </enterprise-beans>
</ejb-jar>
```

We don't need to make any changes to this file.

Running the Bean Inside the JDeveloper Environment

To test the bean, we'll run it inside the embedded application server:

- Right-click on the HelloWorld bean.
- Select Run HelloWorld.

The log window will display messages as the classes are compiled, the embedded server is started, and beans are deployed. If there are no problems, we can next create a sample application to test the HelloWorld bean.

Creating a Sample Application to Test the HelloWorld Bean

To create a sample application:

- Right-click on the HelloWorld bean.
- Select Create Sample Java Client.
- Ensure that Connect to OC4J Embedded in JDeveloper is selected and press OK.

This will create a sample application. It will contain code to create a bean and to call our method but it will be commented out, like this:

```
    // Use one of the create() methods below to create a new instance
    // helloWorld = helloWorldHome.create(  );


    // Call any of the Remote methods below to access the EJB
    // helloWorld.getMessage(  );
}
```

Uncomment the call to `helloWorldHome.create()` and put the call to our bean, `helloWorld.getMessage()`, inside a call to `System.out.println()`, like this:

```
// Use one of the create() methods below to create a new instance
helloWorld = helloWorldHome.create(  );

// Call any of the Remote methods below to access the EJB
System.out.println(helloWorld.getMessage(  ));
```

Now run it:

- Right-click on HelloWorldClient.java.
- Select Run HelloWorldClient.java from the popup menu.

The message *Hello, world* should appear in the log window. If it doesn't, examine each of the error logs by selecting the tabs at the top of the log window for compilation errors or other problems.

DEBUGGING WITH JDEVELOPER

An important feature of JDeveloper is its ability to debug EJBs running in either the embedded server or a remote application server. We'll take a brief look at local debugging here. For information about remote debugging, consult Oracle's JDeveloper documentation.

To debug a program, we first need to set one or more breakpoints in our program. For example, open HelloWorldClient.java by double-clicking on the filename in the System Navigator. Locate the following line:

```
helloWorld = helloWorldHome.create(  );
```

Clicking on the number to the left of this line will set a breakpoint, indicated by a red dot that replaces the line number. Also set a breakpoint in our EJB, HelloWorldBean.java, at this line:

```
return "Hello, world";
```

We'll need to restart the HelloWorld EJB with debugging options enabled. To do this, right-click on the HelloWorld bean and select Debug HelloWorld. This will start (or restart) the EJB in debug mode. Notice that we won't enter the EJB code until a client application invokes it. So next, right-click on HelloWorldClient.java and select Debug HelloWorldClient.java. This will start the application and stop at the first breakpoint.

Notice that, at this point, the debugging icons are active in the toolbar below the menu. Positioning the mouse pointer over each for a moment will cause a tool tip to appear, identifying its function and its associated shortcut key. These are:

- Resume (F9)—Causes program to restart.
- Step over (F8)—Executes current line of code; if it's a method, it calls it and returns.

- Step into (F7)—If current line of code is a method, moves cursor into the method called, opening the source file, if necessary, but does not execute it. If current line is not a method call, executes the statement.
- Step out (Shift-F7)—Executes to end of current method, returns to calling method, and stops execution there.
- Step to end of method—Executes to end of current method, stops before returning to the calling method.

Another important tool is the SmartData view, available under the Tools menu item, which displays a tree view of objects and their attributes. You may wish to spend some time becoming familiar with this and other debug tools.

Packaging and Deploying the EJB—Overview

Once we have the bean working in the JDeveloper environment, we can package it in preparation for deployment to an application server. We'll do this by using JDeveloper in the next section, but first, let's take a look at the steps that would be involved were we to do it manually.

The J2EE specification defines a way to package Web applications and EJB applications into modules and a way to package these modules into an enterprise application. An enterprise application is packaged in an EAR file. The EAR file, in turn, can contain either EJB modules packaged as JAR files, Web applications packaged as WAR files, or both.

- Enterprise application—EAR file
- EJB module—JAR file
    - EJBs (Java classes)
    - Deployment descriptor
- Web application—WAR file
    - Servlets
    - JSPs

Note that, although they are called EAR, JAR, and WAR files, they are all the same type of file—archives produced using the Java jar utility. The extension serves only to indicate what type of contents the archive contains. Figure 11–1 shows the assembly of an EAR file.

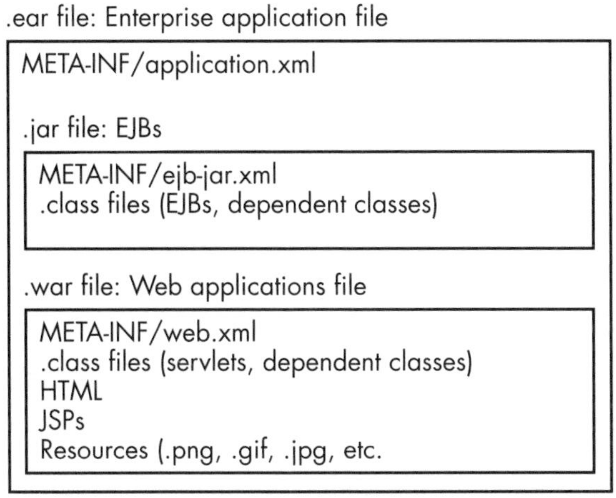

.ear file: Enterprise application file

```
META-INF/application.xml

.jar file: EJBs
    META-INF/ejb-jar.xml
    .class files (EJBs, dependent classes)

.war file: Web applications file
    META-INF/web.xml
    .class files (servlets, dependent classes)
    HTML
    JSPs
    Resources (.png, .gif, .jpg, etc.
```

FIGURE 11–1 Enterprise application archive assembly.

Creating JAR, WAR, and EAR files

Having written our EJB and compiled it, the resulting .class files and the deployment descriptor must be placed in a specific directory structure.

```
META-INF\ejb-jar.xml
classes
```

META-INF is a directory that contains the deployment descriptor, ejb-jar.xml (as presented above), listing all the EJBs that we are packaging in this EJB module (which is only one in this example, of course). The classes that each EJB comprises are also specified in the ejb-jar.xml.

If the EJB's class files were not included in packages, they would be located in the top-level directory as peers of the META-INF directory. But classes are generally organized into packages. In this example, JDeveloper put our interfaces into a package named `mypackage2` and our bean implementation into a subpackage of this, `mypackage2\impl`. The directory structure must correspond to this package structure (as must the entries in the deployment descriptor). The directory and file structure for our HelloWorld EJB is, therefore, as follows:

- META-INF\ejb-jar.xml
- Mypackage2\HelloWorld.class
- Mypackage2\HelloWorldHome.class
- Mypackage2\impl\HelloWorldBean.class

We bundle the EJB and the deployment descriptor into a JAR file using the standard Java jar utility. Assuming that we are in the top-level directory, we could use the following command:

```
jar -cvf HelloWorld.jar *
```

This produces a file, HelloWorld.jar.

If we were building a full-blown Web application, we might also have Web components such as servlets and JSPs which we would also bundle using the Java jar utility. In this case, however, we would use a different extension, calling the file HelloWebApp.war, for example, to indicate that it is a Web module. We'll skip that step here because it doesn't apply to our example.

Once we've created our EJB JAR file and, hypothetically, a Web module WAR file, we can bundle them into an enterprise application archive—an EAR file. Like the EJB JAR format, the EAR requires that we have a META-INF directory with an XML descriptor. This XML file, the application descriptor, lists all the JAR files and WAR files (and possibly dependency libraries and other resources) in the application. This is what the directory structure generally looks like:

```
META-INF\application.xml
ejb-module.jar
web-module.war
```

The EJB JAR files and Web module WAR files are usually placed in the top-level directory, but they can also be in subdirectories; for a large application with many EJB and Web modules, this might make more sense. Their entries in the application descriptor obviously must indicate the directories they are in, if this is the case.

The application descriptor for our HelloWorld application, application.xml, might look like this:

```
<?xml version = '1.0' encoding = 'windows-1252'?>
<!DOCTYPE application PUBLIC "-//Sun Microsystems, Inc.//DTD J2EE
Application 1.2//EN" "http://java.sun.com/j2ee/dtds/
application_1_2.dtd">
<application>
   <display-name>HelloWorld</display-name>
   <module>
      <ejb>HelloWorld.jar</ejb>
   </module>
</application>
```

This is what our directory structure looks like:

```
META-INF\application.xml
HelloWorld.jar
```

To generate the EAR file using Java jar utility, we could run the following command in the top-level directory:

```
jar -cvfM HelloWorld.ear *
```

The well-specified format of an EAR file and its components, such as the EJB JAR file and Web application WAR file, help ensure the portability of an enterprise application between different vendors' application servers. An EAR file can (at least in principle) be deployed on any J2EE-compliant application server.

Unlike the preceding steps—developing and packaging the EJB—the step of deploying the EJB is not specified by the J2EE specification and depends on the application server. OC4J provides an administration tool, admin.jar, in the same directory as oc4j.jar for this task. It's also possible simply to edit the server.xml file (in the OC4J config directory) and add an entry for the new EAR file. The OC4J server will notice the change and deploy it automatically.

Packaging and Deploying the EJB with JDeveloper

One of the unstated points of the preceding section is that packaging and deploying an EJB is the type of well-defined, laborious task that is best automated. Indeed, every application server vendor provides some kind of tool (or tools) for producing and deploying EAR files.

To package and deploy our HelloWorld EJB using JDeveloper, we first need to create the deployment profile, as follows:

- Right-click on the project file, HelloWorld.jpr.
- On the box that appears, Select Deployment Profiles; on the left, select EJD JAR File—J2EE EJB Module.
- In the next box, change the filename to HelloWorld. We don't actually care what the deployment profile file is called, but JDeveloper bases the name of the JAR file, EAR file, and the application name on the name of the profile file. Press Save.
- Accept the defaults presented on this screen.

The deployment profile generates an XML file specific to JDeveloper that, among other things, indicates the name of the EJB JAR file and the EAR file that are to be generated when we deploy the HelloWorld EJB.

The JAR and EAR files aren't generated until we actually deploy the EJB. To do this:

- Right-click on the deployment profile, HelloWorld.deploy.
- Select Deploy to=>OC4J (assuming that you've created the OC4J connection, as described in the previous chapter).

The log window will display the progress as it creates the JAR and EAR files, and invokes admin.jar. If successful, there will be an exit status of 0 (indicating no errors), and the message *Deployment finished* will appear.

To test this EJB, create a sample application.

- Right-click on the HelloWorld bean embedded OC4J.
- Select Connect to Remote Server.
- Verify that the application name is HelloWorld and that the connection to the standalone OC4J instance is selected. Press OK.

This generates a Java file, HelloWorldClient1.java. It differs from the sample application we created above only in that the admin password for the application server and the URL for the EJB are different.

```
env.put(Context.SECURITY_PRINCIPAL, "admin");
env.put(Context.SECURITY_CREDENTIALS, "adminpwd");
env.put(Context.PROVIDER_URL, "ormi://noizmaker/HelloWorld");
```

As before, uncomment the call to `helloWorldHome.create()` and `helloWorld.getMessage()`, and enclose the latter call with a call to `System.out.println()`.

```
// Use one of the create() methods below to create a new instance
helloWorld = helloWorldHome.create(  );

// Call any of the Remote methods below to access the EJB
System.out.println(helloWorld.getMessage(  ));
```

Right-click on HelloWorldClient1.java and select Run HelloWorldClient1.java. This will run the program and display the "Hello, world" message in the log window.

We can also run the EJB client application outside of JDeveloper. The easiest way is to start with the command line that appeared in the message window when we ran HelloWorldClient1.java. We can't simply copy and paste this command as it is to a command prompt, however. First, we need to substitute *java.exe* for *javaw.exe*. The difference between them is that javaw.exe does not use a console window, so if we run our application with javaw.exe from a command prompt, we won't get any output.

We can optionally make a few more changes to simplify the command line. First, we can omit the -ojvm option, which selects Oracle's specialized Java Virtual Machine, OJVM. This is a nonstandard option, and it's not necessary, in any case, because it's the default with Oracle's version of java.exe and javaw.exe. Also, we can eliminate the entries in the CLASSPATH that we don't need for our application, such as mail.jar and jaxp.jar.

The simplified command for starting our application is

```
c:\JDeveloper\jdk\bin\java D:\jdev\jdev\mywork\ejbexamples\
HelloWorld\classes;D:\jdev\Jdk\jre\lib\ext\activation.jar;D
:\jdev\jdk\jre\lib\ext\jndi.jar;D:\jdev\j2ee\home\ejb.jar;D
:\jdev\j2ee\home\jdbc.jar;D:\jdev\j2ee\home\jaas.jar;D:\jde
v\j2ee\home\oc4j.jar Samplemypackage2.HelloWorldClient
```

Instead of typing this by hand at a command prompt, you may wish to write a batch file to run it, instead. The following example is not only easier to understand and maintain, but it can also be adapted for other client applications.

```
@echo off
rem runhello.bat - Run EJB HelloWorld client application
setlocal

rem Java application to run
rem ---------------------------------------------------------
set JAVA_APP=Samplemypackage2.HelloWorldClient1

rem Set these paths according to your environment
rem ---------------------------------------------------------
set JRE_LIB=c:\JDeveloper\jdk\jre\lib\ext
set OC4J=c:\JDeveloper\j2ee\home

rem These jar files shouldn't change much, unless you use
rem additional j2ee features such as JAXP
rem ---------------------------------------------------------
set JRE_CLASSES=%JRE_LIB%\activation.jar;%JRE_LIB%\jndi.jar
set
OC4J_CLASSES=%OC4J%\ejb.jar;%OC4J%\jdbc.jar;%OC4J%\oc4j.jar

rem Set environment variables
```

```
rem ------------------------------------------------------------
set CLASSPATH=.;%JRE_CLASSES%;%OC4J_CLASSES%
set PATH=%JDEV%\jdk\bin\java;%PATH%

rem Run application:
rem ------------------------------------------------------------
java %JAVA_APP%

endlocal
```

Create and save this in the classes directory of your project, for example, as runhello.bat in the following directory:

```
c:\JDeveloper\jdev\mywork\ejbexamples\HelloWorld\classes
```

At a DOS prompt, change to this directory and enter the command runhello:

```
D:\jdev\jdev\mywork\ejbexamples\HelloWorld\classes>runhello

Hello, world
```

Session Beans, Value Objects, and Data Access Objects

In this and in the sections that follow, we'll take a look at a session bean and an entity bean, and see how they both can be used for accessing information in a database. We'll also examine how other objects—value objects and data access objects—can help improve performance and reduce complexity.

Value Objects

One of the potential problems of using a remote object to perform database access is that EJBs often have getter and setter methods for each of their attributes. If these method calls are local, the overhead may be acceptable, but if it's over a network, this can generate a lot of network traffic. One way around this problem is to use a value object to encapsulate all the data and send all the data at once. This is similar to the approach we used in the previous chapter, where we used JavaBeans to pass data from a servlet to a JSP page.

One important difference between the JavaBean we used to pass data from a Java class to a JSP and a value object used to pass data from an EJB to a client application is that the value object must implement the `Serializable` interface. This is because the value object must be serialized before it can be transferred over the network.

Data Access Objects

Another potential problem is that multiple remote objects typically need to access the database; if we have duplicate code in multiple objects, changes will need to be made in many places if the database changes. This problem can be solved by providing a single object, a data access object (DAO) that simplifies and manages access to the database for remote objects.

Session Bean Example

In this example, we'll use a session bean to obtain CD information. Unlike the CMP entity bean in the last chapter where we were restricted to using a single row from a single table, we'll also include information about each of the songs on the CD.

To begin, use JDeveloper to create a new project, CDInfo, and a stateless session bean, also called `CDInfo`, following the steps outlined above. This will create the remote interface CDInfo.java, the home interface CDInfo-Home.java, and the bean implementation class CDInfoBean.java.

We'll add a method to our session bean, CDInfoBean.java, to retrieve the CD information. This method will instantiate a data access object, `CDInfoDAO`, then will call it to obtain the data which is packaged in a value object, `CDInfoModel`.

```
Package mypackage3.impl;
import javax.ejb.SessionBean;
import javax.ejb.SessionContext;
import mypackage3.CDInfoModel;
import mypackage3.CDInfoDAO;

public class CDInfoBean implements SessionBean
{
  public CDInfoModel getCDInfoModel(long cdid)
  {
    CDInfoDAO cdDAO = new cdDAO();
    return cdDAO.createCDInfoModel();
  }

  /* ...*/

}
```

Notice that we must import the DAO and value object classes. We must also declare a corresponding method in our remote interface.

```
package mypackage3;
import javax.ejb.EJBObject;
import java.rmi.RemoteException;
import mypackage3.CDInfoModel;
import mypackage3.CDInfoDAO;

public interface CDInfo extends EJBObject
{
  public CDInfoModel getCDInfoModel(long cdid)
     throws RemoteException;
}
```

These are the only changes we need to make in the EJB itself. Next, we will create the value object and DAO classes.

To create the value object class, `CDInfoModel`, right-click on the CDInfo.jpr project file and select New Class; then, in the screen that follows, enter the class name, `CDInfoModel`. The remaining defaults are okay. The class implements the `Serializable` interface and generally follows JavaBean conventions—with getter and setter methods to provide public access to private instance variables.

```
package mypackage3;
import java.util.Vector;
import java.io.Serializable;

public class CDInfoModel implements Serializable
{
  private long cdid;
  private String artistName;
  private String title;
  private String label;
  private String releaseDate;
  private Vector songs = new Vector();

  public CDInfoModel()
  {
  }
  // getters
  public long getCdid()
  {
    return cdid;
  }
  public String getArtistName()
  {
    return artistName;
  }
```

```
  public String getTitle()
  {
    return title;
  }
  public String getLabel()
  {
    return label;
  }
  public String getReleaseDate()
  {
    return releaseDate;
  }
  public Vector getSongs()
  {
    return songs;
  }

  // setters
  public void setCdid(long cdid)
  {
    this.cdid = cdid;
  }
  public void setArtistName(String artistName)
  {
    this.artistName = artistName;
  }
  public void setTitle(String title)
  {
    this.title = title;
  }
  public void setLabel(String label)
  {
    this.label = label;
  }
  public void setReleaseDate(String releaseDate)
  {
    this.releaseDate = releaseDate;
  }
  public void setSongs(Vector songs)
  {
    this.songs = songs;
  }
}
```

Next, we create a class for storing the information for each song.

```
package mypackage3;
import java.io.Serializable;

public class CDSong implements Serializable
{
  private String title;
  private String composer;
  private int length;

  public CDSong()
  {
  }

  // getter methods
  public String getTitle()
  {
    return title;
  }
  public String getComposer()
  {
    return composer;
  }
  public int getLength()
  {
    return length;
  }

  // setter methods
  public void setTitle(String title)
  {
    this.title = title;
  }
  public void setComposer(String composer)
  {
    this.composer = composer;
  }
  public void setLength(int length)
  {
    this.length = length;
  }
}
```

Finally, we create the data access object, `CDInfoDAO`, that will access the database and populate the `CDInfoModel` with data.

```
package mypackage3;
import java.sql.*;
import java.util.*;
import javax.naming.*;
import java.io.*;

public class CDInfoDAO
{
  Connection conn = null;
  Statement stmt = null;

  public CDInfoDAO()
  {
  }

  public CDInfoModel createCDInfoModel(long cd_id)
  {
    CDInfoModel cdModel = new CDInfoModel();
    try
    {
      getConnection();
      stmt = conn.createStatement();
      // Get CD info
      String sql = "SELECT DISPLAY_NAME(A.NAME, A.SURNAME, A.LOCALE), " +
                   "C.ALBUM_TITLE, C.LABEL, C.RELEASE_DATE " +
                   "FROM CD_COLLECTION C, ARTISTS A " +
                   "WHERE C.ARTIST_ID = A.ARTIST_ID " +
                   "AND CD_ID = " + cd_id;
      ResultSet rs = stmt.executeQuery(sql);
      while(rs.next())
      {
        cdModel.setArtistName(rs.getString(1));
        cdModel.setTitle(rs.getString(2));
        cdModel.setLabel(rs.getString(3));
        cdModel.setReleaseDate(rs.getString(4));
      }
      rs.close();

      // Get song list
      Vector songs = new Vector();
      sql = "SELECT TITLE, COMPOSER, LENGTH FROM SONGS " +
            "WHERE  CD_ID=" + cd_id;
      rs = stmt.executeQuery(sql);
      while(rs.next())
      {
        CDSong song = new CDSong();
        song.setTitle(rs.getString(1));
```

```
        song.setComposer(rs.getString(2));
        song.setLength(rs.getInt(3));
        songs.add(song);
      }
      cdModel.setSongs(songs);
    }
    catch (Exception e)
    {
      System.out.println("createCDinfoModel() - Caught: " + e);
    }
    return cdModel;
  }

  private void getConnection()
  {
    try
    {
      InitialContext ic=new InitialContext();
      javax.sql.DataSource ds =
           (javax.sql.DataSource)(ic.lookup("jdbc/OsirisDS"));
      conn= ds.getConnection();
    }
    catch(Exception e)
    {
      System.out.println("getConnection() - Caught: " + e);
    }
  }
}
```

Configuring an EJB DataSource

In an EJB, we don't register and load an Oracle JDBC driver as we would in a standalone application. Database connectivity is one of the services that is provided by the EJB container in the form of a datasource. This has two benefits. First, portability is improved because we obtain the datasource by doing JNDI lookup, so the datasource can be configured by changing the data-source.xml file instead of editing the source and recompiling the application. Second, because the EJB container is managing database access, it can transparently provide features such as connection pooling, which can improve performance.

Note how we do this in the code above: We call a parameterless constructor, `InitialContext()`, to obtain the JNDI initial context, `ic`. Unlike a client application, where we must provide the JNDI properties for the initial context (either by building a hashtable or by reading a properties file), here the EJB container uses the application's default context environment to create the JNDI initial context. Next, we call the initial context's `ic.lookup()` method to obtain the datasource, using the logical name "`jdbc/OsirisDS`".

Before running the EJB in the embedded EJB container or deploying it to the standalone server, we need to set up the datasource information. We can do this by editing the data-source.xml file. For the embedded server, this file is located in the c:\JDeveloper\jdev\system\oc4j-config directory, assuming that JDeveloper is installed in c:\JDeveloper.

For the standalone OC4J server, it's in the c:\JDeveloper\j2ee\home\config directory, assuming that we're using the one that came with JDeveloper.

We must specify several datasources: one that provides connection pooling, another that supports distributed transactions, and an EJB-aware one that supports pooled connections and distributed transactions.

```
<?xml version="1.0" standalone='yes'?>
<!DOCTYPE data-sources PUBLIC "Orion data-sources" "http://
xmlns.oracle.com/ias/dtds/data-sources.dtd">

<data-sources>

    <data-source
      class="com.evermind.sql.DriverManagerDataSource"
      name="Osiris"
      location="jdbc/Osiris"
      xa-location="jdbc/xa/OsirisXADS"
      ejb-location="jdbc/OsirisDS"
      connection-driver="oracle.jdbc.driver.OracleDriver"
      username="david"
      password="bigcat"
      url="jdbc:oracle:thin:@localhost:1521:osiris"
      inactivity-timeout="30"
    />

</data-sources>
```

Typically in an EJB application, we would use the ejb-location `DataSource`, which is named `jdbc/osirisDS` here.

Testing the CDInfoBean EJB

We can use JDeveloper to build a sample application to test our EJB, as we did for the previous example, by right-clicking on CDInfo bean and selecting Create Sample Java client. Depending on whether you're running the bean in the embedded EJB container or on a standalone container, select either Connect to OC4J Embedded in JDeveloper or Connect to Remote App Server.

We'll need to make the following changes in order to print out information for a selected CD:

- Uncomment the line to create the session bean.
- Add code to obtain a CDInfoModel value object for an arbitrary CD. (In this example, we hard-coded the value of a known CD_ID, 107L.)
- Add print statements with getter methods.

With these changes, the sample application looks like this:

```
package Samplemypackage3;
import java.util.Hashtable;
import javax.naming.Context;
import javax.naming.InitialContext;
import mypackage3.CDInfo;
import mypackage3.CDInfoHome;
import mypackage3.CDInfoModel;
import mypackage3.CDSong;
import java.util.Vector;
import java.lang.Integer;

public class CDInfoClient2
{
  public static void main(String [] args)
  {
    CDInfoClient2 cDInfoClient2 = new CDInfoClient2();
    try
    {
      Hashtable env = new Hashtable();
      env.put(Context.INITIAL_CONTEXT_FACTORY,
         "com.evermind.server.rmi.RMIInitialContextFactory");
      env.put(Context.SECURITY_PRINCIPAL, "admin");
      env.put(Context.SECURITY_CREDENTIALS, "adminpwd");
      env.put(Context.PROVIDER_URL, "ormi://noizmaker/CDInfo");
      Context ctx = new InitialContext(env);
      CDInfoHome cDInfoHome = (CDInfoHome)ctx.lookup("CDInfo");
      CDInfo cDInfo;

      // Create EJB
      cDInfo = cDInfoHome.create(  );

      // Call EJB method to get CD information
      CDInfoModel cdInfo = cDInfo.getCDInfoModel(107L );

      // Print information from CDInfoModel
      System.out.println(cdInfo.getArtistName());
```

```
      System.out.println(cdInfo.getTitle());
      System.out.print(cdInfo.getLabel() + ", ");
      System.out.println(cdInfo.getReleaseDate());
      Vector songs = cdInfo.getSongs();
      for(int i=0; i < songs.size(); i++)
      {
        CDSong song = (CDSong) songs.elementAt(i);
        System.out.println("  " + (i + 1)  + ". " +
                           song.getTitle() +
                           ", " + song.getComposer() + " - " +
                           formatTime(song.getLength()));
      }
    }
    catch(Exception e)
    {
      System.out.println("Caught: " + e);
    }

  }

  public static String formatTime(int time)
  {
    int min = time/60;
    int sec = time - (min*60);
    return Integer.toString(min) + ":" + Integer.toString(sec);
  }
}
```

Notice that we've also added a helper method, `formatTime()`, which takes the time in seconds and formats it into a string, with minutes and seconds separated by a colon.

The sample application prints out information in the following format:

```
Richard and Linda Thompson
Shoot Out the Lights
Hannibal, 1982
  1. Don't Renege On Our Love, Richard Thompson - 4:15
  2. Walking On A Wire, Richard Thompson - 5:24
  3. Man In Need, Richard Thompson - 3:32
  4. Just The Motion, Richard Thompson - 6:16
  5. Shoot Out The Lights, Richard Thompson - 5:20
  6. Black Street Slide, Richard Thompson - 4:29
  7. Did She Jump Or Was She Pushed, Richard and Linda Thompson - 4:45
  8. Wall Of Death, Richard Thompson - 3:42
```

We'll stop here with this example, but we should note that this is more nearly what we would want in the Web application that we examined in the last chapter, where we used a CMP entity bean that JDeveloper created for us. Certainly, creating the CMP bean was a lot easier but we were much more limited in what we could do. Also, because its life cycle is managed by the container, the database is updated each time we call it even though we use it as a read-only object. Here, we don't have that overhead.

Finally, it's worth noting that if this information were being displayed using a JSP, the `formatTime()` method would be a good candidate for a custom tag because it is Java code used for formatting purposes and doesn't properly belong in an EJB, servlet, or controller helper class.

A Bean-Managed Persistent Entity Bean

As mentioned previously, an entity bean differs from a session bean in that an entity bean is persistent—meaning that, conceptually, once an entity bean is created, it continues to exist, and until we explicitly destroy it we can use it and make changes to it, even if the client application that creates it closes or crashes or the EJB container it lives in closes or crashes (once the container is re-started, of course). A Web application, for example, might use an entity bean to store customer orders. If we create an order one day, we can go back the next day or week later, check on its status, and possibly make changes or cancel it.

Of course, an entity bean doesn't really have a continuous existence as a Java object in a virtual reality manifested by the EJB container—this is an illusion it attempts to create. Behind the scenes, the EJB container carefully manages the entity bean's data—typically by using a database—and storing, updating, and deleting the data as required. Another way to look at it is to consider the entity bean to be the set of data associated with a primary key, regardless of whether the data is stored in a database as a database record, in memory as a Java object, or on disk as a serialized object. It is the job of the EJB container to move the data around as appropriate and to keep these different forms properly synchronized in response to client applications.

We don't have to worry about any of the details in the case of a container-managed persistent bean (except when we first create the EJB and map the bean to a database table and its columns by either using the JDeveloper wizard or by writing the deployment descriptor). The EJB container and its deployment tools take care of creating the database code and calling the appropriate methods to create, find, change, or destroy the CMP entity bean.

In the case of a bean-managed persistent entity bean, the EJB container will automatically make the appropriate method calls in response to requests to create, find, change, or destroy a BMP bean, but we are responsible for writing the actual code in these methods to perform the database operations.

In order for the EJB container to perform its database-related duties, we need to provide an implementation for the following methods in the bean implementation file:

- `ejbCreate()`
- `ejbFindByPrimaryKey()`
- `ejbActivate()`
- `ejbLoad()`
- `ejbStore()`
- `ejbPassivate()`
- `ejbRemove()`
- `setEntityContext()`
- `unsetEntityContext()`

Database operations in these methods can be implemented in a number of different ways, using SQL/J, JDBC, Java Data Objects, or another object-relational mapping tool. In the example that follows, we'll use the most usual method, using JDBC.

Creating the BMP Entity Bean Example

To keep this example simple, we'll create a BMP for managing a small set of user information. First, using SQL*Plus, create a new table in the database.

```
CREATE TABLE USER_INFO(
  USERNAME  VARCHAR2(32),
  EMAIL VARCHAR2(32),
  PASSWORD VARCHAR2(32),
  MEMBER_SINCE DATE,
  PRIMARY KEY (EMAIL)
);
```

Next, using JDeveloper, following the same general steps described above, create a new empty project, UserInfo, in the ejbExamples workspace, and in that project, create a BMP EJB named `UserInfo`. The EJB wizard at one point will allow you to define or select a primary key: Click on the selection Built-in JDK class. By default, this class should already be `java.lang.String`; if it's not, select this from the drop-down list, then press Finish.

JDeveloper will create a number of files. These include:

- Bean implementation: `UserInfoBean`
- Home interface: `UserInfoHome`
- Remote interface: `UserInfo`
- Deployment descriptor: ejb-jar.xml

Our job of turning these files into a fully functional BMP will consist of the following tasks:

- In Bean implementation, `UserInfoBean`:
  - Add private instance variables for the data.
  - Modify or add `ejbCreate()` and `ejbPostCreate()` methods, as necessary.
  - Implement the remaining required `ejbXXX` methods.
  - Add additional finder methods, if desired.
  - Create getter/setter methods to allow client applications to retrieve information from the EJB.
- In home interface, `UserInfoHome`:
  - Modify or add `create()` methods to the home interface to the home.
  - Add corresponding finder methods to the home interface, if necessary.
- In remote interface, `UserInfo`:
  - Add abstract getter/setter methods to the remote interface corresponding to methods added to the bean implementation so that the client application can use them.

The Bean Implementation—UserInfoBean

This is the start of `UserInfoBean`, with the imports and instance variables required by the rest of the methods:

```
package mypackage4.impl;
import javax.ejb.EntityBean;
import javax.ejb.EntityContext;
import javax.ejb.FinderException;
import javax.ejb.CreateException;
import java.rmi.RemoteException;
import javax.naming.InitialContext;
import java.sql.*;
```

```
public class UserInfoBean implements EntityBean
{
  public EntityContext entityContext;
  String email;
  String username;
  String password;
  java.util.Date memberSince;
  Connection conn;
```

Note that, in addition to variables corresponding to the bean's persistent attributes, there are variables for the EJB context and for a database connection. The context is necessary because we'll need it later to obtain the bean's primary key. We keep the database connection in an instance variable so we can better manage and reduce the number of times we need to open and close the connection to the database.

ejbCreate() and ejbPostCreate()

These two methods are called one after the other by the EJB container, in this order, when we call the home interface's `create()` method. It's possible to have multiple sets of these methods. The methods in each set—`ejbCreate()`, `ejbPostCreate()`, and the home interface's `create()`—must have matching parameter lists.

Depending on the application's logic, we might initially create a bean with only a primary key, then add additional information later, in which case, each method would have only a single parameter: the primary key.

Here, we'll provide only one way to create the bean, requiring that the client application provide email address, username, and password. We'll automatically initialize the `memberSince` attribute to the current date.

`ejbCreate()` and `ejbPostCreate()` must, between them, set the bean's instance variables and use an SQL INSERT to create a new corresponding record in the database. Some prefer to do all of this in the `ejbCreate()` class and leave `ejbPostCreate()` empty, but here we split the tasks between the two methods:

```
public String ejbCreate(String email,
      String username, String password)
  {
    System.out.println("--- ejbCreate ---");
    this.email = email;
    this.username = username;
    this.password = password;
    this.memberSince = new java.sql.Date
                      ((new java.util.Date()).getTime());
```

```
    return email;
  }

  public void ejbPostCreate(String email,
      String username, String password)
  throws CreateException
  {
    System.out.println("--- ejbPostCreate ---");
    getConnection();
    try
    {
      String sql = "INSERT INTO USER_INFO " +
                   "(EMAIL, USERNAME, PASSWORD, MEMBER_SINCE) " +
                   "VALUES(?,?,?,?)";
      PreparedStatement ps = conn.prepareStatement(sql);
      ps.setString(1, email);
      ps.setString(2, username);
      ps.setString(3, password);
      ps.setDate(4, new java.sql.Date(memberSince.getTime()));
      ps.executeUpdate();
      ps.close();
    }
    catch(SQLException e)
    {
        throw new CreateException("Unable to create new record.");
    }
   }
```

Notice that, to perform SQL operations with JDBC, we first obtain a database connection. We leave the connection open here because it is a high-overhead operation and one that some of the other methods will need to use it soon.

EjbFindByPrimaryKey()

This is the single finder method that we are required to implement. It has one parameter, the primary key. The only real work that our implementation of this method needs to do is verify that a record with the specified key exists in the database. If the key is not found, it should throw a `FinderException`; otherwise, it merely returns the same primary key that was passed in as a parameter.

```
public String ejbFindByPrimaryKey(String email)
throws FinderException
{
  System.out.println("--- ejbFindByPrimaryKey ---");
  if (email == null || email.equals(""))
  {
```

```
      throw new FinderException("Primary key cannot be null");
    }
    boolean success = false;
    try
    {
      String sql = "SELECT EMAIL FROM USER_INFO " +
                   "WHERE EMAIL = ?";
      getConnection();
      PreparedStatement ps = conn.prepareStatement(sql);
      ps.setString(1, email);
      ps.executeQuery();
      ResultSet rs = ps.getResultSet();
      success = rs.next();
      ps.close();
    }
    catch(SQLException e)
    {
      System.out.println("ejbFindByPrimaryKey() caught: " + e);
    }
    if(!success)
    {
      disconnect();
      throw new FinderException("PK email not found");
    }
    return email;
}
```

Notice that whether this returns the primary key or throws an exception depends on the variable success which is obtained by calling the `ResultSet`'s `next()` method; we don't use the `ResultSet` apart from this simple check.

You may be wondering how the record is read into the bean's instance variable. The answer is that, once we return the primary key to the EJB container, assuring it that the record exists, the EJB container will call `ejbActivate()`, followed by the `ejbLoad()` method; the `ejbLoad()` method is responsible for actually obtaining the data from the database.

ejbActivate()

`ejbActivate()` is where we put any code for acquiring resources that the bean needs. In this case, the only thing we need is a database connection.

```
public void ejbActivate()
{
  System.out.println("--- ejbActivate ---");
  getConnection();
}
```

ejbLoad()

This is where we put the code for reading values from the database into our instance variables. Notice that this method takes no parameters even though we need the primary key to obtain a record from the database. To obtain the primary key, we need to call the entity context method `getPrimaryKey()`. We can then use an SQL SELECT statement to read the bean's attributes from the database.

```
public void ejbLoad()
{
  System.out.println("--- ejbLoad ---");
  try
  {
    this.email = (String) entityContext.getPrimaryKey();
    String sql = "SELECT USERNAME, PASSWORD, MEMBER_SINCE " +
                 "FROM USER_INFO WHERE EMAIL=?";
    PreparedStatement ps = conn.prepareStatement(sql);
    ps.setString(1, email);
    ResultSet rs = ps.executeQuery();
    if(rs.next())
    {
      username = rs.getString(1);
      password = rs.getString(2);
      memberSince = rs.getDate(3);
    }
    ps.close();
  }
  catch(SQLException e)
  {
    System.out.println("ejbLoad() caught: " + e);
  }
}
```

Once this method has been called, our bean is ready to use and we can call the business methods that we create such as the getter/setter methods that we'll see below.

ejbStore()

This method updates the data in the database. When this happens is entirely up to the EJB container; we are guaranteed only that any changes we make to the bean will be preserved. We use an SQL UPDATE statement to update the record using the primary key in the WHERE clause.

```
public void ejbStore()
throws RemoteException
{
  System.out.println("--- ejbStore ---");
 boolean success = false;
 try
 {
  String sql = "UPDATE USER_INFO SET " +
               "USERNAME = ?, " +
               "PASSWORD = ?, " +
               "WHERE EMAIL = ? ";

  PreparedStatement ps = conn.prepareStatement(sql);
  ps.setString(1, username);
  ps.setString(2, password);
  ps.setString(3, email);
  success = (ps.executeUpdate() == 1);
  ps.close();
  }
  catch (SQLException e)
  {
     System.out.println("ejbStore() caught: " + e);
  }
  if(!success)
  {
    throw new RemoteException("Failed to update");
  }
}
```

Notice that, because we don't allow the `memberSince` attribute to be changed once the bean is created, we don't need to update it here. Also note that it makes no sense to update the primary key.

ejbPassivate()

This method is called by the container when it is going to put the bean in an inactive state. This may be because the client application closed or timed out, or because the EJB container is running low on resources and decides to let another client use this bean. This method gives us a chance to release any resources and do any necessary housekeeping.

Confusing as it may sound, a bean instance is not associated with a specific set of data. As a performance optimization, the EJB container maintains a pool of bean instances. It may grow or shrink the pool depending on load, but in general, existing bean instances are reused as clients come and go.

To disassociate the bean instance from a specific set of bean data, it first calls `ejbStore()`, then calls `ejbPassivate()`. When the EJB container assigns the bean instance to another client application (or gives it back to ours), it will call `ejbActivate()` to reacquire the resources we need and `ejbLoad()` with the appropriate primary key to associate the bean instance with the right set of data.

The only resource our EJB holds that we need to release is the database connection.

```
public void ejbPassivate()
{
  System.out.println("--- ejbPassivate ---");
  disconnect();
}
```

ejbRemove()

When we want to get rid of a bean permanently, we call the remote interface's `remove()` method. This causes the EJB container to call the bean implementation's `ejbRemove()` method where we must provide code to remove the bean's data permanently from the database using the SQL DELETE statement.

```
public void ejbRemove()
throws RemoteException
{
  System.out.println("--- ejbRemove ---");
  boolean success = false;
  try
  {
    String sql = "DELETE FROM USER_INFO WHERE " +
                 "EMAIL = ?";
    PreparedStatement ps = conn.prepareStatement(sql);
    ps.setString(1, this.email);
    success = (ps.executeUpdate() == 1);
    ps.close();
    disconnect();
  }
  catch(SQLException e)
  {
    System.out.println("ejbRemove() caught: " +e);
  }
  if(!success)
  {
    throw new RemoteException("Failed to delete record");
  }
}
```

Note that we also close our database connection after deleting the record.

setEntityContext(), unSetEntityContext()

The method `setEntityContext()` provides an interface, the `EntityContext`, that our bean can use to access information about the EJB container. We used this context above in the `ejbLoad()` method to get the bean's primary key. The method `unSetEntityContext()` dereferences this context. JDeveloper provides these methods for us; we don't need to change them.

```
public void setEntityContext(EntityContext ctx)
{
  System.out.println("--- setEntityContext ---");
  this.entityContext = ctx;
}

public void unsetEntityContext()
{
  System.out.println("--- unsetEntityContext ---");
  this.entityContext = null;
}
```

getConnection(), disconnect()

These are private helper methods that we create to manage the database connection. They are called from some of the methods above.

```
private void getConnection()
{
  System.out.println("*** getConnection() ***");
  if(conn == null)
  {
    try
    {
      InitialContext ic=new InitialContext();
      javax.sql.DataSource ds =
              (javax.sql.DataSource)(ic.lookup("jdbc/OsirisDS"));
      conn= ds.getConnection();
    }
    catch(Exception e)
    {
      System.out.println("getConnection() caught: " + e);
    }
  }
}

private void disconnect()
{
  System.out.println("*** disconnect() ***");
  if(conn!=null)
```

```
  {
    try
    {
      conn.close();
      conn = null;
    }
    catch(SQLException e)
    {
      System.out.println("disconnect() caught: " + e);
    }
  }
}
```

Notice that the code for connecting is identical to the code we used in the session bean. We use JNDI to locate a datasource specified in the default data-source.xml file.

Business Methods

In addition to writing methods that allow the EJB container to manage our EJB, we also need to write the methods to implement the functionality that our application will require in order to use the bean. These are often called *business methods*, and in the case of entity beans, they commonly consist of getter and setter methods.

Getter/setter methods are identical to the methods that a JavaBean might have; however, it is important to remember that they are executed remotely. This means that the invocation of each method may require a round trip over the network.

```
public String getUsername()
{
  return username;
}

public String getEmail()
{
  return email;
}

public String getPassword()
{
  return password;
}

public java.util.Date getMemberSince()
```

```
    {
      return memberSince;
    }
    public void setUsername(String username)
    {
      this.username = username;
    }
    public void setPassword(String password)
    {
      this.password = password;
    }
    public String getHello()
    {
      return "Hello";
    }
}
```

Possible Improvements

This example is intended to show only a basic BMP bean implementation and it leaves some room for improvement. Because it is likely that all the data will be required by a client application, one improvement would be to add a getter method that returns all the user information in a single value object, as in the previous session bean example, so that only a single round trip is required to obtain the data.

Another possible improvement, also exemplified in the session bean, would be to use a data access object to encapsulate access to the database.

The Remote Interface—UserInfo

As noted previously, the client application interacts with the bean implementation, `UserInfoBean`, indirectly by means of the remote interface.

To be able to call the business methods that we created in the bean implementation, we need to include them in the remote interface, too. Because the methods in the remote interface are called remotely, we need to declare that they may throw a `RemoteException`.

```
package mypackage4;
import javax.ejb.EJBObject;
import java.rmi.RemoteException;
import java.util.Date;

public interface UserInfo extends EJBObject
{
  public String getUsername()throws RemoteException;
  public String getEmail()throws RemoteException;
```

```
  public String getPassword()throws RemoteException;
  public Date getMemberSince()throws RemoteException;
  public void setUsername(String username)throws RemoteException;
  public void setPassword(String password)throws RemoteException;
  public String getHello() throws RemoteException;
}
```

The Home Interface—UserInfoHome

The main use of the home interface is to obtain beans. Typically, there are three ways to obtain entity beans:

- Create a new bean.
- Find an existing bean.
- Find a set of beans.

To create a bean, we need a set of `ejbCreate()` and `ejbPostCreate()` methods in the bean implementation and a `create()` method here, in the home interface, with matching parameters. We can have more than one set of these methods, but as we've seen in the bean implementation, for this sample EJB we have one only set, which takes three parameters, email, username, and password.

```
package mypackage4;
import javax.ejb.EJBHome;
import java.rmi.RemoteException;
import javax.ejb.CreateException;
import javax.ejb.FinderException;

public interface UserInfoHome extends EJBHome
{
  UserInfo create(String email,
      String username, String password)
    throws RemoteException, CreateException;
```

Create methods are optional; if we don't want to allow client applications to create beans, we don't need to provide them. Presumably, beans would be created in some other way—perhaps using a separate administrator application or a bulk loader that imports the data from another source.

In addition to `create()` methods, the home interface can have finder methods to allow us to locate an existing bean or beans. One finder method is required, `findByPrimaryKey()`.

```
  UserInfo findByPrimaryKey(String primaryKey)
      throws RemoteException, FinderException;
}
```

The implementation in `UserInfoBean`, as we've seen, is a method called `ejbFindByPrimaryKey()`. This method is guaranteed to return a single object that implements our `UserInfo` remote interface.

We haven't done so in this example, but we could also have provided additional finder methods that return multiple EJB objects. We might, for example, have declared a method like this in our home interface:

```
Collection findAll()
   throws RemoteException, FinderException;
```

The corresponding `ejbFindAll()` method in the bean implementation would be required to find the primary keys of all the records in the USER_INFO table and return them to the EJB container in a vector. The EJB container would then call the `ejbLoad()` for each primary key to build a collection of `UserInfo` objects.

Deployment Descriptor, Deploying the UserInfo EJB

We don't need to make any changes to the deployment descriptor as generated by JDeveloper:

```
<?xml version = '1.0' encoding = 'windows-1252'?>
<!DOCTYPE ejb-jar PUBLIC "-//Sun Microsystems, Inc.//DTD Enterprise
JavaBeans 1.1//EN" "http://java.sun.com/j2ee/dtds/ejb-jar_1_1.dtd">
<ejb-jar>
  <enterprise-beans>
    <entity>
      <description>Entity Bean ( Bean-managed Persistence )</description>
      <display-name>UserInfo</display-name>
      <ejb-name>UserInfo</ejb-name>
      <home>mypackage8.UserInfoHome</home>
      <remote>mypackage8.UserInfo</remote>
      <ejb-class>mypackage8.impl.UserInfoBean</ejb-class>
      <persistence-type>Bean</persistence-type>
      <prim-key-class>java.lang.String</prim-key-class>
      <reentrant>False</reentrant>
    </entity>
  </enterprise-beans>
</ejb-jar>
```

Following the directions given in the session bean example, you may either run the bean using the OC4J server embedded in JDeveloper or deploy it to a standalone instance of OC4J.

The Sample Client Application

To begin, generate a sample client application using JDeveloper: Right-click on the UserInfo bean and select Create Sample Java Client. Select either Connect to OC4J embedded in JDeveloper or Connect to Remote App Server, depending on where you've deployed the EJB.

The first part of the file is standard, setting up the parameters (which would be in a properties file in production application) to obtain the initial JNDI context, then calling JNDI to obtain the home interface.

```
package Samplemypackage4;
import java.util.Hashtable;
import javax.naming.Context;
import javax.naming.InitialContext;
import mypackage8.UserInfo;
import mypackage8.UserInfoHome;
import javax.ejb.FinderException;
import javax.ejb.CreateException;
import java.rmi.RemoteException;

public class UserInfoClient2
{
  public static void main(String [] args)
  {
    UserInfoClient2 userInfoClient2 = new UserInfoClient2();
    try
    {
      Hashtable env = new Hashtable();
      env.put(Context.INITIAL_CONTEXT_FACTORY,
          "com.evermind.server.rmi.RMIInitialContextFactory");
      env.put(Context.SECURITY_PRINCIPAL, "admin");
      env.put(Context.SECURITY_CREDENTIALS, "adminpwd");
      env.put(Context.PROVIDER_URL, "ormi://noizmaker/UserInfo");
      Context ctx = new InitialContext(env);
      UserInfoHome userInfoHome =
          (UserInfoHome)ctx.lookup("UserInfo");
```

We'll first try to lookup an email address to see whether an EJB with that key already exists. If that fails, we'll create a new EJB for that email address.

```
      // Locate or create EJB
      String email="me@example.com";
      UserInfo userInfo = null;
      try
      {
        userInfo = userInfoHome.findByPrimaryKey(email);
```

```
}
catch (FinderException e)
{
  System.out.println("Bean not found: " + e);
}

if(userInfo==null)
{
  try
  {
    userInfo = userInfoHome.create(email, "me", "kitty" );
  }
  catch (Exception e)
  {
      System.out.println("Caught: " +e);
      System.exit(1);
  }
  System.out.println("Created new bean:");
}
else
{
  System.out.println("Bean already exists:");
}
```

This roughly corresponds to how, in a real application, you might ask users for an email address to see whether they have an account in your system. If the email address is not found, you would then ask the user to sign up for an account by providing additional information.

The next section is intended to exercise all the methods in our home interface to get an EJB and change the data in it.

```
// Access EJB attributes
String username;
System.out.println(" username: " +
      (username = userInfo.getUsername()));
System.out.println(" email: " + userInfo.getEmail(  ));
System.out.println(" password: " +
      userInfo.getPassword(  ));
System.out.println(" member since: " +
      userInfo.getMemberSince(  ));

if(username.equals("delete me"))
{
    // Remove EJB
    userInfo.remove();
    System.out.println("Bean removed");
```

```
          }
          else
          {
              // Change EJB attributes
              userInfo.setUsername("delete me");
              userInfo.setPassword("newpassword");
              System.out.println("Bean altered");
           }
       }
       catch(Throwable ex)
       {
          ex.printStackTrace();
       }
    }
}
```

The first time you run this application it displays all the attributes of the bean that we just created. It then changes the username and password. At this point, you can start SQL*Plus and verify that the EJB container has saved the bean's data in the USER_INFO table.

The second time you run the application the bean will already exist. Once again, the attributes will be displayed, but this time, at the end, the bean will be destroyed by calling the remote interface's `remove()` method. At the end, you can verify the deletion of the record in the USER_INFO table by using SQL*Plus.

CHAPTER 12

Object-Relational Mapping and Java Data Objects

The major premise of this book is that when we design an application in Java, we often find that we need to rely on a relational database in order to store our data. In fact, the majority of business applications are nothing more than a user interface for maintaining data stored in a database.

Throughout this book, we've explored a number of approaches to the problem of using data in the object-oriented environment of Java that we retrieve and store in a relational database.

At one end of the spectrum of approaches is direct database access from Java classes, where we embed relational queries using SQL in our Java code, and map the data to Java objects on an ad-hoc basis (or consume the data in place).

At the other end of this spectrum are Oracle's object-relational features where we create objects in the database and import them into Java, either as weakly typed `Structs` (or `STRUCT`) or strongly typed custom classes, using the `SQLData` (or `ORAData`) interface.

Another approach—and one that avoids these extremes—is to introduce an intermediary between the object realm of Java and the relational regime of Oracle. We saw how this can be done for simple cases using container-managed persistence in EJB. But EJBs come with a lot of baggage that is a major burden (in terms of development, performance, and cost) if you don't need distributed components and the other services EJB provides.

In this chapter, we'll examine an example of an object-relational mapping tool designed explicitly for bridging the gap between Java and relational databases. O-R mapping tools go well beyond a simple one-object-to-one-row mapping. With little effort from the developer, these tools easily support complex object models involving inheritance and composition in one-to-one, one-to-many, and many-to-many relationships.

TopLink, for example, is a mature object-relational product that was originally developed in the early 1990s for the Smalltalk programming language before being rewritten and released for Java in 1996.

The main TopLink program, MappingWorkbench, is a graphical user interface that allows users to map tables to classes. TopLink can use either existing classes or tables, or it can create them. Unlike the simple O-R mapping in JDeveloper (at least the Oracle 9i Release 2 version) which allows only simple, one-to-one mapping between a table and a CMP entity bean, TopLink allows us to model complex relationships between our Java objects, including one-to-many and many-to-many relationships, and to map them to database tables.

Once mappings are established, TopLink can export descriptors that are used to generate wrappers for an application's objects; these wrappers completely hide all details regarding the database from the application and let the developer concentrate entirely on the object model.

TopLink was acquired by Oracle in June 2002, probably with the intention of integrating it with its existing products. We can expect, for example, to see some of its technology used to provide more sophisticated mapping for EJBs in JDeveloper. TopLink features are also likely to appear in Oracle's Business Components for Java framework, as well.

An alternative to TopLink is a relatively new Java technology, Java Data Objects (JDO). As mentioned previously, within six months of the release of the JDO 1.0 specification in April 2002, at least nine commercial JDO implementations were available and several open-source projects were underway.

Every indication is that JDO will be increasingly supported in both new and existing products. (TopLink has limited support for JDO that was introduced before it was purchased by Oracle but it is unclear whether Oracle will continue to develop these features.) The rest of this chapter will be limited to covering JDO but many of the principles are applicable to TopLink and other proprietary object-relational mapping tools.

JAVA DATA OBJECTS

JDO is a standard for making Java objects persistent. As a product of Sun's Java Community Process, it represents the collaboration of developers and vendors with interests in relational databases, object databases, and object-relational mapping technologies.

JDO is not an object-relational mapping technology per se, but rather specifies an API that can be used to manage the persistence of objects without regard to the persistence mechanism, which can be anything from a file-based system to a true object database. Because most JDO implementations use a relational database, this means that these implementations are, in fact, providing object-relational mapping. The beauty of JDO is that Java developers don't have to worry about any of these details—JDO provides transparent persistence. With JDO, you can design everything, including persistent classes, within an object model using standard object design techniques, including inheritance and composition.

No extra Java code is needed to implement persistence. But there is no magic. Instead, a metadata file in XML format is used to declare persistent classes and, optionally, their fields. A special tool called an *enhancer* is used to process the Java classes after compilation to add the methods and attributes, based on the metadata file, that JDO requires in order to provide persistence behind the scenes, as shown in Figure 12–1.

JDO Implementation Setup

The examples in this chapter use LIBeLIS LiDO Professional Edition JDO version 1.2 and Oracle 9i. LIBeLIS and most other JDO vendors offer either limited-time evaluations of their products or community editions that are free for personal and development purposes. Any of these products supporting the JDO 1.0 specification should work with the code presented but see the product information for specifics on the tools that they provide, such as the enhancer and runtime library, and how to set them up and run them.

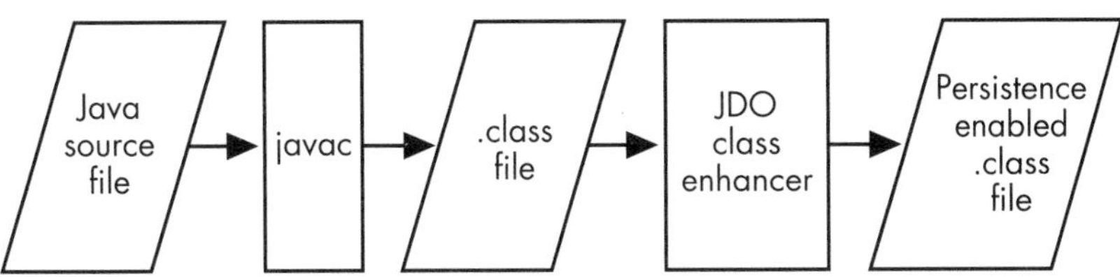

FIGURE 12–1 JDO class enhancement.

After installing LiDO in the directory of your choice, open a DOS window and locate and run the lidoEnv.bat file in the LiDO bin directory. If you've installed LiDO in c:\dev\LiDOPro, for example, you would enter the following command:

```
d:\dev\LiDOPro\bin\lidoEnv.bat
```

This will add the LiDO JDO development tool and runtime classes to your CLASSPATH, as well as set up several other environment variables that LiDO needs. You will need to run this batch file anytime you open a new DOS window to compile or run Java programs using LiDO JDO.

Creating a Persistent Class

There are no special steps required to create the persistent class itself. We'll begin by taking a simple example, a simplified `Person` class, with attributes for name, city, and contact information. We'll use the JavaBean convention of making our attributes private and providing getter and setter methods.

```
// Person
package example;

public class Person {

  private String name;
  private String city;
  private String contactInfo;

  public Person()
  {
  }

  // Constructor
  public Person (String name, String city, String contactInfo)
  {
    this.name = name;
    this.city = city;
    this.contactInfo = contactInfo;
  }

  // getter methods
  public String getName()
  {
    return name;
  }
```

```
  public String getCity()
  {
    return city;
  }

  public String getContactInfo()
  {
    return contactInfo;
  }

  // setter methods
  public void setName(String name)
  {
    this.name = name;
  }

  public void setCity(String city)
  {
    this.city = city;
  }

  public void setContactInfo(String contactInfo)
  {
    this.contactInfo = contactInfo;
  }

}
```

Assuming we are using a directory c:\mywork, this file should be in a subdirectory called *example* because it is declared to be in a package called `example`:

```
c:\mywork\example\Person.java
```

Compile it normally using the following command in the c:\mywork directory:

```
javac example\Person.java
```

Creating a Metadata File

Before we can run the enhancer to alter the class file and make it persistent, we need to create an XML metadata file that describes the class. This file contains several standard lines indicating the XML version, the DTD file that is used to validate the format of the XML file, and the `<jdo>` root element that must contain our metadata. The `<jdo>` element contains the metadata for our class and includes the package name, the class name, and the field names:

```
<?xml version="1.0"?>
<!DOCTYPE jdo SYSTEM "jdo.dtd">
<jdo>
  <package name = "example">
    <class name="Person">
        <field name="name"/>
        <field name="city"/>

        <field name="contactInfo"/>
    </class>
  </package>
</jdo>
```

This file should be saved in the c:\mywork directory, as person.jdo, for example.

Running the Enhancer

To run the LiDO enhancer, at a DOS prompt in the c:\mywork directory, run the following command:

```
java com.libelis.lido.Enhance -metadata person.jdo
```

Notice that it is unnecessary to specify the class file that is to be enhanced or its location; the enhancer works this out from the information in the metadata file.

After the enhancer has been run the `Person` class file no longer corresponds to the Java source file. Most importantly, the enhancer modifies the class bytecode so that it implements the interface `PersistenceCapable`. This is one of the most controversial things about JDO. It's possible to accomplish the same end by using a preprocessor to modify the source code, but this approach is messier and is discouraged by the JDO specification.

Creating the Database Schema

Unlike the enhancer, the tools for creating the database schema are not specified in the JDO specification. This is the step that will vary most from vendor to vendor and that will become easier in the future as JDO implementations continue to evolve and innovate.

We'll create the database schema based on the metadata file by using a LiDO-provided command-line tool, DefineSchema.

First, we'll create a new user in Oracle. In SQL*Plus, log in as database administrator or have the database administrator perform the following steps for you. Create a user *jdoexample* with a password *jdoexample*, as follows:

```
CREATE USER JDOEXAMPLE IDENTIFIED BY JDOEXAMPLE;
```

Grant the user the following rights:

```
GRANT CONNECT, RESOURCE TO JDOEXAMPLE;
```

To create the schema, at the DOS prompt, enter the following command on one line (it's broken up here for legibility):

```
java com.libelis.lido.ds.jdbc.DefineSchema
-dv oracle.jdbc.driver.OracleDriver
-db jdbc:oracle:thin:@noizmaker:1521:osiris
-u jdoexample
-p jdoexample
-m person.jdo
```

Note that you have to modify -db, the option that specifies the database URL, in accordance with your database's hostname and database name. After entering this command, a message will be displayed, indicating whether the schema was successfully created. You can verify this by logging in as jdoexample in SQL*Plus and entering the following query to see the tables that were created:

```
SQL> connect jdoexample/jdoexample
Connected.
SQL> select * from cat;

TABLE_NAME                     TABLE_TYPE
------------------------------ -----------
E_PERSON                       TABLE
LIDOIDMAX                      TABLE
LIDOIDTABLE                    TABLE
```

We can see that LiDO has created a table, E_PERSON, to hold the Person class data, as well as a couple of other tables to hold identity information about objects.

Creating and Persisting an Object

Once we've created a persistent class, we can instantiate objects of the class just as we normally would. But to make them persistent, so they are saved in the database, we need to obtain a reference to a `PersistenceManager` and call its `makePersistent()` method.

The PersistenceManager. The principal JDO class is the `PersistenceManager`. This class has methods that allow us to manage persistent classes, as we'll see now, and methods for obtaining `Query` and `Transaction` objects, as we'll see later.

We obtain a `PersistenceManager` from a `PersistenceManagerFactory`. Like other such factories, `PersistenceManagerFactory` can accept settings either from a properties file with name-value pairs or from a variety of setter methods.

Here, we'll use the setter methods. The exact settings that `PersistenceManagerFactory` requires depend on the configuration but here are the settings corresponding to LiDO and my Oracle database:

```
import java.util.Iterator;
import java.util.Collection;

public class PersonTest
{
  public static void main(String [] args)
  {
    // Configuration parameters
    String PMFCLASS =
           "com.libelis.lido.PersistenceManagerFactory";
    String DBDRIVER = "oracle.jdbc.driver.OracleDriver";
    String DBURL    = "jdbc:oracle:thin:@noizmaker:1521:osiris";
    String DBUSERNAME = "jdoexample";
    String DBPASSWORD = "jdoexample";

    try
    {

      // Obtain PersistenceManager from PersistenceManagerFactory

      PersistenceManagerFactory pmf = (PersistenceManagerFactory)
          Class.forName(PMFCLASS).newInstance();
      pmf.setConnectionDriverName(DBDRIVER);
      pmf.setConnectionURL(DBURL);
      pmf.setConnectionUserName(DBUSERNAME);
      pmf.setConnectionPassword(DBPASSWORD);
```

Once the `PersistenceManagerFactory` is set up we can obtain the `PersistenceManager`.

```
PersistenceManager pm = pmf.getPersistenceManager();
```

Transactions. Persistence operations in JDO are grouped into a unit of work or transaction. Unlike JDBC, this is not an option that we can enable to occur automatically; in JDO, we must explicitly manage our transactions. To do this, we first need to obtain a `Transaction` object that will allow us to mark the transaction boundaries by calling the object's `begin()` and `commit()` methods.

We obtain the transaction object and begin the transaction as follows:

```
// Create and begin transaction
Transaction tx = pm.currentTransaction();
tx.begin();
```

Creating the Person Object. This is the code for creating the object:

```
// Create and persist Person object
Person person = new Person();
person.setName("Bruce");
person.setCity("Asbury Park");
person.setContactInfo("theBoss@example.com");
```

Persisting the Object. This is the code that makes the object persistent:

```
pm.makePersistent(person);
tx.commit();
```

Note that the call to `makePersistent()` makes the object persistent but it is not made permanent until the transaction is committed. If this were part of a larger set of code, `tx.commit()` might not be called until later, pending the success of the other operations.

At this point, you might want to query the E_PERSON table in the database by using SQL*Plus to see that this has, in fact, been added.

Locating and Using Existing Objects

Every persistent object has a unique identifier that is maintained, generally behind the scenes, by JDO. This identifier, the `ObjectId`, is like a table's primary key in a relational database. Although a JDO implementation for a relational database may, in fact, use a primary key in a table for the `ObjectID`, it is not required to do so.

If we already have a persistent object, we can obtain its `ObjectId` by calling the `getObjectId()` method.

```
Object objId = person.getObjectId();
```

If we have an `ObjectId`, we can use it to obtain the object.

```
Person person = (Person) pm.getObjectById();
```

However, except for cases where the application manages `ObjectIds` itself, this presents a chicken-and-egg problem. `ObjectIds` are best left as an internal detail for JDO to manage. It is useful to know that every persistent object has an `ObjectId`, but the details of what `ObjectIds` are and how they are managed by JDO are not important from an application point of view.

We typically will use queries to locate our objects instead. To execute queries, there are two classes that we need to be familiar with: `Extent` and `Query`.

Extents and Queries

An extent represents a set of objects in the database and is similar to a collection except that it has been optimized for use in JDO, where the number of objects that it represents can be arbitrarily large. Because an extent does not retrieve all objects from the database at once, it does not have all the methods of the collection interface such as, for example, a `size()` method.

`Extent` has an `iterator()` method that we can use to retrieve objects from the database like this:

```
// Extent
Extent ext = pm.getExtent(Person.class, false);
Iterator iter = ext.iterator();
while(iter.hasNext())
{
  Person p = (Person) iter.next();
  System.out.println("    Name: " + p.getName());
  System.out.println("    City: " + p.getCity());
  System.out.println("Contact: " + p.getContactInfo());
}
```

An extent is an easy way to obtain all the objects of a given type. More often, however, we are interested in retrieving only objects meeting certain criteria. To do that, we need to use a query.

Queries and the JDO Query Language: JDOQL

The job of a JDO query is to take a set of candidate objects and filter them, returning only those that meet our criteria. We can specify the candidate objects for a query by providing either an extent or a collection of objects (which perhaps we've obtained from a previous query).

In addition to providing an extent or a collection, we usually also provide a filter. (If we don't provide a filter, the query will return all instances of the specified object type.) The filter is a string representing a Boolean value using syntax specified by JDOQL. The rules for forming a JDOQL expression are the same as those for Java and they use standard Java syntax, with a few exceptions.

Equality and inequality operators are the same as Java but they can be applied not only to primitives, such as `int` and `float`, but also to instances of the wrapper classes for primitives, such as `Int` and `Float`. If we have a class, `Circle`, which had an attribute `radius`, we could locate all instances of `Circle` with `radius` greater than 3 by using the following filter:

```
String filter = "radius > 3";
```

Equality and inequality operators can also be applied to strings. For example, we could use the following filter to locate all instances of `Person` named Bruce:

```
String filter = "name ==\"Bruce\"";
```

Although the JDO specification does not indicate how string comparisons are to be implemented, it is clearly intended to have different semantics than standard Java comparisons using `String`. A comparison between two strings using the equality operator is valid in Java but it's not usually what we mean to do and often has surprising results. The Java equivalent of the JDOQL statement above is `name.equals("Bruce")`.

We cannot use assignment operators, post- or pre-increment operators, or post- or pre-decrement operators.

We cannot call Java methods, with the following exceptions:

- `Collection.contains(Object o)`
- `Collection.isEmpty()`
- `String,startsWith(String s)`
- `String.endsWith(String s)`

The JDO specification notes that `String.startsWith()` and `String.endsWith()` support wildcard characters but does not define what they are. In an implementation that is based on a relational database that uses SQL, it's safe to assume that the underlying implementation uses the SQL LIKE operator for comparison, which accepts (%) to match any character or character and (_) to match any single character. The following JDO filter and SQL WHERE clauses are equivalent:

```
String filter = "name.startsWith(\"abc\")";
…WHERE name LIKE 'abc%'
```

Likewise, the following are equivalent:

```
String filter = "name.endsWith(\"abc\")";
…WHERE name LIKE '%abc'
```

Knowing this, we can include wildcards of our own. We can define a JDO filter like this:

```
String filter="name.startsWith(\"%efg\")";
```

This will match a string that contains *efg* anywhere within it, such as *abcdefghijk*.

Filter Parameters

In the filter examples above, the comparisons contained the hard-coded values 3 and Bruce. We wouldn't normally do this, of course. We would instead use a JDOQL parameter—an identifier that acts as a placeholder for a value that we pass in when we execute the query at runtime. We might use the parameter `selectedName` (we'll see in a minute where this is declared) in a filter like this:

```
String filter = "name == selectedName";
```

We need to declare our parameter (or parameters, if there are more than one), but first we need to obtain our `Query` object. We do that with our extent and filter, as follows:

```
Query q = pm.newQuery(ext, filter);
```

To declare a parameter, we call `Query`'s `declareParameters()` method with the declaration in a string, using the same syntax we would use to declare a parameter list for a Java method. This is the declaration for the parameter `selectedName`:

```
q.declareParameters("String selectedName");
```

If our query used multiple parameters, the parameters would be separated by commas, like this:

```
q.declareParameters("String selectedName, int age");
```

When we execute a query it returns a collection, but it returns it as type `Object` so we need to cast it to `Collection`. (This is to leave open the possibility that a future version of JDO may return something other than a collection.) Assuming that the query is expecting a single string parameter, we can execute it like this:

```
Collection result = (Collection) q.execute("Bruce");
```

You may wonder how we would pass multiple parameters. If there are three or fewer parameters, we can simply pass them directly to `execute()` methods with the following signatures:

- `execute()`
- `execute(Object o1)`
- `execute(Object o1, Object o2)`
- `execute(Object o1, Object o2, Object o3);`

The parameters in the call to `execute()` must correspond to the parameters we declared in the `declareParameters()` method. For example, if our filter uses two parameters, `name` and `city`, in that order, the `declareParameters()` and `execute()` methods must correspond as in the following example where `name` and `city` are presumed to be valid Java variables in our application:

```
q.declareParameters("String selectedName, String selectedCity");
Collection result = (Collection) q.execute(name, city);
```

If we want to pass more than three parameters, we can pass any number by putting them in an object array and calling the executeWithArray() method:

```
executeWithArray(Object [] objs)
```

The query `execute()` method returns a collection of Java objects—in the case of this sample code, instances of the `Person` class. We can iterate through them just like we did for the instances we retrieved using the extent's iterator.

```
iter = result.iterator();
while(iter.hasNext())
{
  Person p = (Person) iter.next();
  System.out.println("   Name: " + p.getName());
  System.out.println("   City: " + p.getCity());
  System.out.println("Contact: " + p.getContactInfo());
}
query.close(result); // takes reference to Collection
pm.close();
```

Note that we need to close the `Query` and the `PersistenceManager` because they may have acquired resources that need to be freed.

Variables

In addition to parameters, there is a second special type of element that we can use in a filter: the variable. The semantics of JDOQL variables do not correspond to variables in Java because JDOQL is declarative and not procedural. JDOQL variables are perhaps better thought of as a way of correlating parts of a query and, in particular, queries that include classes containing collections and the individual members of those collections. We'll take a look at variables in the next section when we consider querying nested classes.

Ordering Results

To order the results of queries, we can use the query's `setOrdering()` method. This takes a `String` parameter that lists the attributes to use as sort keys, each followed by either `ascending` or `descending`, in descending order of priority.

Multiple attributes are separated by commas. Valid attribute types are:

- Primitive types such as `int` and `float`, but not `boolean`
- Wrapper classes, such as `Int` and `Float`, but not `Boolean`
- `BigDecimal`
- `BigInteger`
- `String`
- `Date`

The following example selects all persons whose names begin with the letter A and lists them, sorted with `city` as primary sort key and `name` as the secondary sort key:

```
// Query ordering
String filter = "name.startsWith(letter)";
Query q = pm.newQuery(ext, filter);
q.declareParameters("String letter");
q.setOrdering("city ascending, name ascending");
Collection coll = (Collection) q.execute("A");
```

Class Relationships and Persistence

One of the strengths of JDO is that it supports the persistence of related classes transparently. As mentioned previously, this lets us develop object models in Java as we normally would without having to make any special concessions for persistence.

There are two types of class relationships in Java:

- Inheritance—One class is a subclass of another
- Composition—One class contains another

Composition and Aggregation

Of the two types of class relationships, composition is the most common. Composition can take many forms; it can represent one-to-one relationships between classes, one-to-many relationships, and many-to-many relationships. The latter two cases, where the composition involves a collection, are also called *aggregation*.

An example of a one-to-one relationship is that a person may, on our model, have a single principal address. We could model that with a `Person` class that contains a reference to an `Address` class.

An example of a one-to-many relationship is that a person could have various hobbies. We could model that with a `Person` class that contains a vector to hold multiple instances of a `Hobby` class.

An example of a many-to-many relationship is that a person may belong to various clubs and a club can include many members. We could model that with `Person` class that contains a vector to hold multiple instances of a `Club` class and a `Club` class that contains a vector to hold multiple instances of the `Person` class.

As long as we create and manage them properly in Java, persisting object graphs that include complex relationships such as these present no problems for JDO. When we call the JDO `PersistenceManager`'s `makePersistent()` method to persist an instance of the top-level class, all its child objects, the children of child objects, and so on—that is, the object graph—are persisted, as well. We do not need to persist each object individually.

Inheritance

Inheritance, as you are probably aware, is one of the key features of object-oriented languages. Inheritance promotes reuse because it allows us to take a class and create a new one that builds on the original class. For example, if we have a class, `Person`, we can make a subclass, `Employee`, that inherits from `Person`. `Employee` will automatically have all the attributes and methods of `Person`, so all we have to add in the `Employee` class are any additional methods and attributes specific to `Employee`, such as title and department.

Like the support for composition, the support for inheritance is transparent in JDO. If we have a `Person` class and create an `Employee` subclass, we can make the `Employee` class persistent, regardless of whether `Person` is persistent. The methods and attributes that `Employee` inherits from `Person` will be persisted together with those that are specific to `Person`.

A Photo Collection Example

We'll create a more complicated example in order to explore how we create and manage a more complicated object model using JDO.

Let's suppose that the members of a family are avid shutterbugs and have hired us to create a database to keep track of all the photographs they create. At the highest level, we'll group their photographs into `PhotoSessions`. This class will represent all the photos taken by one photographer at one time and place and, like the other classes in our model, will follow the conventions of a JavaBean.

```
// PhotoSession
package example;

import java.util.Vector;
import java.util.Date;


public class PhotoSession
{

  private Photographer photographer;
  private String location;
  private Date sessionDate;
  private Vector photos;

  // getter methods
  public Photographer getPhotographer()
  {
    return photographer;
  }

  public String getLocation()
  {
    return location;
  }
```

```
    public Date getSessionDate()
    {
      return sessionDate;
    }

    public Vector getPhotos()
    {
      return photos;
    }

    // setter methods
    public void setPhotographer(Photographer photographer)
    {
      this.photographer = photographer;
    }

    public void setLocation(String location)
    {
      this.location = location;
    }

    public void setSessionDate(Date sessionDate)
    {
      this.sessionDate = sessionDate;
    }

    public void setPhotos(Vector photos)
    {
      this.photos = photos;
    }
}
```

The `PhotoSession` object model is represented in Figure 12–2.

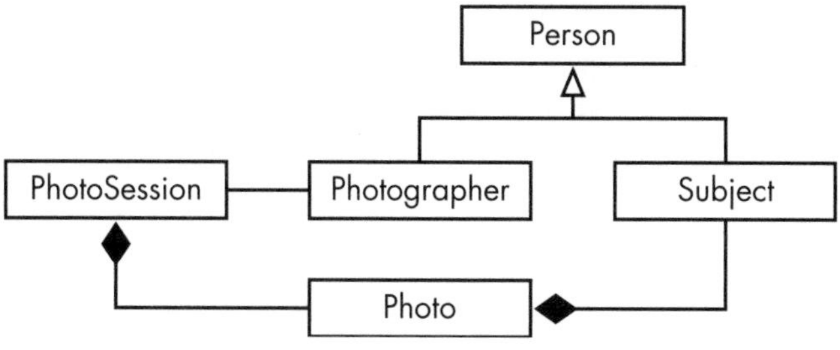

FIGURE 12–2 PhotoSession object model.

The `PhotoSession` class contains an instance of the class `Photographer`, which is pretty much like the `Person` class we created earlier in this chapter. We'll subclass `Person` to create the `Photographer` class and add a little information related to photography, such as the equipment used and a short description of the photographer's photographic experience.

```
// Photographer, inherits from Person
package example;

public class Photographer extends Person
{
  private String equipment;
  private String bio;

  // getter methods
  public String getEquipment()
  {
    return equipment;
  }

  public String getBio()
  {
    return bio;
  }

 // setter methods
  public void setEquipment(String equipment)
  {
    this.equipment = equipment;
  }

  public void setBio(String bio)
  {
    this.bio = bio;
  }
}
```

`PhotoSession` also contains a collection of photographs: a vector of `Photo` instances. The `Photo` class looks like this:

```
// Photo
package example;

import java.util.Vector;

public class Photo
```

```
{

  private String title;
  private Vector subjects;
  private String description;
  private String ucDescription;
  private String notes;
  private PhotoSession photoSession;

  // getter methods
  public String getTitle()
  {
    return title;
  }

  public Vector getSubjects()
  {
    return subjects;
  }

  public String getUcDescription()
  {
     return ucDescription;
  }

  public String getDescription()
  {
     return description;
  }

  public String getNotes()
  {
    return notes;
  }

  public PhotoSession getPhotoSession()
  {
    return photoSession;
  }

  // setter methods
  public void setTitle(String title)
  {
    this.title = title;
  }

  public void setSubjects(Vector subjects)
```

```
  {
    this.subjects = subjects;
  }

  public void setDescription(String description)
  {
     this.description = description;
     ucDescription = description.toUpperCase();
  }

  public void setNotes(String notes)
  {
    this.notes = notes;
  }

  public void setPhotoSession(PhotoSession photoSession)
  {
    this.photoSession = photoSession;
  }
}
```

The `Photo` class contains information about the photograph: title, description (including an uppercase version of the description to enable case-insensitive searching), and notes. It also contains a collection for information about the subjects in the photograph and a reference to the `PhotoSession` instance it belongs to, so we can navigate from any photo to the `PhotoSession` instance that contains it.

The `Subject` class is subclassed from `Person` but adds information relevant to being the subject in a photograph, specifically, age and a description of the subject's position in the photo.

```
// Subject
package example;

public class Subject extends Person {

  private String position;
  private int age;

  // getter method
  public String getPosition()
  {
    return position;
  }

  public int getAge()
```

```
        {
          return age;
        }


        // setter method
        public void setPosition(String position)
        {
          this.position = position;
        }

        public void setAge(int age)
        {
          this.age = age;
        }


      }
```

Notice again that there is nothing in these classes that is specific to JDO. After creating these source code files, we compile them normally using javac.

The Metadata File

To add persistence capabilities to our classes, as we've seen before, we need to create the metadata file that the enhancer will use. It contains descriptions of each class in our model, including information about inheritance and aggregation relationships.

```
<?xml version="1.0"?>
<!DOCTYPE jdo SYSTEM "jdo.dtd">
<jdo>
  <package name = "example">

    <class name ="Person">
        <field name = "name"/>
        <field name = "city"/>
        <field name = "contactInfo"/>
    </class>

    <class name = "Subject"
            persistence-capable-superclass = "example.Person">
        <field name = "position"/>
        <field name = "age"/>
    </class>
```

```
    <class name= "Photo">
        <field name = "title"/>
        <field name = "subjects">
            <collection element-type = "example.Subject"/>
        </field>
        <field name = "description"/>
        <field name = "notes"/>
    </class>

    <class name = "Photographer"
            persistence-capable-superclass = "example.Person">
        <field name = "equipment"/>
        <field name = "bio"/>
    </class>

    <class name = "PhotoSession">
        <field name = "photographer"/>
        <field name = "location"/>
        <field name = "sessionDate"/>
        <field name = "photos">
            <collection element-type = "example.Photo"/>
        </field>

    </class>

  </package>
</jdo>
```

Note that to indicate inheritance, we add an attribute, `persistence-capable-superclass`, to the `class` tag in addition to the existing `name` attribute.

```
<class name = "Photographer"
       persistence-capable-superclass = "example.Person">
```

To indicate that a field is a collection, we use the container form of the `field` tag and include a `collection` tag indicating the type of objects in the collection.

```
<field name = "photos">
       <collection element-type = "example.Photo"/>
     </field>
```

You may remember that, in XML, an empty tag is one that has nothing between the opening and closing tag, such as <tagname></tagname> or the equivalent <tagname/>, whereas a container tag is one that includes data, text, or other tags between the open and close tags.

To create the persistence-capable classes, we follow the same steps as before: Compile the Java source files using javac.

```
javac example\PhotoSession.java
javac example\Photo.java
javac example\Subject.java
```

We don't explicitly have to compile all our Java files because javac can figure out some of the class dependencies and compile them automatically.

Next, we enhance the resulting .class files. The following command will enhance all the classes mentioned in the metadata.jdo file:

```
java com.libelis.lido.Enhance -metadata metadata.jdo
```

One of the drawbacks of the JDO 1.0 specification is that it does not specify support for *evolution*, that is, the ability to modify or extend an existing object model. Depending on the JDO implementation, the easiest (if not the only) thing to do may be to delete the existing schema and rebuild it from scratch.

Before using the LiDO DefineSchema utility to create the extended schema in Oracle, we'll drop the existing schema by dropping the user jdoexample. Log into Oracle as database administrator using SQL*Plus and enter the following command:

```
DROP USER JDOEXAMPLE CASCADE;
```

Next, recreate user jdoexample and grant rights to that user as before.

```
CREATE USER JDOEXAMPLE IDENTIFIED BY JDOEXAMPLE;
GRANT CONNECT, RESOURCE TO JDOEXAMPLE;
```

To create the PhotoSession schema, run the DefineSchema tool using the metadata.jdo file.

```
java com.libelis.lido.ds.jdbc.DefineSchema
-dv oracle.jdbc.driver.OracleDriver
-db jdbc:oracle:thin:@noizmaker:1521:osiris
-u jdoexample
-p jdoexample
-m metadata.jdo
```

Now we can write a program to test the `PhotoSession` classes. The first task is to acquire a `Persistence Manager`.

```
package example;

import javax.jdo.PersistenceManagerFactory;
import javax.jdo.PersistenceManager;
import javax.jdo.Transaction;
import javax.jdo.Extent;
import javax.jdo.Query;
import java.util.Iterator;
import java.util.Collection;
import java.util.Vector;
import java.util.Calendar;

public class PhotoTestAdd
{
  public static void main(String [] args)
  {
    // Configuration parameters
    String PMFCLASS = "com.libelis.lido.PersistenceManagerFactory";
    String DBDRIVER = "oracle.jdbc.driver.OracleDriver";
    String DBURL    = "jdbc:oracle:thin:@noizmaker:1521:osiris";
    String DBUSERNAME = "jdoexample";
    String DBPASSWORD = "jdoexample";

    try
    {

      // Obtain persistence manager from persistence manager factory
      PersistenceManagerFactory pmf = (PersistenceManagerFactory)
          Class.forName(PMFCLASS).newInstance();
      pmf.setConnectionDriverName(DBDRIVER);
      pmf.setConnectionURL(DBURL);
      pmf.setConnectionUserName(DBUSERNAME);
      pmf.setConnectionPassword(DBPASSWORD);

      PersistenceManager pm = pmf.getPersistenceManager();
```

We'll create several subjects.

```
      // Create subjects: name, city, contactInfo, position, age
      Subject rover = new Subject();
      rover.setName("Rover");
      rover.setCity("Anytown");
      rover.setContactInfo("");
      rover.setPosition("Center, front");
      rover.setAge(8);

      Subject mom = new Subject();
```

```
mom.setName("Mom");
mom.setCity("Anytown");
mom.setContactInfo("mom@example.com");
mom.setPosition("Left");
mom.setAge(30);

Subject dad = new Subject();
dad.setName("Dad");
dad.setCity("Anytown");
dad.setContactInfo("dad@example.com");
dad.setPosition("Right");
dad.setAge(30);

Subject jr = new Subject();
jr.setName("Junior");
jr.setCity("Anytown");
jr.setContactInfo("");
jr.setPosition("Center, back");
jr.setAge(3);
```

Now some `Photo` objects that include these subjects in vectors.

```
// photo 1
// - includes subjects, title, description, notes
Vector subjects1 = new Vector();
subjects1.add(rover);
subjects1.add(mom);
subjects1.add(dad);
subjects1.add(jr);

Photo photo1 = new Photo();
photo1.setTitle("Family at park");
photo1.setSubjects(subjects1);
photo1.setDescription(
   "Family standing next to picnic table");
photo1.setNotes("No flash, auto-timer");

// photo 2
Vector subjects2 = new Vector();
rover.setPosition("Left");
jr.setPosition("Right");
subjects2.add(rover);
subjects2.add(jr);

Photo photo2 = new Photo();
photo2.setTitle("Junior and Rover");
photo2.setSubjects(subjects2);
```

```
photo2.setDescription(
   "Junior and Rover playing ball");

// photo 3
Vector subjects3 = new Vector();
mom.setPosition("Center");
subjects3.add(mom);

Photo photo3 = new Photo();
photo3.setTitle("Mom - the diva");
photo3.setSubjects(subjects3);
photo3.setDescription(
   "Mom singing that Shania Twain song");
photo3.setNotes("Flash");

Vector photoset1 = new Vector();
photoset1.add(photo1);
photoset1.add(photo2);
photoset1.add(photo3);
```

Then a `Photographer` object.

```
// Create Photographer - Dad
Photographer photog1 = new Photographer();
photog1.setName("Dad");
photog1.setCity("Cambridge");
photog1.setContactInfo("dad@example.com");
photog1.setEquipment("Sony digital camera");
photog1.setBio("Amateur photographer");
```

At this point, we have all the pieces to create a `PhotoSession` object.

```
// Create Photosession 1
PhotoSession sess1 = new PhotoSession();
sess1.setPhotographer(photog1);
sess1.setLocation("Lakeside Park");
Calendar cal = Calendar.getInstance();
cal.set(2002, 3, 23);
sess1.setSessionDate(cal.getTime());
sess1.setPhotos(photoset1);
```

We also need to update the photos now that they've been assigned to a `PhotoSession`.

```
// Add session reference to photos
photo1.setPhotoSession(sess1);
photo2.setPhotoSession(sess1);
photo3.setPhotoSession(sess1);
```

To make the `PhotoSession` object persistent, including all the child objects, we need to save only the parent.

```
// Make PhotoSession 1 persistent
tx.begin();
pm.makePersistent(sess1);
tx.commit();
```

We'll add one more `PhotoSession` with a couple of photographs so we will have more material to query.

```
// Photos - set 2
Photo mt = new Photo();
mt.setTitle("Cactus mountain and clouds");
mt.setDescription("Mountain,  salt flats, " +
                  "cactus, and storm clouds");
mt.setNotes("About 30 minute exposure on handmade " +
             "photosensitive paper");

Photo still = new Photo();
still.setTitle("Cactus flower");
still.setDescription("Cactus with flower and pear");
still.setNotes("About 8 minute exposure on handmade " +
             "photosensitive paper");

Vector photoset2 = new Vector();
photoset2.add(mt);
photoset2.add(still);

// Create Photographer 2 - Mom
Photographer photog2 = new Photographer();
photog2.setName("Mom");
photog2.setCity("Cambridge");
photog2.setContactInfo("therealboss@example.com");
photog2.setEquipment("oatmeal box pinhole camera");
photog2.setBio("Kodak Instamatic School of Photography");

// Create Photosession 2
PhotoSession sess2 = new PhotoSession();
sess2.setPhotographer(photog2);
sess2.setLocation("Southern New Mexico");

cal.set(2002, 4, 10);
sess2.setSessionDate(cal.getTime());
sess2.setPhotos(photoset2);

// Add session reference to photos
```

```
      mt.setPhotoSession(sess2);
      still.setPhotoSession(sess2);


      // Make persistent
      tx.begin();
      pm.makePersistent(sess2);
      tx.commit();

      pm.close();
    }
    catch (Exception e)
    {
      System.out.println("Caught e: " + e);
    }
  }
}
```

Querying Nested Classes

Querying classes that contain child classes is not very different than querying a simple class, such as the `Person` class earlier in this chapter. We usually start by specifying the extent.

```
Extent extent = pm.getExtent(PhotoSession.class, true);
```

The main difference is that when the class in question has attributes that are themselves objects, we may wish to refer to the attributes of the child objects in our query. In the case of single-value attributes—that is to say, attributes of the parent class that can refer only to a single object—we use dot notation. For example, suppose that we want to find a specific photographer's photo sessions. Each `PhotoSession` object has one instance of the `Photographer` class, `photographer`, and we refer to the `name` attribute as `photographer.name`. We can use this in a query filter like this:

```
String filter = "photographer.name == selectedName";
```

If we want the query to include an attribute of `PhotoSession` that is a collection, on the other hand, such as the vector `photos`, we need to use one of the collection methods, `contains()` or `isEmpty()`. We would use `isEmpty()` to find `PhotoSessions` that have no photographs.

```
String filter = "photos.isEmpty();
```

To find photographs that meet specific criteria, however, we need to use the `contains()` method together with a JDOQL variable. This is how we would locate a `PhotoSession` that contains a photograph with a specific title:

```
String filter = "photos.contains(p) " +
                "&& p.title == selectedTitle";
```

In essence, the filter uses the JDOQL variable `p` to pluck out each `Photo` object from the vector `photos` and test to see whether that `Photo` object's title field matches the variable `selectedTitle`.

The rest of the code necessary to perform this query obtains the query object and declares the parameter `selectedTitle` and the variable `p`.

```
Query q = pm.newQuery(ext, filter);
pm.declareParameters("String n");
pm.declareVariables("Person person");
Collection sess = (Collection) pm.execute("Dad");
```

This method of locating specific objects in a collection can be extended to any arbitrary depth. For example, the `Photo` class contains a collection for the subjects. We can locate a `PhotoSession` that contains a photo that includes a specific person by using the following query:

```
String filter = "photos.contains(p) " +
                "&& p.subjects.contains(s) " +
                "&& s.name == selectedPerson";
```

Here, we need to use two variables—one, `p`, to obtain each photo from the `photos` vector in `PhotoSession` and another, `s`, to obtain each subject from the `subjects` vector in `Photo`. Again, we need to declare the variables and parameters to perform the query.

```
q = pm.newQuery(ext, filter);
pm.declareParameters("String selectedPerson");
pm.declareVariables("Photo p, Subject s");
Collection sess = (Collection) pm.execute("Cactus flower");
```

Navigating the PhotoSession Object

Once we've obtained our results in the form of a collection, we can iterate through the collection to obtain each individual `PhotoSession` object and print out information specific to that `PhotoSession`.

```
Iterator iter = result.iterator();

while(iter.hasNext())
{

  PhotoSession ps = (PhotoSession) iter.next();

  System.out.println("Location: " + ps.getLocation());
  System.out.println("Photographer: " +
                     ps.photographer.getName());
```

To obtain information about the photos, we obtain an iterator for the vector `photos` and use it to iterate through them.

```
Vector p = ps.getPhotos();
 Iterator piter = p.iterator();
 int i = 1;
 while(piter.hasNext())
 {
   Photo currphoto = (Photo) piter.next();
   System.out.println("  " + (i++) +". " +
                      currphoto.getTitle());
   System.out.println("     " +
                       currphoto.getDescription());
```

Likewise, if we want to obtain information about the subjects, we need to obtain an iterator for the `Photo` class attribute `subjects`.

```
    Iterator siter = currphoto.getSubjects().iterator();
    while(siter.hasNext())
    {
      Subject subject = (Subject) siter.next();
      System.out.println("       " + subject.getName() +
                         ", " + subject.getAge() +
                         ", " + subject.getPosition());
    }

  }
}
```

Querying Dependent Objects

The queries in the previous section used the `PhotoSession` class for their extent. Even though we were able to query based on dependent objects, such as photos, the objects that were returned were `PhotoSession` instances. If we want to locate individual photos instead, we need to use the `Photo` class as the extent.

For example, to locate all photographs that contain the word *Rover* in their description, we would use the following extent and query:

```
// Find specific photos:
Extent extent = pm.getExtent(Photo.class, true);
String filter = "ucDescription.startsWith("%" + desc)";
Query query = pm.newQuery(extent, filter);
      query.declareParameters("String desc");
    String searchString = "Rover";
      Collection result =
        (Collection) query.execute(searchString.toUpperCase());
```

Notice that the filter uses the SQL wildcard character (%), together with the `startsWith()` method to allow locating a string anywhere within the description. Also notice that the search is case-insensitive because it converts the search string to uppercase prior to comparing it with the uppercase version of the description, `ucDescription`. (See the `Photo` class above, especially the `setDescription()` method.)

Because the `Photo` class contains a reference to the `PhotoSession` object that contains it, we can locate the `PhotoSession` object, too, once we have the `Photo` object. Here, we display information about the photo obtained from both objects:

```
Iterator iter = result.iterator();
      Photo photo;
      PhotoSession sess = null;
      while(iter.hasNext())
      {
        photo = (Photo) iter.next();
        System.out.println();
        System.out.println("Title:     "  + photo.getTitle());
        System.out.println("Desc:      "  + photo.getDescription());
        sess = photo.getPhotoSession();
        System.out.println("Location: "   + sess.getLocation());
        DateFormat df = DateFormat.getDateInstance();
        System.out.println("Date:      "  +
                          df.format(sess.getSessionDate()));
      }
```

Using Java for Queries

JDOQL is adequate and easy to use for simple, common queries but for complex queries, it may be necessary to use JDOQL to perform a preliminary query in order to thin down the number of candidates, then use Java to perform the final selection from the resulting collection.

Be aware that performing queries using Java is significantly slower than using the underlying database via JDOQL. In some cases, you may be able to avoid using Java by planning ahead for your querying needs and including calculated fields that are maintained by the class's setter methods, such as the uppercase `ucDescription` field in the `Person` class above.

Modifying and Deleting Objects and Object Graphs

After obtaining an object reference by using a query, we can obviously use the information in it in the usual ways: to display it to the user, to perform calculations, or to locate other objects, such as child objects or parent objects, depending on how we've designed the object model. Once we've obtained an object reference to a persistent object, either from a query or by navigating from one object to another object, we can also change the information in the object or delete the object altogether.

Changing a Persistent Object. The only thing special we need to do to ensure that changes are reflected in the database when we change an object—by using our class setter methods, for example—is make sure that the change occurs within the boundaries of a transaction. To do that, we call the `Transaction` method `begin()` before the change and `commit()` at the end.

For example, suppose that we want to change the first instance of *Rover* to *Rover the wonder dog* wherever it appears in the description of a photograph. Assuming that we've obtained a collection result, as shown above, we could change each matching `Photo` object as follows:

```
// Change "Rover" to "Rover the wonder dog"
iter = result.iterator();
Transaction tx = pm.currentTransaction();
while(iter.hasNext())
{
  tx.begin();
  photo = (Photo) iter.next();
  String s = photo.getDescription();
  int i = s.indexOf("Rover");
  int j = s.indexOf("the wonder dog");
  if(i>=0 && j != i + 6)
  {
    s = s.substring(0, i + 5) + " the wonder dog" +
    s.substring(i + 5);
 }
  System.out.println("Changed line to : " + s);
  photo.setDescription(s);
  tx.commit();
}
```

Deleting a Persistent Object. As you might expect, the process of deleting a persistent object is basically the reverse of creating a persistent object. First, we need to call a method, `deletePersistent()`, to delete the object from the database, then we null out the object reference in our object model. Suppose that we've obtained a reference to a `Photo` object. We could delete the object with the following steps:

```
tx.begin();
pm.deletePersistent(photo);
photo = null;
tx.commit();
```

But there is a major difference between persisting and deleting objects. When we created a persistent object, JDO dealt with the whole object graph for us, persisting any dependent objects automatically. This is not the case when deleting a persistent object with dependents, however. Deleting an object such as this `Photo` object will likely cause problems because it is probably owned by a `PhotoSession` object. Deleting the dependent `Photo` object will leave a `PhotoSession` object with a bad reference. To delete a persistent object properly, we need to take our object model into account, removing references in parent objects and deleting dependent objects as necessary.

In our `PhotoSession` application, because of the many-to-many relationships involved, we may wish to manage photographers and photo subjects separately from photo sessions. If this is the case, when we delete a `PhotoSession` object, we would want to delete the `Photo` objects in the collection of photographs that it contains (in vector `photos`) but not the `Photographer` object it references. We also would not want, when we delete the `Photo` objects, to delete the `Subject` objects that each `Photo` object references (in vector `subjects`). Given that, here is the code for deleting a `PhotoSession` object, assuming that we've already obtained a reference to one using a query:

```
// Delete PhotoSession sess and dependent photos
Vector  photos = sess.getPhotos();
Iterator phiter = photos.iterator();
Photo p;
while(phiter.hasNext())
{
  tx.begin();
  p = (Photo) phiter.next();
  pm.deletePersistent(p);
  tx.commit();
}
tx.begin();
```

```
pm.deletePersistent(sess);
sess = null;
tx.commit();
```

Another way of doing this is to put the code to delete the `Photo` objects in a callback method, `jdoPreDelete()`, in the `PhotoSession` class. (See the JDO specification for more information about callback methods.) When the `PersistenceManager` is preparing to delete an instance of the `PhotoSession`, it will call this method first. This callback method, together with the other callbacks such as `jdoPreStore()`, can also be used to maintain constraints in class relationships.

In addition, some JDO implementations may offer vendor-specific extensions that allow specifying cascading deletes in the metadata file so that when an object is deleted, dependent objects are deleted as well.

JDO implementations vary in the extensions they offer beyond the JDO 1.0 specification. There are ways in which JDO 1.0 can be found lacking and it's tempting to choose an implementation that makes things easier. But there is also a value to using only standard features, in case you later find other insurmountable problems, limitations or bugs in the implementation you've chosen, and need to change to another. In fact, if you decide to develop an application using JDO, it's probably not a bad idea to test it on more than one implementation, to make sure you're using only standard JDO.

Index

A

B

C

E

F

G

I

J

S

T

U

V

Java Oracle
Database Development
Oracle SQL
second edition
INTERACTIVE WORKBOOK
Oracle
Web Application
Programming for
PL/SQL Developers
Oracle
DBA
Data Warehousing and
Star Schemas
Oracle
PL/SQL
second edition
INTERACTIVE WORKBOOK

PRENTICE
HALL
PTR

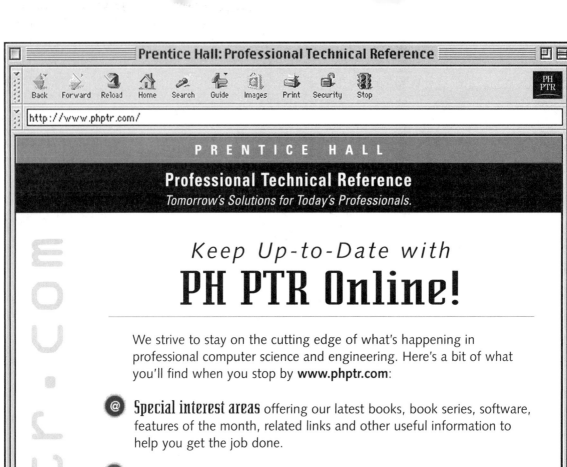